HOW TO RAISE AN ADOPTED CHILD
ADDRESSES THE MOST PRESSING QUESTIONS PARENTS HAVE ASKED ABOUT ADOPTION—

—"Should I refer to my child's *real* mother? Is birth child a term that makes sense?"

—"My husband and I are both high intellectual achievers. How can we ensure that our child measures up to our standards?"

—"My mother tells me that I shouldn't tell my son that he is adopted because he's 'illegitimate.' What should I tell my mother?"

—"How do I handle a teenager who says he doesn't have to listen to us because we're not his 'real' parents?"

—"My eighteen-year-old daughter came home from college expressing interest in searching for her birth mother. What do I do?"

—"I have heard that AIDS among infants is increasing. What kind of information do I need about my child's medical condition and birth parents?"

—"Since I became a single adoptive parent I rarely go out at night and I hardly get to see my friends anymore. How can I restore some of my social life without slighting my child's needs?"

THOUGHTFUL, EXPERIENCED-BASED ANSWERS THAT TRULY HELP ARE READILY AVAILABLE IN—

HOW TO RAISE AN ADOPTED CHILD

JUDITH SCHAFFER and CHRISTINA LINDSTROM are psychotherapists and family therapists, and were cofounders and codirectors of the Manhattan-based Center for Adoptive Families. They are both clinical members of the American Association for Marriage and Family Therapy. Judith Schaffer is the mother of two adopted children and former Director of the Adoption Review Unit of the Human Services Administration, New York City.

The Center for Adoptive Families

HOW TO RAISE AN ADOPTED CHILD

A Guide to Help Your Child Flourish from Infancy Through Adolescence

Judith Schaffer

and Christina Lindstrom

A PLUME BOOK

PLUME
Published by the Penguin Group
Penguin Books USA Inc., 375 Hudson Street,
New York, New York 10014, U.S.A.
Penguin Books Ltd, 27 Wrights Lane, London W8 5TZ, England
Penguin Books Australia Ltd, Ringwood, Victoria, Australia
Penguin Books Canada Ltd, 10 Alcorn Avenue,
Toronto, Ontario, Canada M4V 3B2
Penguin Books (N.Z.) Ltd, 182-190 Wairau Road,
Auckland 10, New Zealand

Penguin Books Ltd, Registered Offices:
Harmondsworth, Middlesex, England

Published by Plume, an imprint of Dutton Signet, a division of Penguin Books USA Inc. This is an authorized reprint of a hardcover edition published by Crown Publishers, Inc.

First Plume Printing, January, 1991
11 10 9 8 7

REGISTERED TRADEMARK—MARCA REGISTRADA

Library of Congress Cataloging-in-Publication Data

Schaffer, Judith.
How to raise an adopted child : a guide to help your child flourish from infancy through adolescence / Judith Schaffer and Christina Lindsay.
p. cm.
At head of title: The Center for Adoptive Families.
1st Plume printing, January, 1991—T.p. verso.
Reprint. Originally published: New York : Crown Publishers, c1989.
Includes index.
1. Children, Adopted—United States. 2. Child rearing—United States. 3. Parenting—United States. I. Lindstrom, Christina. II. Center for Adoptive Families (New York, N.Y.) III. Title.
[HV875.55.S33 1991]
649'.145—dc20 90-46612
CIP

Printed in the United States of America
Original book design by Shari deMiskey

Contents

▪ Acknowledgments vii

▪ Preface ix

1. ▪ An Introduction to Adoption Issues 1
2. ▪ The First Year 30
3. ▪ Ages One to Six 54
4. ▪ The School Years, Ages Six to Nine 79
5. ▪ Ages Nine to Twelve 107
6. ▪ Young Teens, Ages Twelve to Fourteen 129
7. ▪ The Late Teenage Years 159
8. ▪ Special-Needs Adoptions 192
9. ▪ Single Parents 250
10. ▪ The Multiracial Family 271
11. ▪ Emerging Trends 289

▪ Epilogue: Therapy 301

▪ Resources 305

▪ Index 307

Acknowledgments

First, our thanks to Gene Brown, who made this book a reality by helping us turn our clinical experience, research, and knowledge into written words.

A special thanks goes to the original partners in the Center for Adoptive Families, Sherry Bunin, Yvette Obadia, M.D., and Mary Walker. Also to Mary Talen, who helped make those early days at the Center exciting and rewarding. We owe, as well, a special debt of gratitude to Arnold Frucht, M.D., whose ongoing belief in us and support of the Center made many things possible. To those who participated in our Extern Programs, which are the source of many of the treatment strategies and ideas about adoptive family functioning, we are also indebted, as we are to the hundreds of adoptive families who inspired us, with their commitment and openness, to write this book.

It is difficult to adequately thank Ron Kral, coordinator of the Adoptive Family Project at the Brief Family Therapy Center in Milwaukee. We have collaborated with him so often over the past five years that we can no longer separate our thinking on adoption from his. His suggestions, support, and comments on the final manuscript were, as usual, wise and helpful. Ellen Oler, Joyce Pavao, and Mark Schulman read parts of this manuscript and made helpful suggestions. Insoo Kim Berg, David Brodzinsky, Jo Cobb, Betsy Cole, Steve deShazer, Kay Donely, Mary Ellen Eisenberg, Patti Feureissen, Steve Goldstein, Sharon Kaplan, Bob Lewis, and Eve Lipchick have helped us to broaden our thinking and kept us on our toes.

We also want to express our admiration and appreciation to the Board of Directors of the North American Council on Adoptable Children and all the other advocates who have fought for the right of permanence for foster children over the past nearly two decades, as well as the Family Builder's Agencies, who have advocated for national standards of excellence in adoption.

Estelle Rubenstein and Inga Sethness gave encouragement and financial support to get the Center for Adoptive Families going in the first place. The First Women's Bank of New York, the American Women's Economic Development Council, and Malcolm Chaifitz advised us in the early stages.

Finally, and most important, we want to thank Robert and Stacey Schaffer, who reminded us about what it is to be adopted.

Preface

This book comes out of our experiences at the Center for Adoptive Families, an independent treatment, research, and training facility in New York City, which specialized in working with adoptees and their families. Founded by five women, three of whom are also adoptive parents, the Center focused on the special nature of the adoptive relationship.

Our premise is that adoptive families are in some ways different from birth families. Although this may sound obvious, some adoptive parents and adoptees believe that if they can just pretend that they are exactly like birth families, they will be. But when the unexpected happens and their experience diverges from what they take to be normal for all families, they worry that they have done something wrong.

Parents and staff members of agencies we have dealt with through our work at the Center have often remarked on the lack of good models for raising adopted children. They say, "Where in the flood of books about child rearing is the one that speaks to us? Where is our Dr. Spock?" We hope that our book will begin to fill this important gap.

In this book we discuss the various stages of growth and behavior that all children go through, concentrating on complications that adopted children (and their parents) sometimes experience. We begin with infancy and proceed stage by stage to late adolescence. You'll find special topics, such as transracial adoptions, single-parent adoptions, and the adoption of children from foreign countries and of older children treated in separate sections.

For each stage of childhood we offer a model of the broad range of what you can expect from your child. This includes norms for motor development, language acquisition and learning milestones, social and personality development, relationships with peers and family members, and family life-cycle issues that may have some connection to the fact of adoption. We also suggest what you can do if things don't seem to be going quite right.

Since these are models, we emphasize that there are many variations from the norm. Your child may pass through a given stage when he's somewhat younger or older. No child follows the script precisely. We are talking about tendencies and averages, not rigid scientific categories of right and wrong. Some variation from the model is, in itself, no reason for concern.

At the end of each chapter you will find a sample of questions that typify what parents often ask about the subjects covered in that chapter. We trust that the answers will prove helpful and make your own job of parenting easier.

If you would like to contact us, we can be reached by writing:

Judith Schaffer
200 West 90th Street, Ap. 2F
New York, New York 10024

Judith Schaffer
Christina Lindstrom

Cofounders, the Center for Adoptive Families

1
An Introduction to Adoption Issues

What does it mean to be a parent? How do you raise a child? A family about to experience childbirth would already have many of the answers. They learned the basics of parenthood from their own mothers and fathers. As they grew up they also saw other parents caring for their children. Many of these parents-to-be assumed all along that some day they would do the same thing.

When most new mothers and fathers confront a situation for which they have no precedent, they can consult experts. Their pediatrician will tell them what it means and what they should do; if things get a little rough they can ask a therapist. They can read magazine advice columns on how to parent. If they want to read a book about it, they can start with Dr. Spock and go on to hundreds of other volumes on the subject. They can ask friends and neighbors how they did it. If they live in a big city, they can harvest practical advice from the park mothers' grapevine. And, of course, there is always the ultimate help line: the phone call to Mother.

But for adoptive parents, useful information is harder to acquire. Adoption is both the same as *and* different from raising a birth child. While you know as much as other parents do about child rearing, there are likely to be some aspects of adoptive parenthood you never encountered or thought about. When your experience differs from what most other people go through, the standard guideposts drop away. Your own upbringing—unless you were adopted—no longer offers a precedent. Other parents' experience may not always be relevant. You may lack readily available examples that you can copy.

Unfortunately, the mass media, when it deals with adoption, often focuses on the exceptional rather than the norm, leaving people with the negative image of the ill-adjusted adopted child. Though many studies show that adoptees fare well, maybe even better in some ways than their nonadopted peers, this cultural stereotype remains.

Professional expertise in the field is still hard to come by. There is not that much useful literature on adoption, and many social workers, psychologists, and psychiatrists who offer advice on the subject were not adequately trained in the area—or had no adoption-related training at all. They may still cling to classical Freudian attitudes that see adoption as portending possible psychological disaster for your child.

That's the bad news. The good news is that the basic requirements for raising adopted children, for the most part, are the same as for parenting a birth child—love, empathy, patience, trust, and understanding. You will also need a substantial amount of information about what to expect at each stage of your child's development and some advice on how to handle the occasional extra complications involved in raising adopted children.

In a sense you might compare adoptive parenting to an interfaith marriage. In each, the family confronts issues that other families don't. For example, as an adoptive parent you will have to deal with matters besides the usual child-rearing ones, including what others think about your family and how your child reacts to their remarks. But that's nothing you can't overcome.

ADOPTION: THE BACKGROUND

One of the reasons there is so little easily accessible folk wisdom about how to bring up an adopted child is that adoption as we know it—and as you're now experiencing it—is a recent phenomenon. We simply haven't been doing it long enough to become comfortable with it.

Yet adoption is as old as written history. Families in ancient Babylon adopted children. But in ancient and traditional societies, adoption served primarily the function of providing a male heir for religious obligations or inheriting property where a male child had not been born to a family. There was no pretending that it was just as if the child had been born to the family, no thought of keeping the fact of the adoption a secret. For the most part, only males were adopted. Other children who did not have parents either fended for themselves or were informally taken in by neighbors or relatives. The focus was on the family's needs, not the child's. In fact, the present American idea of adoption with the interests of the child paramount is almost revolutionary.

Nineteenth-century methods of caring for orphans form the backdrop for our present adoption practices. Children who had no parents often stayed in orphanages until they came of age. Sometimes they were put to work in factories—there were no child-labor laws—or sent to work on farms in the Midwest and West, actually "farmed out." These children arrived on "orphan trains" from eastern cities and lived with the farm families who came down to the train station and picked them out. The children worked on the farms in return for room and board.

People commonly took in children who were not related to them. American adoption laws became a method of formalizing these relationships. The first state to pass an adoption statute was Massachusetts in 1851. By 1929 all states had adoption statutes. Originally all adoptions were done by private agreements which the courts formalized. Lawyers and physicians often acted as intermediaries. Licensed agencies for placing children were a later development. In many cases, groups of concerned women, often those who did charitable work, set up agencies to search for and screen prospective adoptive parents for their fitness to raise a child.

This adoption system focused on finding babies for white infertile couples. Destitute children were cared for by the state, either by placing them in orphanages or in foster-care families until they grew up. It was not until the late 1960s that public agencies began to place these children in adoptive families.

The laws regulating adoption and their revisions sometimes have negative consequences for adoptive parents and their children. For example, they may create trouble for you or your child if either of you wishes to find more extensive information about your child's birth parents. Most state laws require the sealing of all identifying records about your child's origins. While you might convince a judge to open the file on your child, it is rare that this will occur. Judges usually open files only for serious medical reasons.

In recent years, some changes have occurred, and adopted children have entered their new families in several ways. The first method is the oldest: private agreements formalized by the courts. The private agency method that evolved in the 1920s continues. If you are now engaged in this process or have already adopted your child through it, you know that most child-welfare agencies have strict limitations about who can adopt healthy infants. For example, if you're over forty, it is especially difficult to adopt an infant through the agency channel.

Public child-welfare agencies are mandated by law and public policy to be concerned primarily with the adoption of current foster children who cannot return to their birth families and have had their legal ties with them severed in the courts, or who have been surrendered for adoption. The agency process is, necessarily, somewhat invasive. The social workers who look into virtually every aspect of your life have a duty to protect the best interests of the child; indeed, the law specifies that they do so. They are responsible for making the best possible placement for each child.

Some children have been traditionally considered more adoptable than others. Most in demand are healthy white babies. In the past, children who didn't fit into this category and were considered unadoptable grew up in foster care. Black, Hispanic, and Native American children were among them, as were sibling groups who could present a financial burden to many families if adopted together, and children with health problems or disabilities.

By the early 1970s, some states began to subsidize the adoption of children by the foster families in which they had been placed, making it possible for families of lesser means to join the ranks of adoptive parents. In 1979, the federal government began to take over part of the cost of these subsidies.

Under the subsidy system, federal and state governments pay a stipend to these families until the child comes of age. Besides making the adoption process less dependent on a family's income, the new laws are also intended to encourage minority families to adopt children from similar backgrounds—black families, for example, who might have lower average incomes can now more easily adopt black children. This system also makes it possible for families to adopt children with disabilities involving substantial medical expenses. Previously, such families could have gone bankrupt—and some did—because their medical insurance did not cover children with preexisting conditions requiring care.

The new government policy was not entirely idealistic. Adoption has always had a connection to economics. Not only is it better for the child to be living in a family; it is also cheaper. At present, it can cost as much as $44,000 a year to support a child in a specialized institution in New York—$810,000 over the course of 18 years.

After the Korean War, the adoption of foreign-born children became increasingly common. Today, South Korea, South America, and India are significant sources of children available for adoption.

However, although we do not have statistics to prove it, there are indications that most nonrelative adoptions are now accomplished via the private route. Private adoptions may take place because adoptive parents have heard of someone who must give up her baby. In some states, prospective adoptive parents can advertise their desire to meet a pregnant woman who must place her child for adoption.

Sometimes physicians and lawyers serve as intermediaries. For example, a doctor treating a woman who is about to give birth and wants to relinquish her child might contact a lawyer to find out whether he or she knows of a couple who wishes to adopt a child. The adoptive family often agrees to pay for the birth mother's prenatal and childbirth expenses. Since this can get expensive, such an arrangement is limited to families with sufficient resources to enter such an agreement. These intermediaries are not allowed to profit beyond the fees they earn for providing either medical services or the legal advice and work necessary for formalizing the adoption.

YOU ARE NOT ALONE

Adoption has become a common, everyday phenomenon in our society. According to sociologist David Kirk, one out of every five people in this country has some kind of close connection to adoption. They either have a relative or good friend who was adopted, or they have adopted children or were adopted themselves. Although no accurate data exist, estimates are that there is a pool in this country of about eight hundred thousand adoptees under the age of eighteen.

For several reasons, adoption is increasing. Couples now wait longer to have children, and they often find it more difficult to conceive and to carry a healthy baby to term when they reach the age at which they feel ready to be parents. Many researchers believe that long-term use of the IUD and the pill have contributed to this increasing incidence of infertility.

Because many parents adopt privately and states have not kept systematic records, we don't have accurate national statistics about adoption. (The 1990 census will contain a question about whether you have any adopted children. Your answer will be voluntary.) Most estimates put the number of adoptees in the United States at 2 to 4 percent of the population. That's five to ten million people!

THE STIGMA REMAINS

If adoption has become so widespread, and there are so many other parents who could share their experiences with you, why is it so hard to get accurate information and empathetic support? There are several reasons. We have already mentioned the comparative newness of the process as we know it, and the gap in the knowledge of many professional mental health workers about the dynamics of adoption.

In addition, some people still focus on the stigma surrounding an unmarried birth mother, associating adoption with illegitimacy. Others persist in regarding adopted children as somehow less than "real." They may actually refer to your birth children as your "real (or natural) children," if you have birth as well as adopted children.

One of the most chilling examples of this attitude we have heard was sociologist David Kirk's report of the comment made to a parent whose adopted child had died.

"At least she wasn't your real child," said the consoler, with all good intentions.

GET BY WITH A LITTLE HELP FROM YOUR FRIENDS

Fortunately, there *are* many organizations of adoptive parents who share your experiences and can offer information and support. Adoptive parents' support groups are a common source of help. You may have joined one while looking for a child to adopt. Many parents remain active with these groups after they get their children. Some drop out after the first few years but sometimes get reinvolved when the children are older and run into what appear to be—or actually are—difficulties.

To find a group that meets near you, contact the North American Council on Adoptable Children (NACAC), 1821 University Avenue, Suite S-275, St. Paul, Minnesota 55104, (612) 644-3036. Their newsletter reviews books on adoption and contains articles by adoptive parents about their experiences. There is also a group devoted to the needs of parents who have adopted foreign children: OURS, 3307 Highway 100 North, Minneapolis, Minnesota 55422, (612) 535-4829. If you write to either group, include a self-addressed stamped envelope for a reply.

Adoptive parents' groups can be very useful. One caution, however: their meetings can turn into sessions in which parents merely exchange "war stories," commiserating over "problems" they might be having, rather than focusing on constructive suggestions on how to handle snags in parent-child relationships. Since group meetings are often arranged to bring together parents with children of approximately the same age, you might suggest that the group bring in adoptive parents with older kids, who may already have experienced and overcome the problems you're having. If that doesn't work, a professional skilled in dealing with parent-child issues might help your group focus discussions on solutions.

Just as parents of any child may occasionally require the services of mental health professionals to deal with particularly troublesome behavior or conflicts, so too do adoptive parents. They also need to know where to go to find trained professionals for guidance and, if necessary, therapy, if things seem to be getting out of hand.

Who would you turn to? The professionals most parents call may not fully understand your family complications. In fact, they may be totally unaware of how adoption may or may not relate to your family. Parents often bring in their adopted children with what they assume are adoption-related problems. A therapist may confirm their fears and agree to treat the child with the aim of dealing with the problem of the child's adoptive status.

Yet, in a majority of such cases, in our experience, the whole adoptive family is feeling the effects of the difficulty. The situation may be only partially related to adoption, or not related at all. Adoption may have been a handy peg on which to hang the difficulty. We find it useful to refrain from pointing to one family member who has a "problem"; rather, in our view, it's more effective to encourage members of the family to work together to resolve the issue. After all, they are the *real* experts about their own family. Experience shows that when everybody works together, they can clear up the difficulty, usually within a brief time.

Fortunately, attitudes have been changing in the past ten or fifteen years, and many therapists—particularly family therapists—have begun to treat the occasional difficulties accompanying adoption within the context of family interaction, rather than as simply the inner psychological problem of the adopted child. Should you ever encounter such difficulties, you can get empathetic, knowledgeable help by getting in touch either with the organizations we list in the appendix of this book or by sending a self-addressed, stamped envelope to the American Association for Marriage and Family Therapy, 1717 K Street, N.W., Suite 407, Washington, D.C. 20006. The AAMFT will send you a list of therapists in your area.

While we list these resources so you will know that there is a growing number of trained professionals to turn to, we by no means suggest that you will need to do this; only a very small percentage of families who adopt babies do. Those adopting older children with special needs are more likely to need such services. But you may experience a few more bumps than a birth parent would on the road to your child's adulthood, because adoptive family life is somewhat more complicated.

You may have noticed our use of the word "complication." These are the things in life that you can't do anything about. They are facts—like your child's adoption. However, if you view complications as "problems"—to be solved—you could be creating trouble for your family. You might blow out of proportion something you just need to accept and work around.

What's an example of one of these complications? A family we counseled had a sixteen-year-old adopted daughter. Sarah,* an only child, had always been bright and cooperative, but now she was having trouble in school. When asked to do her share of the chores around the house, she screamed: "You're not my *real* parents and you can't make me!"

Sarah's parents took her to a psychiatrist, who told them that their daughter had poor self-esteem, a natural result of having been given up for adoption in infancy, and thus suffered from trauma and loss. The parents interpreted this to mean that to assure her that they loved her they should be less strict and demanding with Sarah and not "gang up" on her. Afterward, whenever one parent scolded Sarah for not doing her chores or homework or not coming

* All names used in case descriptions are fictitious.

home before her curfew, the other took her side so she would not experience the criticism as traumatic.

The strategy did not work. Now even more worried, her parents began to wonder if some basic flaw in her character, perhaps something genetic, was surfacing. By the time they got to us, Sarah was acting out in very serious ways and her parents were panic-stricken.

We helped them to see that what Sarah was going through was typical adolescent turmoil, combined with a few extra twists added by her efforts to deal with her identity as an adopted child. Her ploy when asked to do something she didn't want to do—saying they were not her real parents—was something that most adopted kids will try once or twice to see how their parents will react. It is nothing to worry about, though it is not easy for parents to hear. Many adoptive parents we have spoken to over the years have taught us that the way to respond is to address the issue at hand. We suggested to Sarah's parent's that they could say something like: "Yes, it's true that we adopted you [the complication], and we can talk about that later. But the issue right now is that your job is to take out the garbage. So take it out."

If anything, it seemed to us that, like many adolescents, Sarah needed clearer, not fewer, limits and rules; she needed better defined boundaries between herself and her parents so she could realistically determine where she stood in relationship to them. Of one thing we were certain: having parents play good cop/bad cop is a sure way to confuse any kid—adopted or not.

The point of the story is that when you try to "solve" a complication as if it were a problem, your "solution" may actually create a problem that was not there before. A little knowledge of what Sarah was experiencing would have put the "problem" in its proper perspective. At issue was her behavior, at that point. She was being unpleasant and giving her parents a hard time. Not exactly revolutionary behavior for a teenager. Knowing exactly what was happening and how to deal with it meant that for her parents, this too would soon pass. And it did.

THE BIG PICTURE

Starting with the next chapter we will accompany you, step by step, through each stage of your child's growing-up process. We will systematically cover infancy through late adolescence, pointing out what to look for, telling you how to handle the trials and tribulations of adoption (while also pointing out the pleasures to come), explaining the sources of behavior that may seem a little puzzling to you, and suggesting various ways to deal with problems that sometimes come up.

We will also show you how the progress of your family through the cycles of family development affects the way you handle adoption issues. All families change as couples decide to have children, start raising them, send them off to school, and then finally launch them into the adult world while they begin to cope with the empty nest. The transition from one stage of your family life to another is where difficulties are likely to occur—particularly in preparing adolescents for independent adulthood.

Families that do not successfully negotiate these transitions may get stuck in old and inappropriate ways of interacting with their children. For example, parents may rigidly insist that they still know what's best for their teenager at all times, when they need to be letting their son or daughter make more decisions for him- or herself. The result could be a child who misbehaves and parents who mistakenly think that they are seeing acting out related to their child's adoption.

Right now an overview of general issues necessarily involved—but not always acknowledged—in adoption is in order. Let's take a look at the big picture.

ACCEPTING THEM FOR THEMSELVES

Mr. Jordan is a black college teacher in New England; his wife is a white therapist. The Jordans have two adopted children: a sixteen-year-old girl and a fourteen-year-old boy of mixed racial background. If you ask the Jordans what's special about being adoptive parents, they'll tell you that if Mrs. Jordan had given birth to their children, they would be watching for the kids' talents to evolve, on the assumption that they would recognize elements of themselves in what they saw. But because they knew little about the children's birth parents, not even where they came from, the Jordans cherished every new talent and characteristic that appeared, especially the ones that were *not* like theirs. For example, when their children are athletic, unlike either adoptive parent, or when they show the artistic talent that their adoptive parents lack, the Jordans delight in those differences.

This illustrates a key element in the successful parenting of adopted children: being open and excited about the innate talents that they display. Such parents don't expect their children to mirror their own endowments, but take pleasure in watching their children's talents emerge and develop.

TEMPERAMENT

All children are born with psychological tendencies. Each child has what developmental psychologists call a temperament. So your child already has inherent characteristics, even if you bring her home within days of her birth. For example, some babies are simply more active than others. One may walk and talk sooner than another her age. However, early or late achievement of these milestones, within normal limits, has no direct connection to intelligence.

Psychologists accept an interrelationship between environment and heredity, although which has primacy for any given trait is never totally clear. For example, the experts generally hold that both influence intelligence as measured by I.Q. tests, although here they accord somewhat more weight to environment than to heredity. You will certainly influence your child's values and personality, but you should not expect to transmit to her your exact values or shape her personality to your specifications any more than you would that of a birth child. Set the best model you can and then hope your child will make sound choices for herself when she is old enough.

What about the worst case? Could there be a "bad seed" waiting to germinate? What if you discover that either of your adopted child's birth parents had some problem—perhaps emotional—that might possibly have been genetically passed on to their offspring?

While children inherit tendencies for all sorts of things, they are just that: tendencies. Environment affects whether those tendencies ever develop. You are not helpless in steering your child away from trouble. In fact, your influence is great. By providing a warm, nurturing family environment, you can minimize the risk.

GHOSTS

Most infants, if adopted before the age of nine months—but possibly even later according to some studies—will take to their new parents as if they were born to them, developing an attachment to them as they would have done to their birth parents.

Children who are a bit older at placement have a history of relationships. Those connections may be to the birth mother, foster parents, foster siblings, or anyone else who cared for them and was important to them. Such ties do not present a barrier to the establishment and strengthening of your own bonds with your child, but it is useful to take them into account. As your child grows up, they may become part of his or her fantasies and may influence some behavior. Even children adopted at birth will have thoughts about their birth parents. This is not only perfectly normal but necessary in developing a clear and strong identity.

Open adoption, in which birth parents remain in touch with their child and his or her adoptive parents, avoids these ghosts entirely. We will have more to say about this burgeoning phenomenon in a later chapter.

UNRESOLVED PARENTAL CONFLICTS

No one approaches adoption with a blank slate. Aside from the anxieties about competence that most parents, birth or adoptive, have, adoptive parents sometimes have unresolved conflicts about their relationship to the adoption process.

If you've chosen adoption because you weren't able to give birth to a baby—the most traditional reason for adopting a child—you might have a lingering sense that adoption is something that's "second best." Perhaps infertility left you with doubts about your ability to parent. Some parents feel insecure about their roles because they actually had to go to somebody and ask for a child. Being judged by an agency may have been especially upsetting.

Others have not yet resolved conflicts with their own parents over the adoption issue. Adult children whose parents oppose adoption may feel great ambivalence over the decision to become parents. Sometimes, if they do adopt, they may have lingering doubts that they are fully entitled to raise their child as his or her parent.

None of these are inevitable, but if you should sense any of these feelings in yourself, discuss them with your spouse and close friends; if you feel they are affecting your relationship with your child, consider getting some professional counseling from a therapist trained to deal with family problems. It is likely that you will need to continue to resolve certain feelings related to infertility from time to time. As our colleague Ron Kral says, "It is like having a small pebble in your shoe. Mostly you are unaware of it, but then you feel it."

SIBLINGS

The Lindner family has two adopted children and a birth child. Over the years, the little girl who was born to the Lindners has talked longingly and with envy about her brother and sister having two sets of parents while she has only one. That's not the reaction most people would expect her to have. Kids often shatter your assumptions about how members of a family with both adopted and birth children will react to each other.

An adoptive family is, first, a family. Where there are siblings, you should expect some rivalry. But you're not likely to encounter anything more serious than that.

"WHERE DID I COME FROM?"

A colleague of ours related a too-familiar story. Joan was adopted in infancy but as a child was never told about it. Being adopted had never occurred to her. But every time she went to a new doctor with her mother there was a discernible tension when the doctor asked about her medical history and her mother sent her out of the room. Finally, Joan asked her mother, "Could it be that you adopted me?" Still unwilling to tell the truth, the mother answered, "No."

There is still too much secrecy and pretending in adoption. If you've had your child since she or he was an infant, look at your daughter or son's birth certificate. Do you see the word "adoption"? In most states, you see what appears to be a document that records an actual birth, with you as a birth parent. This exercise in mythology can be humorous when the certificate implies that two white American parents have somehow (by coincidence?) produced a Korean baby—in Korea, no less.

There is no "correct" level of openness about the subject of adoption. Some families do best by discussing it freely—with their children and with those outside their immediate family. For others, minimizing the differences between birth and adoptive parenting works better.

The extremes, however, don't work. Dwelling on the subject obsessively is not openness as much as it is a way of isolating and hurting an adopted child, however unintentionally. On the other hand, absolute denial can confuse and possibly stigmatize a child, who at some point will inevitably learn that there is a family secret concerning him.

How about telling? When? How? The parents of three-year-old Heather were anxious to be open with her and so they often tried to talk to her about adoption, but every time they brought up the subject she put her hands over her ears and ran from the room. Heather's parents didn't realize that children of this age are too young to handle the subject and all its complexities. At three, a simple account is enough—that she grew in the tummy of another mommy who couldn't take care of her, and that you wanted a baby so you adopted her and took her home and loved her very much.

No matter how you look at it, telling remains, for most adoptive families, a big issue. We suggest that you treat it as you would the question of where do babies come from—frankly, openly, straightforwardly. Give your children the information they want or can handle at their age (more about this later). It's better not to confuse them and give them what they haven't asked for. They simply do not have the ability to understand all the complexities until they are much older. The key is to be responsive without leading your child into those complexities. And when you do discuss the subject with your child, always use "adoption" as a loving word, meaning that she belongs to you.

Believe it or not, some children will want to talk about adoption over and over. The parents of an eleven-year-old brought this situation to us, thinking they had a grave problem. Their daughter asked about her origins every day. Each time the parents responded as openly and honestly as they could. But after six months of this, they began to worry about this confusing behavior.

We assured these parents that they had been open and loving; that was why their daughter could inquire so freely. Despite this, she simply had not settled the issue in her mind and was going about the task of integrating this information into her view of herself in her own way. Eventually, we predicted, she would be satisfied; and before long, she was.

Discussing adoption with a child is a delicate process. You first need to be comfortable with the subject yourself so that your child doesn't sense that the topic makes you nervous. If she does detect that you feel uneasy about adoption—perhaps through your body language or tone of voice—she may not want to bring it up for fear that you can't handle it.

What if your child never asks? Then bring it up yourself every few months. Buy some books about adoption and read them together. You could begin by saying something casual about your memory of getting her from the agency, talking about her adoption social worker, or reading to her a story or book about adoption. If this doesn't start a conversation, don't worry. Some children don't talk about it. But occasionally continue to confirm, in a loving way, that you adopted her.

OUTSIDERS

Almost 30 percent of adoptive parents in one study reported hearing disparaging remarks about adoption from people outside their immediate family. Such sentiments, bad enough coming from total strangers, are worse when they issue from your own relatives. Sad to say, when it comes to adoption, sometimes friends are more supportive than family.

Lack of understanding can be annoying when people who should know better don't. If an adopted child has difficulty in school, her parents may get a call from the teacher or guidance counselor explaining their child's slow progress or misbehavior solely in terms of her adoption. It may have a bearing, but it's not likely to be *the* reason.

Should you let the school know you adopted your child? In a famous study, psychologists told teachers at the beginning of the year that half their pupils were very smart and the other half were at best of average intelligence. In fact, the children were randomly selected for each group. Not surprisingly, over time, the "smart" ones did better, probably because the teacher treated them as if they were smart. If your child's teacher views adoption as a negative, you might do better to avoid the subject unless you're willing to try to educate her. Before you tell her, attempt to get a sense of how broad-minded she is—perhaps through a conversation during open school week. If you find that she's willing to learn more about adoption, supply her with articles about the subject.

If your family looks atypical, people may come up to you on the street and say odd things. Strangers often feel free to be intrusive when it comes to children. We've all heard stories of people who walk up to a pregnant woman, uninvited, and touch her belly. The same kind of intrusiveness can prompt all sorts of comments.

One white woman was walking with her husband, also white, and their dark-skinned Colombian adopted daughter when a stranger walked over and said: "Your child is dark, but you aren't and neither is your husband." They told her that they had adopted their child. She replied:

"Well, what are you going to do if she wants to marry a black man?"

You can feel insulted or invaded by such incidents or you can see them as something you can deal with by educating others as the situation calls for it (although sometimes, in truth, it can be tiresome). You can also treat them with humor or ignore them.

Don't be surprised if you get a lot of unsolicited and useless advice from people you don't know when they discover that you have an adopted child. There are all kinds of misinformation floating around out there. Here are some samples of myths from our colleague Ron Kral about adoption:

Adopted children are less well-adjusted than those born to their parents. There is some evidence that adoptees are referred for mental health intervention more often than children raised by their birth parents. But many middle-class families adopt children and, clearly, they are more likely in any case to use professionals when child-related difficulties arise. The fact that they have adopted means the family has already gone to a lawyer or an agency to get a child in the first place and so may be more willing than birth parents to return to their agency or turn to other professionals outside the family for help.

Since adoptive parents are sometimes more attuned to any little nuance in their child's behavior—especially during the trials of the teenage years—they may be more likely to consult a therapist for the same behavior that other parents would chalk up to the unsettled state of adolescence. Parents who have already had birth children sometimes have an easier time because they are more likely to recognize such behavior for what it is: normal "growing pains."

Adoptees seem more often involved in sensational crimes than nonadoptees. Unfortunately, this kind of sensationalism does sell newspapers. Adoption is not a factor in crime—a poor environment is most likely to blame. True, all adoptive families are not supportive and loving, just as all birth children are not raised in good families. However, the vast majority of adoptive parents are caring and responsive and their children are no more likely to have criminal thoughts or commit crimes than any other normal children.

Only ill-adjusted adoptees want to find their birth parents. If you had been a good parent, your child would never pursue the matter. Why so? Wouldn't you want to know more about where you came from? Girls are perhaps more likely to have an interest in this because they are brought up to be more family-oriented in our society. But it is normal and healthy for any adoptee to be curious about his origins, and you should respect it. This is not a threat to you—your child will remember who cared for him in crucial moments.

QUESTIONS AND ANSWERS

I've been thinking about adopting for a while and have finally decided to go ahead with it. But everybody I speak to tries to discourage me and instead urges that I keep trying to have a child "of my own." What should I tell them?

Tell them: "I'm ready to be a parent." Remind them that you've had plenty of time to consider the adoption alternative. Explain that if you adopt you're either foreclosing the possibility of having a birth child in the future or not, according to which is true in your case.

□

I want to adopt a child but my husband is quite hesitant. Family blood lines are very important to his relatives. I think he'll come around once we have the child, but I'm a little worried. How do I handle this?

If you are counting on your husband to be supportive and join in rearing the child, you and he need to resolve his ambivalence *before* the adoption. Don't assume that he will get over it spontaneously. Some counseling is in order from either your adoption agency or a family therapist.

□

My father-in-law is dead-set against our adopting a child. He says he wants no part of such a "grandchild." What do I do?

Try to reason with him. After the child is yours, encourage him to at least have some contact with his grandchild. Ask at your adoptive parents' group if the organization has an adoptive grandparents' section. Your father-in-law might find it easier to talk to them about adoption. If this doesn't work, for your child's sake you and your husband may have to limit your own contact with your husband's father. Only very occasionally does this lead to the breaking off of a relationship, and you should consider doing this only in exceptional circumstances.

□

I would like to try to conceive even after I adopt a child. What do you think of this?

Sure, go ahead. Lots of families have both adoptive and birth children and thrive on the richness and variety that such child rearing brings.

□

I've considered adopting through an agency. The child they've shown me appears healthy now but her mother was an intravenous drug user. What are the risks?

Discuss this with your agency and your pediatrician. An AIDS test should be performed on babies of intravenous drug users. Even if the child was not born drug addicted there may be a drug-related problem from the mother's use early in the pregnancy and her prenatal care may have been deficient. You should get an indication of this by her birth weight, her Apgar scores, and an evaluation of her scores on the Brazelton Neonatal Behavioral Scales.

□

I have decided to adopt. What kind of information do I need about my child's medical condition and birth parents?

You need to know, at minimum, if possible, the birth mother's history during pregnancy. Was there bleeding during the first trimester, did she suffer from toxemia, diabetes, or have a thyroid problem? What medications did she take? Did she use alcohol or drugs? You will also want to know the baby's birth weight, head circumference, and length, Apgar scores, due date, when he or she was actually born, and any complications connected to delivery such as premature rupture of the membranes, excessive bleeding, or whether it was a cesarean birth. In addition, it would be helpful to know if the infant needed resuscitation or suffered from jaundice, an infection, a breathing problem, or other trouble at birth. You should also find out about congenital impairments including physical defects, if any, and the medical past history of the birth mother and father as well as the present health or cause of death of mother, father, and siblings.

□

How do I prepare my children, birth or adopted, for a new adopted child in the family?

If you have only children to whom you gave birth, speak to them a little bit about the adoption process. Tell them why Mommy and Daddy are adopting this child—"We want another child because we love *you* so much." Then just concentrate on reassuring them that the new child will not displace them—the same thing you would do if you were about to give birth. If your other children are also adopted, this could be a wonderful opportunity to educate them further about adoption and their own origins. If it's an agency adoption, all your children, birth or adopted, will take part in the home-study interviews; again, an education for everyone.

□

My child is five and we haven't yet told him that we adopted him. What should I do?

Start now. He won't understand it fully, but begin. You might want to show him some books that treat the subject on a level that he can now deal with: *Why Was I Adopted?* by Carole Livingston (Lyle Stuart), *Is That Your Sister?* by Sherry Bunin (Knopf), *Our Baby: A Birth and Adoption Story* by Janice Koch (Perspective Press), and *The Chosen Baby* by Valentina P. Wasson (Lippincott). And join an adoptive parents' group and get a sampling of other parents' experience with this issue. Make an effort to take your child to their parties and get-togethers so that he sees other adopted children and begins to understand adoption as a different but normal phenomenon.

□

My child's birth mother was hospitalized for a mental disturbance. What do I tell him about her?

Telling him about his mother's condition depends on his level of maturity and how badly he might want the information. You would be the best judge of that for your child. Short of that, though, you could insist that the agency find out some positive things about her, what she looked like or songs she liked, what hobbies she pursued. Did any other members of his birth family care for him for a while? If they did, try to get similar information about them and relate it to your child.

□

She's finally asked the question I dreaded: "Why was I given up for adoption?" What should I say?

In the old days, they told children that their parents had died. Unless that's the truth, it's not a good idea to fall back on this old solution. Tell her, for example, "Your mommy was only fourteen or fifteen and, while she loved you, she was not able to take care of you." If she answers that her baby sitter is that age, explain that the sitter still has a mommy to take care of *her* and wouldn't be able to take on the job of a parent at that age. Remind her that when something comes up, the sitter has to call *you*, the parent. If you don't have a reasonable explanation, tell the child you don't know and when she gets older you and she will try to find out.

Learn as much as you can about the child's father as well. Sometimes agencies are unable to obtain much information from birth mothers, but try to get as much as you can. If you haven't adopted yet, tell the agency that you want to know about both the father and the mother of your child. The more information you have, the better. You can always use your discretion about how much to tell your child in the early years. *The Art of Adoption* by Linda Cannon Burgess (W. W. Norton) describes how one adoption agency worker is able to get information about birth fathers and why this is important.

□

My child asked me recently why I adopted her. Do I say it was because I couldn't have a baby, or should I just say that it was because I loved her?

Tell her it's because you wanted to be a parent and wanted a child to love and take care of. Later, if you want to introduce the idea of infertility, that's fine. If you feel comfortable with your response, your child will too.

□

How will I deal with comments from other people about my child being adopted?

Read up on adoption so that you can educate people. If you're not comfortable responding to a particular question, you might develop one or more stock replies. Find a style of responding that becomes second nature to you.

□

A story just came out in the newspaper about an adopted child who was convicted of a heinous murder. How do I respond to my child's and neighbors' questions and comments about this story?

Hardly any murderers are adopted and hardly any commit heinous murders. We just seem to hear about every one of these cases. This is what we mean when we say there is a stigma about adoption. Somehow it is newsworthy when criminals are adoptees. Perhaps it goes back to the idea of the "bad seed." Few of the mass murderers we have all read about were adopted as healthy infants into good and loving families. It could just as easily have been a person with diabetes or short hair who did this. In other words, there's no connection.

□

I know that Ronald Reagan is an adoptive father. Do you know of other adoptive parents whose names I would recognize?

Adoptive parents come from all walks of life. Among the more well known are Mia Farrow, Woody Allen, Barbara Walters, Gail Sheehy, and Elizabeth Taylor. Each of the four candidates in the 1988 presidential election has a member of his family who is adopted. Governor Dukakis adopted his wife's son, Senator Bentsen has adopted children, President Bush has an adopted grandchild, and Vice-President Quayle has adopted siblings.

□

My mother tells me that I shouldn't tell my son that he's adopted because he's "illegitimate." What should I say to my mother?

In your mother's day, having a child without being married was more of a stigma. It was also a good excuse for not telling a child she was adopted. Explain to your mother how times have changed.

□

Should I refer to my child's "real" mother? Is birth child *a term that makes sense?*

We prefer *birth child, birth mother,* and *birth father;* or *first mother* and *second mother,* etc. We would also like to point out that most adoptees beyond their mid-teenage years do not like being referred to as *adopted children. Adoptee* or *adult adoptee* would certainly be more descriptive.

□

My husband and I are both high intellectual achievers. How can we ensure that our child measures up to our standards?

You will have a substantial influence on your child's intellectual development but your child may not ever achieve as you do. It's generally thought that a good environment can raise a child's I.Q. by as much as 15 points. That means lots of praise and encouragement from you. But no child will be able to exceed his own genetic potential. That means that if both of his birth parents scored in the average range on an I.Q. test (about 100), your family environment could make it possible, on average, for his score to be 15 or so points higher than his siblings who remain with his birth parents. If your I.Q. scores are in the 130 or above range, that might not seem like very much since his score would more likely range from 115 to 120 or so. Part of the job of being a parent is coming to terms with that—taking pleasure in helping him achieve whatever he can. But bear in mind that even if you give birth to a child, there is a phenomenon that statisticians call "regression to the mean" to contend with. If you're both extremely bright, chances are that even a birth child would not quite reach your level although he would be very bright compared to other children.

□

I am white and I have a three-year-old daughter from Mexico who has a dark skin tone. Recently, a neighbor said:

"Isn't it wonderful that you've taken in this child." My daughter heard this. What should I tell her?

Tell her that this lady is just curious "because we look different and she doesn't understand why." Later you will be able to explain to her about how difficult life is for poor children who live in orphanages and never do get adopted. And, if you wish, tell the neighbor that you are the lucky one to have such a wonderful child.

□

My husband and I have not been getting along for some time and we are considering a divorce. We have two adopted children and we are worried that a divorce would be far more traumatic for them than it would be for birth children. Is this true? What special steps should we take to minimize the trauma for them?

Because your children have already lost one set of parents, another such loss could be particularly difficult for them—unless you both work to minimize the stress to which they are subjected. We have found that divorcing parents with adopted children get through their separation with fewer problems for their kids when they plan in advance to cooperate on the issue of child rearing, if nothing else. These people agree on clear and definite boundaries when dealing with anything involving their children. For instance, when they speak on the phone to discuss the children, it's the only subject they allow to come up. Some form of coparenting, at least for the first—and almost always the most difficult—year is also helpful. Having the kids alternate between living in one parent's home for a week and then the other's is one way of handling this, but you can probably come up with many other creative solutions, depending on your situation.

□

I have just heard that AIDS among infants is increasing. We want to adopt a baby, but aren't willing to adopt one with AIDS. We just don't want to take care of a chronically ill baby who will die in a short period of time. How can we be certain that the baby who is placed with us does not have AIDS?

You have identified a very serious issue, which is only just now beginning to receive public attention. It is likely that you will know whether or not the baby has AIDS if the birth mother and the infant have both been tested. A major complication for adoptive parents who choose not to adopt an AIDS baby is that the birth mother may not, in fact, know that she has AIDS and has, therefore, exposed her fetus to the virus. She herself may not belong to one of the high-risk groups. She may have been infected by a partner who has AIDS or ARC and who also may not have known that he was infected. The baby who has AIDS may appear healthy for the first six months and then begins to deteriorate, usually developing pulmonary symptoms first. Many birth mothers first learn that they have AIDS themselves when their babies become symptomatic and then are positively diagnosed, at which point they are tested. Some attorneys who do independent adoptions, as well as private adoption agencies, are now requiring a series of AIDS tests for pregnant birth mothers who come to them desiring to surrender their babies for adoption. AIDS is a growing concern in many major metropolitan areas and a consideration for families who choose to adopt a healthy infant.

2
The First Year

Was Marsha Harrington doing something wrong? Why didn't her adopted baby cry more? Isn't that what infants are supposed to do? Even on the long ride home from the agency the day she and her husband, Ralph, had claimed her, the baby just lay there quietly while her new mother struggled ineffectively to secure the infant's Pampers with masking tape. Since then Marsha had experienced several moments of panic after rereading Dr. Spock and realizing that she had mishandled diaper rash, among other things. Would she ever make a good parent? Would she have been better at it if she had given birth?

If this sounds at all familiar, remember that child rearing is a process in which all mothers and fathers constantly learn to be more effective parents. *Nobody* begins as an expert. Children are enormously resilient; they are not likely to be hurt by one or even several mistakes.

Child behavior is always a little unpredictable, no matter how much you've read about the subject. Should you ever feel that you are not handling a situation correctly, you can always develop new strategies. Even when your child grows older and realizes that you have erred, you can apologize. In fact, it's important for children to learn that their parents, too, can make mistakes.

We emphasize that no parent is perfect because adoptive parents often strive for flawlessness. They may have undergone painful scrutiny about their qualifications to parent before being given their child. They know that, depending on the law in their state, for the first few months they have their child he or she can, theoretically, be taken back. They realize that their child has no blood ties to them, and thus could lack the automatic loyalty birth parents might assume. And what if she finds her birth mother one day? Will she love her more? One can understand why adoptive parents might feel constantly judged and would believe that they had to be exemplary mothers and fathers.

Unfortunately, in this age of statistics and quantification, it's easy to find "scientific" standards against which to measure your parental competence. Examples of this are the stages of child development, the things that many parents feel that children should do at specific chronological points in their growth—unless, of course, there's something wrong with them. These guidelines are useful when seen as general outlines of what to expect from a child, but they can cause unnecessary parental anxiety when interpreted too exactly. Some parents see them as reflecting on their own skills as parents.

Adoptive parents should exercise even more caution than other mothers and fathers when interpreting their child's "progress" in the developmental process. An adoptee's development will not differ from that of his or her nonadopted peers. But your interaction with your child could vary just enough from the birth parent–child relationship to make you more insecure about any developmental discrepancies you do notice.

THE BEGINNING

Robin Stanton always envisioned herself as an earth mother, her infant strapped to her chest while she shopped, cleaned, and did all the other things that make for a glowing hearth and home. That's why it came as a shock when she discovered that the 2½-month-old baby she had worked so hard to adopt was too heavy for her to carry in that way.

We don't know if pregnancy and the increasing weight she would need to bear would have prepared her physically for that task. However, those nine months would have given her certain emotional advantages. While the entry of a child into a family can briefly overwhelm any parent, the period of gestation does permit birth parents-to-be to gradually prepare for the many impending changes in their lives and absorb what it will mean to be responsible for another human life.

After all, you can read about child rearing, discuss it with your mate and friends, go to classes at the Y, and do all the other things that prospective parents do to get ready for the big day. But if, as it was with Robin and her husband, Allen, and many other adoptive parents, you have two weeks or fewer between hearing that a baby is available and having that wonderful bundle handed to you as *your child*, the feelings can be positively disorienting.

Robin had been on the phone having a long conversation with a friend that Friday, so the woman at the agency had called her husband at his office to tell him that she was putting in the mail some pictures of a child who they thought would be just right for them. The child had been born to a fourteen-year-old girl; the father was a high school senior. The photos and the biographical and medical information came on Monday, and Robin and Allen knew right away that this child was *the one*.

Little Molly might have graced the Stanton household within a few days, but the foster family caring for the infant had become attached to her and asked if they could keep the child for an extra week. That gave the Stantons a chance to rush to prepare a room for their daughter. They spent the better part of an afternoon in a children's furniture store, directing a lot of nervous energy into the choice of a crib, a chest of drawers, and accessories.

A day in advance the Stantons drove to the town in the next state where they would pick up their child, so they would not be tired at the big moment. But they were so excited that they couldn't sleep and instead stayed up all night talking and playing cards. The next morning they arrived at the welfare center an hour early, but when the social worker came out to chat, Robin and Allen couldn't focus on what she was saying. When the agency worker finally come out and handed Robin her blanket-wrapped baby, Robin all but melted. First she sat holding the baby, new mother and daughter staring into each other's eyes, then Allen got his chance to hold the infant and make eye contact. The Stantons can document almost everything that happened that morning with their photo album; they also kept the clothes both they and she wore to give to their daughter as a memento of her arrival.

Robin and Allen didn't realize how much help they would get from friends and relatives. Most of the couple's friends did not have children, but the one woman with whom Robin was close who was a mother (of a two-year-old) brought over clothes, toys, and books on child care. Neighbors dug into old chests to recycle items their kids had used. Robin's in-laws, without being asked, took care of every minor bit of necessary shopping that the harried about-to-be-parents might have overlooked. By the time Molly made her grand entrance, a spontaneous support network had considerably eased the transition to parenthood for the Stantons.

In truth, the only difficulty they had in the first few weeks was a little jealousy from Robin's cousin, Barbara, who drove up to Robin and Allen's country house to spend a summer weekend, bringing along her baby, a birth child, for her first "vacation." Barbara's daughter, Samantha, was colicky, putting everyone's nerves a bit on edge that weekend, while Molly was quiet and peaceful.

It's not unusual for the arrival of an adopted child to turn into a communal affair. One way you can encourage the formation of this helpful network, if it doesn't make you uncomfortable, is to discuss your pending adoption with your neighbors before your child arrives. Answer their questions about the adoption process, and answer their children's questions if they're curious. They may ask you, "How do you adopt a child? Do you know about her parents? How did you choose this child? Were the parents married?"

However, also prepare for some odd responses. At work, one of his colleagues actually came up to Allen Stanton and asked, "Don't you *do* it?" Friends of Robin's, both college teachers, came over to the house and while chatting about the baby awkwardly posed several random questions concerning the birth mother and father. It took a while before Robin realized what they were getting at. They were uncomfortable with the child's "illegitimacy"!

If you already have children, you will have to deal with questions of a different sort. For example, your children might want to know if you could give *them* away, just as the birth parents of your new child did. This calls for some factual reassurance. As a rule, it's better not to tell them that the baby is coming until you get the call. First, you won't experience till then the full emotional awareness that you are about to receive the child, and you might communicate to your kids a little of the "unreality" that the event may hold for you. Also, holding off this information blunts the effect on your children of any last-minute delays or hitches in the adoption.

Many adoptive parents overlook the potentially "communal" aspect of their own relationship to their child. In an age when men have increasingly taken on the role of co-nurturer in their families, adoptive parents have a unique opportunity to foster more equality in parenting, beginning with the time they first bring their child into their home.

Because of the lack of a physical connection to the mother for nine months in adoptive parenthood, an adopted child can "belong" as much to the father as to the mother;

there is less of a proprietary relationship built into the connection between the mother and the child. Feeding is the crucial element, since it is during feeding—ordinarily the mother's sphere—that a baby is most conscious of his relationship to his care-giver. Robin Stanton chose to give Molly a bottle, making it equally possible for Allen to feed the child. (Should you prefer to breast-feed, you might want to discuss it with the local chapter of La Leche. It is a difficult and complicated process, however, unless you have given birth to a child already.)

In our experience, adoptive fathers generally do get more involved in the rearing of their children. Feeding the child is an opportunity to begin raising her so that she grows up with positive images of, and feelings about, men, and we urge you to consider taking advantage of it.

START OFF RIGHT

In preparing for parenthood, one of your first tasks is to choose a pediatrician. Any parent should choose this doctor with much care. Since you will have to establish a relationship with this professional, depending on her for advice about your child's health as well as treatment for specific conditions, the doctor's attitude and personality are as critical as her medical skills. The way she makes you feel about your parental competence and the degree to which you can feel confident in her ability to keep your child healthy will go a long way toward giving you peace of mind.

As an adoptive parent, you will want to be even more selective than birth parents in choosing a pediatrician. This is the last person you can allow to have prejudices about adoption. A woman we know was shocked when her eight-year-old adopted daughter related this to her about her pediatrician. The doctor was examining the child one day and the girl asked this previously sensitive and gentle man if he knew anything about her birth mother. "You're a very ungrateful person," he replied sharply. "How can you do that to your parents?" Whatever *that* was, it had thrown him into a tizzy. Fortunately, the exchange had no traumatic effect on the girl because her mother quickly reassured her that it was okay to ask such questions. The mother also began searching for a new pediatrician.

You also don't want to stay with a pediatrician who will not acknowledge that your child *is* your child. For example, if the adoption has not yet been made final and the doctor, noticing your child twitching, says, "Look, I think this kid is going to be hyperactive. Why don't you return her to the agency before it's too late?" you should reconsider your choice of doctors.

Many adoptive parents have already had difficult experiences with doctors through the drawn-out process of dealing with infertility. If you underwent this ordeal, you may have had the feeling that you were being acted upon, repeatedly pushed toward trying "one more" procedure in an attempt to repair you as if you were a defective automobile. Therefore it is important that you find a pediatrician who is not just one more person in a white coat about to take charge of your life. She certainly should not be sending out signals that you are less than adequate because you adopted rather than gave birth to your child.

How do you select this important person? You could begin with a referral from a friend, relative, or neighbor. Also ask any other adoptive parents you know for a recommendation. Inquire at your adoptive parents' support group for the names of physicians they have found to be both medically competent and sympathetic to the needs of adoptive parents. When you interview a prospective doctor for your child, bring up the subject of adoption. Ask her about her experiences with other adoptive families and what, if anything, in particular she's noticed about their children. Would she feel uncomfortable not having a full medical history for the child? Watch for any prejudice or discomfort she exhibits during the conversation. In general, does she make you feel comfortable when discussing adoption?

Your pediatrician can also advise you about the later medical problems for children whose histories may include poor prenatal care or drug and alcohol use by the birth mother, as well as low birth weight and low Apgar scores. Then you will be better able to make an informed decision about whether or not a particular child would be right for your family.

Once you've selected a pediatrician, talk to her about how you plan to discuss adoption with your child, when you'll first bring it up, and how much you plan to tell him. This is important because the doctor might later say something to your child about adoption and you want to make sure that you and she are saying the same thing.

Make sure you give the pediatrician every bit of information you have about your child that might be relevant to caring for him. The agency or lawyer should have given you a full report which you should share with the pediatrician, but supplement it with anything else you know or have already observed.

Bring your child in for an examination as soon as possible after he is placed with you. This enables your pediatrician to advise you on any condition that needs immediate treatment and it establishes a baseline of information for how your child should be when his health is "normal." This will prove useful anytime something seems amiss. For example, the doctor can check his reflexes to see how he responds to stimulation under average circumstances.

THE TIES THAT BIND

Ed and Marge have two children: Roberta, adopted at age six weeks, and Philip, adopted when he was seven months old. Roberta was pure pleasure to raise, but Philip had more than his share of problems in his first few years, and whenever they arose his parents blamed them on a lack of sufficient bonding between mother and son. Marge had been seriously ill at several crucial points in Philip's young life, but they did not consider that fact, since adoption seemed to be a more convenient explanation for the child's difficulties.

"We weren't with our child from the beginning, and that's why we're having this problem now," goes an occasionally heard explanation from adoptive parents for any problem that arises in their child's development. The image of the newborn infant in his mother's arms, bonding to her in one of the most intimate ways one human being can create ties to another, is an attractive one. But inspiring as it is, it can evoke some mistaken conclusions about the relationship between parents and infants.

The literature about the ties between a child and her first nurturer concentrates on the way the adult has bonded to the child, more than how the child has developed ties to the care-giver. In our experience, and in some of the recent writing on the subject, such as that by psychologist Jerome Kagan, the quality of care-giving more than the identity of that care-giver has greater significance for roughly the first nine months of the baby's life. To be sure, a baby needs consistent physical and emotional nurturing from one set of care-givers during that time and will suffer if she doesn't get it. But whether that sustenance comes from one person or several, as happens in a large family, from a birth mother or a sister or an adoptive mother or father, may not be crucial to healthy development.

People who adopt infants may thus develop emotional ties with a child similar to those the child might have developed with her birth parents. This doesn't mean that people who adopt older children can't form deep and enduring ties with their child, but the quality of that relationship may differ at least somewhat from one created near the beginning of the child's life. We will have more to say about that later when we discuss the adoption of children with special needs.

How about the bonding process from your end? It comes naturally for birth parents, who are raising a child to whom they have a biological connection. By taking care of your adopted child you will also establish some deep, enduring ties to her without thinking much about it.

However, we also know that sometimes adoptive parents may have doubts about whether they are fully entitled to raise as their own a child not born to them. Psychologists say that such parents have not fully "claimed" their baby. When that happens, the parent-child relationship may not take hold as strongly as it should, possibly producing difficulties for the family when the child gets older. It doesn't happen often, and you can take some steps to ensure that it does not arise in your family.

Periodically remind yourself that this is your child and that you will do your best to raise her, that you *are* her parent. Don't second-guess yourself if you make a mistake in your child-rearing work. You are entitled to your quota of mistakes, a quota most parents easily fulfill.

New parents often feel trapped and burdened by their awesome responsibilities. You and your spouse are bound to at least occasionally have ambivalent feelings about your child. That's normal and not a sign that you are not bonding with the child.

"Is there an adoption equivalent of postpartum depression?" we are sometimes asked. In a word, yes. Becoming a parent has to be a little anticlimactic after all you've gone through to get a child. Now you notice how much laundry you have to do. If you were a working woman who quit or took a leave of absence from her job, you may suddenly find yourself home alone with an infant who is all feelings and no intellectual stimulation at all. What's more, there are times when nothing you do can comfort your baby.

While ordinarily none of this threatens the bonding process, you should talk it out with your spouse and friends to vent your feelings. It's important for you to see that you're not alone in experiencing these emotions; any mother, birth or adoptive, can confirm that. One important way you can counter the effect of this letdown is to find ways of being out in the world without your baby from time to time.

TEMPERAMENT

Mike Wagner was worried. He and his wife, Lena, had two children: five-year-old George, who was born to them, and seven-month-old Debbie, who they adopted when she was three months old. Mike's relationship with his son was not always smooth, yet he still derived much enjoyment and satisfaction from his interaction with the youngster. But where Mike had always felt a closeness to George, his ties to Debbie were somewhat problematic. Sure, he loved her, but from a bit of a distance. The chemistry between the two seemed slightly off, and Mike was concerned that he and his daughter were missing a one-time chance to establish a close familial bond. Mike was also beginning to wonder if there wasn't a simple explanation for this problem: Debbie wasn't his "real" daughter.

He needn't have worried so much; and it wasn't helpful to look for an answer in the adoptive relationship. The chemistry between parent and child can be a little off at any time in the child's development, starting with infancy, and it can happen in any family. It involves people with different temperaments coming together in an intense relationship. In families with more than one child, a parent will always feel a different kind of kinship with each. He or she develops different levels of attachment and "like" with each child. That doesn't mean that the parent doesn't love the others. Nor does the favorite always remain the same, since children often change as they grow, especially after infancy. Clashing chemistries only call for professional intervention when they prevent a mother or father from effectively parenting.

It used to be fashionable to blame the mother (and sometimes the father) for children's difficulties. Current research by child development psychologists and especially by Drs. Alexander Thomas and Stella Chess indicates that while most babies are what they call "easy to handle," a small number appear to be born somewhat fussy or overactive and are, as a result, more difficult to handle. Others, fearful or oversensitive, are somewhat slow to warm up to people. Although babies are born with these characteristics, they are not static, however.

It is important to remember that a child's personality develops through interaction between her own inborn tendencies and her environment, so that certain qualities can change as a result of experience. Just as the easy-to-handle baby can, if reared in particular ways, develop as a difficult child, the opposite can be true as well. Some psychiatrists and psychologists have hypothesized that adopted babies may be more likely than other babies to be more difficult to handle, or slow to warm up to others. As a possible explanation, they suggest that because the birth mother is considering surrender of her baby to adoption, she is likely to be under greater stress during her pregnancy. Because this stress can affect the prenatal environment of the developing fetus, the result may be a greater risk for certain temperamental difficulties. While this is interesting and certainly should be studied by researchers, at this time there is no evidence to confirm this hypothesis.

DEVELOPMENT: INITIAL STAGES

Ruth Roland could have worried when her adopted daughter approached the age of two without ever having said a word. Many mothers would have worried about that. But Ruth already had three birth children—all sons—and she knew how much each child could vary, reaching developmental milestones at different times. Since the brothers adored their little sister and seemed to anticipate whatever she wanted, the child did not yet have a need to speak—at least, that's what their mother reasoned. Besides, the pediatrician had said there was nothing wrong with the bright-eyed girl.

Ruth had deftly avoided a potential trap for any parent: the temptation to take a model of child development too literally and to overlook the peculiarities of a particular child. When parents interpret the stages of development too precisely, as tests that their child must pass on the road to normality, they undermine their ability to respond to the specific, idiosyncratic human being in front of them. If they are adoptive parents and yield to the temptation to see a missed or late stage of development as connected to adoption, they could truly be creating something out of nothing.

Of course, parents should never ignore anything that seems out of the ordinary about their child's development. But there is no clear connection between when your child reaches a developmental landmark and the nature of his future development. A missed milestone is no cause for alarm, although a pattern of veering far from the norm would be reason to consult your doctor.

Unfortunately, friends, neighbors, and relatives can sometimes add to the pressure on you to produce a "normal" child, with their constant questions: "Has she talked (rolled over, sat up) yet?" "Has she taken her first step yet?" "Since she's taking so long, don't you think you should have her tested for some possible problems?" If you're hearing this, just tell them that your pediatrician has checked her and she's fine.

"Normal" development covers a lot of territory—witness the descriptions of these babies, all normal:

Jimmy. This child never seemed to sleep. He expressed a constant need to be held and cried a lot, and his mother felt that she could do nothing to comfort him. Within weeks of getting him she was feeling drained and had to go back to work, hiring a baby-sitter to help with the child care. Jimmy was always a vigilant baby, alert to everything going on around him. He didn't like toys—only adults. He rolled over at the age of one month, pushed himself up and tried to crawl at five months, walked at seven months, and taught himself to read at age two.

Bill. This was a much more self-sufficient child. He needed considerably less contact with people than did Jimmy and did not reach out to be held. He was content to entertain himself, sitting in his crib playing with stuffed animals or listening to music. He was also happy when his parents put him in front of the TV. Bill's parents feared he would never roll over and he didn't sit up by himself until the age of ten months; he was sixteen months old before he took his first step alone.

Alice. She shared some traits with the other children, but the combination of characteristics made her an entirely different kind of child to be with than either Jimmy or Bill. Alice was responsive to attention and affection from adults, but also liked quiet time by herself. She rolled over at three months and began to walk unaided at thirteen months. Alice liked to play with toys and be around adults, but she was shy with noisy children. Overall, Alice was not a child you would think of as adventurous.

These traits in your child's early stages tell you nothing about his intelligence. Some kids, for example, are just more inwardly oriented; they may become avid readers. Shyness and inhibition are the temperamental characteristics that tend to remain most constant from infancy into adulthood—but the way you bring him up will diminish or strengthen even them. So how your infant appears to you now will not give you the full picture of what he'll be like when he's twenty-one.

By all means read the fine guidebooks to early child development by experts such as Benjamin Spock and T. Berry Brazelton. They are good "ages and stages" guides to early childhood, but don't try to use them like Bibles. There are also videotapes available at your local video store with information about child development: *Baby Comes Home* (Karl/Lorimar), *Creative Parenting* (A&M), and *What Every Baby Knows* with Dr. T. Berry Brazelton (FHE).

Ultimately, the only person qualified to write the book on *your* child is *you*. Unfortunately, you won't have the full and accurate picture of any particular stage for your child until he or she has passed through it, making its predictive value worthless.

That you adopted your child also makes her first few years an open book when it comes to her physical development, since you may have little or no genetic information upon which to make an educated guess about how she'll look. For example, your pediatrician should be able to give you some idea of whether your child will be tall or short, but her skin tone will take a few months to develop and so will her eye and hair color, and the doctor will not be able to predict them.

If you can, cultivate an attitude of "benign curiosity" toward your child's development. Sit back and watch the patterns emerge; experience the mystery of it. But if you're among the many people who feel anxious doing this and yearn for more control, we have a suggestion. Give yourself observation tasks. Note (perhaps literally, in a notebook or baby book) how your child responds to other people, when she rolls over, what she does if you put your finger or other object near her. Record all the milestones: when she first drinks from a cup, takes her first step, says her first word. Watch how she reacts to people in the supermarket who go "kitchy-koo." In effect, you will be training yourself to respect the essence of your child—and to appreciate her for who she is.

A FAMILY AFFAIR

Those first few months with your child will be hectic, and at times you may feel that you have a little less control over your life than you'd like. It would be nice if you could just concentrate all your energies on developing a relationship with your child and giving her the nurturing she needs. But there is a social component in any kind of parenthood, and adoptive parents often have to devote more energies to this side of raising their child than do birth parents.

If you adopted through an agency, you were probably required to discuss your relationship to your parents and in-laws and their attitude toward your intention to adopt. Those relatives, and your own and your mate's brothers and sisters, can be a source of support in your efforts, or they can become one of the complications of adoption with which you will have to deal; or perhaps they will be some combination of the two.

Even if your parents or in-laws expressed strong reservations about adoption, they may sing a different tune—perhaps a lullaby—once they're holding their grandchild. It's much easier to resist an idea than to remain cold toward a child. But if they still don't warm up to your youngster, or if they observe what they consider to be a hitch in her development, you may have some work to do to either win them over or to at least make sure that they don't let your son or daughter know about their prejudices.

If you think that your child is beginning to sense his grandparents' ambivalence about him, structure his time with them so that the family is involved in some activity, such as going to the zoo, rather than just having dinner together. You might also confine visits to Grandma and Grandpa's house to those times when other people will be around, thus diffusing any negative feelings the grandparents have.

Even if you and your mate have more or less resolved your infertility dilemma, your relatives could still be hung up on this issue. This is particularly true for potential grandparents who have a strong desire to pass on their genes. If this is bothering your parents, you could see if your adoptive parents' group has a program to help adoptive grandparents adjust to their new status, and check with your adoption agency because they may also have such a program.

In its extreme form, your parents' ire might even sound something like, "How can you bring a stranger into the family? I'll be damned if I'll have my name on some—some *bastard*. Why don't you keep on trying to have a child? I've heard about another fertility doctor." You may also hear talk of "bad seeds," or sense an active scrutiny for flaws in your child even when the grandparents have seemingly given you their blessings.

What can you say to your parents if they feel this strongly about it? Here's a possibility: "I know that you have some strong views about this, but I'd appreciate it if you would think it over. Johnny can't change his background, but you can modify your objections. This is our decision, mine and my husband's. I hope you can come to terms with our decision, but it's final. Johnny is our son and, we hope, the grandchild you will come to love."

In some families, resistance to accepting an adopted child as a grandchild may emerge at holidays, such as Christmas and Thanksgiving, or at other occasions for family gatherings. The prejudice may come out in the form of showing favoritism to birth grandchildren over your adopted youngster. If that happens, you could say: "Look, I understand how you feel, but I don't want to expose my child to discrimination, so please try, at least consciously, to treat them equally."

Perhaps you would be more comfortable responding differently. Think about a time when you wanted something from your parents and you had to convince them to change their minds. Couch your argument in the way you did then; adapt it to your style.

Adoptive parents we have spoken to have also found it helpful to introduce reluctant adoptive grandparents to other people who have adopted and are enthusiastic about the process and can tell them of the satisfactions that come with it. Perhaps your spouse's parents as well could speak to your mother and father. They may be more willing to listen to somebody their own age. A clergyman's voice on your side might also help.

Some people have such deep-seated feelings about illegitimacy and the background of the child who will carry on their name that they will stubbornly cling to their antiadoption prejudices no matter what. If this describes your parents' or in-laws' sentiments, you may have to put some emotional distance between them and yourself. Should this become a constant irritant, you might even consider moving away from them to diffuse a perpetually tense relationship. In rare cases, adoptive parents have decided to break off their relationship with these relatives rather than subject their child to their hurtful remarks and behavior and possible emotional abuse. But we stress that this is a last resort, used only after you've tried everything else.

FRIENDS, NEIGHBORS, AND STRANGERS

Many adoptive parents discover that their friends are their greatest resource—often more helpful than their own parents. As for friends who are not supportive of your adoptive parenthood, it would be hard to imagine how your friendship with them could survive, since for many years parenting will consume so much of your time, energy, and attention. Could you feel comfortable with people who devalued this activity?

Neighbors could be very helpful during your child-rearing years. They are repositories of advice and folk wisdom if they have kids, and they're close by should you ever have to deal with an emergency. When your child gets a little older, you may find yourself exchanging baby-sitting chores with other parents on the block or in your building to your mutual advantage.

These are good reasons to bring the neighbors in on this new part of your life, if you're comfortable doing it. As we previously pointed out, it can help to invite them over before you get your child to share your feelings and information with them. Talk to their children, who probably have many questions to ask if they've never known an adoptive family. Talking to kids about adoption may also give you some good practice before you have to respond to the questions of people who have more hardened attitudes on the subject.

Adoptive mothers often find themselves bombarded by questions from birth mothers—"park mothers" in big cities or over-the-fence, neighboring parents in more rural areas—about what adoptive parenting is like. Remember that they're still sorting out their feelings about their birth children, so it may be difficult for them to assimilate what your parenthood is all about. For example, they might be thinking that if you can love a child as your own even though she's not related to you by blood, what does that say about love? They will want to compare their experience to yours, and their questions are likely to be neither malicious nor critical, but rather philosophical and affectionate. They could ask you questions like:

"Can you love her as much as a child to whom you might have given birth?"

"What's it like not to carry her for nine months and then have her handed to you?"

"Do you ever think about your child's birth parents?"

"Do you ever think about what your birth child would have been like?"

"How does your husband (wife) feel about the baby?"

"Who wanted most to adopt?"

"Do you feel like you missed something not going through a pregnancy?"

Perhaps at first you will feel a little uncomfortable responding to these questions. But even if you do, try to see them also as an opportunity to give some thought to how you feel about the issues they raise, which you might not have had time to deal with in the work and excitement of getting and caring for your child. Most often, such questions come from a benign, neutral perspective, so they offer you an opportunity for introspection without the need to defend yourself.

Strangers, unfortunately, are often another matter. Their questions, at their worst, can be intrusive, hurtful, totally insensitive. An adoptive father we know who was in the supermarket with his eleven-month-old adopted Korean child actually had a stranger walk up to him and say, "Gee, you must have adopted her. How much did she cost?" Or you may hear people say dumb things about adoption right in front of you when they don't know that you are an adoptive parent. If they know that you adopted your child, they may ask you about the adoption in her presence, even if she is old enough to understand the question, as if she were invisible. A stranger's remarks can create awkward situations. For instance, you might be introduced to somebody as a new mother, only to hear, "You sure got your figure back fast."

This won't happen constantly, but it's worth preparing yourself to deal with even occasional thoughtless remarks or comments. There is no single correct way of handling these reactions to adoption. You could change the subject or ignore a comment, give a short response and then go on to something else, or, if you're up to it, educate people with straight, comprehensive answers and explanations. It depends on your temperament or how you're feeling at the moment when it happens.

One strategy we learned about from a client could prove useful to you. It offers you the chance to take the initiative and thus diffuse awkward or painful situations before they get a chance to develop. He always waits for a stranger to say something complimentary about his son—most people will do that with a child—at which point he tells him that he adopted the child, catching the stranger on the upbeat.

QUESTIONS AND ANSWERS

My husband and I went through so many infertility tests and had to look so hard for an agency that had the right available child that finally getting our baby has seemed almost anticlimactic. How can we put all the negative memories aside so that we can parent our child?

It's understandable that you feel that way. Achieving any long-sought goal often leaves people with such feelings. It will take time for you to adjust to this new part of your life. Try not to pressure yourself to feel any particular way. You might also want to remind yourself that getting your baby and raising your child are two separate processes. After a few months of parenthood the travails of getting your baby will start to seem like memories that do not impinge on your present status: parents of a child.

□

We adopted privately. Next week the court probation officer is coming for an inspection and we are nervous wrecks. Our child is colicky and we're afraid that if she cries incessantly during the visit the officer will think that we've been abusing her. Are we overreacting?

Every adoptive parent gets nervous before the visit of a probation officer or social worker. We can reassure you that the aim of such visits is not to see if you are being perfect parents; rather, it's to root out the occasional abusive parents. It's rare that such visits result in a child's removal from a home. To feel more in control of the situation, get a note from your pediatrician to the effect that your child has some digestive problems and that her crying does not reflect mistreatment on your part. You're very unlikely to need the note, but having it will probably make you feel better. You could take control of the way your house looks—perhaps even put out some fresh flowers. Try to view the visit as a collegial experience in which you will exchange thoughts about being parents with the court officer, rather than as a confrontation.

□

When we brought our baby home there was a great outpouring of interest, warmth, and empathy from our friends, neighbors, and relatives. In fact, so many people have been trying to participate in caring for him that I'm starting to feel crowded out. Our child's positive response to everyone who has come over strengthens that feeling. There are times when I feel as if I do not have a special place in his life. It's all getting to be too much. How can I get all these well-wishers to back off a little?

Parents often find it necessary to consciously develop boundaries at this time. One solution is to make yourself and your child unavailable for at least several hours each day. Other new mothers take the phone off the hook or find some other way to control contact. Try it.

□

I know that babies in carriages often draw the interest of, and comments from, strangers. But I think that my child is getting more than his share because my husband and I are dark-complexioned and our adopted son has blond hair and blue eyes. I'm not ashamed of being an adoptive parent, but I am getting very tired of answering the same old questions about how we got him. How can I get people to stop bothering me?

It's okay not to discuss your child's adoption at all with strangers. You don't owe them an explanation of anything and if they press the issue you can tell them that you would like to discuss it but that you don't have the time at the moment. With neighbors, though, you might want to try to be patient and answer their questions, since you're likely to interact with them socially and your child might eventually play with their children. You could also view the questions of neighbors you don't know too well as an opportunity to make new friends.

□

While talking about my new adopted baby with my best friend and her six-year-old son, the boy remarked, "What did he do wrong? Why did his mother give him up?" That made me feel sad and I don't know how I'm going to respond to other comments like that, especially from my son as he gets older.

You can respond to this and similar remarks by saying that "his mother couldn't take care of him and she loved him enough to make sure he was raised by a family who could care for him." Add that you feel lucky to be his parent.

□

Lately I've had the feeling that our pediatrician is uncomfortable with our adoption. She doesn't say anything outright, but the gaps in our child's medical record appear to bother her. Besides constantly referring to the incomplete records, she puts our child through what I regard as an inordinately large number of painful medical tests. No other adoptive mother I speak to has a similar story about her child. Is it time to switch doctors?

Tell the doctor why you're feeling uneasy about the way she's treating your child. Ask her if there is a special medical condition which she is trying to isolate. Make it clear that you prefer less testing and ask her straightforwardly if she can come to terms with the lack of complete medical records. Remember that physicians depend a great deal on precise medical histories. More and more inherited tendencies for illness and chronic conditions are being uncovered. For example, a physician can, if she knows there is diabetes in your child's family, insist that he stay slender as a preventive measure. Suggest that she consult with the adoption subcommittee of the American Academy of Pediatrics if she would like to have more information about the general subject of caring for an adopted child. If this conversation leaves you with any doubts about her attitude, look for another physician. Some adoptive parents have told us that older doctors seem to be more comfortable working with skimpier records and don't seem to feel the need to subject children to an excessive amount of testing in order to fill in the blanks.

□

When I look at my adopted child in her crib at night I can't help thinking that I don't deserve to have such a beautiful, sweet, wonderful baby. Why would I feel this way?

It might take you a while to feel that you fully deserve to have your child, perhaps because you did not experience the nine months of pregnancy or childbirth. In time, as she responds positively to you, you'll know that you made the right decision and that your daughter is lucky to have you as a parent.

3

Ages One to Six

These are years of amazing growth for your child. She will get bigger, walk, talk, explore her world, and formulate increasingly complex ideas about her experiences. *Your* growth is also important during this stage. It is vital to your family that you successfully make the transition from being part of a couple to being a parent. This is a formidable job for any new parent, and sometimes considerably harder for adoptive parents, who have to overcome an additional obstacle.

The excitement and work of caring for a baby can take most of your energy and time. However, as your child becomes old enough not to need your constant attention, you may surprisingly find yourself thinking of something you probably thought you had put behind you: infertility, if this was the reason you turned to adoption. It's not unusual for this issue to reappear for adoptive parents in their child's early years. If it doesn't come up spontaneously, questions from other mothers about the relative difficulty of your labor, how soon you got your figure back, or the hospital in which you gave birth could bring it to mind again.

Coming to terms with infertility is a major developmental task for adoptive mothers and fathers at this time.

To grow into the role of parents, you may have to acknowledge the probability that you will not give birth to a child. Unfortunately, doing this requires you to buck a strong social stereotype, since giving birth to children is seen by many in our society as a mark of adulthood.

Perhaps you sense that your own parents don't fully view you as an adult, even though you are raising a child, because you didn't become a "natural" parent. If it was your spouse who had the fertility problem, they may subtly suggest that you might have done better to have married someone else. If you encounter this, you can ask them to speak to members of the grandparents' division of your adoptive parents' group, who may be able to put your parents at ease about having an adopted grandchild. Sympathize with your parents' distress over not having a biological grandchild, but make it clear to them that you've resolved this issue for yourself.

Dashed expectations of procreation can also strain marriage ties. Wives sometimes wonder if their husband's love will survive the disappointment of not having their own biological child, even though they have, in fact, become parents.

If you still have substantial doubts about whether you are a "real" parent—an adult—you might also be uncertain of your right to exercise full parental authority in raising your child. Your child will need your firm guidance through the early years, so it's very important that you deal with any reservations you still have by discussing them with your spouse, other adoptive parents, friends, or if necessary, a therapist.

It's worth repeating: If infertility still bothers you, you're not alone. Many adoptive parents struggle to deal with it. It will probably always be in the back of your mind. To keep infertility from growing into a major problem that interferes with your becoming an effective parent, talk it out whenever you realize that it's troubling you.

YOUR PARENTAL STYLE

In your child's second year, she begins to shed her baby fat and her size, weight, and body type start to become clearly defined. Her physical appearance is now a more dramatic reminder that she was born to another couple. Yet she has probably already begun to reflect many of your family's shared characteristics. You may recognize familiar hand gestures, facial expressions, and smiles in her mannerisms. Perhaps she's already picked up some of your family code words. If you're beginning to think that she even resembles you or your spouse, you're not unusual. Adoptive parents—and others—often make this observation about their adopted children.

While you began to interact with her the first time you and she made eye contact, that interaction has gradually taken on a different quality. Now your child will be walking and talking and in every way possible making her presence known throughout your home. A force to be reckoned with, she will fully take her place in your family as an individual with tastes, sensibilities, needs, quirks—and opinions. A relationship, in the fullest sense of the word, is evolving between you and her.

As this relationship develops, you will establish a style of child rearing and start to define your family's characteristic way of interacting. Along with psychiatrist W. Robert Beavers, former president of the American Association for Marriage and Family Therapy, we believe that there is no single standard of family interaction against which all families should measure themselves. There is a wide spectrum of possibilities between strict and traditional and progressive and democratic. Your formula for success in child rearing and family interaction will depend much on the combination of your own and your spouse's upbringing with the goals you have set for yourselves.

However, we think there *are* some procedural rules worth keeping in mind to ensure that your family continues to work well. Since you are just now putting your own rules into place, this would probably be a good time to look at them and fine-tune them if necessary before they become too solidified. From researchers in the field and from our own practice, we can suggest that the following tips help promote the functioning of any kind of family:

- Try to remain open to disagreements and make sure family members always feel accepted despite differences of opinion.
- Let there be no doubt about who is running the family. Parents should act like parents.
- Make sure your children know what's expected of them. When you talk to them, do it on their level. For example, instead of telling your child that "Mommy likes a neat house and we all need to cooperate to keep it that way so I would like you to pick up your toys," say to your child, "Please pick up your toys." And then get down on the floor and help him.
- Teach respect for individual boundaries, both physical and psychological. Children should realize that they can't barge into your bedroom any time they want to; and you should be aware that by about the time your youngster is six, it's appropriate for you to knock before entering his bedroom. Similarly, family members should also avoid being invasive by telling others in the family how they should be thinking or feeling. For instance, if your child falls and starts to cry, don't run over and tell him, "Don't cry, it doesn't hurt."
- All family members should be able to make mistakes without being humiliated.
- Accept the changes that must come with your child's development and be ready to adapt your family to those changes. For example, when your child has gained the competence and maturity required to do something appropriate to his age level—and his

peers are allowed to do it—let him do it. That could range from permitting a nine-year-old to play with friends without close supervision, to allowing a sixteen-year-old to date.

PREPARING YOUR CHILD FOR THE WORLD

Parents today, adoptive and nonadoptive, can consult experts on child care and development through widely available and inexpensive books such as the Boston Women's Health Book Collective's *Ourselves and Our Children* (Random House), Stella Chess, Alexander Thomas, and Herbert G. Birch's *Your Child Is a Person* (Penguin), T. Berry Brazelton's *Toddlers and Parents* (Delta), Benjamin Spock and Michael B. Rothenberg's *Baby and Child Care* (Pocket Books), and Burton White's *The First Three Years of Life* (Prentice Hall). We will not attempt to offer a comprehensive view of the early years of childhood, already covered so well in these volumes. However, we will focus on certain areas that are sometimes difficult for adoptive parents.

One negative interactive style for which adoptive parents are particularly at risk is the overly child-centered family. They share this with parents of first-borns and only children, and indeed, adopted youngsters often fit into these categories as well.

As an adoptive parent you worked hard to get your child, and the temptation is to hover over him. It's not unusual for adoptive parents to be overprotective. Of course, at the age of one, your child will try to climb into, or on, or reach out for just about everything that's accessible to him. You will have to childproof your house to keep your explorer from hurting himself. (*Keeping Your Kids Safe: A Handbook for Caring Parents,* by Gene Brown, is a good guide to this aspect of child rearing.) Also you might rent the videotape *Baby-Safe Home* (Embassy) with David

Horowitz for information on this subject. Two other tapes—*Too Smart for Strangers* (Disney) and *Strong Kids, Safe Kids* (Paramount) would be best utilized by watching them with your child so that you could answer any questions that arise. But falls are a part of life, and they will happen no matter what you do. An occasional scraped elbow or knee is not too high a price to pay for some important learning experiences, and they're nothing to worry about.

Emotional overprotectiveness is an equally important issue. Your child needs a balance of attention and distance from you; otherwise, he will grow up thinking he's the center of the universe and will experience difficulty in developing satisfying relationships with others. If you overreact to his misbehavior, he will learn that breaking the rules is the way to get your undivided attention. If you pay too much attention to him when he's sick, you will be teaching him that he can get people to care for him by being helpless.

Balance is also the key to launching your child on the road that will eventually take him to a state of healthy autonomy. At about the age of one, he may cry when you leave the room. The awareness of how dependent he is could have frightened him, causing the tears. But he's also curious and wants to be on his own. This ambivalence about dependence and independence is a central theme in the second year and will recur through much of your youngster's early childhood years. Your job is to help your youngster develop a healthy combination of connectedness and self-reliance.

Behavior resulting from this ambivalence could give you some tough moments—as it does for many adoptive parents. For example, you may have noticed that your child occasionally likes to get away from you but does not want you to leave him. When scared by the prospects of separation from you, a parting he can't control, your two-year-old may run to you and cling. If it's a necessary separation—say, leaving him with a baby sitter while you are out—you may have to resist some heartrending sobbing and possible hysteria aimed at reversing your decision.

Temper tantrums are normal behavior for many children in the one-to-four age range. They have nothing to do with adoption and will usually play themselves out after a while. But if you are ambivalent about your right to stand firm and let his temper tantrum run its course, vacillating about a decision that causes him such visible distress, he will learn an effective method of getting his way at any time. If he can work that on you, how will he interact with others—people who do not see his wants and needs as their highest priority? So you will just have to remind yourself that you know best about what is good for him and the family of which he is an integral part.

DISCIPLINE

Your child must realize that the world does not revolve around him and that he can't always get what he wants, when he wants it. To help him learn this, you will have to develop techniques that will enable you to make him hear and heed a particularly important word whenever you say it. Unfortunately, he has his own uses for that word.

No! In truth, one-year-olds already know the concept and, if they talk, are likely to favor this word. But when you start to hear it often from your two-year-old, you know you have your work cut out for you. It is comforting, though, to realize that so many other parents are also experiencing this negativity and that it even has a name: "the terrible twos." Do you think you might be having a bit more anxiety over this phenomenon than does your neighbor, who is a birth parent? Many adoptive parents do. Some adoptive mothers and fathers interpret this rebellion as a sign that their child doesn't like them. Could they be doing something wrong? Does their child act this way because she senses that they are not her "real" parents? Will their child still love them if they stand firm?

This is your child's first major manifestation of independence—a moving away from you. While it might be natural for you to respond by questioning your parental competence, you're not likely to be doing anything wrong to elicit this obstinacy and you would be mistaken to let your anxieties influence the firmness with which you respond to your child's refusal to cooperate. Action is required rather than long lectures. Kids have short attention spans. Letting them have their way could cause trouble and give you real reasons to doubt your ability to parent. They not only need limits at this point, they are also beginning to ask for them and it's your job to supply them.

You will be setting many limits for your child now—presenting him with your own "nos." He needs to learn where he can't walk, what he can't touch, when he shouldn't interrupt. Your child will have to learn not only rules for safety, but also that he must consider the needs and rights of others. Remember, two-year-olds have small vocabularies and very little judgment or common sense.

Adoptive parents sometimes feel guilty about disciplining "another person's child." While we can understand that you might have doubts about your entitlement to impose discipline on your child, you need to realize that you not only have the right and obligation to do this, it is also an expression of your love for your child.

Believe it or not, we've had adoptive parents come into our office, towering over the four-year-old they have in tow, and complain that they can't "control" their child. We find it hard to believe that these adults are so helpless that they can't deal with a small child.

Usually, you can effectively control a one-year-old's behavior through direct physical action. If he's doing something that could endanger him, lift him and carry him away from the source of the danger; or distract him by taking away the object he should not play with and exchange it for something else that interests him. When you tell him "No" or "Don't do that," say it in a steady, firm tone of voice. Let him hear the seriousness with which you view his misconduct; you should not confuse him by saying no with a chuckle or bemused expression. He needs to get the message straight.

As your child gets older and you become aware of just how much and what kind of misbehavior you and your spouse will tolerate, stick to the limits you set. If your youngster is carrying on, don't try to be too patient and understanding. Remind her that "this is the way we do it," without a long and involved explanation and defense of why that's the case. If she still doesn't do it your way, correct her immediately. Then, if necessary, some consequence or punishment for the misbehavior may be in order. We feel that small and brief but sure punishments work best—ten minutes in her room, for example. And don't allow any back talk when you're correcting her.

If this all sounds a bit stern, remember that disciplining only accounts for a small part of the time you spend with your child. Take a "firm but friendly" approach to correcting him, as Dr. Benjamin Spock suggests, and he'll accept it in that spirit. Your child wants you to set limits for him; he knows when he's getting away with too much. Don't worry, he will love you just as much after you impose discipline, though he may like you less at the moment.

While we will not cover every kind of misbehavior you are likely to see, we think it's important that you stay alert to types of misconduct that can easily be blown out of proportion. The way that adoptive parents interpret their young child's behavior is perhaps even more crucial than the comparable perceptions of birth parents. In some instances you might be tempted to resort to a handy explanation for misbehavior: your child's adoption. Unfortunately, that pushes into the realm of pathology actions that probably have their roots in something much more mundane.

For instance, many children of three or four will be

fascinated by and use bathroom language. This sometimes shocks parents and gains attention for the child. If you are surprised by such words coming from your adopted child, and possibly vulnerable to someone making a silly observation like, "This language reflects the child's lower-class roots," you could create an adoption problem where none exists. You might start doubting that you can truly affect your child's character and behavior. Children outgrow this. It is just a phase.

It can really upset some people to hear a little child spouting such words. Ideally, you will be able to understand his fascination at this point in his development and be reassured that it is likely to stop when he outgrows this stage. It has nothing to do with class or adoption. But if you can't let it go, try not to express shock. That gives your youngster a message that he can use words to get to you. Just correct your child, tell him why you don't like it and make up new funny words with him; if he persists, you may wish to have a consequence for such behavior to remind him of your disapproval.

Another type of behavior that many parents, including adoptive mothers and fathers, are prone to mistakenly regard as serious misconduct, is what they perceive as "lying" from their three- or four-year-old. Adoptive parents sometimes think this is related to their child's origins. Children of this age have vivid, active imaginations. They love to make up stories and, because of their cognitive development at this stage, may sometimes blur the boundary between reality and fantasy. They are not willfully distorting the truth, trying to put something over on you; they have no bad intent. They're just acting their age and they shouldn't be punished—or regarded as sick—for it.

Don't be hard on yourself if you realize that you've occasionally given in a little to fears that such behavior is adoption-related. Take it as an opportunity to prepare yourself to recognize these incidents for what they are in the future. So much of this is uncharted territory; you simply need to try to do your best knowing that all parents make mistakes and kids survive quite well despite that fact.

One way you can avoid making too much of a minor incident is to try to train yourself to be open to more than one explanation of why your child has acted in a particular way. If you have no reason to believe otherwise, assume that the most benign explanation is the correct one. What if you find this difficult to do? You could practice on the little mishaps and mischief that arise with any child of this age.

Dr. W. Robert Beavers, former president of the American Association for Marriage and Family Therapy, offers the following as an example of the many ways parents could interpret the simple act of their three-year-old spilling a glass of milk at the table:

1. It was an accident, involving no motive.
2. The child was trying to get back at her mother for something.
3. The child was expressing hostility not connected to the parent.
4. The child was tired and anxious and likely to make a mistake at the time.
5. The glass was too large for the child's fingers.

Depending on the context, any of these explanations could have been correct. The point is not to immediately seize on the same explanation every time to the exclusion of others. Parents who do that may be seeing a "symptom," which suggests that a diagnosis and treatment will logically follow, possibly turning a trivial event with a simple explanation into a major crisis. Child rearing is a tough enough job without making it unnecessarily tougher.

TELLING YOUR CHILD ABOUT ADOPTION

An adopted child, four years old, went up to his mother one day and asked, "Where did I come from?" His mother, who was relieved to be asked such a direct question, finally had an opportunity to use the response she had carefully prepared when the youngster was two. She told him how he had grown in another mommy's tummy, and how that mommy had brought him to the agency, which gave him to his adoptive mother and father, who brought him home and loved him very much. "Is there anything else you would like to know?" his mother added, partly looking forward to and partly dreading the dialogue she thought would follow. The child looked quizzical. "Yeah," he replied. "Johnny next door said he came from Ohio. Where did I come from?"

Understandably, when, how, and what to tell an adopted child about the way he joined their family is one of the prime concerns of adoptive parents. They sometimes get very anxious about "doing it right." Fortunately, fewer and fewer people think that the answer is keeping adoption a secret from their child. Unfortunately, there's still a lot of confusion about how to go about telling a youngster the truth.

There are only two things surrounding the issue of telling that could harm your child: keeping it a secret, or using the information as a weapon in a moment of anger. Your family's style will determine the mechanics of telling. For example, some parents begin when their child is in the cradle, calling their infant their "beautiful adopted baby." Others wait until their child asks about childbirth, usually when asking about a pregnant woman he had observed, or a friend's mother.

Some parents pick an arbitrary age at which they think their child should hear the story. While that's not likely to do any harm, you should realize that no matter what you tell your child, she will not fully understand the concept of adoption until she is considerably older. In fact, kids are usually at least fourteen or so before the impact of their adoption can completely sink in.

Until about the age of five, your child's cognitive abilities will not really be up to the task of making sense of what she hears about adoption. That might surprise some parents, who tell their child the whole story and then hear her relate it accurately to someone else. The catch is that the child is largely parroting words, not grasping their meaning, although she may have begun to understand some of the simplest aspects of the process.

Psychologist David M. Brodzinsky, an authority on adoption, illustrates this by relating his attempt to see how much a four-year-old understood about adoption and childbirth. He asked the child, an adoptee, to describe the adoption process. The girl related how "the baby grows in one mommy's tummy and then comes out at the hospital and a new mommy and daddy come and adopt the baby and love it forever." Not bad for a child her age. And where, Brodzinsky asked her, do babies come from? "The baby grows in one mommy's tummy and then comes out at the hospital and a new mommy and daddy come and adopt the baby and love it forever," the child replied, indicating that the child was too young to understand fully the conceptual difference between birth and adoption.

It's helpful for even your young child to start to become comfortable with the vocabulary of adoption and to have at least a simple explanation of the process to supply if anybody asks him about it. When he does begin to understand it in greater depth, it will be not because of the passing of time and the gaining of experience, but rather because he has reached a new stage of cognitive development. Simply put, his mind will be capable of handling more complex ideas.

We think that the most useful approach to telling a child about her adoption is to let the child set the agenda, rather than delivering a lecture when you think she should be ready to hear it. If you've been using the word *adoption* all along, your two- or three-year-old may one day say, "My cousin says he wasn't adopted; why am I adopted?" There's your opening.

When you reply, give her a simple answer. "We wanted

to have a baby and we couldn't," you could say. Then tell her in as uncomplicated a way as you can how she came to be in your family, but nothing more unless she asks. If you exhaust her with a long story, she may hesitate to ask you about adoption again. Read to her from books for children about adoption, such as *The Chosen Baby* by Valentina P. Wasson (Lippincott), one of the classic books children seem to love. You could also follow up by reading bedtime stories to her from books that have an adoption theme. The stories of Thumbelina and Heidi are fine for this purpose. If you notice that an upcoming TV show will treat the adoption theme on a kid's level, watch it with her so you can answer any questions she raises.

Tell your child as much as she seems to be able to deal with. Make sure she's satisfied with your answers. And always balance your description of how you got her with a statement about how much you wanted her and how much you love her. Her experience in your family will reinforce her perception that you love and care for her regardless of how she came to be with you.

The inevitable questions about childbirth offer a good way of bringing up adoption. If your child asks you about a pregnant woman he's seen, tell him where babies come from and then explain that another person carried him in her womb and that you adopted him. If he asks why, explain that the other woman couldn't take care of him and that you got him because you wanted him. Make sure you convey the idea that putting him up for adoption was an act of love by his birth mother—that everyone concerned had his best interests at heart. By the time he's older he may begin to question this, but then gradually he will be able to see the situation in a broader context.

Of course, the reality of it is never quite so neat and tidy. No matter how carefully you frame your answers, you'll probably hear "But why?" over and over. Or she may come back to you with different questions that you might think you sufficiently answered in your response to her initial questions. For example: "If this child [in the pregnant woman's womb] can stay with her mommy, why couldn't I?" Don't let it discourage you. It's natural for your child to ask you again about material you know you went over thoroughly. In young children this stems partly from their enjoyment of having the power of getting you to respond. But it derives even more from the nature of the process of taking in and assimilating this information. That will last for years.

What if your child seems unconcerned about adoption and never asks, or after hearing about it once, does not bring up the topic again? Generally, this is not a cause for concern. Every adoptee wonders why he was given up. But some kids are less prone to talk about it. Bring it up yourself, from time to time and every time he reaches a new stage of development—certainly when he starts school—perhaps by referring to a movie you saw or book you read that had a story that reminded you about how you got him through adoption.

Always be careful not to use anything relating to your child's adoption in a flippant, teasing, or angry way. For example, don't tell your child, "We got you from under the cabbage patch." Nor should you ever connect your child's misbehavior to adoption. There's a difference between hurtful remarks from a stranger and similar comments from you. Your child assumes that you know her better than anyone and your words would have an immensely greater impact.

While it's difficult, sometimes impossible, for a parent to apologize for angry remarks tied to their child's adoption, kids are resilient. Some children can shrug it off; others will take it as a challenge and try to prove their parent was wrong. But even those energized by this kind of abuse pay a price. One adoptee we know was goaded to achieve a Ph.D. in psychology by such treatment, partly to prove her mother wrong. But it also causes her great pain to this day.

SIBLINGS

On the day that Al and Sue Brookens took home Julie, their adopted daughter, the social worker handling the adoption made sure that five-year-old Carl, the Brookenses' adopted son, was in the middle of the ceremony. In fact, as soon as the parents got to exchange loving looks with their new daughter, the social worker handed the baby to Carl and said: "This is your baby."

Agencies know that when a new adopted infant enters a family, it's important that children already in the home begin immediately to form an attachment to the baby. The older child should not be made to feel external to the process. The phenomenon of sibling rivalry is present here as much as in any other family, so it's important to get the new sibling relationship off to a good start.

If you become parents for a second time, the adopted child you already have might react negatively to the addition to your family before the new child even arrives. "Can we send her back if we don't like her? Can't we get two cats instead?" and the like are normal reactions. Acting babyish is another common reaction to a new sibling. Unless such behavior is constant, it will do no harm to give in to it. But if it continues for three months or more, you might want to consult your pediatrician.

You can help ease the transition to becoming a two-child family by acknowledging your older child's frustration at having to share your attention with a sibling. It often helps to enlist the first child as a "helper" in taking care of his sibling, but of course you should supervise any help he gives you with the baby. You can also point out the privileges he has because he is older—going to the zoo with you, for example, while his little sister can't.

If you took pictures of your first adopted child, it would be nice if you did the same for your second. But the reality of it is that most parents don't make as complete a photographic record of their second child as they did of their first, so it's not worth the guilt feelings it can provoke. However, if you adopted your second child but gave birth to your first, you might want to be more self-conscious about taking those pictures of your adoptee. She could be a bit more sensitive to any family pattern that might suggest that she is any less your child than is her sibling.

Talk as much to the new child as you did to your first adoptee about adoption. We note this because it's only natural to slack off a bit after you've already gone through the process once. Remember that your second child has not experienced any of this and the attention is as important to him as it was to his older brother or sister.

If you've given birth to your second child and are nursing him, your adoptee may ask: "Did you do that to me?" If you didn't, explain that Mommy and Daddy held her close and smiled and sang to her while feeding her from a bottle. You could also use the question as another opportunity to discuss adoption with her.

Sibling rivalry can be unpleasant and disruptive. Your older child may express hostility by holding the baby too tightly or pinching her too hard, all the while saying how cute the new child looks. One mother we know became worried when it was too quiet in the next room where her three-year-old and her newly adopted baby were. She got up to look and found the older child holding the baby near the back door of the house. "I told you not to pick her up and carry her," she admonished her son. "I didn't," he replied in all innocence. "I rolled her."

That can happen in any family. But in an adoptive family, certain additional problems can result from sibling rivalry. Adopted kids are vulnerable to teasing from birth children that takes adoption as its theme. Remarks like "You're adopted and I'm not" hurt. So make it a rule in your home that nobody can use adoption to taunt or tease. And, naturally, avoid ever adding to possible tensions yourself by making comparisons between your children.

Don't overlook your birth child's possibly ambivalent

relationship to adoption. It would be normal for him to have fantasies about adoption and his own origins. If he does raise questions about the subject, answer them as carefully and clearly as you would similar queries from your adoptee. And make sure your birth child knows that it's okay for him to ask.

SEXUALITY

Marjorie Parsons and her husband had adopted a boy and a girl. While giving the children a bath one day when the boy was four and the girl was three, Marjorie noticed that her children were starting to touch each other all over. Marjorie was a sophisticated parent who had read extensively about child development and knew that her kids were just being naturally curious about each other's bodies. But the incident nevertheless unnerved her a bit. She had heard just enough scare stories about adoption—"bad seeds," incest, and the like—to have at least a few fears in the back of her mind.

These fears prey on the minds of many adoptive parents—it's one of the most frequent difficulties that they have when trying to square normal child behavior with the distorted ideas and misinformation about adoption that we all hear at one time or another. In our experience, adopted children are no different from other kids when it comes to expressing sexuality. They are curious and they explore their own bodies and sometimes those of their playmates—playing doctor, for example, is normal for four-year-olds. Parents who may not realize that most kids do this could be shocked by such behavior and incorrectly ascribe it to adoption.

Just as some kids are more curious than others, children vary in how physically affectionate they are with their parents and siblings. If you can, return your child's affection for you in kind. Should she unknowingly cross the boundary of propriety, straightforwardly tell her that there are some parts of your (and her or his) body that are private.

If your child seems to be extraordinarily affectionate, it could be from some insecurity for which he wants reassurance. Any kid can feel that way, adopted or nonadopted. Don't be afraid to respond to it. Most likely it's a stage he will soon get over. By the age of five or six it's also normal for kids to express something akin to a romantic attachment to their opposite-sex parent (more about this in the next chapter).

Children between the ages of three and six who show great curiosity about where babies come from are behaving well within the normal range. When your child asks such questions, use them to talk about adoption and her origins. This might be a good occasion to once again take out your favorite adoption book for kids, such as *The Chosen Baby*, and read to her from it.

There are many books that are useful for answering your child's questions about sexuality. Among them are Margaret Sheffield's *Where Do Babies Come From: A Book for Children and Their Parents* (Knopf) and Sara Bonnett's *Making Babies: An Open Family Book for Parents and Children Together* (Walker). Also useful is the videotape *Where Did I Come From?* (LCA). The latter should be viewed together with your child.

PLAYMATES AND NURSERY SCHOOL

By the age of two, kids are old enough to sit next to each other and play separately—a phenomenon called "parallel play." Don't worry if your child does not interact at all with the child busily moving blocks around right at her elbow. Kids this age have little empathy for others and do not share; they're just not yet developmentally ready to socialize fully.

Nevertheless, it's beneficial for your child to spend time

in this activity because it helps her get used to being with other children. A two-year-old may be timid and need all the practice she can get being in the presence of other kids. In fact, it's a good idea to encourage even this limited socializing by taking her to the park or playground and bringing her over to visit your friend or a neighbor who has kids her age.

Most children begin to play with others at about age two-and-a-half or three. (If your child is still completely a loner by four, you might want to consult your pediatrician about it.) Inevitably, as she gets older and begins to actually play with other children, the issue of her adoption may come up at some point. In these early years, the tone of anything other kids say to her is likely to be benign. For example, the parent of one of her playmates may tell her child that your youngster was adopted. That child then might ask your child a straight question about the subject.

If your child seems a little thrown by having to respond to such a question, reassure her that all kids are curious about any way they differ from others. Before you suggest how she should handle it, ask her what she would like to say. In her childhood interaction with others, it will often be a good idea to help her to work out and rehearse a response to anything requiring a reaction, rather than intervening and helping her directly. This will help build her confidence in her ability to handle her relationships with others.

Now that your youngster is taking her first tentative steps outside the safe confines of your family, you may start to encounter some situations in which you will have to decide whether to bring up the fact of her adoption. For instance, it might be appropriate to mention it if you become friends with the parents of your child's playmates. If you do tell them, don't be surprised to discover that there are a lot more adoptive families around than you had realized.

If you send your adopted child to nursery school, you may want to tell her teacher and the school's administrator that your child was adopted. Talk to them and try to get a sense of how they feel about adoption. You might ask if there are other adopted kids in the school. If there are, request that the school put your child in their class, if possible. Also make it clear that you will serve as a resource of information about adoption should the teacher need facts to answer a question raised by another child in the school.

QUESTIONS AND ANSWERS

My two-and-a-half-year-old adoptee is becoming willful and has begun to have temper tantrums. I'm very worried that he's inherited some kind of emotional problem that we knew nothing about when we adopted him. My husband says I'm overreacting. Is he right?

Unpleasant as this phase may be, that's all it is—a phase, common to all children. You might find it reassuring to read some child development books to see just how normal it is. However, you may also be observing the result of a rather fragile disposition, inherited by your child from his birth family. That would still not be a cause for alarm. A recent study by Finnish psychiatrists and psychologists indicates that even adopted children born to mothers hospitalized for schizophrenia can grow up healthy in healthy adoptive families.

Try to observe what happens just before he has these tantrums. It could be some sort of stimulus, such as too much noise, the presence of too many people, or the need to choose between one thing or another that is setting him off. You could avoid placing him in the kinds of situations that create the tantrums.

□

I'm wondering how much longer I can continue to take my four-year-old to her grandparents'—my husband's parents'—house. They have never been comfortable with her adoption and they continue to favor their birth grandchildren. Now my daughter is becoming aware of their favoritism. We have tried to discuss this with them, but we don't seem to be able to get them to reexamine their attitude.

If your spouse, who knows his parents best, can't come up with a way to overcome their resistance to accepting your child, you may have to limit contact with them. They are, after all, the grownups, and they will have to do the changing. There's nothing your daughter can do to change her adoptive status. And if you don't protect her from this cruel treatment, she could grow to resent you for it.

Perhaps you could just see them for dinner occasionally, without your child. You may also have to leave them out when you invite your other relatives to your home. Let them know why you feel you need to do this and perhaps that will start to bring them around.

□

My four-year-old says that she wishes that she came from my womb. I wish it too, and thinking about it makes me cry. Is this a serious problem?

If it's still that much of an issue for you, it would probably be a good idea for you to talk to other adoptive mothers, friends, perhaps even a therapist about it. It's okay to tell your child that you wish you had given birth to her, although stress that the most important thing for you was to become a parent. At the same time, emphasize that you love more than anything that she's your daughter. Also remind her that giving birth is a brief experience and that the long period of time that you have had her and will continue to raise her is more important to you.

□

My two-and-a-half-year-old insists on playing by himself. Somebody told me this might be a sign of antisocial behavior. Is there anything to that?

Your child should be encouraged to play with his peers. Yet some children, often only children, genuinely enjoy playing alone. Your child needs to be given a chance to play with or near other children. Help your child by bringing one child to your home and gently assist in getting your child to play with her for a short time. Each time they play together, gradually lengthen the time that they play, judging by how your child appears able to tolerate it. Then introduce more children gradually. Behavior is a matter of temperament. If you would like to find out more about the subject of temperament, read *Your Child Is a Person: A Psychological Approach to Parenting Without Guilt* by Stella Chess, Alexander Thomas, and Herbert G. Birch.

□

My adopted child, age two-and-a-half, has begun to call every woman he sees "Mommy" and every man "Daddy." Does this have anything to do with adoption?

Any child of this age might use these terms generically for a while. It's nothing to worry about.

□

My neighbor walked into her daughter's bedroom the other day and found her playing doctor with my four-year-old adopted son. Now she won't let her daughter associate with my child. She also says that this happened because my child was adopted. What should I tell her?

Playing doctor at this age has nothing to do with sexual promiscuity—and certainly nothing to do with adoption. It's simply a child's healthy curiosity about his and others' bodies. Try to explain to your neighbor the facts of the matter. If she just won't hear it, you'll have to limit your child's contact with her child, certainly until things cool down. Children of this age do need to be supervised, however, when they play together.

□

My three-year-old has been taking her older sister's favorite toy. I know she's young, but my husband and I worry that this stealing could be setting a pattern for the future. We're also wondering if this could be the beginning of some kind of complex related to adoption.

The problem here is in how you're framing your dilemma. Your child isn't "stealing." Kids don't have a fully developed sense of what is theirs and what belongs to others until somewhere between the ages of five and seven. Until then, honesty is an abstraction. At the age of three, your child's conscience is in the process of developing. You could help it along by offering her guidance and correction every time she takes something that doesn't belong to her so she will eventually learn to respect the rights of others, but don't expect her to really grasp it until she is older. This has nothing to do with adoption.

□

We are considering adopting a second child now that our first adopted child is four years old. Our daughter is easygoing and bright. Both my spouse and I work at demanding professions and the time that we have to spend together as a family must, of necessity, be quality rather than quantity time. We, therefore, want our second child to be as healthy and enjoyable as our first. We have recently learned that infants born to mothers who have used cocaine even once during their pregnancy are likely to be quite handicapped. What are the facts about this and how can we ensure that the baby we adopt has not been exposed to cocaine as a fetus?

You are correct in being concerned about cocaine's effects on the fetus even when used occasionally during pregnancy. It appears, from recent research, that cocaine use during pregnancy almost certainly damages the central nervous system of the growing fetus and may damage other organs, as well. Cocaine or "crack" appears to be far more damaging to the developing fetus than other narcotics or alcohol. It is unlikely that you will be able to know absolutely whether or not a baby has been exposed to cocaine prenatally unless the birth mother has lived in an entirely restricted facility during the entire nine months of pregnancy. Sometimes cocaine was used in the first trimester, before the mother knew she was pregnant. Unfortunately, this is also when cocaine does the most damage to the fetus. Usually the characteristics of a "cocaine baby" are the following: low birth weight, small head circumference, small size, prematurity, a piercing cry, and muscular rigidity. These infants are difficult to comfort, feed, and interact with and require a great deal of parental time and attention. They will be likely to require intensive parenting to ensure that they can develop to capacity. These infants suffer from permanent damage to the central nervous system rather than withdrawal from narcotics. Researchers at the present time believe that the central nervous system damage will manifest itself, as the child grows, in attention-deficit disorders, hyperactivity, and school difficulties. High birth weight, normal head circumference, high Apgar scores, and high scores on all of the scales of the Brazelton Neonatal Behavioral Assessment Scales (BNBAS) should be useful in helping you to determine whether you should adopt a particular newborn.

4
The School Years, Ages Six to Nine

From age six on, the outside world increasingly affects your child's thoughts and behavior. Now she begins her formal school career. Where once you and you alone stipulated rules, limits, and moral tenets, you must now vie for influence with teachers and your son or daughter's school friends.

Going to school is the beginning of separation from the family—completed in late adolescence—and it can be a little trying for parents. If this is your first child, your family has never experienced this break; if your last child is starting school, his or her departure is the first intimation of the empty nest.

Some adoptive parents seem to have a particularly hard time with this process. They experienced less control than other parents over the way their child entered their family; now, just a few years later, they find themselves required to graciously begin to relinquish their parental omnipotence. If these parents still harbor doubts about their right and ability to effectively parent, they may wonder if they have adequately prepared their child to cope with the outside world.

This separation drama is played out against a backdrop of the child's dawning realization—as the result of comparing herself to her classmates—that it's different to be adopted. While a full understanding of her origins is still probably about seven or eight years away, she can now put into words the sometimes confused notions she may have about her relationship to you and her birth parents.

If no major problems have hindered her development, you should be confident that you've given your child enough resources to respond appropriately to the people and situations she will encounter. However, you should stay alert to the difficulties that her adoption may present to her in these years. For example, while it's not likely to happen, an occasional teacher or school guidance professional may misinterpret your child's minor classroom difficulties as problems stemming from his or her adoptive status. The parents of one of your child's friends might show prejudice toward your youngster—making things rough for her with her peers—under mistaken impressions about adoption. Or thoughtless adults could congratulate your child: "Weren't you lucky to be adopted!" These or similar events would require you to do a little educating. It is an adult responsibility which requires adult intervention. Your child is too young to handle it herself.

FEARS AND FANTASIES

The questions that some children this age ask about their background become more pointed—and more challenging than the ones they previously asked. When Jimmy was seven, he asked his adoptive mother if his "first mother" knew her, and if she didn't, how could she just give her her child? Wasn't he sufficiently valuable for his birth mother to want to know his adoptive mother before handing him over to her? His mother responded in a way that you could when faced with a similar question.

His mother first asked Jimmy if he could think of any reasons why a girl might do this. Among other reasons Jimmy said, "If she didn't know anybody who could take care of a baby." She then explained to Jimmy that in some kinds of adoption, when a mommy didn't know anybody who could take care of her baby, she goes to a place called an adoption agency. Here there are people called social workers who ask the mommy how she wants her baby taken care of and who then try to find a family that will give the baby just that kind of care and love. That's what they did for his birth mother. Jimmy's mother also told him that she wished that she had been able to meet his first mommy and that she had been able to decide if she liked his adoptive mother. But the social worker did that for them.

What if Jimmy had entered the family through private adoption and had asked the same question? Then his mother could have told him that some birth mothers get to choose from descriptions of several possible adoptive families, and that his birth mother chose the ones she liked best. When responding to any question from your child about his birth mother's motives, it is helpful to stress the positive, even if you do not have all the facts.

Jimmy's question falls within the typical range of thoughts, observations, and remarks about adoption that you may hear from a child of this age. As he moves out into the world, he will come into closer and more frequent contact with other families, which can be a constant reminder that his background differs from that of most kids in an important way. He may respond by questioning how that came about, and what that should mean to him. No matter how often, openly, and rationally you may have discussed this with him, his burgeoning imagination may well come up with creative, and possibly disconcerting, embellishments.

On the bleaker side, adopted kids at the age of nine may wonder, with fear, if their birth mother might return to take them away. At this stage, they consider such a turn of events as a real possibility. If that should happen, they wonder, to whom would they belong? Your child is still too young to understand the legal aspects of adoption that would reassure him that he belongs legally with you.

At age seven, Adam began waking up in the middle of

the night, crying out as the result of nightmares. When his parents went in to comfort him, they discovered that he had dreamt that his "real" mother had returned and wanted him back.

After some time, Adam's parents calmed him by reassuring him that "you are our son now, a real part of our family. No one will ever take you away."

Adam's parents reminded him that someday he would move away, probably first to go to college and maybe later to have a family of his own. But they reassured him that this would happen only when he was ready, not before. "And even then," they added, "we won't stop being your parents. You won't need us so much then, but you'll still be our son." Comforted, Adam went back to sleep.

Misunderstandings can also occur during this period as a consequence of punishment for bad behavior. Since, if she misbehaves, your child knows that you will discipline her, she may "reason" that she was given up for adoption because she was bad, perhaps for crying too much. (Similarly, children caught up in the middle of their parents' divorce may think that they could have prevented the split if only they had behaved better.)

If your child expresses such thoughts, tell her: "Parents don't give up children for adoption because they are bad. Sometimes, though, if a parent knows she can't take care of her child in the way that she should, she may decide to let another family, who *can* raise a child, bring her up. It's hard for a parent to give up a baby and making that decision means she loved you very much and wanted the best for you."

Although it is more likely to show up later, some kids in this age range begin to speculate about who their birth parents "really" were. It is usual for children at this time of life to add imagination to facts to try to understand things. Sometimes they dream up idealized biological parents who were famous, powerful, beautiful, talented, and very loving people. Children of this age see things in more extreme forms—either all good or all bad.

Such idealizing of the unknown may arise in response to the gibes of playmates who belittle your child's birth parents or emphasize his lack of knowledge of them: "You don't even know who your real parents are!" Not yet capable of dealing with the reasons why a birth parent would give her up, your child may well respond with a vivid description of what she has imagined: "My mother was a famous movie star."

What if you overhear your child making up a story like this? It's no cause for alarm. Your son or daughter is responding to a stressful and ego-threatening situation with the best weapon he or she now has: imagination. It's nothing to worry about. Stories about glorified birth parents are as harmless as the conversations children sometimes have with imaginary playmates.

Normal children of six or seven—adopted or not—indulge in a good deal of fantasy play, and some of it is about things that may trouble them: accidents, sickness, killing, and death in general. Seven-year-old Michael, for example, plays violent games with his Masters of the Universe figures. They kill each other, sometimes first cutting off their opponents' limbs. You might hear your child link such fantasies to adoption, imagining, for example, violence perpetrated on a birth parent—although it's not common. If you do hear this and it does not become obsessive—he does not become totally preoccupied with it or change his behavior as a result—you should not worry.

There is some disagreement among experts about whether adopted children of this age are likely to be ready—or want—to voice anger about the reality of their parents' rejection of them early in life. In our experience we have found that the expression of such feelings at this age is relatively rare. But the issue could arise.

Johnny Coleman, age six, flew into a rage one afternoon. When his mother managed to calm him, he explained: "A boy in my class said my mother didn't want me. She didn't like me, and that's why she gave me up for adoption. I hate her, I hate her!"

Should your adopted child say something like this, you will have to accept it. Your child *was* rejected; that's a fact of life from which you cannot protect him. It's OK for him to be hurt and even angry about it. If you hear these sentiments, acknowledge your child's pain and mirror what he says. It is important for him to be able to talk about how he feels. It is not important at this moment for you to explain anything, but, instead, to listen to him and comfort him for his perfectly normal feelings.

Some children like to be held when they cry, others prefer that you keep your distance, while still others get upset if you even look at them while they weep. Respect your child's style. Don't try to pretend that his bad feelings aren't there, because then he might doubt their reality. Don't tell him how sad he makes you feel when he is sad. It could seem as if you were trying to substitute your pain for his.

If you hear your son or daughter suddenly express strong feelings about adoption, or if your child has nightmares or anxieties that weren't there a few days ago, the cause might very well be something seen on television. Ask her about it; if she did see something on television, discuss it with her. You can use this to have a vivid conversation about adoption, perhaps more open than any you've previously had. Try to make the most of it, but be cautious not to push it too far. Your child will let you know when to stop, either by telling you he now wants to do something else or by visibly losing interest in the subject.

Adoption is a romantic, dramatic, and compelling subject, one that's ripe for television treatment. Not long ago, for example, "Punky Brewster," a popular TV show, featured a story about a kid who was put up for adoption but ended up instead in an institution. Finally, through some melodramatic plot turns, he found his way back to his birth mother and he confronted her. She refused to speak to him at first, but then she cried and apologized and the two were able to stay together. That's powerful stuff for a six- or seven-year-old adoptee.

"Mr. Rogers" and "Sesame Street" have also dealt with adoption. There's no reason to shelter your child from such broadcasts. They are sensitively and honestly handled. If you can, watch them with her. Do so in order to be aware of and sensitive to issues they raise. It is a wise adoptive parent who scans TV listings for such programs.

What if your child in this age group shows little or no interest in discussing his adoption? It would be a good idea for you to introduce the subject yourself once in a while if he doesn't initiate this conversation. However, ask yourself, are you sure that the reticence is entirely on his part?

A colleague of ours recently organized separate adoption support groups for several adoptive mothers and their six-year-old adoptees. The mothers, in their group, said that their children hardly ever talked about adoption—certainly less than they had expected them to. Their kids, on the other hand, painted a much different picture when they discussed their adoption among themselves. They said they didn't bring it up because they knew that it made their mothers sad and they "didn't want to hurt Mommy's feelings." One child even said that it might be a good idea if the videotape being made of their sessions could be shown to their mothers to help them feel more comfortable in discussing adoption.

"HAPPY" BIRTHDAY?

Birthdays had always been happy affairs for the Johnson family, who have two adopted children, Jeremy, eleven, and Jennifer, eight. On Jennifer's eighth birthday, Mrs. Johnson noticed that Jennifer seemed a little blue. That day, Jennifer chose to spend more time alone in her room than was typical for her.

Mrs. Johnson finally knocked on Jennifer's door and upon entering found her daughter staring out the window. "What's up, Jen?" she asked.

"It's my other mother, Mom. I think about her on my

birthday and I wonder if she's thinking about me. Do you suppose she remembers what day this is? Do you think she misses me?"

Though somewhat surprised by her daughter's questions, Mrs. Johnson reassured her. "Of course she remembers you; you were so important to her that she made a hard decision to let you go to another family who could love you and bring you up the way she wanted."

Jennifer seemed satisfied with this response, so Mrs. Johnson let it rest at that point even though she could see that Jennifer remained a little distracted for most of the day.

Birthdays are momentous events for most children. Pride, new freedom (for example, to stay up later and do more things without parental supervision), and increased status among their peers for being "more grown up" are some of the benefits that often accompany the birth anniversary. But for some adopted children, this is a day of intensely ambivalent feelings.

Put yourself in their place. What would this day mean to you if you had been adopted? Besides being a joyous occasion, it might be a powerful reminder that there is someone out there who gave birth to you and with whom you do not share this event. You could be acutely conscious that while other kids your age were celebrating a specific event about which they could learn all the details from the central characters in that drama, you were commemorating . . . what?

It's sometimes said that adopted children carry around with them a certain amount of sadness that birth children do not have. There may be an element of truth to this. It would not be unreasonable for some of them to have a sense of loss and incompleteness, because of a gap in their life history and because, in a sense, they were rejected. They are different from most other kids in an important way. And this is the day that, once a year, may dramatically confront them with this fact.

We do not mean to suggest that birthdays are melancholy affairs for all adopted kids. But it would certainly fall within the range of normal behavior if your adopted child had some mixed feelings about this day. *Where is the mother who gave me up?* she might be thinking. *What is she doing on this day? Is she thinking of me? Will she call?*

Adoptive parents should not diminish the importance of birthdays, since rituals and celebrations are important to everybody; and playing down your adopted child's birthday would single her out as different from her peers. Some adoptive parents, especially those who adopted older children, also supplement birthdays with another commemorative occasion: adoption day. This is the anniversary of the day your adopted child joined your family. It should never take the place of a birthday, but it's a special day your whole family can enjoy and be part of. In fact, some adoptive family support groups hold very moving candlelight celebrations each month to honor kids whose adoption anniversaries fall within that month.

FACTS OF LIFE

Alice walked into her children's bedroom and found her adopted son and daughter in bed together, touching each other's bodies. These were her first children, and Alice became deeply concerned that what they were doing was unnatural. She had heard that adopted children didn't develop incest taboos like everyone else. Now she became increasingly worried about leaving them alone together. In response to her anxiety, the children's behavior became more difficult.

We reassured Alice and her husband that kids were naturally curious about each other's bodies. What she had seen was not at all unusual with children close to one another in age, and that it had nothing whatsoever to do with adoption. We also told the parents that no research showed a likelihood that adoptees would engage in sex with their adoptive siblings.

Also unrelated to adoption, although sometimes mistakenly connected to it by parents, is the overly enthusiastic affection common to children of this age. Boys talk about marrying their mothers and girls act adorable with their fathers. A parent's misinterpretation of this normal stage of growth can lead to problems.

When Bill Roberts, a stockbroker, offered to read bedtime stories to his six-year-old adopted daughter, he wasn't quite prepared for the way she would cuddle up to him as she climbed on his lap. He was prepared even less for his response: an erection. The thought of discussing the incident with his wife gave him a chill. Preoccupied with what he assumed to be his unacceptable thoughts and feelings, Mr. Roberts began staying late at the office, channeling his anxieties into hard work. His wife felt confused about his attitude toward her and about the distant relationship that she perceived was developing between her daughter and her husband. That they had adopted because of her infertility made the whole situation seem even more painful. Before long, the Roberts had to seek counseling for their increasingly shaky marriage.

Had Mr. Roberts realized that flirtatious behavior by little girls with their fathers—and little boys' romancing of their mothers—is within the range of normal behavior for this stage of development, his family could have nipped this problem in the bud. Kids of this age may want to cuddle up in bed with you as well as sit on your lap. Aside from looking for affection and attention, they are also beginning to unselfconsciously mimic adult behavior.

Depending on the level of physical affection with which they're comfortable, parents' reactions to such conduct may vary from delight or amusement to fear that they are doing something wrong to provoke it. With a daughter, some people link this behavior to sexual irresponsibility they assume to have been part of the birth mother's traits if the child was born out of wedlock. They fear the same behavior is beginning to germinate in their daughter and that she may be a "bad seed." Fears of your child's origins coming home to roost are groundless—it just doesn't happen that way.

It is important if your child appears flirtatious to remember that such behavior is normal at this age. If you get ruffled and completely withdraw physically, your child will sense that something very disturbing has happened and you may begin to create a problem where none existed.

If you are uncomfortable with so much physical contact with your child as he or she grows older, gently move the child away. Substitute sitting next to her for holding her on your lap if this makes you more comfortable. Do it calmly and without alarm and your son or daughter will eventually accept these limits in the spirit in which you offer them.

Of course, there's the other side of the matter. If you enjoy extra attention from your kids (without, of course, actually encouraging seductiveness) you can just sit back and delight in being the apple of their eye, even if they occasionally overdo it.

Jill and Ron Melanick had three sons by birth. Ron recalls leaving for work every day with a " 'bye, Dad" from his sons and not much else. But when his adopted daughter reached the age of six, she made it clear that Daddy's departure was a terribly sad time, and his homecoming a signal for great demonstrativeness. Ron loved every minute of it.

DISCIPLINE AND LIMITS

Since your child is entering a period in which his interaction with people outside the family will increase significantly, it's important that he know and live up to the standards of conduct that you and others will require of him. Some adoptive parents have a bit of difficulty with this. They may still be unsure of how much "right" they have to discipline their child, since he was not born to them. They may also have heard that adopted kids, by nature, have low self-esteem, and they are thus wary of being too strict with their child for fear of giving him an "inferiority complex." And some adoptive parents, because they have worked so hard to get their child to love them as if they were his birth parents, fear that disciplining him could cost them that hard-earned love.

However, it is crucial that you come to terms with any ambivalence you may have at this time. If you tell him that he is doing something wrong and then don't follow up on it, your child will sense your ambivalence. Some parents convey their mixed feelings nonverbally. For example, a parent may laugh nervously while scolding his child, confusing her about the message he is trying to get across.

If you want to avoid fruitless power struggles in the years to come, be firm about standards of conduct now. Otherwise, before you know it, he will be too big to control physically, and you will have nothing to fall back on to help influence his behavior. Your child needs to feel confident that you know what you're doing. He requires standards at this age, so you need to impose them—unilaterally.

Avoid justifying your style of disciplining, since your child is still too young to do much abstract thinking. When you tell him what you're going to do and why you're going to do it, speak to him in short sentences. Say, for example, he stayed out late when you said he couldn't. You should say, "I want you to come home on time. As punishment, you can't go out to play tomorrow." Kids this age think very concretely and tend to obey older people, so it should not be too hard to establish your authority and respect for your rules in this way.

Most kids can behave reasonably well if they know what's expected of them and if the consequences for not behaving are clear, logical, and certain to follow misconduct. Emphasize consistency and fairness when you discipline. There is no single correct punishment for transgressions; most parents find that children of this age can accept any fair punishment. But keep it in proportion to what the child did wrong. For example, you wouldn't want to ground him for a month because he came in fifteen minutes late for dinner. One evening without TV is probably sufficient. Another reason to avoid excessive punishments is that they may require major inconvenience to yourself. You have to supervise—staying in, for example, to make sure that he stays in.

Remember that when you discipline you may hear some of the back talk that each adopted kid thinks he patented. Aside from the common "You're not my real mother" line, be prepared for something like, "Why did you adopt me if that's the way you feel about me?" Respond by saying that you will discuss adoption at another time, but right now you are dealing with the issue at hand and nothing else.

Sometimes families have so many rules that children can't tell what's really important. We saw one family in which an eight-year-old son seemed uncontrollable. After a few conversations with all concerned, however, we could see that the parents needed fewer, clearer rules if they wanted to develop their child's inherent ability to behave. To him, his parents seemed out of control, constantly making demands and criticizing and threatening punishment for all types of transgressions without any limits. To help the situation we asked his mother and father to pick out five rules that were important to them—for example, that their child get dressed for school promptly, keep his room neat, wash his hands after coming inside, etc.—thus helping them to create their priorities. Then we asked the boy to choose four out of the five that he could adhere to during the next week, which provided him with a sense of participation and control. They were to record each time he obeyed a rule rather than the times he broke them. It didn't work miracles, but it did enable them to start rebuilding a relationship of understanding and respect and to establish a basis for acceptable behavior.

Another issue that arises at this age is that kids try to stretch the limits you impose on them as they increase their demands for independence, such as, "Why can't I ride my bike past the corner? Betty's mother lets *her* do it!"

If you're not sure of where your restrictions stand vis-à-vis other parents, ask around. As a reality check, talk to other parents with children the same age as yours and see what sort of limits they set. You could also discuss the problem with members of an adoptive parents' support group. In addition to being a source of practical information, the parents will understand what you're feeling. And if, for some emotional or physical reason, you feel your child does need a little extra protectiveness for a while, give it to her and don't feel guilty about it.

OFF TO SCHOOL

In all likelihood, the transition from taking care of a preschooler or nursery school child to being the parent of a first grader will occur without a hitch, but don't be hard on yourself if it does give you a few jitters. (Nor should you worry if your child shows a little irritability, bed wetting, or cranky eating habits, which are not abnormal for this stage.) Giving up your child to the care and influence of strangers for a full day makes many parents—birth and adoptive—a little queasy, even though you probably share in your youngster's excitement over preparing for this big change in his or her life.

Adoptive parents may be somewhat more protective of their kids, viewing them as slightly more fragile than birth children. While it is natural to feel this way, try to keep from becoming overprotective both for your child's sake and your own. She needs to start the arduous task of making her way in the world, and you must begin the equally difficult job of letting go.

For some children, the prospect of going to school all day and separating from their mothers for that long is a difficult one. Your child may cling to you, implore you not to put him through the ordeal, cry, promise you he will be good, or imply that forcing him to go will harm him irreparably. If this behavior does not abate, discuss it with your child's teacher. Your son or daughter may need a smaller class or different kind of school for a while.

Most children don't have this hard a time, but if your child does, try to find out if adoption is involved. Perhaps someone has said something hurtful to her about her being adopted. Maybe other children have asked her about adoption and she's having a hard time explaining it to them without you there to help her. Or being away all day at school could be triggering some sad feelings about her birth parents that your child has yet to master. If the problem is adoption-related, it's still important that she know you can protect and comfort her at school by talking to her teacher about the difficulty.

Address your child's fears as he communicates them. For example, he may fear that the other kids or the teacher won't like him, that he won't be able to do the work, or that the school is too far away. He may even say that he needs a nap and a full day of school makes him too tired, or that there are too many kids in the class and they are too noisy. What he's really saying is that he fears the unknown and that it's the first time he's ever been somewhere for so much time where there's no one who loves him more than anything else in the world.

Assure him that you understand what he is feeling and that there are other kids who are probably feeling the same way. Talk to him lovingly but firmly, making it clear that he will have to go to school and will soon get used to being there all day, but will suffer no diminution of your love in the process. Explain to him that going to school is his "job," just like going to work every day is your job or that of your spouse. Point out that this is a difficult experience at first and that he will soon be able to handle it more comfortably.

Many schools allow parents to spend part of the first few school days with their child so that he may gradually acclimate himself to the fact of separation. If your child's school does not do this as a practice, you could ask for permission to be there at the beginning, maybe in the hallway rather than in the classroom. The drawback is that adopted children already have to deal with the fact of being different; if yours is the only kid whose parent has to tag along, you may set up a more difficult situation for him. You might try pointing out the possibility that other kids may make fun of him if he needs you with him (although you should make sure he realizes that *you're* not making fun of him). Kids at this age will do almost anything not to stand out in this way.

Should your youngster have a real problem with this separation, and if his birthday is near the cutoff for your school district, you may be able to keep him back in half-day kindergarten for an extra year. But don't opt for this too quickly, since it will separate him from kids his age who live nearby. Before you decide on this option, consult with school personnel about their experience with children who adjust to a full day of school more slowly. They may suggest a gradual process of building up to a full day for him.

If you do choose to keep him in kindergarten again, use the year to get him gradually involved in some kind of socializing activity in the afternoon and a full day of camp in summer.

TO TELL OR NOT TO TELL THE TEACHER

Many parents wonder if it's a good idea to tell the teacher of their child's adoption. You could wait to talk to the teacher when your child starts school, hoping to get a good sense of her attitudes and character from conversations with her and from what you have been told about her by other parents. While talking to her, try to see how she regards people who are different—those who have disabilities, for example. Consulting other adoptive parents familiar with the school beforehand would be an even better way of coming to a decision. If you've met other adoptive parents who have children in the school, try to find out what they know about your child's present teacher and others she may get in the future. If you're a member of an adoptive parents' support group, seek out parents in your group who know something about your child's school and learn all you can. You will probably turn up some useful information.

The advantage of confiding in the teacher is that you can freely discuss with her or him any adoption-related problems that arise at school. For example, while it will not necessarily happen, your child could have a dispute with another pupil who taunts him with something like: "At least *I* know who my *real* mother is." If you informed the teacher of your child's adoption and she knew your feelings in the matter, she could handle such incidents as you would.

Still another reason to familiarize the teacher with your child's adoption is that you can talk to her about potential difficulties your child may have with the curriculum. A prime example is the "family tree" that third-graders often have to draw. For your adopted child, who should occupy the branches? Does she need two trees? Will hers look like an alien organism when compared with what her classmates draw? Does this project make any sense for her?

You and the teacher might have to do some intensive brainstorming to come up with a creative solution to complications like these—and you can only do it if you both understand what's involved.

If you feel comfortable letting school authorities know that you adopted your child, try to get him into a class with at least one other adopted kid, since that will take some of the edge off the important "difference" in his life. Even schools that ordinarily assign pupils to a class at random may honor your special request if you convince them that it would ultimately enhance your child's ability to adjust to school and his classmates.

BEHAVIOR IN SCHOOL

It's important that her teacher find your child's behavior acceptable. This is probably the first major encounter your youngster has had with any adult outside the family who she has to impress but who doesn't have to like her. Thus this interaction serves as a model for much of your child's future social activities. Also, a teacher's attitude toward her pupil colors the way she treats the child, which in turn will affect the youngster's chances of succeeding in school.

Influential factors here include your child's appearance—neat dress and haircut—her manners, her ability to listen to and follow instructions, and, in general, to play by the teacher's rules. Teachers are only human and do not like all kids equally, so it behooves your child, within limits, to learn how to get along with this important adult.

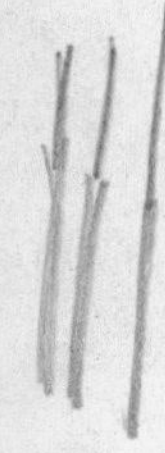

While attitudes are changing, if your child misbehaves in class you still may have to deal with teachers, guidance counselors, and psychologists who have prejudices about adoption or lack knowledge of the subject. For instance, in response to your son's cutting up in class, and with his adoption in mind, the school psychologist may say that your son has low self-esteem, a poor self-concept, or poor impulse control, or that he's hyperactive. But just as a person is not necessarily depressed because they are feeling sad, your child is not by definition any of these disturbing sounding things simply because he's a little rambunctious.

"Hyperactivity" is a typical behavioral problem that arises in the first grade: the teacher thinks your child simply can't sit still and pay attention for long enough periods of time. But one person's hyperactivity is another's liveliness and curiosity. It's not natural for a child this age to want to sit still and focus on something dictated by an adult he barely knows, especially when the process is new to him. After all, until now he has spent much of his young life running around, and it's hardly realistic to expect him to turn on a dime.

Such diagnoses, often considerably less scientific than they sound, may reflect the teacher's and guidance counselor's personalities more than your child's behavior. This is particularly true for adopted children. Because of the stigma attached to adoption, teachers are often as likely as others to blame adoption for behavior they find difficult to control in the classroom. In one study, teachers asked which kids in their class were hyperactive described 43 percent of the boys in the room that way. On the other hand, your child could end up in a class with many passive kids, thus appearing "hyperactive" or overactive by contrast.

We have seen so-called "hyperactive" children in our office who sit in their chairs and pay attention, leading us to conclude that somebody must be over-diagnosing their "condition." If your child is so labelled, speak to the teacher or school psychologist about it and insist that they specify the behavior on which they based their evaluation. If your child is overactive only at certain times or in certain places such as school, the overactivity is more likely to be due to stress or immaturity, both of which you can help him with. Ask them to define what's normal for kids this age in terms of getting up and walking around the classroom. This will help you and your child to set limits and to work for more self-control and a successful adaptation to the school's norms.

Even if her teacher errs on the side of too much self-control, your child will have to meet her standards in order to succeed in that class, unless you put her in a more progressive school.

Joanne, a second-grader, had been labelled disturbed because she was getting up from her seat and walking around too much in the classroom. We asked her to keep a diary (she loved to write and draw pictures), paying special attention to those times she was able to control her behavior. She soon noticed that she was able to control herself most of the time. She was already doing it. She just needed to do more of it. Joanne's mother told her daughter's teacher about this activity, encouraging her to expect positive changes in

Joanne's behavior. With the girl's efforts and her teacher's positive attitude, Joanne soon adapted to her school's standards of decorum. You could try the same technique if your child is having this kind of problem.

A small percentage of children—adopted and birth—do have acute behavioral or social adjustment difficulties at school. Jenny, for example, was by nature a shy child and had considerable trouble establishing relationships with the other pupils in her class. While her peers were beginning to engage in after-school activities with their classmates, she remained a loner. In fact, the occasional interaction she did have with the other children tended to be in the form of unpleasant confrontations.

What Jenny was experiencing may have been partly adoption-related. Adopted kids, if they are in the common position of being the first or only child in their family, have grown up primarily in a world of adults. They would naturally have to work harder to establish peer relationships, since at this age they have had less practice with them. But this is also true for biological children who are first or only children. Jenny's parents dealt with their daughter's social awkwardness by inviting a neighbor's child Jenny's age over for several minutes every few days, gradually increasing the time the children were together and gently intervening when it seemed that the friendship they had hoped for was in danger of foundering. Over time this technique worked, and Jenny was able to begin making her first tentative moves toward friendship with other kids, first with one child, then with two at a time, and then with a larger group of children.

If your child has behavioral problems in school, it is best not to act too quickly if school guidance personnel suggest individual psychotherapy as the solution. Some practitioners will zero in on adoption as the root of her problems, which isn't very useful as it is a fact that can't be changed. We suggest that you first speak to the teacher and family and friends about practical, limited ways of dealing with the difficulty. Then check with an adoptive parents' group. If none of what you try works and you and your child do seem to have a legitimate problem, search for a family therapist who understands how members of families can interact to resolve problems and who will help you to find solutions for the immediate difficulty at hand, rather than attribute everything to adoption.

LEARNING DIFFICULTIES

While there are such things as learning disabilities, a more common phenomenon is often mistaken for them. Some kids, because of their temperament, just take longer than others to pick up basic learning skills. They achieve educational milestones at a later age, the tendency for which may be inherited. But this is a matter of tempo—nothing more. It does not reflect on their intelligence or foreshadow any future inability to learn.

Like temperament, varying styles of thinking can also mislead parents into thinking that their child has a learning problem. Bob and Sheila Worth have encountered this phenomenon with Harry, their adopted nine-year-old son. Bob, a school principal, and Sheila, a CPA whose score on her certifying exam was one of the highest in the country, have expressed some concern about Harry's B's and C's in school. Given their talents and background and the A's that their two younger birth daughters consistently earn, they find it hard to see why Harry doesn't do better.

But Harry literally sees things another way. At this stage he shows more of a flair for drawing than for words. His style of learning differs from his parents' and sisters'. While it is still too early to know if his affinity for art will mature into real talent, clearly he marches to the beat of a different drummer, and his individuality is not a cause for concern.

We each tend to perceive the outside world with a little more emphasis on seeing, hearing, intellectualizing, or feelings than others might. We all have a little bit of each of these four major styles, but lean more toward one. Anyone can have a child who takes in the world differently than they do, but the odds of this happening may be greater with adoptive parents, since genetics may play a role in determining a child's predominant style.

Parents often come into conflict with their adopted and birth children who may have different cognitive styles—ways of understanding things. A couple who value high intellectual achievement and who find it easy to conceptualize when dealing with problems may feel frustrated with a child who spends little time reading and is indifferent to the pursuit of high grades, even though he's willing to devote several hours a day to socializing with friends. His largely intuitive approach to navigating past the pitfalls of life is also likely to be disconcerting. It can be even more annoying when his siblings manifest a style with which their parents are more comfortable.

If you find this happening with your adopted child, first remind yourself that there's more than one way to interact with the world. Then enjoy it, because your child is going to be his own person no matter what you do, and his differences from you and your spouse—and possibly from his siblings—on this account can enrich your family life.

On a mundane and very practical level, pick up cues from him when misunderstandings arise. For example, if you tell him to do something and then ask, "Do you hear what I'm saying?" and you get a halfhearted response, it could be that you're trying to get a visually oriented person to respond to an auditory metaphor. Listen to the way he talks. For example, if he frequently uses the word *see*, you can assume that he thinks visually. If you know he's visually oriented, say instead, "Do you *see* what I mean?" or "Let me show you how I want you to do it." Believe it or not, cognitive styles actually operate on this level and you'll have a better chance of making your point.

If you have more than one child, it's easy to fall into the trap of using the style most often used by the kids stylistically closest to you. Make an effort to relate to each child using the style, expressions, and imagery with which he or she is comfortable.

REAL LEARNING DISABILITIES

Misunderstanding aside, there *are* such things as learning disabilities. What's more, adopted children, according to one study, seem to have them in a slightly higher proportion than children raised by their biological parents—roughly 20 percent of adopted boys (it occurs in boys much more often than in girls) as opposed to about 10 percent of birth kids. What's the reason for this? We don't know for sure, although with adopted children it may have something to do with the birth mother's high anxiety during her pregnancy, poor nutrition, drug and alcohol use, or poor hospital care at birth.

Learning disabilities include dyslexia, audio perception problems, language-based difficulties (in which the child has trouble expressing what he thinks or interpreting what he hears), and short attention spans. Dyslexia, for example, is a disability that may affect speaking, reading, and spelling. The child may read from right to left, have trouble telling a *d* from a *b*, and, therefore, find it hard to concentrate.

The odds are that your child has none of these disabilities, or will learn or can be taught to compensate for minor ones. A diagnosis of a learning disability could be more indicative of poor teaching, many unruly kids in the class, or an overcrowded classroom. You might also be hearing the familiar overreaction to any learning difficulty—no matter how slight or brief—involving an adopted child. Even if the teacher or guidance counselor cites examples to show you how the disability has manifested itself in your child's work, you should retain some healthy skepticism. But don't ignore it, because your child could become demoralized by how difficult his work can be for him.

The school will probably suggest a series of tests. To

take them, your child may have to travel to the nearest regional medical center and be tested by strangers, which could intimidate him and affect his performance on the tests. Or he might just be having a bad day when he takes the tests. Don't hesitate to have him tested privately to give you a second opinion in the matter. For information about where to have him tested, call the local chapter of the Association for Children with Learning Disabilities. If you can't locate it, send a self-addressed, stamped envelope to the Association for Children with Learning Disabilities, 4156 Library Road, Pittsburgh, Pennsylvania 15234.

What if he does have a learning disability? Sometimes learning difficulties are not related to overall lowered intellectual functioning, a worry that frequently plagues adoptive parents. They can be compensated for. Albert Einstein, for example, was late in learning to speak and may have had dyslexia. Leonardo da Vinci, another well-known genius, probably had the same condition. You can take specific action to deal with learning disabilities. Your child will probably need supplemental instruction (or a different school) in a class with a low teacher-to-student ratio. The Association for Children with Learning Disabilities can provide you with information about where to find such instruction.

In other cases these learning difficulties are associated with lower measured intelligence. Special schooling may be required to enable your child to achieve his full potential as well as maintain his self-esteem.

QUESTIONS AND ANSWERS

My eight-year-old, who's usually talkative and open with me, has been much more secretive lately. I have a feeling that he's been thinking about his birth mother. What should I do?

There are times when adopted children do think about their birth parents, and they are often hesitant to share these thoughts with their adoptive parents. If you sense this is happening, make it clear to your child that you are receptive to a conversation about his biological parents, but don't push the matter. You could introduce your child to books about adoption, or attend a family event at an adoptive parents' group as a way of stimulating a discussion.

Adopted children are often more curious about their birth mothers than their birth fathers. There is a simple reason for this. Adoptive parents usually know more about their child's birth mother, and can give more information about her to the child.

Birth fathers have rarely been involved in the decision to place an infant for adoption for a variety of reasons. Most babies surrendered for adoption are born to unmarried women. Married fathers always had clear rights concerning the surrender of a child for adoption. Only recently have unmarried fathers been given rights related to the adoption of their babies. In some cases fathers didn't even know that a baby had been conceived. In others they denied paternity in an effort to avoid responsibility for the mother and infant. It is also much less expensive and time consuming to an agency and attorney if the mother states that she does not know who the father of her baby is when she gives the baby up for adoption. Otherwise the father would have to be consulted which would cost time and money. He might also, if consulted, decide against adoption. For these reasons most adoptions occur with little real knowledge of who the birth father is.

□

I overheard my son telling his friend that his "real" father was a famous baseball player. I happen to know that his birth father was a high school dropout who was successful at very few things, and baseball was not among them. Should I tell him what I know, or just let him think what he wants to think?

It's common for adopted children to idealize their birth parents (as well as any parents) at this stage. It's their way of coming to terms, over time, with the fact that they know little about these people. So let him tell the story the way he wants to—for now. You could speak to him *alone* and assure him that his birth father has many positive qualities because you can see them reflected in your son, but it isn't likely that being a famous baseball player is one of them. It will only be a problem if he can't let go of the fantasy as he grows older.

□

I'm very concerned because I keep catching my son in lies. When I ask him a direct question, he will frequently lie to keep from getting into trouble. I've tried punishing him, but nothing—taking his bike away, not letting him watch TV, etc.—seems to work. I ask him why he's lying, but he won't tell me.

Most children do lie a little; if you follow the lie with punishment you can usually make the point that this is unacceptable behavior. Clearly, you need a different approach. In our experience, a child can't say why he's been lying, so it's best not to pursue that course. Also, it's usually not a good method to ask your child questions for which you already have the answers; when you do this you're just setting yourself up for a disappointment when you don't get the truth. Instead, tell him that you already know what he did and discuss that; don't give him the opportunity to lie his way out of it. It's also helpful to look at times when your child might have lied but didn't; point them out to him and commend him for them each time they occur, to further reinforce the fact that he is already truthful, he just needs to be truthful more often.

□

After a difficult beginning in first grade, my daughter is finally going to school without a fuss. However, the teacher tells me that she is not socializing well with the other children. I'm worried that she would still prefer to be home with me.

She could still be adjusting to school, which for some kids takes a while. If this persists beyond the middle of the year, she may need a different kind of school with a higher ratio of teachers to children to help her with this difficulty.

□

We believe that it's particularly important that our adopted daughter feel accepted at school. However, she has a teacher who seems unusually strict and overly critical of her. What should we do?

One thing children have to learn as they grow up is how to survive all kinds of teaching. You could turn this apparent adversity into a positive experience by helping your daughter to devise a strategy for getting along with her teacher while acknowledging that this person may very well be unpleasant. To help your child, get her to record each time she interacts with her teacher when the teacher is not being awful. Your daughter could also watch what the other kids do to get the teacher to respond positively to them. Have her pay attention to what she or another child are doing to make this interaction positive. When she can pinpoint what works, she will feel more in control of the situation.

If the conflict between your daughter and her teacher seems to be getting out of hand, ask for a conference with the teacher and a guidance counselor or the principal. (We have been told by people who have had this experience that schools respond more readily to parents if the father as well as the mother comes to school. While this is not how we would like it to be, it is nevertheless the reality.) Should that not work, try to get the principal to transfer your child to a different class. Aside from dealing with the problem of an excessively strict teacher, this would also help keep your daughter from getting an undeserved reputation as a troublesome child, a tag that she could find hard to get rid of as she proceeds from grade to grade.

□

Having learned that our adopted son has some learning disabilities, I'm wondering how to talk about this with members of our extended family—especially my brother-

in-law, who thought adoption was not a good idea in the first place and who will now probably say, "I told you so."

Is it necessary to discuss this with your brother-in-law or other relatives? If your child needs extra tutoring, how likely is it that they will know? It is not uncommon for parents who have children with learning disabilities, whether adopted or not, to have a difficult time trying to help relatives understand these difficulties. Learning-disabled children often complain that they have been called stupid and lazy, even by their teachers. There are a number of organizations that you can contact for assistance with the many issues that you will be facing, such as adequate diagnosis, finding an appropriate educational program, and dealing with some of the family issues. The first is the Mayo Clinic, 200 First Street, S.W., Rochester, Minn. 55905 (507) 284-2511. This is ideal for families who want a complete evaluation by a number of specialists under one roof. They will confer with one another and report their comprehensive findings to you. Another is the Association for Children and Adults with Learning Disabilities mentioned previously: 4156 Library Road, Pittsburgh, Pennsylvania 15234 (412) 240-1515. A national association with local chapters, membership is open to parents and professionals. Information on educational programs and support systems for families is available from local chapters. Two other organizations that could be helpful are the Foundation for Children with Learning Disabilities, 99 Park Avenue, New York, New York 10016, and the Churchill Center, 22 East 95th Street, New York, New York 10130. Remember most learning-disabled children are not adopted and most adopted children aren't learning disabled. Resources for Children with Special Needs is an organization that can recommend schools, camps, and other activities to parents who have children with a wide range of physical, emotional, and developmental handicaps. They are located at 200 Park Avenue South, Suite 816, New York, New York 10003.

5 Ages Nine to Twelve

Welcome to the age of divergence. Children between nine and twelve years old mature physically and emotionally at widely dissimilar rates. Differences between the academic progress of your son or daughter and his or her friends may also become evident. It's also likely that your child's activities will coincide less and less with yours and, if you're married, your spouse's, as your youngster's relationships with his or her peers take on greater importance.

At this stage, each child begins to come into her own. Her physical, mental, and emotional maturation make her stand out as an individual, separate from her parents. Her skills, talents, and idiosyncrasies become clearer to outsiders as well as family members. By the age of twelve, aware of this budding maturity, she will begin to move toward a greater autonomy.

Birth parents can often predict with some accuracy certain aspects of their offspring's likely physical characteristics, maturation rates, and intellectual or artistic tendencies. For some adoptive parents, however, this drama can resemble watching a mystery movie where you feel as if you have few clues about how it will turn out. Yet it's just that mystery that can make being an adoptive parent interesting as you watch your child develop talents and skills you might not have yourself.

For any parent who worries about how close his or her adolescent's development approaches the "norm," this can be a complicated time. Your child can be "too short," "too tall," "too developed" (or "undeveloped"), or "too babyish"—and yet still fall within the broad range of normal for her age.

School becomes more of a challenge in this period. Students, having acquired basic skills, begin to deal with substantive subjects. Now the school can identify "underachievers" and start putting bright kids on the fast track to academic success. Families oriented toward high achievement may find this particularly trying if their adopted child does not show the same level of interest or ability in academics.

It's important to maintain some perspective on your child's performance in school. If his grades are not what you think they should be, is it perhaps because he is more mechanically or artistically than academically inclined? Find out from the school if your child is performing up to capacity. If he's not, you can get tutoring for him or help him with his homework yourself. If he is doing all he can, make sure you convey to him your pride in his motivation and accomplishments even if they don't match your aspirations. In fact, work on obliterating any sense of disappointment by remembering that each child has different—not inferior—capabilities.

Preadolescents also begin to move out of the family's orbit. Friendships, hanging out, music lessons, scouts, 4-H, dance classes, and organized athletics take up more of their time. They may begin to read more—girls often love biographies at this age—and daydream. This is also the age of the true friendship, when same-sex pals share confidences, hang out together, and form cliques which, unfortunately, can sometimes lead to the exclusion of others.

THINKING ABOUT ADOPTION

Your child now realizes even more clearly than he did when he was younger that he has two sets of parents. Yet, believe it or not, in spite of the conversations about adoption you may have had with him, he is still quite likely to have some doubts about his permanent status as a member of your family because most kids under the age of fifteen can't fully grasp the complex principles that underscore the legal process that has terminated the relationship between him and his birth parents and created a legal bond between him and you.

Nightmares or fantasies about his birth mother returning to reclaim him are still possible and within the range of what is normal. If you encounter this phenomenon, let him know that other adoptees have this fear, too. Remind your child that you love him, that he is yours forever, and that someday he will be able to fully understand the laws that make this so. Show him the adoption decree or certificate of adoption which says that he is your legal child.

More likely, your child will express increased interest about her birth parents. For example, she may want more information about what they look like, what they like to do, what talents they have. She may also want to know about the size and makeup of her birth family, especially whether she has birth brothers and sisters and who they live with.

In this period of renewed interest, your protestations that you don't know more than a few bare facts about her background may no longer satisfy her. To respond to her curiosity, you might try going back to the adoption agency to learn more about her birth parents. Sometimes, parents forget some of the information they did get from the agency in the excitement of finally receiving their child. However, since rules and regulations have loosened in the last five or ten years, you may discover that the agency can now tell you more than they could at the time of the adoption. So this may be the ideal time to do some more investigating of your child's background.

If you haven't discussed adoption with your child for a while, this might be a good time to bring it up again. For example, you could give her *How It Feels to Be Adopted* by Jill Krementz (Knopf), to read. It's a collection of thoughts about adoption by teenage adoptees, written in the kind of honest language with which kids are comfortable.

STIRRINGS OF REBELLION

Just after his tenth birthday, Jeremy announced that he would no longer wash the dishes, make his bed, or do any other "women's work."

Mr. and Mrs. Anderson, who equally shared household responsibilities, were taken aback since they saw themselves as good role models for their adopted son. Though they suspected that Jeremy's attitude was the result of the influence of a new friend, they did not challenge Jeremy's right to his views but rather told him that as a member of their family he was expected to do his chores. Jeremy said nothing.

Over the next two days Jeremy did his chores, though he grumbled a bit. His parents chose to ignore his comments and instead complimented him on how well he was fulfilling his responsibilities.

On the third day, Jeremy refused to make his bed. His parents simply reminded him that this was one of his tasks and said no more about it.

When Jeremy came home that evening, he found that his favorite video game was missing. When he asked where it was, his parents told him that because he had not lived up to his responsibilities they had removed it.

The next day, Jeremy made his bed and his parents returned his video game. This pattern of Jeremy refusing to do a task of his was repeated every few days for nearly a month, with each test followed by a consequence. By the end of the month, Jeremy's behavior was clearly improving and the discussion of what is or is not "women's work" was put to rest.

Parents of children this age may justifiably feel that their youngsters are testing them. Children may begin to come home late from play or from organized group activities. They might also talk back or act up in school, especially as they approach adolescence. It is even within the realm of normality to see one or two instances of petty theft at this stage.

Adopted boys, some research has shown, tend to temporarily act up a bit around the age of eleven, and it's possible that an incident or two of stealing could be one way a boy misbehaves. Perhaps this is how he is trying to master his feelings of sadness or anger over being adopted. But *no* research has pointed to theft as a characteristic of adoptees.

Adoptive parents may doubt their "right" to discipline their child or feel incompetent because the youngster might have "inherited" bad behavior traits, making it "useless" to even try to get the child to behave. If they feel that way they are not likely to be clear and firm when the child does something wrong.

What should you do if *your* child steals? This has no more significance than any other kind of misbehavior unless it becomes chronic, and it's important not to overreact. Remember, this testing of the limits indicates that your child wants you to reestablish the kinds of limits and boundaries that will make him feel safe and secure. Let him know the rules. And make sure he understands that there are consequences for breaking them.

If petty theft starts to become a pattern, make sure your child understands the significance of what he's doing. Probably the best way to do that would be to make him return what he stole and apologize to the storekeeper. If he continues to steal, you may need some help. Family therapists are especially good at nipping this in the bud.

Life at this age can sometimes resemble a battle for control between parent and child. The battleground can vary from slowness in getting dressed that delays the child's departure for school to an overt challenge of your right to impose discipline. Kids who pose problems in this area are trying to find their limits. Should they gain the control they ostensibly want, they will not feel that the adults around them can take care of them. The best thing you can do for them here is to make sure those behavioral limits are present and well-defined so they can develop a sense of themselves through the boundaries you create for them.

For those rules which are absolute for you, this is not the time for ambiguity. If you've been a little tentative—perhaps a little less demanding of good behavior because your son or daughter was not born to you—it's important to get it straight in your own mind that you have a right and obligation to set behavioral standards and, if necessary, to punish.

The consequences of misbehavior do not have to be dire, just consistent. If you still hear lines like "My real mother wouldn't punish me this way," tell your child that while you have no idea what his birth mother would have done in similar circumstances, you've decided that this is best for him. Don't allow your child to bully you, and make sure that he or she can't play one parent off against the other. In fact, if your youngster has been behaving especially bad lately, look into the possibility that you and your spouse might be undercutting each other, with one parent criticizing behavior that the other is in some manner portraying as cute either overtly or covertly; or perhaps one of you is giving permission for something that the other has banned. If you are a two-parent family, it is important that you function as much like a team as possible when it comes to setting clear limits on your child's behavior.

On the other hand, it's also important that you confirm your child's growing sense that you are not omniscient. It's always good for children to understand that their parents can make mistakes, and to expect an apology from these all-important adults when it's appropriate. If the adults they love and respect act that way, kids will grow up to do the same. Acknowledge that you've made an error and learned from it, as all people do from time to time.

By the time your child approaches adolescence—at the end of this age range—he will begin to realize that not all rules are absolute. He will see that different families have different ways of doing things, and may insist on an explanation and justification when you lay down the law as you see it. As he matures, acknowledge the points he makes when they're legitimate, and let him begin to play a role in negotiating behavioral limits that are not absolute. Possible activities now open to negotiation would include the hour at which he must come in from play, whether he can use public transportation by himself, and whether he can spend less time doing homework if he finishes his assignments accurately and quickly.

To the difficulties that some families have with disciplining, adoption can add a few extra twists. Fred Larkin couldn't understand what was happening between himself and his son; their relationship was degenerating into one of constant confrontation. It was especially painful to Fred because through his son's eleventh year, they got along so well. For his part, Bill complained that his father was picking on him, singling him out for constant criticism while his younger brother, a birth child, "got away with it."

To an outside observer, something besides the normal tensions between preadolescents and parents had clearly arisen in the Larkin family: their twelve-year-old's height. Bill was a slim but towering five feet nine inches in a family characterized by men of short stature. Fred Larkin, at five feet six inches, felt a little uncomfortable with his young upstart. He had not expected to have such a tall boy. Never totally sure of his authority over his adopted son, the height disparity between the two had put him on edge, aggravating whatever conflicts they might have had. Once aware of his feelings, Fred was able to see Bill's behavior in perspective and respond to it appropriately.

Sometimes an adopted child's good looks or superior

intelligence can cause her parents to have uncomfortable feelings toward her. As well as pride, an uneasiness could result, and this, too, could affect the way they discipline their child. They may be harsh with a child who is making them feel inferior by contrast.

On the other hand, adopted children sometimes get away with behavior that would bring down parental wrath on birth children. Biological children, of course, resent this patently unequal treatment. But adopted kids don't like it either, since it reinforces their sense that they are different. In fact, when we asked a large number of adopted children what advice they would give to adoptive parents on raising their kids, the adoptees all responded that they should treat the adopted children the same way parents treated their biological children.

At times, of course, differences in age, gender, and temperament may make it necessary to treat a child differently from her brothers or sisters. But on the whole, fair treatment should be your aim. How can you tell if you're treating each of your children fairly? It's not easy; you might think you're doing it when, in fact, you're not.

Janet Wilson thought Joe, her adopted son, was taking advantage of her. He rarely did his chores when he was supposed to and usually had to be reminded before he would start them. Joe said that she demanded more of him than his brother Frank. To help clarify this disagreement we asked Mr. and Mrs. Wilson to keep a chart for a week of all activity related to chores in the family.

One week later, Mrs. Wilson had graphic evidence that her perception of what was going on did not match the reality of her family pattern. She and her husband permitted the intellectual, bookish Frank to forego some of his chores if he was in his room reading, while they made Joe, who liked to spend his free time outside playing with his friends, more consistently fulfill his family obligations. The Wilsons were more likely to favor their birth son because his inclinations matched their own, while they saw their adopted son's activities as frivolous and not sufficient to excuse him from raking leaves or changing the cat's litter.

If you think that you might have a similar problem, first ask your children if you treat them fairly. If they don't think that you do, try keeping a record, like the Wilsons', of how you treat each child. Beyond that you could ask friends and relatives if they think you're even-handed when it comes to your treatment of your children. Outsiders can sometimes see things more clearly.

DIFFERENCES IN INTERESTS

Now that your adopted child is getting old enough to share some of your interests and activities—hobbies and sports, for example—it can be frustrating to discover a divergence over what you and he like to do with spare time. The Robinsons were having a great deal of trouble with this dilemma. Mr. Robinson, a computer consultant, liked nothing better than to take a busman's holiday after work and tinker with his home computer. Mrs. Robinson taught art and loved to paint whenever she could make time for it at home. Their eldest adopted son took after his parents and his favorite activity was simply to read. But their ten-year-old adopted son came out of a different mold. He wanted attention and action. He liked games and outdoor sports.

This is the sort of thing that could have developed into a real problem, alienating the youngest child from the rest of the family. But instead they decided to meet their younger boy halfway. The Robinsons found some active pastimes that everybody could enjoy together at least once in a while, and Mr. Robinson discovered that he could blend his interests with his son's proclivities by playing video games with him. They also spent enough time exploring what their youngest son liked to do to discover some quiet activities—playing Monopoly and card games—that would engage him.

Normality, of course, is not at issue here. What's

"normal" in terms of interests and talents varies with a person's temperament. When these tendencies clash within a family, as they well might in an adoptive family, there are usually specific and uncomplicated solutions that parents and children can work out together. That could be something as simple as encouraging an athletically inclined youngster to sign up for a supervised program at the Y or for an after-school gymnastics club so he can work off steam and do the things he likes to do and then be ready to participate in more sedate activities. If you have younger children, consider hiring a young, energetic baby sitter. This could give you the chance to pursue your own interests without always having to go along with the activities your child favors; you could continue allocating some periods of time to joint activities, and he could still have plenty of opportunity to engage in activities which suit him best.

OSTRACIZED

We're coming to an age that can be a danger zone for any child who is different. Children are now verbal enough to wound with their words but not yet old enough to appreciate the full impact that their words can have on others. Furthermore, they are in the clique-forming stage; and what good is a clique if you can't find somebody different from you to exclude?

Nevertheless, parents need to bear in mind that the ostracizing of a child is not always as simple as it may appear. Group dynamics can get complicated; sometimes a scapegoat plays a role in his own isolation. If your child comes home from school and tearfully relates how he approached a group of boys, asked that they include him in their games, and then was told to "get lost, we don't play with adopted kids," there may be more to it than that—especially if it happens more than once. Kids are usually not singled out just because they're adopted, although you can't discount the possibility that prejudice about adoption could be motivating some children. The kids who are excluding your child are more likely to be using adoption-related taunts and epithets when some other and more basic conflict is actually causing trouble.

Try to find out why the other kids won't accept your child. Get as much information as you can from your youngster about the background of the conflict. What's the history of his relationship with these kids? Exactly what did he and they say this time? What happened just before the incident? Perhaps he could talk to someone close to both him and them, maybe a teacher, to get an objective opinion about what occurred.

Some of the characteristics and behavior that may alienate kids this age are extreme silliness and immaturity, lying, exaggerating, sarcasm, bullying, buttering up the teacher or acting like a know-it-all, and snitching to the teacher on what other pupils have done.

Since you can't be with your child all the time to protect him against this kind of pain, it's very important that you help him to develop a workable problem-solving technique he can use to deal with or, better yet, to prevent such incidents in the future. For example, ask him to focus on how he gets along with these kids when there is no conflict—the times he's asked them to let him play and they said yes. How did he get them to let him into their games? What did he do differently and how can he do more of it?

Some kids gain acceptance by zeroing in on the things they have in common with others, such as following the exploits of a local sports team. Sometimes a child needs coaching on a particular sports skill that will impress the other kids. If it's your son who's having these difficulties, make sure his father gets involved in helping him work his way out of trouble, since fathers can often relate more easily to the ways boys of this age interact socially.

If the other kids know that they're getting to your child, they may step up their efforts. A sense of humor, on the other hand, will often deflate ribbing before it turns ugly.

The idea is to concentrate on those interests and skills that will earn him acceptance from his peers or at least blunt differences when they arise.

You can pursue other courses of action if a persistent problem develops and your child seems stuck in his isolation. If the situation requires it—and if it doesn't make you or your child uncomfortable—you could sign him up for karate lessons. These would help him to focus on self-protection and building up his self-confidence, not on revenge. Encourage him to look for other friends. If he attends a large school he can almost certainly find groups of kids with interests and temperaments close to his. If you're not part of an adoptive parents' support group, you might join (or rejoin) one, so he can meet other adopted kids his age.

Throughout this trying time, make sure your child knows that you're sorry this is happening to him and that you don't like it one bit. Echo the painful feelings he describes. For example, if he says, "I feel so lonely," reply with, "Yes, I can hear that you feel very lonely." But try to keep the emphasis on what he can *do* to change the position he's in. Stress problem solving over self-pity. *P.E.T. (Parent Effectiveness Training)* by Dr. Thomas Gordon (New American Library) offers good examples of this style of reflective listening and problem solving.

SUMMER CAMP

Many children in this age group go away to camp for the first time. For you, it may trigger thoughts of the time, not so far distant, when your youngster will go off to college or go to work and leave your home for good. But your child will probably be focusing exclusively on the separation at hand. Most kids experience some trauma when going off to camp for the first time. An adoptee is not likely to manifest anything different from her peers, although there's always the possibility that you will see something a little out of the ordinary.

As the end of June approached, Marsha Goldstein thought her adopted daughter, Cindy, wasn't going to make it to the camp bus. Although the idea of going away to camp had excited Cindy—who had, in fact, asked to go—the closer the big day came, the more anxious she got. She began to interpret her mother's willingness to let her go as a sign that she was no longer wanted by her family.

Mrs. Goldstein helped Cindy deal with her fears by first listening to them. She agreed with her daughter that going to camp for the first time is scary for all children, and she told her that even kids who have gone to camp before sometimes get scared when that first day rolls around again. She also pointed out that many kids get homesick and that the camp staff knows how to help children feel better when they get the away-from-home blues. And Cindy's mother reminded her that she would already know some of the other girls at the camp because they came from her neighborhood.

Finally, Mrs. Goldstein, knowing that homesickness usually runs its course in about two weeks, got Cindy to agree to try camp for at least that long with the guarantee that if she needed to come home early, her mother would come and get her. Aware of the possibility that her daughter's adopted status could influence the fantasies that Cindy might have about leaving home for an extended period, Marsha Goldstein reminded her that she would always be part of the family no matter what. She emphasized that wherever Cindy went—on a visit to Grandma's, away to camp, on a school trip, off to college, and finally into her own house or apartment—her family would always be there for her and their home would always be hers.

Though still wary, Cindy tearfully left for camp, and her subsequent letters told of her adventures and only occasionally mentioned her homesickness.

SEXUAL AND EMOTIONAL MATURITY

Perhaps no other aspect of preadolescents' lives more dramatically reflects the theme of divergence than their physical development—and the disparity between it and their level of emotional maturity. Important anatomical and physical changes occur in girls at this stage: their bodies start to fill out and they begin to menstruate. Boys are generally about two years behind in their physical development. They are likely to begin to put on muscle and height after age twelve; by twelve and a half they may get erections, masturbate, and have wet dreams (it is normal for girls, too, to have masturbated by this age). These developments are occasionally disconcerting for parents, and can be particularly jarring for some adoptive parents.

In well-nourished, middle-class youngsters, the onset of menstruation is, to a great extent, genetically determined. Therefore, birth parents can estimate when this might occur in their daughter, but adoptive parents usually have no idea when it will happen. Generally, girls begin to get their period between the ages of nine and fifteen (on the average, at twelve or thirteen), with athletes and dancers often beginning to menstruate at the high end of the range. If you have a daughter, you should be prepared to deal with this important event in her life before she begins to menstruate. Since you are not her birth mother and therefore have no idea when she might begin, it's best to assume that she will start at the lower end of the age range so you can prepare her early. Try to have some discussions with her by age nine so that if she starts early it will not come as a surprise to her.

Mrs. Johnson had been meaning to do this with Emily, her ten-and-a-half-year-old adopted daughter, but just hadn't found the time. Then one day Emily frantically called her mother at work during lunch period from the school pay phone. "Mommy!" she screamed through her tears, "I'm dying, I'm bleeding to death!"

Though surprised, Emily's mother, with a few questions, quickly figured out that her daughter had started her period and told her to go the nurse's office and wait there for her.

Mrs. Johnson left work and after a quick stop at the drugstore drove quickly to her daughter's school where she found Emily still sobbing. Putting her arms around her daughter, she rocked her gently until the sobs subsided. Then she explained briefly what Emily had to do to take care of herself, showed her how to use a sanitary napkin, and answered her questions.

After some time, Emily was calm enough to return to class and Mrs. Johnson went back to work. Before they separated, her mother told Emily that they would have a special dinner out to discuss the changes Emily was experiencing and to celebrate her growing up.

While this manifestation of growing up is not likely to cause much of a problem for you, some adoptive parents do find it brings up some uncomfortable feelings and memories. If infertility is still a painful subject, this evidence of your daughter's possible ability to reproduce could leave you with mixed feelings, perhaps even a little jealousy. For some parents, it is a reminder of what they once considered to be their failure.

For others, it may awaken thoughts of a birth mother who bore their adopted child out of wedlock, and the fear that history will repeat itself. You need to remember that there is no connection between a birth mother's past and your child's own future sexual conduct. The only thing that might produce this linkage would be if you treated your daughter as if she "had it in her." In fact, the most important element in the formation of her sexual values is your communicating to her your beliefs about what constitutes a responsible attitude toward intimacy and sexuality.

If you do have some fears that your daughter will repeat her birth mother's experience, talk them out with your spouse to avoid putting too much emphasis on them and having them influence the way you interact with your child.

Try to convey a lack of tension in discussions with your daughter. It is an important goal as you help her understand her changing and maturing body.

The beginning of menstruation does require some frank talk with your daughter. If sexuality and bodily processes are difficult topics for you to discuss, as they are for some families—and your daughter is not yet studying these subjects in school—you might want to ask your pediatrician or some other competent adult to discuss it with her. In big families, older children sometimes tell the younger kids. Or your daughter might feel more comfortable talking to an aunt if she has one whose age falls somewhere between her own and yours. You might also take a look at these books: Planned Parenthood's *How to Talk with Your Child About Sexuality* (Doubleday), Lynda Madaras's *What's Happening to My Body? Book for Girls* (Newmarket Press), Lynda Madaras's *What's Happening to My Body? Book for Boys* (Newmarket Press), and Ruth Bell's *Changing Bodies, Changing Lives* (Random House).

If you do feel comfortable talking about sex, the best approach is to wait for your children to come to you with questions and then to answer them matter-of-factly.

Adopted children sometimes wonder about the sexual relationship between their parents. Your youngster, at this age, knows that she was born to another woman, and that the act of procreation involves sex. If you don't have any birth children, she might ask you if you and your spouse ever have sex. It's a good idea to decide beforehand how much of your privacy you are willing to have breached to satisfy your child's curiosity should this question come up. Acknowledge that married people have sex, but you can answer questions about specific details with, "That's a private matter between your father (mother) and me." However, do explain to your child that people who are unable to conceive children still have intimate relationships and that sex can be for pleasure as well as reproduction.

Occasionally, parents, whether adoptive or birth, overreact to their children's sexual curiosity. For example, it's perfectly normal for a ten-year-old boy to peek through his sister's bedroom door as she undresses if she didn't close it all the way. If you encounter this behavior and it is unacceptable in your family, make it clear to your son that such conduct is unacceptable and that there are consequences for repeating it, and ask your daughter to close her door when undressing. But don't make more of it than you would if he had broken any other family rules; and, if you can handle it, offer to answer directly any questions he might have that provoked the peeping. Most important, we can assure you that such behavior is not adoption-related, but rather normal curiosity in a developing child.

Adopted kids are no more sophisticated than those raised by their birth parents, so it shouldn't surprise you if you get fantastic questions about sex and reproduction that seem totally absurd. For example, one ten-year-old we spoke with was absolutely convinced that when a baby was born the mother's vagina came out with the infant. (He was an only child!) Another was certain that boys, too, had periods, and felt sure that all the grownups were trying to keep it a secret from her. Whatever the question, try to be as patient and honest as you can be. Sex and intimacy are confusing topics for almost everyone, so understand that developing a healthy and mature attitude is a complicated process for your child.

QUESTIONS AND ANSWERS

We feel it increasingly necessary to discipline our eleven-year-old. However, we now realize that when she was little we never made it clear to her what our values were. Is now too late to start?

No. In fact, she will be able to understand your values and standards more easily now than she could have at an earlier age, when children obey rules because the people setting them are older and more powerful than they are.

Eleven-year-olds, on the other hand, are on the verge of understanding the intrinsic merit of a value system.

However, you have to start being very specific about your rules and what's expected of her and realize that it will take time for her to adapt to this new order of things. If your child is going to become active in Girl Scouts, for example, establish a rule that she has to come straight home. As she gets older and stays out more often, either set a curfew or at least make it clear that she must call and tell you where she is if she's out past a certain time. She may test you, and you will have to be prepared to deal with this. You and your child both have to believe that your rules will not be broken without consequences. You have to convince yourself that you mean business and will pursue the matter.

□

My twelve-year-old adopted son is ashamed because his six-year-old adopted sister tells people that they are adopted. Does this mean that he has some emotional problem related to adoption?

It doesn't sound like there's anything wrong with your son. Twelve-year-olds don't like to have attention called to the things that make them different from their friends. Sympathize with your son; acknowledge that little sisters can sometimes be a "real pain."

□

My nine-year-old daughter sometimes likes to pretend that she is my birth child. Is there any harm in my going along with her?

There's nothing wrong with your daughter having this fantasy—it's a compliment to your parenting that she feels that way—but it would be harmful for you to play along with it. The next time she expresses these feelings, try responding, "It sounds to me like you feel like it would be nice if I had given birth to you and you weren't adopted." Then repeat back to her what she says without making any judgments so she will feel safe expressing these normal feelings.

□

I told my ten-year-old daughter that if she wanted to find her birth mother, I would help her. That seemed to make her a little uneasy. Did I make a mistake by suggesting this now?

Yes, your offer was premature. She is still too young to understand the legal connection created by adoption. She may be worried that if her birth mother appears she may have to make a choice about whom to live with. Tell her that you meant that you would help her look some day—if she wanted to—when she's much older. Assure her that you are the mother she will live with until she leaves home.

□

In our family, it's normal for girls to get their period for the first time at age twelve or thirteen. My adopted daughter has just started her period at age ten. What will this mean? Should I treat her any differently?

The timing is more related to genetic factors than anything else. It has no significance for predicting her behavior, nor does it mean that she will be prematurely sexually active. These days a lot of parents feel they have to follow a biological time clock. But just because she got her period doesn't mean you have to start treating her as if she were a mature woman—any more than you would just because she has started to use cosmetics. She's still a girl, with the emotional makeup of a girl—it's important to treat her like one and not as if she's suddenly more mature.

□

My nine-year-old adopted son, who has never had behavioral problems, has suddenly become impossible to handle. He beat up his little sister, threatens to run away at least once a week, and has started to misbehave in school. Is this something that adopted boys tend to do at this age? It's a little frightening.

While it doesn't necessarily happen, it's not unusual for boys of this age, adopted and nonadopted, to act up as your son is doing. Paradoxically, he may respond to feeling confused and out of control by testing your willingness to maintain control of your family and, especially, of him. Winning this battle of the wills would be the worst thing that could happen to him. It's important now to reestablish clear limits for him and not let him think that he is more powerful than you. For example, if he refuses to go to school, take him firmly in hand and transport him to the school. If you have been a little lax in asserting your authority over him, you need to insist on it now. The child wants you to use a firm hand, reassuring him that you are able to take care of him.

Be reassured that this phenomenon can occur in any family. We recently treated a family with four children, three birth and one adopted. Both parents have Ph.D.s. But that didn't help them with their adopted child, who was driving them to distraction. When either his parents or sisters gets mad at the boy, he says, "You don't want me to be in this family and I don't want to be a part of it." Then he goes out into the garage to sit in the car for a few hours. We explained to the parents that, contrary to his actions, he wanted them to stop him from acting out this way. What they had to do was not let him leave the house and reach the car. Instead, they had to sit him down and explain in a clear way what his place was in the family and what he could and could not do.

□

My ten-year-old adoptee behaves well at home but misbehaves terribly at school. We've been to his school to talk to his teacher and guidance counselor, but his misconduct continues. What's going on and what should I do?

Kids this age have a lot of nervous energy; and as we just noted, many of them, especially boys, may act in a very disruptive manner. It's not likely to have anything to do with adoption. Since your child is acting this way only in school, unless he has a particular problem at school, it sounds like it's just easier for him to blow off steam there than at home. This often happens when a family is highly structured and fairly strict and the school is a somewhat looser environment. The child chooses the path of least resistance, acting out where he knows the consequences will be minimal. If your child is well behaved at school and acts out at home, the situation is probably reversed.

Since you have more control over your home environment, try making some adjustments there. A more relaxed family structure in which your child has a greater voice in what limits you impose on him—say, in how late he can stay out and play during the summer—might take some of the steam out of his rebelliousness at school. Also, try enrolling him in an after-school program that emphasizes physical activity so he can harmlessly burn off some of the energy he's now channeling into disruptive behavior.

□

Every year our family has vacationed together but this year our adopted daughter wants to go away to camp. My husband is willing to go along with this, but I'm upset because I've always looked forward to these family vacations.

Peer relationships become more important to children at the upper range of this age group and will build to a crescendo by age fourteen or fifteen. Many of her friends are now probably going away to camp, and she may not want to be the only kid who still has to vacation with her family. Since she's adopted, being like her peers may be very important to her. So there's nothing wrong with her wish to go to camp. And for you, it's the beginning of a letting-go process. Now would be a good time to start to confront and prepare for the fact that in a few years she will be moving away from joint family activities in even more substantial ways.

□

We are a two-career family and caring for our three-year-old birth child has become quite a burden. Our nine-year-old adoptee has volunteered to help out, but we wonder if he's old enough to take on this type of responsibility. What do you think?

Nine-year-olds are quite competent to help out in this way with adult supervision. Child care calls up the best in these youngsters. It also gives them a sense of responsibility and reinforces the notion that adoptee or birth child, they are a highly valued and integral part of the family.

6 Young Teens, Ages Twelve to Fourteen

Families begin to undergo a basic change when their children reach adolescence. Until this time, most families operate upon the principle of a parent's authority. For the most part, you set rules of behavior for your child and you made sure that your youngster obeyed them. But with the coming of adolescence your child needs—and will often demand—more autonomy. At this stage your son or daughter must also develop a greater sense of responsibility. You will have to arrive at a point where you begin to trust her to make good decisions for herself. All this is in preparation for a time—no longer so distant—when your youngster will leave home and be responsible for herself.

The successful completion of this transition is a tall order under the calmest of circumstances. Unfortunately, many of the conditions and experiences that characterize adolescence make for turmoil. Hormones often appear to be running rampant. At the same time that adults ask them to be more independent and to develop more internal controls, adolescents' bodies and emotions may feel most out of control. In junior high school, the nurturing, constant presence of one teacher—usually female—is suddenly replaced by a group of subject teachers, men and women, who have less focused contact with your child. Your child is increasingly influenced by his peers, and the misunderstandings between parent and child, which are anything but amusing, begin to cloud your family's life. And there are the heavy issues regarding sex, alcohol, and other drugs to contend with.

An added complication is that as your child gets older, he will have less need for your supervision. You have to begin to let go and prepare for the empty nest that may now be no more than six or seven years down the line. Sometimes adoptive parents find this harder to do than birth parents.

Marge Jones, a forty-five-year-old housewife, couldn't understand what was motivating her twelve-year-old adopted son, Bobby, to disobey her. After school he went out to play with his friends for about three hours before he had to come in to have dinner and do his homework. She thought it perfectly reasonable to require him to check in with her every hour or so during his play time. He thought that was ridiculous at his age and responded by not only not staying in touch but often coming in late for dinner as well.

When faced with such unrealistic demands, kids tend either to comply, stifling their appropriate urge toward more independence, or they defy almost all parental limitations, meeting overprotection with an overreaction. Marge could have checked with other parents in her neighborhood to determine the norm for kids Bobby's age. However, she and her husband, a fifty-one-year-old automobile dealer, after years of battling against infertility and enduring a long wait to become adoptive parents, were holding tight to what *they* thought was best for the child they had worked so hard to get.

Adoptive parents, who had to go through a struggle to get their child in the first place, may have more of a need to try to delay their child's independence than do birth parents. When the time comes to begin the separation process, they are likely to be older than biological parents at a similar stage of their child's development, and thus possibly a little less flexible in their adaptation to change. They may also wonder how strong their ties to their child will be once he moves out into the world, and if those ties would endure were he to look for and find his birth parents.

For some families, an additionally troublesome factor at this stage could be one of the very features of their family that the adoption agency was so pleased with at the beginning of the adoption process: a wife as full-time homemaker. Until recently it was rare for an adoption agency to place a healthy infant in a family in which the wife worked. In rural areas this still often holds true. Thus women who adopted more than one child may have been required to remain at home for many years, making it difficult for them to begin a career. One could easily understand why, without a career outside the home, a mother might feel especially reluctant to part with the person who has occupied so much of her life.

When parents don't deal with their feelings about their child's moves toward autonomy, they could end up inappropriately drawing their youngster into the part of the family transition that is rightfully their job. Their child, responding to his parents' inability to let go, reverts to immature behavior, thus justifying continued "mothering." It can become a vicious cycle, with the actions of parents and child provoking more of the same from the other. Parents who have difficulty with this process should discuss it with their mates, friends, or, if it really gets sticky, a professional trained to help with such obstacles.

A DAY IN THE LIFE

Life can seem like a whirlwind for parents of an adolescent. A thirteen-year-old comes home five minutes before dinner, gets on the phone almost as soon as she's in the front door, with barely a "hi" as she goes by. You thought you knew all her friends, only to find one Saturday evening that the cast of characters has undergone a sudden and inexplicable change. Just when you felt familiar with her likes and dislikes, she sounds like she's borrowed another person's tastes and sensibilities. Even the way she dresses can be disconcerting at best and absolutely disturbing if she chooses to pursue the far(out) fringes of teenage fashion. What's more, she may claim that she wouldn't be caught dead participating in the family activities that she formerly enjoyed so much.

Emotionally, she may seem totally incomprehensible. She's up one minute, down the next, short-tempered, and passionate about everything. She may come home from school devastated by something one of her girlfriends said to her; yet when that same girl calls, your child gets off the phone smiling. When you ask her what happened to the sworn enemy she was denouncing ten minutes ago, she doesn't know what you're talking about. She's capable of responding to a new style of pants with, "I would *never* wear *that! No* way!" But when she sees her best friend wearing it the next day, she has to have it or she'll "die."

Boys, too, can experience mood swings in this period. Many parents of sons of this age complain that their once cheerful, talkative boy now acts sullen and doesn't speak much of the time. Sure, he's as vocal as can be when participating in or watching a sports event, but at home he spends more time in his room than with other family members, just as an adolescent girl may do. If your family tends to be gregarious, you might view this as strangely uncharacteristic of your family style. But rest assured that this could happen in any family, adoptive or not.

What happened to the sweet and somewhat predictable kid you knew? No wonder our popular culture is full of images of uncomprehending parents trying to fathom the ways of these aliens in their midst. Almost all parents find this period at least a little trying, and adoptive parents perhaps more so, since they may wonder if this adolescent turmoil is really a symptom of emotional disturbance arising from their child's genetic background.

Parents also sometimes interpret their adolescent child's occasionally erratic behavior as symptomatic of something they did wrong in raising her. But if your teenager's conduct strikes you this way, it's more likely that you are looking at coping mechanisms, not pathology; she's struggling with her mixed feelings about the rapid changes in her body and the world that adults expect her to master. The easiest way for her to respond to these pressures is to accept the marks of meaning and belonging that our culture offers her—the dress, music, language, hair styles, ways of interacting with parents, and super-attentiveness to the attitudes of her peers.

If she was having serious problems beyond the ordinary travails of teenagers, you would probably know it. For example, spending a good deal of time at home in her room without her friends is not necessarily a cause for alarm. But if that were combined with other unsettling behavior, such as a sudden change in her eating habits, a hysterical response to your simplest request, no peer relationships, a refusal to go to school, an inexplicable and abrupt decrease in her grades, and/or an unwillingness to obey family rules when she had not acted this way before, it would suggest a problem. The key is the presence of more than one symptom over time.

If your adolescent's behavior starts to look like this, you could say to her, "I see some changes in your behavior and I wonder what they mean. Is there anything you'd like to talk about?" If she seems reluctant to open up to you, you could add, "If you don't feel like talking about it now, I hope you'll feel free to sit down and talk when you're ready."

Bear in mind that a certain amount of turmoil and unhappiness naturally accompanies the experience of adolescence. These are transitional years, and change on this scale rarely comes easily. Fights between friends, rejection by a boyfriend, a party that flops, or a breakout of acne are part of the pain of being an adolescent. You can't completely shield her from pain—negotiating difficulties is part of growing up—and you certainly should try to avoid becoming more upset about whatever is bothering her than she is.

As an adoptive parent, it's crucial that you realize that adoption in itself does not cause any serious adolescent difficulties. Yet adoption can have a bearing on almost every major aspect of adolescence, and while the connection may be more subtle than it was in earlier stages of growth, it is just as important to understand it now as it was when your child was younger.

HORMONES OUT OF HARMONY

Puberty is, first, a physically unsettling time. If you looked at a graph showing when girls first got their period, the curve would peak at ages twelve and thirteen. A similar graph demonstrating when boys first experienced ejaculation would hit a high point between ages thirteen and fourteen.

Kids grow proportionately as much at this stage as they did in infancy. It's not unusual for them to begin their twelfth year retaining the characteristic look of their early years, and to approach their fifteenth birthday already beginning to resemble the way they will appear when they are full-grown adults.

However, unlike the beginning of their lives, they are now very much conscious of how they are changing. Girls, who may yet see themselves as children, must come to terms with bodies that increasingly suggest maturity and sexual awakening, while many boys must deal with increments of height and muscle implying a manhood that, they usually sense, is still a fiction.

There is a good deal of research which suggests that taller, handsomer, and earlier-developing adolescents are more popular with their teachers and peers. Since looks have an important bearing on popularity and self-image, anything that mars an adolescent's appearance is a serious matter. Acne, crooked teeth, mousy straight hair, shortness, and breasts that are either too big or don't appear on schedule are just a few of the obstacles along the way. Most parents offer advice to their children to be patient because, with age, these worries will pass. But your child doesn't have your experience and may find it hard to accept on faith, no matter how much he trusts you, that there really is a light at the end of the tunnel.

Your adopted child is in a somewhat tighter bind concerning certain physical flaws of adolescence than are other kids. We know that inheritance plays a role in the manifestation of physical characteristics that often trouble children in this age group—for example, the oily skin and the production of certain hormones that forms the basis for acne. Nonadopted children often get some measure of comfort when they hear from a relative how he, too, had this problem but outgrew it by the time he reached his twenties. A family photo album may offer graphic proof to back this up. Indeed, such facts give children some reason to hope that their development will follow a similar course.

Adopted children don't have these kinds of experiences to fall back on. Unless you were fortunate enough to get detailed information about your child's birth parents, you can't reassure him about his short stature because his father and uncles all shot up at about the age of seventeen; maybe they did, but you have no way of knowing it.

However, even without a family tree from which to draw comfort, you're not helpless in ameliorating the effects of these adolescent difficulties. Boys can compensate for their lack of height with extra muscle or athletic skill, to name just two ways. If your son is short for his age, you might buy him a set of weights—they make them for younger kids—or sign him up for gymnastics classes at the Y or at the after-school center. The girl who seems too tall and feels awkward can take dance classes and develop a sureness and control of her body. If she's overweight, don't criticize her; rather, assist her to devise a workable diet and an effective exercise regimen. Don't buy tempting snacks. Attractive and appropriate clothing can help take the edge off her disappointment at not developing the way some of her friends have.

If your son is not being picked for basketball choose-up games or your daughter is negative about her height because most of the boys won't dance with a girl who is taller than them, you could point out short men or tall women whose accomplishments and renown your child admires—perhaps Woody Allen and Michael J. Fox for boys, Lauren Hutton and Grace Jones for girls. Ask your daughter, also, to notice how other tall girls she knows get along and to make note of the specific things they do that seem to work (from style of dress to the ways they carry themselves) and help her to review these characteristics from time to time.

For either sex, acne is, to some extent, medically treatable, so get a referral to a good dermatologist. Orthodonture, also, though expensive, can improve your teenager's appearance over the long run. Despite the fact that braces are not exactly attractive, they are often considered a status symbol at this age.

Sometimes, these complications can lead to sibling rivalry. If your adopted daughter's skin is broken out and she has still not developed breasts, while your older birth daughter went through this period just two years ago without a complexion problem and with an attractive, lithe body that even her friends envied, your adoptee may have one more stress to deal with.

If your adopted child is comparing herself unfavorably to her sibling, you are not without ways to comfort her. For example, you could show her pictures of movie stars looking no more glamorous than her when they were her age (magazines such as *People* often run such pictures). But if her sibling is making this comparison, you should act decisively. Make it clear that such teasing violates family rules. Should the brother or sister bring adoption into the teasing, consider it a punishable offense.

JUNIOR HIGH SCHOOL

It might be comforting at this tumultuous time in their child's life if adoptive parents could at least think of the intense ups and downs of adolescence as occurring within the supportive framework of a nurturing educational institution. Unfortunately, just when they really need stability and close attention, adolescents enter junior high school, which reflects the outside world much more than did their elementary school.

The transition from one type of school to another seems to be an especially vulnerable time for some adopted boys. They are slightly more likely than nonadoptees to have behavioral difficulties in school at ages eleven and twelve, although their problems are not monumental and usually fade by the time they reach high school. Why this happens is not altogether clear.

For all kids, the change from elementary to junior high school is a revolution and thus a major stress in their lives. Socially, it is almost an instant end to their childhood. They may not yet be going to coed parties and dating, but now they are surrounded by kids who do and who talk about it a great deal. Although the pressure to get good grades so they can get into college is not yet upon them, it's in the air; they constantly hear that by the ninth grade their marks will start to "count."

Adoptees face additional pressures. In junior high, they no longer stay in one room all day under the watchful eye of a single teacher. Now they move from room to room and from subject to subject every hour. Their teachers emphasize subject matter, not general educational and social skills. While teachers encourage them to their full potential, they are not as concerned with making their students feel good as elementary school teachers probably were. Losing the close contact with one teacher they had in elementary school might evoke fantasies some adopted children have of abandonment. Further, the sudden plunge into a world of adolescent cliques and the necessity of making a new set of friends may also enhance their feeling of being different from other children.

Your interaction with your youngster's school and its staff also changes. If you used your child's primary school teachers as allies in dealing with adoption-related complications, you will find yourself likely to have a more distant relationship to this new set of teachers. Unless your child has become a problem in their class, they will want to discuss his achievement, not his social adjustment.

Your child is less likely to require the protection of grown-ups, so you will probably not need his teacher as an ally to keep adoption from becoming an issue at school. The exception would be something serious, such as harassment from a bully. But while that represents progress, it may also undermine any feeling you had that by staying in touch with the teacher you had some control over how your child did in school.

If your child does have some difficulty at school, try to narrow down the possible source of the trouble. Until Jill Worthington took this approach, she thought her daughter was developing some kind of complex.

Jody Worthington was getting stomachaches in school. While the school's cafeteria hardly rated four stars, it certainly wasn't that bad—and her pediatrician had eliminated a medical basis—so her mother figured that the sudden illnesses must be emotionally based. She decided to do a little detective work and charted the occurrences of her daughter's malady. In less than two days she solved the mystery. Jody was all but doubling over when confronted with Ms. Wilson's social studies class. The teacher was demanding, sarcastic, ironic, and judgmental, while Jody was gentle and straightforward.

To help her daughter cope with this situation, Mrs. Worthington asked her to play observer for two weeks. She told Jody to note the specific things that Ms. Wilson did that upset her and anything that Jody was able to do to make things easier on herself. Jill also told Jody to see how the other kids managed to deal with the teacher. It turned out that Jody was very bothered by Ms. Wilson's sarcasm when she called on Jody and she did not know the answer. The kids who were not bothered by this unpleasant practice were those who had taken extra time to prepare for the class and were able to volunteer before being called upon. Jody took the hint, and her little bit of extra preparation time cured her stomachaches.

Home routines not conducive to studying could be the cause of poor performance in school. Perhaps you have two youngsters sharing a bedroom. If so, make sure each has access to a quiet area for enough time each day to do homework. In one family we know of, the parents solved this dilemma by allowing one of two brothers who shared a bedroom to do his homework in the bedroom temporarily vacated by their older sister, who was away at college.

Another boy, Timmy, seemed like two different people at his junior high school. He was either alert and on top of everything, or else virtually inert and out of it. The secret ingredient turned out to be informal after-school choose-up sports. On days when he engaged in them, he would come home, have his dinner, do his homework, watch TV, and go to sleep, awakening the next morning rested and ready for another day. On nonathletic days he was restless, stayed up late, and paid for it the next day with a bleary-eyed presence in class. When his parents brought him to us and we saw the pattern, we encouraged them to get him into an organized program of athletics to help him work off the excess energy that's natural for a boy his age.

In other words, the first thing to look for when school difficulties arise is connections. What time of the day does the trouble occur? Does it seem to coincide with particular activities or teachers? Sometimes family tensions, such as an argument with a grandmother who lives with you, play a part in how your child will behave or perform academically in school the next day. Also, focus on the good days and see what happens then to find out what your child did to cause things to go right. If you can figure out what happens when things go well, you will be able to increase their occurrence, thereby improving the situation.

School performance in the junior high school years starts

to take on added significance for many teenagers: college looms on the horizon. As an adoptive family, you may feel the pressure even more than other families. People who have adopted often think they must try a little harder to be good parents; they really work at it. While this is a good thing, the down side is that they sometimes see their child's academic progress and achievement as a measure of whether they have been doing their job well. That's why we would like to put the question of schoolwork at this age in some perspective.

For the most part, kids this age do not focus on their studies. As we have already pointed out, they have a good deal to contend with outside the classroom; and they are very much aware that their grades, at least until the ninth grade, "don't count" towards college admission, if this is their goal.

In the past, experts have discussed the subject of motivating children in early adolescence to like school and to want to study. Parents subsequently believed that if they could just find the right emotional button to push, they would see results. But in recent years we have come to realize that any such approach is questionable, at best, simply because there's no good reason for children to enjoy their studies now—they would most likely enjoy doing other things. That's not true for the few kids who always place in the top percentile of their class but, remember, they are the exception, not the rule.

On the other hand, at this age, children must learn the basics of a broad range of subjects and must develop good study habits if they want to go on to higher education. So you do need a way of getting them to fulfill their responsibilities. One approach is to think about your child's homework and getting good grades as his tasks, as his work. Happiness is not the issue here. Think of these responsibilities as akin to your family's rules for behavior. They are what he must do and he simply has to do them to the best of his ability.

Christopher Davidson wasn't doing *any* homework at home in his first year of junior high school. When his parents questioned his lack of homework, he said that he finished it in school. But when the first marking period brought C's rather than the solid B's their son had earned in elementary school, they began to worry. They had adopted him as an infant and they knew that his birth parents had not done well in school. Did they expect too much from him academically?

The Davidsons conferred with Chris's teachers, asking them what grades they thought he should be attaining and how much homework he should be doing. The teachers thought the youngster could be getting B's and they felt that two hours of homework per night would bring him to that level. Consequently, Chris's parents told him that they would expect him to do two hours of homework every night. They would supervise it, and if he didn't have an assignment, they would give him one from his textbook. After that, his time would be his own. The result: beginning with the next marking period, solid B's.

Having noted that academics are not a high-priority activity with most teenagers, we should also point out that school does have great significance for adolescents. After all, it's in the school hallways and at the lockers that they interact with some of the most important people in their lives: their peers.

FRIENDS

It would be hard to overstate the influence of her peers on this stage of your child's development. They will have a lot to do with how she talks, thinks, and dresses. They define what's "in" and what's "out." When you think it necessary to counter their influence on any given issue, you may find yourself swimming upriver against a very strong current.

Kids at this stage have a deep-seated need for acceptance by their peers. For adopted kids, this may be all the more reason for them to push their birth circumstances into the background if they aren't friendly with peers who are adopted. They know that kids their age are quick to categorize others, so they are not likely to make much of their adoption, for fear of being introduced to their friends' friends as Jane or Johnny, "who's adopted."

One thing all adolescents share is the experience of sometimes feeling out of control. Their bodies and emotions just won't cooperate. This phenomenon is at the root of many teenage customs: they try to create a safe environment so they can know what to expect. It can mean making their room look a certain way; hanging out at a familiar place, like McDonald's (their home room in junior high school fulfills somewhat the same purpose); carrying their music with them in the form of personal stereos; and blending into a familiar background of clothing styles, such as cutting out parts of their tee shirts, that you might regard as weird at best.

Your adopted child might seize upon these and other badges of identity with an even greater relish than his friends. He may feel that his world is more out of control than theirs, since he knows less about himself. He may welcome any way open to him to create stability and familiarity, so don't worry about weird haircuts or clothing fads he adopts because they are in.

An adoptive parent who has been enormously involved with her child may find it difficult to acknowledge that her youngster is now taking her cues from her peers. Are they the right bunch for her? Do they drink or fool around with drugs? What are their families like?

All parents, of course, have some of these anxieties about their child's friends. But for adoptive parents, extra anxiety could enter the picture. For example, if your child came from an ethnic or racial group different from yours, he may now seek out friends with whom he has that characteristic in common. That's only natural. We are all, to some extent, drawn to people who are like us in some way. While your child does share your family's "culture" with you, there are certain traits he may want to identify with that you simply can't supply.

This may be difficult for you to accept. His friends could

look and speak differently than you do, come from another social class, practice a different religion, have values that clash with yours. They may aspire to be carpenters and mechanics while you hope your child will go to college.

When an adolescent does seek the counsel of an adult, he may sometimes go to the parent of a friend, rather than to you. This has nothing to do with adoption. Kids tend to hang out at one house in particular, and adults in that family are sometimes convenient sounding boards and sources of advice. If this happens, try not to view it as a rejection of you. There is just enough distance between your child and these adults to make it possible for your youngster to raise issues he might not be able to with you. For him, it's a safer way of dealing with topics that might literally hit too close to home if he brought them up with his own father or mother.

One way you can get some control over this situation is to get your child's friends to spend more time at your house. In general, kids will go where they feel comfortable and accepted. If you have delicate antiques and white carpeting, they may take that to mean that they're not welcome. But even if your living room is not conducive to hanging out, you could set up other areas of your home in such a way that your child and her friends will feel welcome.

A finished basement, for example, oversized pillows on the floor, a good stereo system, a Ping-Pong table, and a VCR well stocked with movies appealing to this age group should serve as an effective enticement. If you have less room, another attraction is a kitchen that always seems to have all the right foods. Potato chips, chocolate chip cookies—whatever is currently in—will make your home appealing. You could also encourage your child to bring his friends over on a Saturday night to make pizza, franks and beans, or whatever people in your section of the country consider a fun food. If your youngster hosts a pajama party, you might feed the kids pancakes made from scratch for breakfast.

On the other hand, you'll have to be very discreet if you encourage the kids to hang out at your house. If you appear to be a little too anxious to have them around, it could backfire and turn them away. Adolescents don't like to have adults fuss over them, try too hard to be friendly, and, especially, ask them too many questions. So while you're understandably interested in knowing as much about your child's friends as you can, you'll probably have to remind yourself once in a while that much of their relationships will have to remain a mystery to you.

What if you know enough about one or more of your child's friends to know that you don't like them? The first thing you should ask yourself is whether this friend represents a real danger—does she use drugs or alcohol?—or is this just a matter of chemistry and you don't like her because of her personality, values, or something even more undefinable. Unless this friend does represent a clear danger to your son or daughter, you're better off withholding criticism. It's good for your child to get to know all kinds of people. You can't protect her from everything, and if you've given your youngster a clear sense of right and wrong, you can be confident that she will probably not get too close to the wrong kind of people.

PRIVACY—AND YOUR WORST FEARS

The privacy issue occupies the border area between your need to know and your child's compelling desire to carve out an increasingly larger part of her life that is hers alone. She is struggling for control and autonomy; you're trying to let go gradually and graciously, all the while knowing that you still have to do much of the steering until she can safely take over directing her own life.

Parents must accept that their children have some feelings and facts which they need to keep to themselves. You have to respect that need. As an adoptive parent, you might find this a little hard to do. In our experience, adoptive parents, more than birth parents, tend to be concerned with what their child is thinking. They may feel that if they knew more they could help more. But this only works when your child wants to talk to you about something.

With fewer role models than birth parents have, adoptive parents may want reassurance from their child that everything is going fine in her life, that they are doing a good job of parenting. But it's not a child's job to reassure her parents. If you have these feelings, seek the reassurance from your peers—friends, relatives, or an adoptive parents' group.

Though it may be tempting, especially if you're feeling anxious, never try to read your child's diary or eavesdrop on his phone conversations. It might also be a good idea to tell him to lower the volume on his telephone answering machine, if he has his own, so that you don't inadvertently hear something you'd rather not.

Serena Martin, thirteen and a half years old, turned her answering machine off when she went to the country for a weekend to stay with a friend. Her mother, thinking her daughter had forgotten to push the "on" button, turned it on. The volume was high enough for Mrs. Martin to hear what she took to be a juicy message from one of Serena's friends, bragging about the hot time she had had the previous night with her boyfriend and alluding to Serena's similar relationship with another boy. In fact, the message was ambiguous, and it could as easily have been referring to necking on a park bench as to anything that might have been occurring in a bed. But Serena's mother now had to live with considerable anxiety, for to question her child would mean acknowledging her eavesdropping.

If your child were drinking or using drugs on anything more than an experimental or occasional basis, you would certainly know it without having to overhear references to that fact. Observation of your child's behavior is the key here, not your behavior, which your child could interpret as snooping.

Having accepted this, how do you stay in touch with what your child is doing and thinking? Contrary to notions fostered by our popular culture, parents *can* communicate with adolescents. One way to go about this admittedly difficult task is to avoid conversations that are really one-way interrogations. You might begin by being open yourself. Show your child that you're willing to talk about things that have happened to you and how you felt about them. Even if you've never tried this approach before, you can start now and probably get a good response.

Carla Hopkins, in trying to empathize with her son's dismay at being falsely accused of cheating on a test, said to him, "It's funny, I was thinking about what happened to you the other day and remembering a weird experience I had when I was your age. I also had a teacher who thought I had cheated on an exam. To see if his suspicion was correct, he gave our class two different tests, but he didn't tell us. When he checked the answers he discovered that my girlfriend, who sat in the row next to mine, was the one who was copying the answers." She commiserated with her son about the unfairness of it all and about how hard it was to get somebody to listen to your side of the story. While her youngster remained somewhat upset, the raw pain did ease a bit and he appreciated his mother's response.

You might try talking to your child while you're both engaged in the same activity, like cooking or making repairs around the house. Establish lines of communication with talk about subjects that interest both of you, such as planning trips and family weekend activities, politics, sports, what's going on with your relatives, and the like. By establishing the habit of talking freely, you make it more likely that he will approach you if he has something more personal or urgent to discuss.

Recent studies indicate that a tendency toward alcoholism may be an inherited characteristic. In fact, adoptive families have participated in a few of the studies on the subject. We emphasize the tentativeness of the results of these studies and that we are dealing with a *tendency*, not an inevitable fact. If you know that one of your child's biological parents was an alcoholic, you should make an extra effort to teach your youngster that drinking is inappropriate at his age. Alcohol can disrupt the process of hormonal change during puberty, exacerbating an adolescent's normal ups and downs. It can also keep a child from learning and performing up to his capacity. Set an example by not making alcohol too much of a presence in your home. If you do not know of any alcoholism in his family background, there's less reason to be concerned, but keep an ongoing awareness of this issue. Controlling alcohol intake is an important lesson for all youngsters.

Some signs that your child may be abusing drugs and alcohol are certain behaviors that have lasted more than one month. They include:

- impulsive behavior
- suspiciousness
- aggressive behavior, provoking family arguments
- inability to meet important responsibilities to friends and family members
- failure in school
- money difficulties
- legal difficulties related to the illegal purchase of drugs or alcohol
- accidents, especially in automobiles

If you note these behaviors in your adolescent, it is important to seek advice and assistance immediately from a drug and/or alcohol program. Again, remember we are not talking about occasional experimentation, but rather a clear pattern of developing dependence on highly addictive substances. The current drugs of choice among today's teens are alcohol, marijuana, cocaine and cocaine derivatives such as crack, and amphetamines. Because of the highly addictive nature of some of these drugs and the serious damage they can cause, often in a very short time, it is important for parents to become educated about the signs of substance abuse.

SEX

Girls in this age group daydream a lot. They may talk—especially among themselves—of having a family. For adopted girls, an especially poignant aspect of these thoughts relates to the possibility that some day they will finally have biological relatives they know and can love. While this is of course also true for adopted boys, we've observed that girls seem somewhat more interested than boys in this subject. However, this could change as the role of the male in our society shifts more toward that of nurturer.

Having their own family can also give adoptees a sense of increased control over their lives, something they experienced even less of while growing up than did other kids. Even if they were adopted as infants, they knew less than did nonadoptees about where they came from and about what they could anticipate from their future. Their own biological child would provide a connection to both past and future.

Most adoptive parents can sympathize with such thoughts; the only problem involves their worry about the timing of the family creation process. By the time they are fourteen, some girls are beginning to approach the age at which their birth mothers conceived them. That's enough to make some adoptive parents a little uneasy. Could their daughter follow in her mother's footsteps?

As we have pointed out, early sexual activity is not an inherited characteristic. Your daughter's sexual behavior depends on what values you have instilled in her. But since it's not unnatural for parents to have at least a few fears that there might be something to a genetic connection, when your daughter reaches this age it could be helpful to remind yourself that there's no correlation between her future sexual activity and her birth mother's past.

It's also important that you do not criticize her birth parents' sexual indiscretions. Adolescent adoptees are often sensitive about such criticism, hearing it as an attack on themselves. If you do insult her mother or father, even without meaning to, she may not tell you. Should you realize that you have hit a sensitive spot, by all means apologize and attempt to clarify your concerns.

During these years, the interaction between boys and girls is uneven. By age fourteen there are often dances and coed parties, but the girls—adoptees and nonadoptees alike—are likely to be more on the lookout for relationships than are boys in the same age group. As a result, fourteen-year-old girls sometimes seek out older boys, increasing the chances that they could become sexually involved.

How should you talk to your adolescent about her sexual maturation? Don't hesitate to make your views clear on what you consider appropriate social behavior for your daughter: she should know your standards. Emphasize the difference between being a child and being an adult. Point out to her that she simply hasn't had enough experience of life to make certain judgments—about the difference between love and infatuation, for example. At this age, your child is capable of understanding that such guidance is for her own good and the setting of rules in this matter can actually relieve some of the peer pressure on her to get prematurely involved with someone.

What if she's stubborn about not conforming to what you say is best for her? If she says, "All the other girls are doing it," say, "I feel that you are too young now and will be too young for some time. There's a difference between being thirteen or fourteen and being eighteen; you're just not ready." If she replies that "you don't know, I am ready, you just don't know me," you could respond: "We may disagree, but I'm the adult and I've been there. I was your age, and I know about it. It would be too hard and complicated if you got sexually involved while you have a lot of growing up to do."

Make sure your child knows about birth control. While schools are handling this issue at the junior high level in some parts of the country—and thus your child may even know more than you about this subject—that may not be true for your area. By the time your daughter reaches fourteen, you can send her to a gynecologist with the assurance that she will get straight information from a professional. You could also give her *Changing Bodies, Changing Lives* by Ruth Bell (Random House).

Impress upon your daughter the seriousness of abortion—no matter what your particular views on the issue—and that she should not regard it as just another means of birth control. This is particularly important for adoptees, since there are indications that frequent abortions may affect a girl's fertility. Should your youngster impair her ability to bear children through too frequent recourse to abortion, she could destroy the possibility of ever having a blood relative she knows.

And don't neglect your son. Male adoptees often speak of their desire to have children—blood relatives. It's important to protect your son from and educate him about those things which appear to decrease male fertility, including diseases such as mumps and drugs like marijuana and cocaine. Aside from making sure that he knows about the mechanics of birth control, and the importance of using condoms, you should impart a sense of personal responsibility to him about the prospects of possibly creating another life.

YOUR EVOLVING FAMILY

Although it may seem like a minor aspect of your adopted child's life compared with some of the other issues we've just discussed, the sharing of household chores at this age plays a major role in the successful evolution of your family and your youngster's growing maturity. In fact, we prefer *responsibilities* to *chores*, since this word suggests the family role that your child is beginning to play: that of an autonomous yet contributing member of the household.

Occasionally there are adoptees who were spoiled because their parents felt that they had to bend over backwards not to make too many demands on them. With these parents, we point out that one of the greatest gifts you can give a child is a sense of responsibility. Knowing he can do what's required of him as he matures gives him confidence in his ability to take care of himself, enhancing the growth of his sense of autonomy, so necessary for a successful passage into adulthood.

What's more, parents who excuse their adopted children from household duties are depriving them of a feeling of belonging, of being truly a part of the family that has raised them. This often results in the child feeling singled out and different from other members of the family. In fact, adopted kids have come to us complaining that they were not being given enough work to do around the house. Since you and your child don't share a genetic history, the bonds that come from the sharing of responsibilities are perhaps even more important than they might be in a birth family: they are part of the necessary creation of family rituals and the establishment of a family history.

Even the process of deciding who will have which responsibilities in your family is integral to your child's development. At this stage, such decisions should come about more by negotiation than by fiat. By the age of twelve, children have begun to develop a sense of empathy. Until this point they had to be told to do something, simply because you said they should and you might punish them if they didn't do it. But now they fully understand the concept of fairness and they can imagine themselves in somebody else's shoes. They can understand that if they don't help you, you will have to do it all. The significance of this new level of comprehension for single-parent families and for parents of latch-key kids is of obvious importance.

There is no one "right" way of delegating responsibilities. A good general principle to bear in mind, however, is to try to match each person in the family to the tasks they either like the most, or to those jobs they find the least onerous. For example, maybe you don't mind doing the laundry but hate to shop. If so, see if your youngster is willing to take on some of the responsibility of bringing home the groceries. Remember that the process of dividing these responsibilities can be just as important as the actual assignment of specific tasks.

If you suspect that you might be expecting too much or too little from your child when it comes to these tasks, check with other parents, adoptive and nonadoptive, to see how this process works in their families. In a family with more than one child, a little sibling rivalry could show up over these assignments. If that happens, keep in mind that children of different ages *should* have different responsibilities, and if a twelve-year-old, for example, has to do more, then he should also have more privileges.

For adoptees, it can be especially valuable to have this sense of responsibility for shouldering one's share of work carry over beyond the family into the broader social realm. While it's always an admirable value to feel the need to perform community service, adoptees can perhaps derive an even greater satisfaction from such work than others. It gives them a sense of connection to the community, to a past and to a future, that the lack of blood relatives may have left them without. In fact, many of the adoptive families we see are active in church or synagogue affairs or other community activities related to religious groups. This work seems to give them a feeling of transcendence, an important but often overlooked component of emotional development.

MONEY

According to a certified public accountant recently quoted in the *New York Times*, many people feel "more comfortable talking to children about sex than about money." However, while your child can go elsewhere to learn about sex, she will have to come to you to learn about money, at least initially, since for her you are the only source of it.

This could be especially important for an adoptee. Everyone feels more secure if he can handle money. Since the fact of adoption leaves some adoptees with question marks about themselves and their origins that nonadoptees do not share, it behooves you not to leave your adopted child uncertain about this important part of life.

Also, the feeling of having been given much without much being asked of them is an observation that some adoptees have made about their lives. They say this made them feel never truly part of their families. So it is especially important for adoptive parents to make sure they teach their child the value of money.

As with family duties, the interaction on this subject between you and your child should be changing as she passes through early adolescence. When she was younger, you probably just gave her what you thought she should have, and that was that. But now allowances become more a matter for negotiation. Here, too, she should develop a sense of responsibility—and a feeling for the relationship between her allowance and your family's income.

Many adoptees live in adoptive families with far higher income levels than those of their own birth families. Adult adoptees have reported that this has troubled them and often made them feel that they were "rescued" from poverty and should feel grateful. Some don't feel that they rightfully should share in the family wealth. By teaching your child control over money you are reinforcing not only her sense of personal responsibility, but also your confidence that she can handle "family money" as a "family member."

One of the things you could negotiate with her is the matter of which purchases she would like responsibility for and which you will still buy with or for her—clothes, for instance. The advantage to giving her money to buy her own clothes is that it forces her to budget her funds and make choices from several possibilities, thus preparing her for adulthood. On the other hand, this arrangement may not work if she is not yet able to delay gratification. You might try adding such money to her allowance on a small scale; perhaps it could initially just cover shoes or sweaters. As she proves her ability to handle her funds, she could have more responsibility for her own purchases.

Kids this age should also have savings accounts to help them begin to see the connection between current income and future needs. But don't be surprised if your child resists the idea of putting away a sizable amount of money earned from a part-time or summer job. She's still too young to have a true intellectual and emotional grasp of that connection.

Should your child work? Notwithstanding economic necessity, we think it's a good idea to encourage adolescents, but not to force them, to get a part-time or summer job, such as having a paper route, baby-sitting or lawn-mowing. Besides offering them more control over their destinies, it also gives them a better sense of life. Just as your child's initial foray into the world of school made him cope with adults who would not necessarily love him automatically, dealing with a boss is a good preparation for interaction with people who will judge him primarily on his performance.

THEIR THOUGHTS ON ADOPTION

For some children at this stage, adoption begins to fade into the background as a source of confusion in their lives. Most likely by the time your child reaches fourteen he will have a full legal and psychological understanding of adoption's significance. But if he ever had any overt preoccupation with the process, he may have put it behind him. The odds are that in the place of the adoption questions he might have asked in earlier years, you now will hear silence.

QUESTIONS AND ANSWERS

The shock of junior high school has been too much for my child. She did very well in elementary school but she seems isolated and confused now and can't establish relationships with her teachers.

It might be a good idea to talk to the guidance teacher at your child's school. If your child has just entered junior high, she may just need a little extra time to adjust. This is more likely to happen with only children, a category that includes many adoptees. It also crops up more often in families that have moved recently, or to children whose friends from elementary school have gone on to private or parochial school. If the trouble persists, she may need a different school that offers more individual attention.

□

My son has been coming home later and later. We tried setting a formal curfew, but he's just ignored it. We're worried and running out of things to say to him. What should we do?

When adoptive families have come to us with a child who stays out past his curfew, it's almost always part of a pattern of misbehavior—and not the major part at that. If lateness is not a temperamental characteristic with your child—for example, is he simply less attentive to time when making appointments?—then you should sit down with him and try to see what's bothering him.

As to the mechanics of setting a curfew, it's often best

accomplished when parents get together and establish a community norm. For example, when Arthur, Bob Franklin's son, reached the ninth grade, Bob and his wife, Kay, joined with the parents of Arthur's friends to establish a common policy on parties, dates, and the like. They decided that 12:30 A.M. on weekends would be a reasonable limit for this age. Parents were encouraged to telephone the parents of kids having parties to determine if adult supervision would be present. By going public and acting together, the parents were able to get better cooperation from their kids, who knew where they stood and who couldn't play one set of parents off against another.

□

Every time my husband and son sit down to negotiate anything from allowance to studying and acceptable grades, it ends in a fight. I'm worried that this has something to do with our only son being adopted. Could there be a connection?

The transition to the negotiation style of family interaction is difficult for many parents. There may or may not be a connection between adoption and the difficulties you are experiencing, but try this negotiating technique and perhaps you won't need to make the connection. Have your husband and son each argue his case for five minutes. Your son could go first, with your husband taking notes while your son talks. Then it's your husband's turn to present his case while your son takes notes. Now each spends five minutes talking about what the other has said. At this point, they might want to separate and come up with list of solutions before coming together again.

The intent of this exercise is to get them to listen to each other, something that few people who argue do. Once they've established the habit of listening, they can begin to narrow their differences and seek areas of compromise, since they know what's important to the other and why.

□

My adopted child had a drink at a party this past weekend and got very giddy—more so than the other kids. We heard that there is a genetic predisposition to alcoholism. We know virtually nothing about our youngster's birth parents and we are worried. Are we overreacting? Should we discuss the possible connection between alcoholism and his genetic background with our child?

Treat this matter as you would if there were a possible history of diabetes in his birth family. His adoption is a legitimate issue here and you should be vigilant if your son exhibits a special sensitivity to alcohol. It's appropriate to discuss this with him, and you might find it easier to do this by introducing an expert into the discussion. By going as a family to see a genetic counselor, you can remove this subject from the realm of moralizing and give it a medical-scientific context—thus adding some distance when you need it. He will find it easier to hear what he needs to hear in this objective setting.

□

I've heard there's nothing to worry about if your child doesn't talk about adoption. My thirteen-year-old adopted son has nothing to say on the subject, and I am worried. Could you help me to feel better about this?

You can never be sure what's on a child's mind. Assuming you have been open and honest about his background, you have to trust that your son would come to you with anything that now significantly troubled him about his past.

□

I have two adopted daughters, eleven and twelve. The other night they were watching a TV program about a girl who discovered that she was adopted and searched for her birth mother. My children burst into tears, left the room, and have since refused to talk about it with me. All my subsequent attempts to get them to talk it out have failed. What should I do?

While this must have been upsetting for all of you, it's highly unlikely to have caused any permanent problems for your children or any change in their feelings about you. But if you want to be sure that no harm was done, perhaps you could ask one of your relatives to talk to them. Also, ask other adoptive parents if their kids had similar reactions and how they did or would handle it.

□

I wish my daughter had more friends; she's so shy. I've heard that adopted kids have lower self-esteem than other kids. Could this be the source of her isolation?

Some recent studies suggest that adopted kids' self-esteem is at least as high as other kids'. Unless there are some other problems and if this is not new behavior, you just may have to accept shyness as her temperamental style. Shyness appears to be characteristic of the inborn temperaments of some people and may have to be accepted as such by parents both adoptive and not. It is important for parents again to respect their children's unique personalities. A shy individual can be encouraged to be a bit more outgoing, but to expect her to change entirely is unrealistic. If this is a change in behavior, however, then you should worry. If it is more of the same and just bothering you more, then you should sit back and observe the ways in which your daughter interacts with friends and whether this is satisfying for her. You should then accept her for who she is and encourage her to do more of what works for her.

7
The Late Teenage Years

Matt Thomas, a lawyer and CPA, never thought he'd have to deal with this particular adoption-related complication: there he was, a man in his early fifties, walking down the street with a vivacious and attractive 17-year-old girl on his arm. Had she resembled him, nobody would have looked twice. But Laura, his adopted daughter, did not look like him, and the two drew more than one or two inquisitive stares from passing strangers.

It wasn't the first time this father had encountered insensitive behavior by strangers. For adoptive parents, that sort of thing comes with the territory. But this day Matt was in the mood to deal with it with his sense of humor. When he caught a disapproving look, he nodded, smiled, and put his arm around Laura. She was delighted to go along with this bit of playfulness, participating in their private joke by throwing him an adoring glance.

Matt's wife grinned when he told her about the street byplay. It seemed just like yesterday that they were agonizing about when and how to first start discussing the subject of adoption with that delightful three-year-old child who had entered their lives via an agency. For them, the "problems" of adoption had certainly changed.

TIME FLIES

Where did the years go? Chances are the child you once picked up and carried around is almost big enough to carry you. By late adolescence your youngster has completed most of his physical growth. His emotional development has also progressed, although more unevenly. On some days his good sense may make you forget that you're still talking to a child, while at other times you may wonder if he'll ever be able to get both feet into adulthood.

Your child needs you less now than when he was younger, and he decides when he requires your attention. Some adoptive parents may experience this as a rejection and begin to worry about how their youngster will regard them once he achieves his independence. But if your relationship with him as been solid, there's little to fear. Your ties to him need not be any less deep and satisfying now that he's older, just different. You will be less a caretaker, your discussions more intense and egalitarian.

Don't be surprised if you feel sadness as well as relief at your child's maturing into adulthood. You've been through a lot with this almost-adult, from dealing with scraped knees to soothing emotional hurts (not to mention the mountain of laundry you've done over the years!). Before long you will hardly see him around at all.

Much has been asked of you. As we pointed out in response to one of the questions at the end of chapter 2, it is often said that adoptive parents have to establish "claiming" behavior when they first get their child, that they must possess their child, make him their own, not see him as the "other," an outsider. Yet for your child to grow into an autonomous human being, you also had to begin to redefine that claim by the time he was six years old, as he took his first steps outside the family, differentiating himself from you. Less than two decades later, you have to relinquish the remnants of the claim you worked so hard to establish.

The fruits of your labor, once your adoptee has grown up,

are likely to be continuing love and close family ties. Now your child is fully capable of understanding the significance of adoption—and the central role that you have played in his life. At this point, the fact that he was born to someone else and possibly spent some time with a foster family is heavily outweighed by the many years you have spent nurturing him. He knows that *you* are his parents. We have, in fact, often noticed he may even be more appreciative of your efforts than birth children are of their parents' labors.

With your child approaching the point where he will leave home as an independent person, you can also look forward to the next stage of family development, in which you can be more independent, as you were before you began to raise your child. You can anticipate peace and quiet around the house, fewer responsibilities, and more free time to pursue *your* interests.

Adoptive parents are typically a few years older than the average birth parent when their child joins their family. If that description fits you, you are now even more likely than the parents of your child's friends to be entering your peak career years and may be especially looking forward to your youngster's autonomy. You could probably use more time and energy to apply to your job—or to a full-time career if you interrupted work to be a homemaker.

As the time approaches for your child to leave home, particularly if she is an only child, you may need to work at making a smooth transition into the next stage of your marriage. A good part of your relationship with your spouse has been bound up in the process of child rearing. That period is ending.

If the thought of an empty nest unsettles you, try focusing on specific issues. Then you'll start to realize how much you can do about shaping your life once the kids are on their own. For example, if you've played the role of full-time mother and homemaker, start planning for new activities, a renewed career, or an entirely new line of work. Look into the possibility of taking refresher courses at the local college; make an appointment to see a career counselor to discuss the possibilities open to you. You can find professional career counselors in most cities; and don't overlook the books and pamphlets in the careers section of your public library.

Many fathers who have been heavily involved in their child's athletic activities suddenly find themselves at sea when their youngster moves on to college. But that needn't make for empty Saturdays. What did you like to do with your spare time before your child was old enough to need you to help the team? This is also a good time to explore new interests and activities as well as to resurrect old ones.

It may occur to you that without day-to-day, child-centered activities, you and your spouse will have less to talk about. But that needn't be the case, especially if you're both active pursuing new projects. And now you have the opportunity, with fewer distractions, to redefine and enjoy your identity as a couple. Dinners out, weekends away, heightened interest in new careers—all of these can add new sparkle to your relationship and solidify it.

CREATING THEIR OWN IDENTITY

Of course, your child-rearing work isn't quite over yet. As we pointed out in the previous chapter, the teenage years are formidable for parent and child for good reasons. At this age it can be very unsettling when the child you thought was becoming more mature and independent suddenly reverts to juvenile behavior. But contrary to what you may have heard, your youngster will not have to pass through some kind of pathological version of a teenage identity crisis, just because he was adopted.

In the past—and in a few pockets of resistance today—some mental health professionals suggested the inevitability of serious problems for adoptive families, caused by their adolescent's Herculean struggle to establish her identity and autonomy with respect to two sets of parents, birth and adoptive. In our extensive experience with adoptive families, we find no basis in fact for these theories.

Indeed, to the extent that all adolescents have to come to terms with who they are, adoptees may have a heard start on other kids. Because of some of the complications built into adoption—especially the most basic one: being different—your adoptee has probably already had to deal with the identity question and has had practice figuring out who she is in relation to her parents and other families. It began when you first told her that she was adopted.

We would also like to emphasize that tension and conflicts between parent and teenager are not as inevitable as they are often portrayed. In fact, we've often observed that parents and their teenage adoptees have less trouble with each other than other families do. We suspect that's because many adoptive parents have fewer expectations about how their child will turn out than the mothers and fathers of birth children. Because of this they are less likely to try to force their adoptee into a mold dictated by their family traditions. They find it easier to stand back and give their child breathing space, room to find his own way.

While teenage adoptees do not necessarily experience an identity crisis, and may even have a head start on determining their identities, they still have a few more complications in their lives to deal with than do other teenagers. These kids are still trying to figure out who they are, and why they were given up. Sometimes that leads them to, say, act out a bit in school. Then parents might bring the youngster to a therapist thinking their child was experiencing a major crisis when in fact it just might be something that needs to be talked out and handled in one or two sessions. Adoptive parents tend to have more education and income than the average parent and that also disposes them to take advantage of therapy for dealing with such difficulties. The bottom line is that preoccupation at this age with adoption-related identity issues will not make your child crazy, but some kids need a little help in sorting things out.

It is important to realize that even if your teenager has little to say about adoption, it may still be on his mind. One sixteen-year-old teenager responded strongly to a question about what her feelings were when she thought about her birth mother: "When I think about her, it's with anger or sadness, never with benign curiosity. I am sad that she gave me up and angry at her for getting pregnant before she could take care of a child." Other teenagers have answered this kind of question just as fervently, and in almost the same words.

Your role in this stage of your adolescent's process of coming to terms with herself is similar to what it has been for some time: be there for your child, offer her support, listen to her, and bring up adoption from time to time.

DISCIPLINE AND CONTROL

Whenever possible, the way to resolve differences with your child when she reaches late adolescence is through negotiation. We can't say this too often. Even more than when she was younger, your child now needs to realize that she can sometimes make a point and "win" if she gives you good enough reasons, that you did not predecide an issue before you discussed it with her.

Parents sometimes have trouble maintaining the flexibility required to make this give-and-take mode of family interaction work. They may have been more comfortable and effective when their child needed them to lay down the rules unilaterally. But such firmness, which once served the purpose of creating much-needed limits for a preadolescent, may now take on the character of rigidity in this new stage of family development.

Some kids will rebel if their parents persist in imposing hard-and-fast rules at this point in their development, creating problems between parents and child that need not be there. On the other hand, some adoptees are generally less rebellious than their nonadopted peers at this age because of excessive gratitude for all their parents did for them through the adoption process. And here parental rigidity may aggravate their passivity and acquiescence.

What if you simply don't feel comfortable exercising less parental control after it's functioned so well for you for so long? First, if you can monitor yourself and acknowledge that you're having this difficulty, you've already won half the battle, since what's required is not a change in your personality but simply a change in the way you act under some circumstances. You don't need to *become* more flexible, but you do need to *act* that way.

It isn't magic and it is workable. Here's how to do it: Every time you hear yourself dictating something to your teenager simply because you think you know what's best, stop yourself. If there's a bone of contention, instead of saying, "You must" or "You have to," you could say, "It's more comfortable for me that you do———this way, but I also realize that you feel more comfortable handling it the other way; so let's talk about it." Remember that you have to decide each time that you'll listen to and consider what your child says and not just pretend to negotiate and then hand down the law.

For example, suppose your daughter wants to come home from her Saturday date at 2 A.M. but you think midnight is more reasonable for someone her age. You could begin your negotiations by going over the facts of the matter: the standards for your community and her "crowd" in the activity in question, whether the event is chaperoned, the weather (if she's driving or being driven), how responsible she's acted with other privileges you've granted her lately, whether she's going out in a group or will be on an individual date, and anything else that's relevant.

Besides letting the facts influence your agreement, always look for opportunities to engage in a little give-and-take. For example, resolving the disagreement over a curfew might involve the child having to give in a little this time but, in return, getting an extra, different privilege or permission to stay out later for something scheduled next month. This give-and-take process can be as important as resolving your differences, since it builds trust and a sense of fairness that will strengthen your overall relationship with your child.

Adoptees, especially, need to know that they are trusted to act reasonably well outside the home, particularly if they've given you no cause to think they will do otherwise. They may interpret the lack of trust to mean that you do not quite consider them a full member of your family. If you're finding it difficult to extend this trust, you should discuss it with your mate and consciously work on it.

Are we asking you to totally give up your standards and make everything negotiable? Not at all. Every parent has—or should have—bottom-line values about basic safety and health, especially when it involves things like drugs and alcohol, and other issues, such as school attendance, that are nonnegotiable. But we are saying that when your child is this age you can't be everywhere, acting as a constant monitor, so it is purely practical not to fight it out every time you disagree. Besides, by now you need to trust that you've done the job of imparting your basic values to your child.

What if you've made a mistake and either haven't given in when you probably should have or have given in when you shouldn't have? The sun will still come up the next morning. Don't be hard on yourself. For both you and your teenager, each little crisis of adolescence is a learning opportunity, and you rarely learn something without making mistakes.

IF THE GOING GETS TOUGH . . .

The typical teenager thinks he knows everything, at least some of the time. "Mom, you don't know *anything*," he may reply, rolling his eyes, to what you thought was a quite cogent observation on your part. It's best to deal with this type of remark with a sense of humor whenever you can.

However, he still needs discipline when he breaks family rules. If anything, he may need it a bit more than his nonadopted peers, since reasonable nos, with sanctions for transgression, add clarity and structure to his life, which has already had enough haziness.

What if you run into some serious behavioral difficulties with your teenager and he does not respond at all to appeals to reason? After all, you can't ground him forever without imprisoning you and him in the house. What do you do when all else fails?

Battles for control at this stage of your child's development are not a good idea. He's certainly too big to control physically. Rather than engage in a struggle to get him to do something specific—such as coming home at a reasonable hour—if nothing else works, try changing the rules, making *your* behavior unpredictable.

Here's an example of what we mean: the Loftons were having trouble with fifteen-and-a-half-year-old Tom, their adopted son. He seemed to be two people. At times he acted, if anything, slightly mature for his age, and was a pleasure to be with. Then there were the periods when he behaved as if he were writing the rule book for teenage behavior as he went along, acting as he saw fit. *This* Tom was especially evident in his unwillingness to pick up his sneakers from the living room, the one room his adoptive parents especially wanted to keep neat.

Tom's mother, after trying everything reasonable she could think of to get her son to cooperate, took his sneakers, which he had dropped next to the coffee table while watching TV the night before, and hid them in the refrigerator. The next morning, when Tom reached into the refrigerator for some milk to pour over his cereal, his hand brushed against something that was not on his breakfast menu. From then on his sneakers were to be found neither in the living room nor in the refrigerator, but rather under his bed, where they bothered no one.

While most parents worry about their kids rebelling,

disobeying, and running a little wild, the opposite kind of behavior is at least as much cause for concern. When a child does not rebel it is often because his parents have had a hard time allowing for more individuality and independence to emerge. Occasionally, one parent, especially, will try to maintain a child's dependence, encouraging the youngster to stay within the family orbit rather than move out into the world.

While some adopted children respond to this situation with rebellion, others take the path of submission. They may fear a withdrawal of parental love if they dare to be too different. Their unwillingness to buck the wishes of their parent may be reinforced by guilt at wanting to become more independent when they know how much their adoptive parents have done for them. These adolescents do not talk about their future plans, have few ideas separate from their parents', are a little too cooperative. They spend too much time at home and relatively little away with their friends; in fact, their social life is nil.

If this describes your child, or if you notice that your mate is having trouble giving up control over your maturing youngster, then you should seriously consider at least some short-term family therapy to resolve this difficulty before it creates serious problems for your child.

SCHOOLWORK: NOW IT COUNTS

Although your child is now making many decisions for himself, there are still some things about which you know more than he does. No teenager, for example, is capable of fully appreciating the significance of dropping out of high school—any more than he can fathom the idea of his own mortality or just how bad drug or alcohol dependence can get. It goes without saying that high school dropouts in this society start adult life with the odds heavily against them; staying in school and doing as well as he can is something that you will have to impose as a matter of discipline if necessary.

However, if your teenager is not doing well in high school, it may be because his school is not tapping his talents. He may have more of a flair for the graphic arts than for strictly academic work. Perhaps he has an intuitive rather than an analytical bent, with an aptitude for creative writing that his school's standard English curriculum is stifling. He might not score well on standard tests, but could possibly shine in a program that stressed creative skills.

You could investigate alternatives to his school's regular program of studies. For instance, "City as School" might be just the thing for him. This increasingly popular program, which uses the community as a classroom, allows kids to absorb and apply knowledge in the outside world by serving as an editorial assistant on a newspaper, for example, or as an apprentice at a theater. If he's bored because he's not being challenged enough, look into the possibility of his taking courses for advanced placement at a nearby community college, where he can study just about anything that interests him.

College, however, is another issue, one that sometimes unsettles adoptive parents. Your adopted child may not have the intellectual bent that you think of as characteristic of your family. Or perhaps she'd like to see a little bit of the world before committing herself to another four years in the classroom. Should conflict arise over this issue, negotiating a compromise that preserves her independence while keeping her on a course that you know is best for her is the key to helping her to keep her options open.

While you have to be careful not to confuse what you want for your child with what she wants for herself, you can insist that she work hard enough in high school so that she will still have the choice of whether or not to go to college. And the only way to insure that, as we have noted, is to make sure she does at least several hours of homework each night. If she's having trouble with a particular subject, get her a tutor. To find one, call one or more of the colleges in your area and arrange to have their placement office put your requirements in their listings. If public school is really overwhelming your teenager, you might want to consider putting her in a private school—perhaps only for a year—where she can get more individual attention.

Remember that if she decides against going to college when she graduates from high school, it's not necessarily the end of her academic career. Many eighteen-year-olds take a year off from school at this point and go to work to see what life is all about. In fact, in Europe this is fairly standard procedure. The ones who return to school often do so with better motivation and a clearer idea of where they're going than do their peers who went directly to college from high school. Or she could take courses at night at a community college while working during the day, giving her a taste both of work and higher education.

The costs of adoption and the values that guide adoption workers and attorneys who place healthy infants make it likely that you and your spouse went to college and, therefore, may expect your child to do so, as well. It is important to remember that your child is a product of both inherited tendencies from her birth family and the environment you have raised her in. A son or daughter's talents and aptitudes may lead the child in a different direction. Vocational or technical training programs may prepare a person better than college to do what he or she likes or is good at—for example, word processing or auto repairs.

An example of a child who found a happy career without college training is Susan Ryan, whose adoptive parents both have Ph.D.s. They were not entirely comfortable when their daughter, a bright, hard-working young girl, opted not to go to college. During the summer before her senior year in high school she worked at a clothing store, part of a large chain. Two weeks before graduation Susan took a full-time position at the store. Within a month she was promoted to floor supervisor. She worked hard and she loved it. Now the chain has offered her an opportunity to join their management program. Not only have her parents overcome their misgivings, they've started to brag about their daughter's accomplishments.

IF YOU HAVE YOUNGER CHILDREN . . .

If your family includes younger children, adopted or birth, you may face the necessity, and the opportunity, of having your teenage adoptee act as an assistant caretaker. For most of the world's families, the economics of survival dictate such an arrangement, although we often tend to see this as somehow impinging on the natural freedom of the child asked to help out. It is also, however, an opportunity. For an adoptive family, the need to have an adolescent look after younger siblings enables parents to tell their adopted child in the most basic way any parent can that you trust him and that he is an essential part of the family.

If your adoptee cares for a younger brother or sister, make it clear to the younger child that you've authorized your teenager to act in your name. Set clear limits about what punishment the older child can mete out for misdeeds. "Debrief" your adolescent after he has spent time supervising his charge, pointing out any corrections in his supervision style that you feel are necessary. Don't criticize mistakes he's made in front of his younger sibling. Emphasize ways he can do his job better. Remind him of the successful strategies he's used when his task has gone smoothly.

In arranging for your teenager to share in child care, keep in mind that between school, after-school activities, and homework, kids his age often have a very long day. Depending on how rigorous the schools are in your community, that could account for as much as thirteen hours of his time each weekday and a good part of the weekend. Also, he is in the midst of forming his own identity apart from the family—a necessary task at his age—in preparation for complete independence. So you will have to balance these demands on him with your need for help with the younger kids.

If your teenager serves as the family baby-sitter, he deserves compensation as well as recognition for his work. That could be money—a raise in his allowance—or increased perks. Since he is showing a high degree of responsibility by caring for a younger child, you could reward him with a later curfew or increased access to the family car.

What if your child really hates taking care of a younger brother or sister? Unless economic necessity forces the issue, don't make him take on the job. If you have more than two children, try letting the middle child do the baby-sitting. Your eldest can fulfill his family obligations in other ways.

DATING

Julie Edwards, a conservative, somewhat shy woman, almost didn't have to describe her fears. She arrived at our office with her fifteen-and-a-half-year-old adopted daughter, Mary, whose heavy makeup, tight, revealing clothing, and affected air of sophistication was causing her mother a great deal of anxiety. While she didn't get straight to the point, it wasn't long before Julie reached the crux of her concerns: the possible relationship between Mary's adoption and what her mother viewed as her daughter's sirenlike demeanor.

Julie Edwards's situation was somewhat unusual. Parents don't usually come to us saying that they're worried about the effect of adoption on their teenage daughter's sexual behavior. It's not often that obvious and straightforward, yet it's sometimes there in the background. We can occasionally hear it in their voices. Their anxiety level about their daughter's sexual habits has a different quality to it than that of nonadoptive parents.

We would therefore like to make it clear that there are no scientific studies which indicate that teenage girls act out sexually because they were adopted. That doesn't mean that no adopted girl—or boy—has ever acted irresponsibly in matters of sexuality. When it comes to sexual activity, today's teenagers live in a world that differs substantially from the one in which you grew up. The opportunities and pressures to get prematurely involved have increased enormously. Contrary to what many people think, the teenage pregnancy rate has not risen, but the average age at which teenage pregnancies occur has dropped. No study shows that adoptees are more likely to get pregnant than nonadoptees.

If anything, the adopted teenagers we've known, boys and girls, as a group tend to be somewhat more responsible and straightlaced than their peers about sexual involvement. When we got a few of these kids together for a discussion of this subject, we heard remarks like: "I think people should be more careful about having babies," and, "People should consider how they're going to be able to feed and take care of a child before they have one. They should be more responsible."

Adopted kids have been conscious of issues of relationships and intimacy since childhood because of their awareness of the importance of these subjects in their family history. Consequently, they may be more likely to feel clearer on where they stand about sexual relations, and more self-confident that they can deal with it.

Nevertheless, we realize that most adoptive parents have special concerns when it comes to teenagers and sex. These days that's only natural. The core of the matter usually turns out to be communication. Parents would like to know where their kids stand on sexual limits, what they've been doing about birth control if they have decided to be sexually active, if they are now having sexual relations with anyone, even what their children know about sex (it's amazing what some kids don't know, even at this age). Their children, not surprisingly, volunteer none of this information.

The first thing we do in this situation is to point out that sex, along with other loaded subjects such as drugs and alcohol, is an issue that parents can discuss with their children, just as they speak to them about other areas of life. If you're having trouble dealing with these matters, or your child is approaching these years and you're anticipating some problems and can't imagine how you would bring up topics like these, you might find it helpful to look at this interchange we recently had with a concerned parent.

When Ann Bronson came to us, Joan, her sixteen-and-a-half-year-old daughter, had been acting a bit more secretively than had been characteristic of her in the past. The daughter also had recently acquired a steady boyfriend:

THERAPIST: It seems to me that you're a pretty concerned parent and I can understand why, what with the way things are these days, you have some concerns about this issue. Is your daughter a fairly responsible girl?

Bronson: Yes, we've given her what we think are good values, and for the most part she's lived within those guidelines, at least in other areas of life. But somehow, we're feeling a little uneasy when it comes to Joan's relationships with boys and the possibility that she might get sexually involved.

THERAPIST: Has she cooperated in family matters and manifested no more than the normal amount of teenage misconduct?

Bronson: Yes, we couldn't say that she's been a "bad" kid, that's for sure.

THERAPIST: Well, then what would have to happen to reassure you about your fears? How could your daughter set your mind at rest?

Bronson: I'm not sure.

THERAPIST: I'm hearing from you that Joan is a pretty cooperative girl; it sounds like she would be willing to talk to you about her social life, at least to some extent, if you bring it up in a respectful and unprying way.

Bronson: Yes, I suppose so, although it sounds like a very touchy subject to bring up in any way with a teenager.

THERAPIST: Do you *want* to know how she feels about it? Enough to ask her?

Bronson: Do you think she would actually discuss how she feels?

THERAPIST: Well, you know her better than I do.

Bronson: I guess that while we don't let it all hang out all the time around our house, we tend to be honest and open in our family when the occasion calls for it.

THERAPIST: How do you bring up other touchy subjects in your home?

Bronson: Nothing fancy; one of us just says something like, "Gee, I've had something on my mind, can you spare a minute to talk?"

THERAPIST: And it usually works?

Bronson: Yes.

THERAPIST: It sounds like you have your method.

Ann Bronson got mixed results from her conversations with her daughter about the teenager's love life. Joan did start sleeping with her boyfriend, although her mother tried to talk her out of it. But on the other hand, Joan was willing to discuss it with her mother, she did use birth control, and she kept her head about the whole situation. When the boy started pressuring her to spend too much time with him, causing her schoolwork to suffer, she broke off the relationship. If anything, Ann Bronson's determination to "be there" for Joan, offering advice but also listening to her child and not trying to control her life, brought mother and daughter closer.

If your teenage daughter is determined to get sexually involved with someone, it's almost impossible, short of locking her in her room, to prevent it. But you can point out that just because she's had sexual relations with a boy, it doesn't mean that she has to continue to be sexually active. You can insist that she take a responsible approach to birth control—which these days means the use of condoms and spermicide containing Nonoxynol 9. And you still determine what happens under your own roof. You have a perfect right to say no if she wants to have her lover sleep over at your house.

Talking about sex with your child or providing her with information will not increase the chances of her becoming sexually active. Knowledge is always helpful, not an incitement to harmful behavior.

Adoptees (and their families) also have some anxieties about dating with which nonadoptees never have to contend. Jill Rosenberg's parents felt strongly that their adopted daughter should date Jewish boys, and for more reasons than one. They hoped that she would marry within their faith. But they also thought that confining her dating to Jews would avoid the chance that she might end up on a date with one of her birth siblings, since her birth parents were not Jewish.

The possibility of an adoptee dating her birth sibling isn't just theoretical: it's happened. Teenagers tend to gravitate toward people who are like themselves. And if an adoptee lived in a medium-sized city or town, was brought up there and adopted nearby, and had several birth siblings, her chances of having this experience would increase.

Even the remote possibility of this incestuous scenario occurring should alert adoptive parents to the importance of doing everything they can to secure from their adoption agency as much information as possible about their child's birth siblings. It's also one of the reasons why New York State is moving toward giving adoptive parents an opportunity to adopt any birth siblings of their adopted child who come into the state foster-care system.

Adoption may enter a teenager's romantic involvements in another way. Roberta thought she was saying something totally innocuous when she referred to her cousin Bob's adoption while talking to Sue, Bob's girlfriend. But when Sue's mouth dropped, Roberta realized that she had just spilled the beans: Bob had never discussed his adoption with Sue.

By adolescence, adoptees must decide for themselves who they will tell about their family origins and when and how much they will tell. Bob's parents might have had some ideas on the subject, but it was no longer in their hands.

There are sometimes reasons to hold back this information. Prejudice against adoptees still exists in many quarters. Enough scare stories appear in the media to provoke anxiety in some people about a "bad seed" repeating her birth mother's behavior, or possible genetic defects resurfacing from previously unknown generations. It would not be a good idea for an adoptee to hide the circumstances of his birth from someone with whom he had become seriously involved romantically. But how about her parents? What if he sensed possible prejudice on their part? If they seemed inordinately curious about his family background, already speculating about their potential grandchildren, he might feel on his guard, since some people still obsess about "blood lines."

Unfortunately, no one can lay down hard-and-fast rules about how to handle such a situation. Each person must decide for him- or herself what feels right.

LEAVING HOME

Do you sometimes feel like you're running a motel? The car is a fitting symbol of this stage of your child's life. With a car—whether it's your child auto, the family car she borrows, or a friend's—she can put distance between herself and the rest of the family, stopping by occasionally to grab a bite to eat and change her clothes. The automobile also represents the emotional distance from the family that she must be creating for herself if she is to successfully break away and lead her own life as an adult.

The process of breaking away could be a bit more difficult for your adoptee than for other adolescents. He knows, on some level, the extra work that you did in getting him. Even more important, he realizes that you really wanted him; unlike birth parents, you weren't forced to keep him. That's a heavy responsibility to place on the shoulders of a young person. The child may view his impending departure from the family as an ungrateful act, even disloyalty.

These thoughts may also reinforce an adoptee's feeling that he has known less about himself than his friends have about themselves. Who in his family did he look like? From where did he get his red hair? What if his adoptive parents had not taken him? When he needs to begin taking control of his own destiny, he may not feel entirely secure at the wheel.

There is a type of activity we recommend that helps prepare many youngsters, including adoptees, for the time when they must stand on their own. Wilderness programs, such as Outward Bound, give kids a sense that they can master their environment and gain control over their lives—prerequisites for independent living. Through activities such as rock climbing, long bike trips in which they must fix their own flat tires, and sleeping out in tents in cold weather, these programs force kids to push themselves physically beyond what they thought were their limits. You can find such programs in the advertisements for summer camps in your Sunday newspaper. You might also try attending a camp show, since these programs often take space at the shows.

SEARCHING FOR BIRTH PARENTS

June Tyler remembers when the thought first hit her. Her adopted children were nine, ten, and twelve years old. She had just seen a human-interest feature story on the evening news about an adoptee who spent seven months trying to find her birth parents, only to discover that her birth mother lived in the next town, a mere ten-minute drive away. "My God," June thought, "what if my kids want to look for *their* birth mothers?" And then she quickly suppressed the thought because it was simply too painful.

Fortunately, with time, June realized that she had no control over whether her kids decided to search, and that if they did search it would do her and them no good if she feared what they might find. So she read all she could on the subject to make herself feel as comfortable as she could be with it and to be able to offer help and guidance if her kids asked for it.

Of all the aspects of adoption that adoptive parents may have to deal with, searching for a birth parent is one of the most loaded ones. Few adoptive parents approach it with complete peace of mind. The questions it raises are almost unavoidable:

- Will my adoptee find someone she likes better than me?
- Will she still consider me her parent?
- Will I have to establish some kind of relationship with her birth parents if she finds them?
- Should I help her if she asked me for my help?
- Will she play me off against a biological parent?
- Will we both discover something about her relatives we would just as soon not know?

It is understandable that an adoptive parent's imagination might simply run wild at the various possibilities. But only a small percentage of adoptees—perhaps fewer than 10 percent—ever go through with a search, although our society's increased openness toward adoption records may eventually result in a rise in the number. Among adoptees who try to find their birth parents, women seem to outnumber men. In fact, women appear to have so much more of a desire to know about family roots than do men that when a married male adoptee decides to search, it's often at the prompting of his wife, regardless of whether she is an adoptee or not.

Not every adoptee who says she will search fully pursues the sometimes arduous task of looking for someone who may have left a very faint trail. For many adoptees, simply finding more information about their birth parents may be enough to satisfy their curiosity, and they never carry it through to the final step of actually locating a birth parent. Discovering their original name, for example, is often a momentous occasion, making their birth parents seem much more real and diminishing their interest in continuing the search. On the other hand, some adoptees who intend to do nothing more than uncover facts they don't know have their curiosity piqued and decide to go on and look for their biological parents.

Searching is neither "good" nor "bad." It's simply something that some adoptees do and others don't. We should point out, though, that a recent survey of adult adoptees who had searched suggested that, whatever the results of their search, most were glad they did it. They also felt that *the search brought them closer to their adoptive parents.* Interesting, isn't it?

Even if your adoptee is among the relatively few who engage in a search, the odds are that he will not pursue it until he is at least in his twenties. The Adoptees' Liberty Movement Association (ALMA), the most well-known organization that assists adoptees looking for their birth parents, won't help an adoptee—unless her adoptive parents agree—until he or she is at least eighteen years old.

Adoptees most often initiate a search either when they plan to marry, when they're thinking of having a child, or when their adoptive parents die, possibly because they might have felt disloyal if they had begun a search while their adoptive parents were alive. That last occasion is particularly poignant, highlighting the irreducible fact that, in at least a narrow sense, the child did have two sets of parents. And it's another reminder that birth parents are likely to be younger than adoptive parents, usually by at least ten years.

If your adoptee wants to make the effort to search, offer to help, but don't push your help on her if she doesn't ask for it. Adoptees who look for their birth parents are going through an emotional process that must unreel at its own pace. The timing and the agenda of this profound experience must be the adoptee's alone.

The mechanics of the search may vary from state to state, depending on local laws concerning such activities. In Connecticut, for example, adoptive parents have to give their permission before the state will grant adoptees access to their birth records. We know of one fifty-year-old man whose eighty-year-old adoptive parents stymied his desire to seek out his birth parents when they refused to approve his search.

There are about 250 search and support groups in the U.S. who help adoptees find their birth parents. For example, Orphans Voyage was founded in 1953; ALMA, in 1973. An adoptive parents' organization, the North American Council on Adoptable Children, only began in 1974, and Concerned United Birth Parents (CUB) got its start in 1975. That last group shows the increasing organization of birth parents looking into what happened to the children they gave up.

There are twenty-eight state-operated adoption registries containing information from both adoptive children and birth parents, but their usefulness is severely restricted because regulations governing their use vary from state to state and there is little cooperation between registries. The International Soundex Reunion Registry is more helpful. This data bank, begun in 1975, has 43,000 registrees and has already matched 1,750 adoptees with a birth parent. Adoptees can register at any time, but their file is not activated until they reach their eighteenth birthday.

The actual search may produce results in a week. Or it could require months, even years of spadework. Some people hire private detectives—there is now a subspecialty of professional searchers—to assist them. Others need only the additional information they can get by going back to the adoption agency and asking more questions. A typical clue would be the name of the hospital where the child was born and the date of her birth. Even at a major metropolitan medical center, there's a limit to how many babies could have been born there on one day.

If the agency from whom you received your child told you that her birth parents had died, don't assume that to be the final word. Return to the agency and find out on what evidence they based this assertion, because it may not have been accurate. By the way, this is an excellent reason not to tell your adopted child that her birth parents had died unless you know this to be the case.

For some people, life goes on hold while they search; occasionally the investigation becomes a little obsessive. And the process can get bumpy. Early in their search they may experience an emotionally bruising encounter with an agency or court. It's not uncommon for personnel at these organizations to suggest that an adoptee should be grateful for her adoption and that she is wrong to be curious about her past.

What if the search is successful? What might be its consequences? Steve Brady began his search for his biological mother after the birth of his first child. Four months of checking hospital records, local newspaper files in the library, and numerous telephone directories, led him to the woman he was looking for. She had married about a year after giving birth to him and had since had three children—a family much like the one in which he grew up. He was gratified to have found her. It gave him a sense of having closed an important gap in his life. Yet, somehow, he was also a little let down.

There was nothing special about her. If anything, after the initial encounter, he felt he had very little to say to her.

The results of these searches, even when they are successful, are often less dramatic than you might imagine. The birth mother, who by now may have assumed almost mythical proportions in an adoptee's mind, is likely to prove very ordinary. If the child to whom she gave birth is now a teenager, the birth mother was probably just a college or high school student who "got in trouble." That's the way it was especially before abortion became widely available.

Meeting the adult child she never knew may, of course, be a deeply moving experience for the birth mother. Just because she gave the child up for adoption doesn't mean that her baby hasn't occupied a big place in her thoughts through the years. But that doesn't mean that she and your child will necessarily establish a close, intense, and continual relationship. Remember that in searching for birth parents, your child is trying to fill in a gap in her or his life. What rôle might there be for the birth mother in your adult child's life now if she is found? It's very hard to predict. Your son or daughter already has a mother: *you*. Or as a teenager who met her birth mother remarks in Jill Krementz's *How It Feels to Be Adopted* (Knopf): "In my view I have only one mother and that's the mother who raised me and mothered me—who gave me food and shelter and love while I was growing up. That's my definition of a mother."

Another adoptee recalls of her search: "I had a very happy adoptive home. I wasn't looking for anyone to replace the family that raised and loved me. But I felt as though there were a lot of questions I wanted answers to about my background. When I went to have my own children, I couldn't tell the doctor how much I weighed when I was born—things like that."

Occasionally both adoptive and birth parents can share an adoptee's pleasure at a reunion. One adoptee we know of spoke on the phone to her birth mother from 10 P.M. to 4 A.M. after she finally was able to discover her phone number. The adoptee wanted her adoptive mother to meet her biological parent, and eventually they agreed to a get-together. The two older women became so engrossed in looking over family photos—from both families—that they didn't notice it when the daughter who brought them together quietly slipped out of the room, leaving them alone to reminisce about their lives and the very important person they had in common.

An adoptee might also run into difficulties with the birth mother he had worked so hard to find. She may want more involvement in his life than he had anticipated giving her. If this happens, it's important for the adoptee to establish clear boundary lines so there will be no confusion as to what the nature of the relationship will be.

If your adult child does establish a close relationship with his birth family, it is more likely to involve his birth siblings than his birth parents. And even that may be a mixed bag. Al Dawson, one of three adopted children, at the behest of his wife, sought out and found his birth mother and four half-brothers. Two of his brothers welcomed him warmly and became his friends, while the other two have never given him anything but the cold shoulder. Of his two sisters in his adoptive family, incidentally, one has no interest in searching and the other has always expressed some interest but never bothered to proceed beyond the talking stage—even though their mother made it clear to all three that searching was fine with her and that she would help if asked.

Sometimes the search ends with a relationship established not with a birth parent but with a birth grandparent. This can occur when a woman does not want to tell her husband and other birth children about the child she bore out of wedlock and gave up for adoption. Perhaps she became pregnant while her husband was in the service, or a similar circumstance. There is no place in her life for even a casual relationship with the child, but the woman's mother may feel entirely different about it.

Cindy Roland's birth mother rebuffed Cindy's attempt to establish a relationship with her when the adoptee located her after an eight-month search, although her birth siblings welcomed her. Periodically, Cindy would try again to interest the woman who had given her up for adoption twenty-eight years before to at least maintain casual ties, but to no avail. When her birth mother died a few years later, Cindy went to the funeral and poignantly recalls feeling like a "shadow" at the service.

We even know of situations in which an adoptee found his birth mother within his adoptive family. A birth uncle and aunt might have served as adoptive parents, raising the child because another woman that the child now calls his "aunt" was, unbeknownst to the boy, actually his birth mother. She may have been a high school girl who got pregnant, could not deal with the stigma of "illegitimacy," and worked out a solution with her family that enabled her to maintain ties with her son.

Occasionally it's the birth parent—usually the mother—who searches for and finds the adoptee she brought into the world. This is still relatively rare, although it may happen more often with increased consciousness raising in birth parent groups. Although the chance of it happening to your child is remote, remember that if it does, you are still your child's legal guardian. You don't have to relinquish any control just because the birth parent has appeared on the scene. In every sense except the strictly biological one, you are the parent. Especially at the initial contact, you would have no idea of the birth parent's state of mind or needs. So you must play a role in supervising any contact the birth parent has with your child.

Should this happen to your family, determine what the birth mother has in mind. Does she just want to know how your daughter is doing? Does she want a relationship with her? If so, what kind? What does your daughter want? A child could feel overwhelmed trying to negotiate two sets of parents, especially during adolescence. You and the birth mother, in establishing the terms of her participation in your child's life, must therefore make sure that everything you agree to is in the youngster's best interest. If you are having trouble reaching such an understanding, you, the birth mother, and perhaps your child might want to seek counseling from someone experienced with adoption matters.

QUESTIONS AND ANSWERS

I have children ages ten, thirteen, and fifteen. The fifteen-year-old is adopted. I work full-time and I'm a single parent. My thirteen-year-old is better than the eldest child at caring for their ten-year-old brother when I'm not home, but someone told me that I should put the older boy in charge of the preadolescent simply because of his seniority. Also, won't the fifteen-year-old, because he is adopted, feel less than a full member of the family if I bypass him for this important responsibility?

Ideally, each child's responsibilities should mesh with his temperament, abilities, and interests. You may not have a real problem at all if you can come up with important tasks that you can entrust to your fifteen-year-old that make him feel that he is an important family member. For example, since a fifteen-year-old is usually more mature than a thirteen-year-old and better able to handle emergency situations, you could put your oldest child in overall charge of the house while you're away, with the thirteen-year-old specifically assigned the "lesser" task of caring for the youngest child. You could also have the oldest child do most or all of the shopping, showing him that you trust him with money responsibilities.

□

Believe it or not, I've never found the right time to tell my sixteen-year-old daughter that she's adopted. When she was little I wanted to wait till she was older and could understand it better. But as she got older, it became harder and harder to tell her. What should I do?

It's never too late to tell a child that she was adopted. If you doubt your ability to handle the task, consult a family therapist for help. Some time ago a couple came to the Center for Adoptive Families for help with belatedly telling their fourteen-year-old son that they had adopted him. We worked with them, practicing the way they would talk to their youngster. When the big moment came, the boy responded, "Big deal, I've known about *that* for years. I just knew you didn't want to talk about it." And when you think about it, between neighbors, friends, and relatives, a lot of people knew about the adoption and could have let the child know, purposely or inadvertently.

Of course, once the boy's parents had gotten their "secret" out into the open, the hard work had just begun for them. Now they had to build a relationship of trust with their son, gaining his acceptance of their promise that they had not kept other serious facts about his life from him.

This kind of thing happens more often than you might think—and at later ages. We spoke to a therapist who was treating a family with two adopted daughters, ages twenty and twenty-one. When the daughters had to miss a session, the parents took that opportunity to inform the therapist that they had adopted their kids but had never told them the truth about their origins. The therapist pointed out to the mother and father how much energy they had wasted keeping such a secret and showed them how it had affected the way they had interacted with their children. After a few more sessions without the kids present, the parents were able to share with their children this important fact about their lives.

□

My oldest child, who we adopted, has chosen to go to a college halfway across the country rather than to the one nearby that we thought he would attend. It's making me feel very sad. Should I mention that to him, or keep it to myself? His adoption has never really given him any trouble and I certainly wouldn't want him to have any second thoughts about how much my husband and I support him.

There's nothing wrong with telling your son that you have mixed feelings about his going away—that's not an adoption issue. Let him know that you're happy about his increasing maturity and ability to function independently, but that you'll also miss him.

□

My eighteen-year-old daughter came home from her first Christmas vacation from college expressing interest in searching for her birth mother. My daughter is so far away most of the time now that I wonder what it will mean for our relationship if she goes through with her search and it's successful.

If this were happening while your adoptee was living at home, you could be supportive and let her know how much you stood behind what she was doing. But the geographic distance between you and her puts her more on her own, complicating matters. Still, ask if she'd like you to help in any way with the search process—perhaps you can check some records that are easier for you to get to. Also tell her that if her search brings up any feelings that she'd like to talk out with you she should feel free to call about it any time.

□

I've read your chapter on the late teenage years and I recognize my son in the child who doesn't rebel at all, who makes no move to break away from the family and seems to have no plans for the future. I also see myself in the parent who has trouble adapting to a relationship with a child based more on negotiation than authority. What can I do about this?

It is encouraging that you can see the problem and not pretend it isn't there. That shows that you're already on the road to dealing with it. Have you talked to your son about what he plans to do as an adult? That would let him know that you expect him to start acting on his own more in the near future and might prompt him to start thinking along those lines. Also, begin trying to be more conscious of any signals you might be giving him to stay a child and remain dependent. Work at building some distance from him. Take progressive steps to encourage his independence—say, for example, encouraging him to do his own laundry. And when he disagrees with you on anything, even mildly, make a point of acknowledging your differences but show him that you respect him and his opinions.

□

I understand that our sixteen-year-old adopted daughter needs the freedom to go out and date but my husband is resisting. He's more conservative than me and comes from a strict background. He also keeps mentioning to me the fact that she was born out of wedlock and he doesn't want to see history repeat itself. I know we can trust her. How can I handle this?

From what you tell us, it sounds like you have come to a basic disagreement over an important issue in child rearing, one that couples often take to therapy to hammer out an acceptable solution. However, before taking that step, why not try finding out from your husband what it would take to convince him that he could trust his daughter to have the kind of social life most kids her age have, and to act sensibly? For example, maybe he'd be more comfortable allowing her to go to parties if he knew there was at least one adult in the house. Ask him what your daughter would have to do to earn his trust, and then have a family discussion about it. This might make the problem for him more one of evaluating information than of abstract moralizing and vague suspiciousness. And by all means get him to read the parts of this book that discuss parental fears that their adopted child will repeat a birth parent's unwise behavior.

□

We've just moved to a new neighborhood and our teenage adoptee has asked us whether he should tell the kids he meets here that he was adopted. What do you think?

The one course that is never helpful is to keep adoption a secret under any circumstances. Other than that, at his age, it's something he must decide for himself in each instance. For example, let's say that you've been to his high school and met his homeroom teacher. She tells you that from your appearance she would have never guessed that you and he were related. The thing for you to do would be to change the subject and afterwards ask your son if he would be comfortable having her know about his adoption.

□

My husband and I think that some of the kids our adopted daughter hangs out with experiment with drugs. One of my teenager's birth parents was a heroin addict and our daughter was born addicted and had to be kept in the hospital until she withdrew from the drug. I read about the possibility that alcoholic parents may pass on an enhanced sensitivity to alcohol to their children, and I'm concerned that my adoptee could now be especially at risk for drug addiction should she ever try even a small amount of the stuff. Is my anxiety justified?

We don't know of any long-term studies that have yet established a tendency of kids born to addicts to be especially sensitive to drugs when they grow up but it seems logical to assume that this might be the case. However, until we have more knowledge of the long-term effect of prenatal exposure to narcotics, it would be a good idea for you to take extra precautions to alert your daughter to the harmful effects of drug use, just in case.

□

My adopted daughter has been insisting that I buy her expensive clothes that she says she just has to have. I get the feeling that she thinks I should do this to make up for the fact that she was adopted and never knew her biological parents. She even once said that "if you were my real mother you would get them for me." I have been feeling guilty and I was wondering if there's a way for me to get a handle on this before it goes too far.

It's all right to say no. If you do, she may react rather strongly, but she has to learn that there are limits to what she can have—that's part of growing up. It's also important that you not fall into the trap of confusing the giving of material objects with getting your child to love you. If she continues to demand those purchases, tell her that her birth mother would have set the same limits.

□

My son has no interest in looking for his birth mother, but I am curious to know what she is like. Would it be harmful for me to search for her?

We can understand your curiosity, but this is a dilemma. You could be opening up something that has repercussions for your child. Maybe he's not interested now in searching, but he might be when he gets older. If you had already done it, you would have foreclosed the possibility of his experiencing the process of seeking her out. We think your best course of action on this matter is no action.

□

I'm a foster parent. I expect to adopt the seventeen-year-old boy placed with me once the twelve-month waiting period is over. My problem is that I don't know how to establish a father-son relationship with him. I've read your chapter on older teenagers but it doesn't seem to speak to my situation.

Little that has been written about adoption addresses your concerns. Separation from caregivers and establishing an individual identity are at the core of what your boy needs to do at this point of his life, and you will build a relationship with him against this backdrop. Try to aim for an ongoing friendship with him, and then see what else develops out of the mix of your personalities.

8 Special-Needs Adoptions

At the ripe old age of twelve, after six years in foster care, Jessica was a veteran of five foster homes. Her wanderings through the world of foster care began suddenly, two days before her sixth birthday. With guns drawn, the police had arrested her mother's boyfriend, a drug dealer, and his accomplice, Jessica's mother. A policewoman handed Jessica a large plastic garbage bag, gave her a few minutes to fill it with possessions—she didn't even need the whole bag—and hustled her off to the nearest child-welfare shelter.

Social workers in the state's foster-care system described Jessica as a child who found it difficult to trust anyone, especially an adult. She was combative; when told to do something, she often responded by yelling. She had a hard edge for a girl her age, and a seriousness and intensity that belied her youth.

But Jessica was also feisty, carried herself with dignity, had a droll sense of humor, and projected a certain vulnerability despite her toughness. She showed a tender side when in the presence of younger children, taking it upon herself to protect the youngest and most vulnerable. Jessica was a fighter—and a survivor. While many people thought she lacked any charm whatsoever, there were others who could appreciate the good qualities that could make for an engaging child if only they were given the chance to flourish. A family finally did adopt her.

The population of children available for adoption through agencies has changed substantially since the mid-1970s. All too often these children have heartbreaking stories to tell. Jessica is not necessarily the typical special-needs child readily available for adoption today; but, unfortunately, she is far from extraordinary.

About 90 percent of children available from agencies now have special needs. What almost all of them have in common is that they are older than the babies that most people prefer when they seek to adopt a child, and that many of them have been through the wringer. It's not for nothing that they ended up in foster care, and their experiences in the foster-care system itself often add to the stresses that have burdened their young lives.

Eddie, a fifteen-year-old, has seen many foster families, and he put it this way:

> It bothers me that everyone except me has control over my life. It bothers me that I am the way I am. If I could change my ways I could be able to live somewhere. It bothers me when people trap me or use past history against me to make me feel bad. And it really bothers me the most that they always seem to change my life around every time I get into a relationship with someone special. But to put this into its simple terms, life bothers me.

In everyday language, *special needs* refers to youngsters who are not likely to join a family and then just blend in effortlessly after a brief, uneventful period of adjustment. Too much has happened to many of them; they often have psychic wounds that need time to heal.

If adoptive parents have to work harder than birth parents, then parents who adopt children with special needs must work harder still. The number of complications are greater, and sometimes there are real problems, ranging from immaturity to violent behavior. These children differ from adoptable infants in a crucial respect: they have a difficult history, much of which they remember. That fact will make a difference in their relationship with their adoptive family.

We are not suggesting that a child's past defines her future possibilities. That her father deserted his family and her mother was a drug addict who neglected her daughter doesn't tell us how a youngster will do in a loving, nurturing environment. But neither can we tell you what you can reasonably expect as she grows up, as we have done for children adopted as infants. Because of the difficult environment from which she comes, this child may not act according to the ages and stages outlined in child-development books—her behavior may not even correspond to the typical behavior of other adoptees that you've read about in this book. Some of what you know about child development will apply to her, but you would be mistaken to rely too much on her chronological age in anticipating her behavior and responding to her needs at any given time. Her particular life history and how she acts in your home are better indications of what she needs from you, especially for the first few years she's with you.

Older children may have lived with one or more foster families. They may have survived physical or sexual abuse or both. Under the best of circumstances, you have to assume that their emotional development has suffered at least temporary setbacks because of the instability and stress they've experienced. We can't emphasize that too much. Even if the older child you adopt has remained emotionally intact after being abandoned, taken from her home by the police when her family had deteriorated past the point of no return, or survived the death or imprisonment of one or both parents, these terrible experiences will have taken a toll. There is always a price to pay.

"All you need is love" does not suffice as a guideline for raising a special-needs child. If there is a rule of thumb in raising these children, it is: hope for the best, but don't count on it. Anticipate problems, and be willing to work long and hard to alleviate them.

THE OLDER CHILD: FORMULAS FOR FAILURE AND FOR SUCCESS

If you are thinking of adopting an older child but have not yet done it, you should know that people who have adopted older children, despite the difficulties involved, tend to think that they made a good decision and would do it again. For example, in a survey of 177 families in the Midwest who adopted children with special needs, conducted by Katherine A. Nelson, 93 percent expressed satisfaction with their experience, and 20 percent of these described their experience as excellent or good. How do you think a similar group of birth parents might respond to such a survey about how they viewed parenthood?

Good agency preparation of these parents and a close match between the child's characteristics and what the parents felt they could cope with often had a lot to do with this high level of parental satisfaction. But it also stemmed from patience and hard work on the part of the parents. As an adoptive parent of one of these children, you will have to telescope into a brief period of time much child rearing that other parents can spread out over many years. Contrary to what some theorists still maintain, you will not have to repeat every stage of childhood that you missed experiencing with your new son or daughter. However, it can go slower than you expect or hope.

Some people flounder in this job because they seriously miscalculate the amount of work required to successfully parent a special-needs child. Among the people most likely to have a hard time raising these kids are those who may think that in adopting an older child they've skipped his most dependent years and thus most of the work. Similarly mistaken are couples who married at a relatively older age and think that not having to deal with an infant will minimize the demands on their energy.

Others run into trouble because they know little about child development and child rearing in general, not to mention the unique requirements of raising a special-needs child. That's why families that already have at least one child, birth or adopted, and have been through the development process in some way before may have a slight advantage.

For example, the infant and five-year-old that the Henrys adopted together were their first children. Almost immediately they ran into difficulty with the five-year-old. Whenever Jeffrey misbehaved, his parents asked him, "Why did you do it?" He either said that he didn't know or else made up a reason. That happens to be normal for any kid his age, but his parents had no experience with such a response, assumed he was lying, and that this had something to do with his life before he joined their family. They brought him to a therapist, creating a problem where there had been none.

The age of adoptive parents may also work against them. People who adopt older children are themselves often older than the average adoptive parent. They are further removed from their own childhood and may find it harder to empathize. Few adoptive parents have personally experienced the traumatic childhoods of their children and may find it difficult to understand entirely how a child might feel when exposed to some of the stresses that kids adopted beyond early childhood have had to experience.

We have worked with parents who had enthusiastically adopted and effectively raised older children whose behavior had made their placement very difficult: fire-starting, inappropriate sexual behavior, and chronic bed-wetting, to name a few kinds of disturbing conduct. One of the secrets of being able to transcend even these extreme problems is making a good match with an older child in the first place.

Parents who did well were often those who found out everything they could about the child offered to them. If you are currently in the process of adopting an older child, tell your agency that you have read that these adoptions work best when parents have every bit of information about the child that can legally be given to them.

Successful parents also tended to be honest with themselves about any characteristics that they probably just couldn't stand. For example, some people, if they had to, could tolerate bed-wetting, but fighting would be the last straw and could cause them to seriously reconsider the adoption. Similarly, some parents may be more comfortable with a child who responds to difficulties by withdrawing; other parents are more comfortable with a child who is more active, even if it is in a negative way. Many others drew the line at lying or stealing. They would not take a child with those traits, even if they feared the agency would not offer them another youngster. Many agencies use the Achenbach Child Behavior Checklist to help potential adoptive parents rate their tolerance for specific misbehavior. If you are at the stage of choosing a child and your agency has not provided you with this guide or something like it, ask them to do so.

Successful special-needs adoptions are also usually found among parents who make sure that bringing an older child into their life does not erode their intimate relationship with each other. They do not allow the adoption to overwhelm their marriage, forcing them to give up their own lives to be with their kids all the time. They let their child know what adult couples are about by acting the part.

However, such couples also tended to be somewhat more child centered than other adoptive parents, taking more of their identity from being parents. Often they were people who had already raised other children, birth or adoptive, to adulthood, and responded to their now empty nest by adopting one or more special-needs children.

Those who have been manifestly successful in raising special-needs kids can get a lot of attention from agency social workers, desperate for good homes for new children coming into the system. The special-needs child that Ed Baron adopted was thriving, so although he never returned to the agency to adopt another youngster, he kept getting calls from them offering him other kids. Fortunately, like many of the more successful of these parents, he knew when to say no. Ed realized that he had enough work and didn't want to risk putting too much stress on the child he already had. He knew his limits. Bringing a new child into your family is always stressful. Be certain that the members of your family can tolerate such stress before you do this. List some recent stressful experiences and think about the ways your family members responded to these events.

THE IMPORTANCE OF PREPARATION

Information about your child's background is one important thing that will give you a clue about what to expect from him. So make sure you get all the general medical, neurological, dental, psychological, and educational data the agency has. You also need to know what experiences he's had in foster care. Get all this in writing or tape record all discussions with your social worker, because when you go through the adoption process you may be initially overwhelmed by the experience and forget the details. Agencies often tell us that they gave adoptive parents the necessary facts about their child when the parents can remember no such thing. Both may be right.

If it's at all possible, arrange to have your doctor and dentist examine your child right after you get him. To be an effective parent you should know for sure what your child's health needs are. Is he a child who will need special medical treatment or close observation of a condition that may require future care? Since the agency has legal custody until the finalization proceedings, they may be unwilling to pay for your own physician and you may have to do so, so bring up this issue with your social worker.

It's by no means a sure thing that the social worker at the agency will tell you everything you need to know. In a big urban agency, the social worker who arranges the adoption may not be the same person who has had direct and continual contact with the child. The person you deal with may be working from a sketchy case record.

If you are dealing with the person who has worked with the child, her loyalty may be to the child, understandably enough, who she may have been involved with for several years. She may be anxious to get him into an adoptive family, since that's probably the only chance the child will have of leading a satisfying and productive life. She may, therefore, withhold some negative information—perhaps that a grandparent was schizophrenic or a parent a drug addict—thinking that revealing such information might turn away prospective adoptive parents.

Jan and Robert Stone had undergone difficulties with their adopted daughter, Melissa, from the age of five months until she entered school. Their pediatrician, whom they consulted, was as confused by Melissa's behavior as they were. The Stones blamed themselves for not giving Melissa all of the love and attention she needed. One evening, they accidentally met their adoption worker at a social event and asked her whether there was anything she could remember that could shed light upon some of their daughter's difficulties. The worker, who had been a pioneer in special-needs adoptions, admitted that Melissa had been born addicted to heroin and had undergone withdrawal from the narcotic over a four-month period in a municipal hospital where it was unlikely she received more than custodial attention. When the Stones asked her why she withheld the information the social worker admitted, "I was afraid you wouldn't take her if I told you about this and I knew a loving family would make up for her early experience."

The big turnover at many agencies often makes for a

young and inexperienced staff who may not be fully trained about the development of even the average child. Schools of social work rarely offer courses on older-child adoption, and the literature on the subject is still very thin, so these social workers are not likely to have even much theoretical knowledge or practical experience with the issues involved.

However, the bottom line is that the adoption may not work if false or missing information colors your expectations about the child. Also, a social worker with whom you do not feel comfortable will unnecessarily add to the work you are already taking on. Between the home study process, placement, and supervision, you may be dealing with this professional for as long as two years. You don't want a difficult and burdensome relationship with her. If you feel you're not getting the whole story, or if the chemistry between you and the agency's social worker is way off, request a new worker or try a different agency with which you can cooperate more easily. For help in finding a Family Builders Agency, specializing in special-needs adoptions, write to the National Resource Center for Special Needs Adoption, P.O. Box 337, Chelsea, Michigan 48118, (313) 475-8693, and enclose a stamped, self-addressed envelope.

We would like to note an encouraging recent trend among some agencies toward not only freely providing the information they already have, but also making extra efforts to fill in the gaps by bringing together in one place bits and pieces of data that make for a comprehensive picture of what has happened to the child so far in her life.

Families usually act as their child's historian, providing her with a record of her life, her roots, as she develops. Photographs of her document much of what her parents say about her early life. All kids in families also share memories with their parents to see if they are based on reality. But children in foster care often have, at best, a hazy notion of where they've been and what has happened to them. Unless someone in the system has been careful to compile a comprehensive account of the child's life history, the child may, in effect, have none.

Now some adoption agencies are taking the admirable step of recording the life history of their children as far as they know it. This often takes the form of "life books" for the kids. These scrapbooks include information about foster families the child has lived with and the circumstances under which the youngster left, places she's visited, and things she's done. They contain photographs as well as text, creating a substantial biography of the child. Since youngsters under the age of six sometimes have trouble separating fantasy from reality, the books help them to develop a sense of their real past, performing a therapeutic function for them, as well as giving you a fine introduction to your child. But at any age, life books are a good idea.

Ideally, the agency should do this task before placing a child. But since the social worker has to see your child monthly after making the placement, she could also do it then. If your agency doesn't perform this service at all, press them to do it. Be persistent. If the social worker says she's overloaded with cases, doesn't have the time, and can't pass on the task to someone else, ask to consult with her supervisor (going through their chain of command should help you to avoid unnecessary confrontations).

Adoptive families we speak to tell us that several services are important in the successful adoption of older children. Adoption subsidies pay for medical and other services and may help you defray costs you are more likely to incur with these kids than with other adopted youngsters, such as tuition for special school, or after-school activities. Make sure your social worker explores every kind of financial help for which your child qualifies because of her status as a hard-to-place child or her handicaps.

Also make every effort to get counseling from the agency on the problems involved in adopting an older child. One of the factors related to the success of older-child adoptions in a recent study was group preparation of the parents who were going to adopt these kids. This "group home study" process evolved in response to pressure from parents' advocate groups who realized that people about to adopt special-needs kids needed better training than they were getting.

In group preparation, prospective parents meet in weekly sessions—typically about ten. They view videos showing why kids come into foster care, learn parenting techniques such as P.E.T. to make them feel competent and less helpless, and discuss special-needs adoption with adoptive parents who have already successfully raised such kids. At this point, people who had an unrealistic notion of what they would be contending with in a special-needs adoption have the opportunity to change their minds while it's still relatively easy to do so. The process also enables adoptive parents to start forming their own informal support networks. And joining with others like themselves gives adoptive parents a feeling of strength and empowers them to view the agency social worker more as a partner than as an adversary who can arbitrarily affect their lives.

REALISTIC EXPECTATIONS

In the Nelson survey of parents who adopted older children, 62 percent of the adoptive parents said their child had at least some emotional or behavioral problems. Some adoptable older children do not manifest dramatically negative behavior. But anybody who adopts an older child should realize that expressions of grief, anger, hostility, manipulativeness, or overt aggressiveness are well within the range of normality. Such children may cling to you and express excessive gratitude for the most trivial favors; or they may be exploitative, or perhaps hell-bent on constantly provoking other people into confrontations.

Boys, especially, are often restless, jittery, unable to do anything for more than twenty minutes at a time except watch TV. If they are truly hyperactive, they may give the impression that they are motor-driven regardless of the event: they may constantly try to climb on objects and not be able to await their turn in group games. Such children may be bossy and stubborn and have trouble tolerating any kind of frustration. Sometimes they can also fool you with their street-wise sophistication into treating them as if they were older than their years. To survive in very difficult environments, many of them learn to mimic adult behavior and they often know how to "play" an adult, manipulating to get what they want.

Children who have survived traumatic experiences such as sexual abuse, rape, physical abuse, removal from their birth family because of the violent behavior or criminal activities of their parents, or constant moves in foster care, may exhibit symptoms of posttraumatic stress disorder (see page 242) or clinical depression. Adoptive parents can't always predict when normal family activities might resurrect the child's memories of that trauma. A family move, for example, could set it off.

Most adopted older children will exhibit behavior in their adoptive families that is at its worst mildly or moderately disruptive—and that mainly in the first two or three years of the adoption. The worst of it may show up only at school and not be evident in your home at all, or only at home and not at school, or everywhere. Usually such conduct is the consequence of what worked for them in the difficult environments in which they lived. That behavior helped them to survive, but although it is inappropriate in their current circumstances, it has become a habit they need to unlearn. You will need to show them good reasons to unlearn it, and that takes time.

In view of their background, to expect too much from adopted children with special needs—and to expect it too soon—is to set up both you and the child for disappointment and possibly failure. One of the most potentially disastrous expectations would be that you and the child will quickly come to love each other after a brief getting-to-know-each-other period. If you think about it, how could that happen in the initial stages of your adoptive parenthood? You barely know the child, and his first reaction to his placement with you is likely to include considerable wariness, at the least. Would you really expect him to walk into your home and start loving you, a stranger, almost immediately?

We've heard heartrending tales from these youngsters. For example, a child may be told by a foster family that she will stay with them permanently, only to wake up one morning to find her bags packed. Or a social worker may have come to her foster home and told her she was taking her to visit the child's aunt, only to have the destination turn out to be an institution. No wonder the child has learned not to trust anyone over the age of eighteen. Only in the movies do people shed the weight of such a past in one sudden and dramatic catharsis, although your family environment will eventually begin to bring out her best.

An added complication: more often than not, a child's primary caretaker in her adoptive family will be the mother. Unfortunately, many of these children trust women the least, since they may already have been given up by several foster mothers and had to deal with female social workers who they felt had let them down—not to mention whatever mixed feelings they have about their birth mothers.

That doesn't mean that the older child you adopt can't learn to trust you. Think of his capacity to trust as a muscle allowed to atrophy, or perhaps never used at all. You wouldn't begin to exercise that muscle by lifting two-hundred-pound weights; instead, you would start slowly, gradually working it into shape.

The most practical initial approach is to concentrate on appreciating those characteristics of the child that caused you to adopt her. Let yourself grow to like her first. Draw your satisfaction from the tiniest progress she makes. That could be as simple as the first time she lets you read to her at bedtime and hold her hand while you are doing it. If love follows, it will do so in its own time. Sometimes, with difficult kids who have been brutalized by adults, it may take you a long time to get past the "like" stage; in truth, developing nothing more than a workable caretaker relationship constitutes a success with some of the most difficult older children. And that is a success to be proud of!

NEITHER HERE NOR THERE

As in any adoption, you face a period before the adoption of a special-needs child is made permanent—usually six to eighteen months. This may last longer than the similar wait before the adoption of an infant reaches completion because there is more counseling involved.

Your interaction with an older child is considerably more complicated than it would be with a baby, and ideally you would have much more freedom of action than you will actually have during the preadoption period. Unfortunately, you will have to take on the job of a parent for that time—probably of a child with some problems—without some of the usual parental responsibilities and decision-making powers.

Legal custody of the child still rests with the agency. They have the final say in everything from how you can discipline your child to what kind of therapist your child visits. In an emergency, your child's school may contact the adoption agency, and may not call you. We came across an appalling incident in which a school that had information about an adopted child's birth mother called *her* when a problem arose, even though the child had already been legally adopted. Also, you may need your social worker's permission to take your child out of the state or even to have him stay over at his adoptive grandparents' house. Emergency medical care must be approved by your worker as well.

Establishing a good relationship with the social worker will help make the adoption process easier for you. Sometimes adoptive parents, discovering the abusive treatment their child may have received in foster care, and already forming a bond to her, vent their fury at the social worker, who they think should have protected their child. But you're not likely to know the full story of what happened to your child, nor how much, if anything, the social worker you're now dealing with had to do with it or could have influenced the child's treatment. Scapegoating the social worker is not in your interest, and you should do your best to avoid it.

The social worker on your child's case is required to see her alone periodically. This could possibly hamper your ability to parent the youngster, encouraging her to think that she can keep secrets from you, discussing them only with the social worker. Should you and the youngster come into conflict, the child could play up to the social worker, getting her to place further limits on your ability to use your discretion in caring for the child. This is a difficult but not uncommon problem among special-needs adopters.

Try to get the social worker to share with you any important information she gets from the child during this period. Ask her to discuss with you, away from the child, any problems and conflicts that arise, to bolster your authority. In matters that directly concern the child, urge the social worker to bend the rules a bit, if necessary, so you may be present when they're discussed. Tell her you want to do things in a family context as much as possible. Acknowledge that she is still in charge in that she is responsible for monitoring the adoption, but try to negotiate with her a gradual withdrawal of her status as *the* authority figure in the child's eyes. She's probably overworked, so she may be quite agreeable to this.

If the finalization process seems to lag, press your attorney to get the court to set a date. When that day comes, don't assume that you will find a festive air in the courtroom. While it is not frequent, some judges fail to make it easy or joyous for anybody at the end. Sometimes judges are prejudiced about adoption and concerned with the sacredness of blood ties. "Judicial discretion" allows them quite a bit of leeway. For seemingly no reason judges can, and occasionally do, order an additional home study after all work preparatory to adoption had been thoroughly done. Believe it or not, in one recent case in a large city, a judge would not permit a child with AIDS to be part of the adoption finalization in his court and he ordered psychological tests for the adoptive parents to probe their "motive" for the adoption. We've also observed judges who give parents a hard time when they adopt children of another race. An attorney who handles a large number of child-welfare agency adoptions can protect you and your family from these experiences.

Your child may be anxious as the time for finalization approaches, partly because every transition is stressful and also because he most likely has never had anything good happen to him in a courtroom. For this reason, many adoptive parents feel it's important for them and their child to plan a small celebration for him at home or at their church or synagogue after the legal proceeding. Some religious groups are developing ceremonies for families who adopt, and if you haven't inquired at your place of worship about this practice, it might be a good idea to do it now.

WELCOME TO THE FAMILY

The best general advice we can give you about how to act with the older child you've recently adopted and brought home is to go *slow*. Don't crowd in on him. He's been through a lot in his few years. Your warm home and good intentions notwithstanding, entering yet another environment is stressful to him, and it may not take much to overwhelm the youngster.

His room should not be overstimulating. Keep it sparsely furnished and paint it in a subdued color. You needn't feel that you have to make up for all the toys he never had. Leave only a few toys out if he's young enough to have them, and store the rest, introducing them into his life gradually. He probably does not know how to care for his toys—you'll have to teach him.

If he's your only child, remember that only-child status is probably something new to him. He may have been part of a large birth sibling group, or had brothers and sisters in the foster homes in which he's lived. Living with other children would have allowed him to share complaints about the adults in the house, getting confirmation of his feelings and allowing him to blow off steam. He may feel more at ease with children than with adults. Suddenly, if in your home, he finds himself the focal point of the family with no other children to distract attention from him, it may be the first time he's ever experienced having nowhere to hide.

Anger may be the most usual kind of emotional intensity he has ever experienced from adults, provocation the only way he's ever learned to get attention. So even if your instincts tell you to take him right to your heart, back off a little and let him signal when he's ready for closer ties and something approaching the parent-child relationship with which you're familiar.

Have you assumed that she will start off calling you "Mom" and "Dad"? She might, but let it be her choice. Some special-needs kids will begin calling their adoptive parents by their first names. As soon as you can after she's placed with you, ask her how she wants to address you—let her know she can call you Mom (or Dad) if she wants to—and what she'd like you to call her if she seems to have a nickname.

As an overall approach to finding and adapting to *her* rhythm of fitting into your family, use the observation method we introduced in chapter 2 (page 44) when we discussed how parents can deal with their anxieties about how an adopted infant will develop when they may lack important knowledge about her family history. Give yourself an assignment to note when your child seems most satisfied, most content. In time, you'll develop a profile of your child that may help you predict how she'll react to most new experiences.

Most parents want to be physically affectionate with their children and to have that affection reciprocated. But since your child may have received mostly painful physical contact from authority figures, you will have to move carefully here. See when your child comes to you. Does he like it when you physically reach out to him? Does he respond positively to your arm around his shoulder? To a hug? Some kids like to be kissed, some don't. If your child doesn't, don't press the issue, because that certainly won't get him to accept your affection. Sit on a chair next to his bed and read bedtime stories to him. After a while you might try touching his arm as you read. With some kids you may never be able to have close physical contact, at least until they're bigger and feel more self-confident and less afraid.

Observe which activities your child enjoys; see when he takes the initiative to join in and when you have to invite him to participate. When you find something he likes, do more of it. If bike riding is what he likes rather than talking, for example, emphasize that activity. Many adoptive families have found that camping trips are a special way of relating to a special-needs child. The family has a chance to interrelate away from the normal distractions. They work together at the simple tasks which camping requires and ones which each family member can contribute to in some way. She only has the family to relate to. It is also unlikely that there will be any environmental cues to remind her of former experiences of abuse or neglect.

Try a variety of activities to draw him out. For instance, he may not feel up to joining the conversation at the dinner table, but a board or card game after dinner might make him talkative. Pick something simple that will not make him feel like a failure, and remember that he may have a short attention span at the beginning, so be willing to suspend the game when he appears to lose interest.

These kids often have a lot of physical energy, so try some activities that focus on movement. Individual athletic games are a good bet, although stay away from team sports at least at first if your child finds it difficult to relate to large groups of people as many special-needs adoptees do. You might also do something like baking bread that requires a lot of physical exertion (without a food processor, so you have to knead the dough).

It may sound strange, but your first job as a parent adopting an older child is to teach him to be part of your family. Every family is different, and their dissimilarities range from the seemingly trivial—are kids allowed to eat while watching TV? are they required to make their bed as soon as they get up in the morning?—to basic values concerning manners, cleanliness, acceptable language, and religion. Don't assume that your new child will know what's "natural" around your house, no matter how normal it seems to you.

Kate Simpson, then six years old, was already a veteran of several foster families when she was placed for adoption with Ellen and Harry Simpson. Things were going reasonably well in the first few weeks but the Simpsons still got the feeling that something was on their daughter's mind. When Kate didn't say anything, Mr. Simpson casually asked her if there was anything bothering her. There was: how to make the bed. Every family she had ever lived with had different rules about this mundane duty. Kate was confused and concerned, since she liked the Simpsons and wanted to fit into their family. When Mr. Simpson demonstrated their version of hospital corners, Kate had one less thing to worry about.

Nothing is too obvious for you to explain. Your child will not be hurt or insulted when you point out your family customs, since by doing this you are in effect telling him that you want him to be part of your family. In fact, we urge you to be as straightforward and as authoritative as you can about how you like things done. If morning showers are the house rule, let him know it from day one. If you care how the table is set, show him the right way. But don't flood him with too many new customs at once. Let him master one or two at a time.

You never know when rituals that seem obvious and appropriate to you will take your adopted older child completely by surprise. For instance, you could have knocked Frank Sheridan over with a feather when he greeted his nine-year-old at dinner on the boy's birthday with a birthday cake on the table and a gift-wrapped present set down next to it. Richard, who had lived with Frank for only three months, was startled and didn't know what was going on. He had no experience of this ritual, didn't know how to act, and seemed very uncomfortable. Frank, of course, had expected to see his son's eyes light up.

To your older adopted child, the activities your family enjoys as well as your rituals may seem like they come from another planet. Do you celebrate Thanksgiving? Do you like to go to museums, plays, concerts? Do you take it for granted that most people at least occasionally eat in restaurants? Don't assume that your child has done any of these things—even once—or that he will take to them in time simply because you like them.

By all means introduce your child to these new experiences, but do it gradually. The first time you take him to a museum, for example, limit the visit to fifteen minutes or a half-hour; unless, of course, he takes to it with relish, in which case let his enthusiasm and your physical endurance set the limit. Take him to a Little League game as a spectator and see how he reacts before signing him up for a team. Share with him anything you like, but do so with subdued expectations so that if he's bored, you won't be sorely disappointed.

Eating in a formal restaurant with your child might be a trial more than a treat unless you acclimate her to the experience first. It's quite possible that she's never seen the inside of any restaurant other than one that serves fast food. Why should she know how to act? She has no precedent in her life for this strange activity.

Fortunately, you can practice at home how to act at a restaurant. First, don't bring the food right away. It may not have occurred to you that waiting for food involves a kind of delayed gratification, which always entails trust that something you want or need will come to you if you are patient. Little or nothing in your child's background may have proven that to be true for her.

If you frequent better restaurants, place cloth napkins, maybe even candles, on the table. Is it the custom in your family that children first tell their parents what they want, and then the parents tell the waiter? If so, explain it to her, since there's no reason she should be able to figure it out for herself. Once she seems to get the picture, you might want to do a "practice run" by going to the restaurant just for dessert.

Meeting your neighbors, friends, and extended family is also something the child should experience a little at a time. It's natural to want to throw a big party to celebrate the arrival of your child. After all, it's a proud moment in your life. But it's hardly likely that the child will be easily able to handle it. Think back to your own childhood. Can you remember a social function at which friends or relatives of your parents, people you didn't know or couldn't remember, came up and all but overwhelmed you with their attention, questions, and comments? Imagine how your adopted older child would feel about meeting a flood of people when she is still trying not to see you as a stranger.

People outside your immediate family will feel a little differently about your adopting an older child than they would if you had taken in an infant. You may hear questions like, "Aren't you afraid his character is already formed and that you won't have any effect on him?" To that you could reply with information about special-needs kids—their difficult past and their potential for growth and achievement once they are secure in a nurturing environment. If they tell you you're a saint for putting up with such a child, you might want to respond with humor and tell them that your child is a saint for putting up with *you*.

SCHOOL

Should you get your child in the middle of the school year, he will have to endure still one more stressful situation. Not only will he be the new kid—always rough on any child—but he may also have a name different from yours, since you will not yet have finalized the adoption. In a small town or close-knit neighborhood, where families often know each other at least slightly, his status as an adoptee will make him stand out, accentuating the last quality he needs right now: difference. You might be able to avoid this problem by arranging for the school to call him by your last name, assuming that's all right with your child and the adoption agency.

Parents adopting older children should prepare for the distinct possibility that their child will need special attention in school. Many things may have adversely affected your child's ability to concentrate and learn. For example, special-needs children may have had mothers whose use of alcohol or drugs during their pregnancy affect their child's ability to learn as quickly as other children. If your youngster moved around a good deal, he may have had big gaps in his education. Good grades on his academic record might be deceiving, especially if he spent time in institutions such as residential treatment centers, where the emphasis was probably on controlling emotional and behavioral problems rather than on academics. And if you adopted him at the age of seven, eight, or nine (this is especially true for boys), he's come to you when many kids are restless in the classroom; the instability in his life up to this time is not likely to improve that tendency.

You will probably have to serve as your child's advocate at school. It's a little like having a relative in the hospital. The doctors and nurses always seem to be a bit more attentive to patients when relatives visit frequently and speak to the attending medical personnel. If possible, make sure the child's adoptive father makes his presence known, since schools often seem to respond more readily to a father who takes an active interest in his child's education. Mike Harper did that with his son, Rod, who had been acting up at school. Mike dropped in on Rod's class once in a while unannounced—with the teacher's permission—and sat in the back of the room to observe. Rod actually enjoyed the extra attention; and the teacher viewed it positively too, seeing it as a sign that Rod's parents cared and that the youngster's chances of doing better were therefore enhanced. In turn, that made her pay more attention to the boy.

The educators in your town may not have much experience in dealing with children with your youngster's needs. Also remember that their responsibility is to all the kids in the system and they are not likely to appreciate a child who makes their job harder. If your child is disruptive in any way, school personnel will not view your child's interests as paramount. So you'll have to become the expert in the field and help the school find alternatives if your child doesn't respond well to standard pedagogical and disciplinary methods.

When you meet his teachers and guidance personnel at the school, make it clear that you think he may need some *temporary* help while he adapts to your family as well as the role of pupil. Doing this should enable your child to take advantage of any extra services the school may have, such as resource rooms, individual counseling, and tutoring, while avoiding his placement in a special class and possibly having him permanently labelled as a troublemaker or poor student. Ideally, what he needs are small classes, clear rules, and appropriate reading material to ultimately bring him up to his age level academically.

Unfortunately, our public schools have a good deal of trouble dealing with a child who is undereducated. In fact, such a classification does not formally exist. Instead, school personnel are often all too comfortable calling kids "neurologically impaired" or "emotionally disturbed." So you will have to be vigilant and resourceful to keep these labels from adhering to your child.

If your child is disruptive, the school may have him evaluated by a psychiatrist. They may even insist that he be medicated with a drug such as Ritalin, commonly prescribed for hyperactivity. This should only be a last resort and even then its use should be strictly limited. Ritalin occasionally has side effects that are serious and irreversible. Even when it works the way it's supposed to, it may leave a child somewhat "stoned." A friend of ours gave it to her adopted son for a brief time and got this response the first time she administered the medication: "Mommy, I feel very tired; is this the way you feel all the time and is that why you behave?" Try everything else possible before you resort to this.

Family therapy that uses a structural model is especially useful with children who are overactive and disruptive. The Philadelphia Child Guidance Clinic, 34th Street and Civic Center Boulevard, Philadelphia, Pennsylvania, 19104 (215) 243-2773, have pioneered this model of working with families and children. They should be able to recommend a therapist or clinic near you with expertise in this approach.

If your youngster develops academic or behavioral problems that seem intractable, consider placing him in a school with a higher teacher-student ratio where he can get the special attention he needs. You might use your adoption subsidy monies to help you to finance this special schooling if your local school district will not pay for it.

For a cheaper but effective alternative to private school, consider sending him to one of the private after-school learning centers you can find in storefronts in many cities these days. These organizations provide children with high teacher-to-student ratios and give the kids frequent tests to measure their progress. If you don't know where to find one, your child's school guidance counselor should be able to help.

ACKNOWLEDGING THE PAST

Helen Weiner felt relief. The foster parents of Jackie, the ten-year-old she had adopted three years ago, were moving halfway across the country. Helen really didn't care for them. She didn't like their manners, the way they kept their house, or their failure to set academic standards for their own children. But she put up with having a relationship with them because Jackie loved them and they still meant a great deal to her.

Sensitive adoptive parents will recognize that an older child arrives with emotional baggage. He's had time to develop relationships with other parental figures; unlike other adoptees he may have known his birth parents—perhaps all too well. And you may have to develop a relationship with some of these people. It's a different experience from adopting an infant, of course, unless you got your child through an open adoption process. If you never gave it too much thought before the adoption, it would be well to consider its importance now, because in adopting your child, you took in with him all the relationships that are central to his life. So while you welcome him to your home, leave some room in your family for the family ties he's already developed.

Agencies often encourage adoptive parents to meet their child's current and about-to-be-former foster family to help the child make the transition from one family to another. For one child we saw in our practice, who had been shuttled around to many homes, we brought her foster mother into the therapy to act as a sort of grandmother, giving her blessings to the child's adoptive family. You need not establish a relationship with your child's former foster family as a matter of course, but it could be helpful if your child has obvious enduring emotional ties to these people.

There is no hard-and-fast rule about how to handle your child's relationship with a former foster family. You could take him for an occasional Sunday afternoon visit to his former home, or have a child from that family stay overnight with you if your child remains close to him. But short visits, telephone calls, and letters are probably preferable to overnight stays, since you want to do everything you can to encourage your child to shift his loyalties to your family. However, you might want to remain especially flexible if your youngster shares an ethnic or racial background with the foster family that you and he do not have in common. In that case, this tie may be even more important.

Negotiate the terms of any continuing relationship with the foster family at the very beginning of the adoption. For example, if a relationship does continue, you will have to come to an agreement about how to handle the possibility that your adopted child may bring up important matters about himself with the foster family that he is not yet comfortable discussing with you. That could range from the type of food he is used to eating or anxiety about competing in team sports at school to doubts about whether he's liked enough by his adoptive family to remain with them.

THE PARENTAL CHILD

The Andersons adopted two children: nine-year-old Patricia and her thirteen-year-old brother, Ronnie. The boy liked his new family, and wanted to stay. He especially liked his new adoptive father. But Patricia was having a hard time. She had developed a close attachment to the mother in the foster family they had been staying with and under the stress of separating from her, the girl's asthma began acting up. Realizing that his sister was profoundly unhappy, Ronnie, against his own self-interest, began to systematically misbehave in a way and to an extent that forced the Andersons, an experienced adoptive family of special-needs children, to begin family treatment.

Siblings placed together come with their own behavioral patterns. On one hand, brothers and sisters have a model for a close emotional relationship: their ties to each other. That bodes well for their developing a similar relationship with you. On one hand, some interactions between siblings can cause adoptive parents a considerable amount of trouble. This is particularly true of the parental child phenomenon. Here the oldest child sees himself as a caretaker for his siblings.

When the therapist engaged by the agency to see Ronnie spoke with him, he revealed the essence of his problem. "Don't you ever just feel like having fun and being a kid?" the therapist asked him. "Lady," he replied in a flat tone of voice, "are you joking? I've *never* been a kid. I was born old."

Ronnie and Patricia each eventually got what they wanted. After they were returned to the foster family from which they had come to the Andersons, Ronnie misbehaved again. This time he was acting for himself. The brother and sister were separated, Patricia staying with the foster family she had liked and Ronnie getting a second chance, alone, with the Andersons.

The parental child is not neurotic. His sense of duty is likely to be a response to an objective situation. But that doesn't mean that such a child is necessarily stuck in that role forever. Louis, for example, took on this heavy responsibility at an early age when his mother, a prostitute and drug addict, locked him and his four brothers and two sisters in their apartment when she went out. Louis would break out of the apartment so he could steal food for his siblings and himself. When he was later adopted with his two sisters, Rose and Anna, he understandably did not quickly surrender his position of guardian. Fran and Howard Jensen, Louis's adoptive parents, had to find a way to transfer his authority over Rose and Anna to themselves, since the boy needed to live the life of a child as much as his sisters, and the Jensens needed to have their authority as parents accepted by all three children so they could protect and nurture them. They made the transition gradually, telling Louis, "You've known your sisters longer than we have, so we hope you'll help us to discover what kind of care they need. You've done a good job of watching after them, but there are many things they need now that you can't provide. Besides, you need some time off, too, from all the responsibilities you've had to take care of. We would like to convince you that you can begin to trust us to take care of the girls."

Succeeding with a parental child means working with him and not just trying to move in and usurp his authority, since he's not likely to give it up under those circumstances. You have to validate his perceptions and compliment him on the job he's been doing. It may even be necessary to treat him as if he were considerably older than his years, since he's been acting the part—at least in one segment of his life.

When we have worked with these children in family therapy, we've found that the younger children are often in a bind regarding loyalty. We've often had to work, over a period of time, to get the older child to give the parents permission to assert authority with the younger siblings.

Parents should openly acknowledge the sibling pattern to each of the kids and be explicit about the new relationship. Make it clear to the parental child that there is now someone else to care for the younger brother or sister. Give him credit for watching over his sibling, but tell him that you will shoulder much of that responsibility now. Let the parental child know that there may still be times when his sibling will come to him for help; at other times the younger child can go to their parents. And remind him that he is now free to act his age and enjoy his childhood.

If you're in this situation, remember that you have to earn the trust of all the children. The relationship they have forged has worked for them under very difficult conditions. They won't give it up until you prove to them that you are trustworthy and consistent, and that will take time.

SOME UNPLEASANT FACTS

There's a good possibility that the older child you adopted was physically or sexually abused. Or your child may come from a family in which antisocial behavior was the family norm. Perhaps his birth parents expected him to steal or to sell drugs. Or he may have had a parent who was mentally ill.

It's not uncommon for a special-needs child, two or three years after her placement, when she feels safe, to act out symbolically to show what happened to her. For instance, she may dance in a manner that suggests she has had sexual experiences inappropriate to her age. Or a child may tell her adoptive parents directly about the sordid details. Naturally, adoptive parents feel outraged when learning what their child had to endure, especially when they hear it directly from the victim. Adoptive parents often respond to such horror stories with bitter characterizations of the birth parents, particularly of the birth mother, thinking that their empathy will comfort the child. But that's a big mistake.

Nothing good ever comes from denouncing your child's birth family, no matter how upsetting their behavior may have been. Your child will resent it. If you're truly enraged, after comforting her, go out for a walk and burn off the anger with physical exertion. When you're feeling calmer, sympathize with your youngster and tell her how sad you feel that she had to go through such an ordeal, and promise her that in your family it would be inconceivable that any child would ever be beaten, made to go without food, forced to do terrible things. Even though she may already have lived with you for several years and you've gained her trust, continue to reassure her anyway; she'll appreciate hearing it again.

As awful as your child's early life experiences may have been, it might be useful for you to at least try to see her birth parents' behavior in perspective, since she probably retains some kind of loyalty to them and it could help you to empathize with her. Her birth mother and father may not have been fortunate enough to have parents as loving and caring as you; their economic and social circumstances may have been dire. Try to imagine them as victims like the child you adopted, because that's what they were.

Further, if the adoption agency's description of the birth parents influences your view of them, remember that social workers had to build a good case in court so they could have your child removed from her original home; they were not trying to paint an objective portrait of troubled human beings. So their files may contain a description of the birth parents at their absolute worst. Yet your child's appealing characteristics must have come from somewhere; in the midst of the terrible troubles in her family there must have been at least a glimmer of warmth.

DISCIPLINE

Kids who have been shunted around from foster families to institutions and back again have a harder time dealing with complexity and ambivalence than do other children. More than other adopted kids, they need clear rules of conduct consistently enforced. It's important that they come to see you as an adult who can take care of them and that you can tell them the right thing to do in most situations. Besides kindness, they need predictable, fair, and equal treatment from you. So don't waste time agonizing over the hard life they've led. Give them their share of household chores as you would any other child. And tell them what sort of behavior you expect from them.

All parents have to correct their child's conduct, but discipline is a delicate subject with these children. If your child was abused by a birth parent or other adult, avoid all physical punishment. Find other ways to control his behavior, such as sending him to his room (but not if isolation was a theme in his upbringing) or taking away some of his privileges.

You would think that Renee and Peter Thompson, a teacher and CPA living in New York City, would have had no trouble devising an effective way of getting their eleven-year-old adopted daughter, Susan, to comply with their standards of behavior. They already had two grown birth children and they knew something about parental discipline. But Susan was running rings around them.

Susan had entered foster care because her mother was a chronic alcoholic whose boyfriends subjected her daughter to frequent beatings. Six months after she was placed with the Thompsons, the preadolescent was still teasing her hair, using eye shadow and lipstick, and dressing to kill. What's more, she was complaining to her social worker in the northern, rural part of the state where she came from that she missed the country and wanted to return to the foster-care system in that area. The worker was getting jumpy and the Thompsons knew it. That pushed her adoptive parents to enter therapy.

After some conversation it turned out that the Thompsons, feeling sorry for Susan because she had been through so much, had been letting her stay out as late as she pleased, buy whatever clothes she wanted, and generally make up her own rules of conduct. When they had the temerity to decide that she needed at least some limits and that her freedom had gone far enough, the girl all but laughed in their faces. When they tried to take away her TV and other privileges to get her to change her behavior, she told them that she didn't care, a response that demoralized her parents and caused them to quickly back off.

It was pointed out to the Thompsons that they knew how to raise kids and should be able to set limits on their adoptive daughter. They replied that no punishment they tried worked. They had also attempted to reason with Susan, bringing her into their discussions of what constituted acceptable behavior, but that hadn't produced anything positive either.

Susan was quite up-front about where she thought she stood. "They can't make me do anything," she proclaimed defiantly. Further conversation clarified the nature of the problem in the Thompson family. The parents were allowing their child to blur the boundaries between her and themselves when they let her into their discussions of what to do about her actions, and they simply were not standing firmly enough when they made attempts to change her behavior.

The essence of effective discipline is not the specific punishment or how long it lasted but rather the conveying of a tone of seriousness to their daughter. Brief but sure punishment is almost always the best kind. Susan had to understand that her parents meant it, that if they said something would happen, it would. Threatening without following through was worse than no punishment at all, because it encouraged Susan to hold her parents in contempt. They had to see their threats of punishment as a promise that they would keep. By acting consistently, with no ambiguity, they would also be teaching their daughter that she could always trust them to do what they thought was best for her.

The Thompsons got the point. The next time Susan went against their wishes, they discussed it among themselves, excluding their daughter, as suggested. They concluded that a week without her bike might change Susan's attitude, and they informed their daughter of her punishment. At first, she was indifferent; but this time her parents were adamant. After a week without the bike, when it became clear that now her parents would not back down, Susan actually displayed some contriteness. Not that she turned on a dime. Two weeks later the Thompsons told us that Susan had called them, well past her curfew, from Times Square. We told them to call the police the next time she did that, and to let Susan know that that's what they planned to do.

An interesting thing happened after that. Over the course of several sessions—it took about nine or ten in all—a gradual transformation occurred not only in Susan's behavior but also in her appearance. Bit by bit the heavy makeup and other marks of pseudosophistication disappeared to reveal the eleven-year-old underneath. Given the strain of her childhood, innocence was perhaps something she would never know, but at least she was now both acting and looking like a child, to her parents' enormous relief.

Another family in treatment felt they needed to use corporal punishment on their adopted child to get him to mind them. These parents had tried all of the normal types of discipline and they were willing to use these methods at first. They were concerned that if, when these other methods didn't work, they couldn't use corporal punishment that they would not have a last-resort threat. As they raised their other children they had resorted to occasional spankings. They themselves had been spanked as children. They didn't like changing what had always worked for them. Because we were unsure of the child's experiences in former homes and couldn't absolutely rule out that he had been abused, we were reluctant to allow them to use corporal punishment, but we also didn't want them to feel incompetent as parents of this difficult child with special needs.

To create a strategy that would enable them to handle the child's misbehavior without doing anything inappropriate, we agreed with them that it was the scariness of the noise of a slap, not just the hitting itself, that is effective in getting a response from a child. We suggested that they clap their hand against a book not too near their child's ear to produce the desired result. It made the parents feel less helpless, and it got the child's attention without hurting him.

There is also a legacy of physical and sexual abuse that might present a serious impediment to the smooth integration of an older child into your family beyond limiting the kinds of sanctions you can use to impose discipline. It involves a survival mechanism that the child may have once legitimately used but that is now grossly inappropriate. Many kids know that if they're unhappy and want to lash out at you, they can charge *you* with child abuse.

If that happened a whole investigation might ensue. The people who investigated you would not be obliged to return to tell your neighbors and others who were interviewed that the accusations proved unfounded. By comparison, this experience would make your adoption home study seem like a lark.

Kids usually threaten to turn you in before they actually try it. If your child should make such a threat, take it seriously. Even if your child is already adopted, call your agency worker right away and tell her that you want this threat included in your child's record. Send a follow-up letter to the agency with details of the incident, such as what the youngster did, what you did, and the precise threat. Such a record can help you in the event your child makes a complaint against you. Ask your agency worker to help you and your child develop an alternative way for your child to get help if he is angry with you. Remember that it has been his experience that parenting figures are untrustworthy and sometimes brutal. He may feel the need, for a while, of having someone outside the family available to him when he is angry at you or scared while he learns to trust you. Something you said or did may have triggered a memory for him of a time when somebody did, in fact, abuse him. A family therapist who works with the whole family, but agrees to see just your child from time to time, should be helpful to both you and your child as you work to build a trusting relationship. Try also discussing his grievances with him, aiming to come up with other ways he could express, and you could deal with, his unhappiness. And tell him that if he did carry out the threat other people would interfere with your home life, preventing you and him from becoming a family.

Fathers of girls who were sexually abused should be particularly aware of their child's past when they act affectionately toward their daughter. A confused adolescent girl with a history of abuse may not know how to differentiate affection from abuse. Try to gauge her limits by first making small gestures, such as placing your hand on her shoulder. If she's comfortable with that, then you might hug her. In other words, let her give you clues as to how you should act.

SERIOUS MISBEHAVIOR

You will need patience, persistence, and the willingness to act firmly if your child has major behavioral problems, such as stealing or inappropriate sexual conduct. We are not saying that you should expect the older child you adopted to do these things, but in our experience such conduct is not unheard of for these children.

Dealing with a child who has serious behavioral problems can wear down even the best parents. Should you encounter misbehavior on this level, family therapy should probably be the first order of business. Also, for your sake and the child's, take advantage of any institutional assistance you can get, such as the local Big Brother program. Get together with other parents who have adopted older children and take in each other's kids for a brief time, allowing one set of parents time off from their responsibilities. Perhaps a member of your family would be willing to take her for a few days, a week, or a month to give you a respite.

If you can afford it, consider sending your child to boarding school if it will help.

If her conduct is troublesome enough you might have to consider placing your child for a time in a residential treatment center, as a last resort, where she can receive close supervision. This might have echoes of abandonment for her, but remember that you will be visiting her regularly, calling her, writing to her, and bringing her home for weekends and it's still better than letting her push you beyond your limits, possibly resulting in the abrogation of the adoption. We have had the experience of two children who spent time in residential treatment and they returned home greatly improved. Be certain that the residential treatment facility that you choose isn't one that believes adopted children have to be "rescued" from their adoptive parents. As unbelievable as it sounds, some of them actually believe that their institutions are better for children than living with their own families. Residential treatment center staff have often only had experience with children who have problems related to brutal treatment by their parents. They may have difficulty understanding that your child came to you with certain difficulties that had nothing to do with you.

If your child steals, it may be because he has not had things of his own and needs to learn the difference between his property and others'. It could be behavior necessary for survival in the environment he came from. Or he may be testing you. If nobody has ever loved him or treated him well, he might be telling you through his behavior: "You may think I'm cute, but other people haven't trusted me and why should you?"

Should you encounter this conduct, make it absolutely clear to the child what is and is not acceptable in your family; you may have to do this over a period of time until he realizes that stealing will keep him from becoming a full member of the family. Meanwhile, take precautions to secure your valuable possessions and those of any other kids in the family. Put locks on doors and desks, even though it's unpleasant.

If you have other children, you will need to pay special attention to their feelings in the matter. After all, to the normal emotions associated with sibling rivalry you have just added a very complicated element. Besides not trusting the new child, his brothers and sisters may be embarrassed by his behavior at school and with their friends in the neighborhood. Reassure them that you will protect their property, that their new sibling is passing through a difficult period of adjustment, and that he will settle down. Also tell them, in your adoptive child's presence, that he is acting this way because he is not yet able to control his temptation to steal, but that you are helping him to learn how. Make it sound like a problem rather than some inherent evil lodged in the child.

If you have entered family therapy, sessions need to be focused on your children's concerns as well, perhaps in sessions which, from time to time, include only the children in the family.

If your other kids panic and simply want to get rid of the newcomer because of his outrageous activities, tell them you know that they're going through a hard time but be sure they understand that their new sister or brother is here to stay.

We realize that having a child who steals can be an emotional drain on adoptive parents. But we emphasize that if you're firm in asserting the wrongfulness (both morally and personally) of such behavior and stand your ground, he's likely to abandon the habit. Since this is the sort of thing that's useful to talk over with parents who have had similar experiences, seek out other people who have adopted older children and had to deal with this behavior. If you can't find them in your local adoptive parents' group, check with the North American Council on Adoptable Children for your local chapter.

Bear in mind that your family's attitude toward this kind of problem is as important as your child's behavior. Few children are inherently bad; most problems have solutions, and there are ways out of virtually every seemingly dead end.

Liz Trent and her husband, Paul, for example, thought they were really up against it and were ready to throw in the towel. Their fourteen-year-old adopted son, Jack, was stealing from their three birth children, and he was showing no remorse when caught. The Trents could put up with a lot from Jack, but they found his apparent lack of a conscience in this matter chilling.

When Jack and his family came into therapy the focus was not on thievery, at least initially. First the therapist established that in other ways he was an integral and contributing member of the family. His parents, for example, proudly talked about the way he helped his younger sisters with their homework. It was only after taking a session to lay this groundwork that the therapist asked him why he stole. "I don't know," he replied. "I see something that I want and a little voice in my head says don't do it, but I don't always listen." You mean it's like hearing a transistor radio? he was asked. He agreed. So maybe he had to turn the volume up. Yes, he nodded, with a smile.

At that point the therapist knew that Jack would soon realize that if he tried a little harder, he could hear his conscience on a regular basis. But just as important, his parents now understood that his conscience was there all along. Their child was not hopeless, and they were capable of giving him the help he needed to get on the right track, to hear and heed his already existing conscience more often, and to stop stealing.

The same difficulties early in life that might lead a child to steal could, paradoxically, also cause her to do something just the opposite. Sometimes older adopted kids will hoard food when they first join a new family. If this happens, don't let it offend you. It's not a comment on your caring and generosity but rather a reaction to a life of uncertainty and deprivation. She'll get over it, but in the meanwhile you might respond to this behavior by leaving a basket with some special treats in her room each night, telling her "this is yours." After a while, she'll realize that the food supply won't run out.

Over the years we've discovered that many children not described in the adoption agency's records as having been sexually molested were in fact abused in this especially terrible way. This type of violation sometimes confuses a child about the nature of his sexuality to the point where he behaves sexually in ways improper for his age. He may even act as a sexual victimizer himself.

How might you know if your child was sexually abused? Some of the signs include acting frightened when near a male (true of boys as well as girls), premature sexual activity, and a heightened interest in sex. However, such behavior is not a definite indication of abuse. Perhaps your child came upon a couple having intercourse and his knowledge and interest stems from that incident.

If your child acts out sexually, you will need to first set up sleeping arrangements that discourage this practice. For example, you could have the child sleep in a bedroom next to yours so you can see anyone going by, institute an "open door" policy in the house, with kids using the bathroom to change, and have two boys or two girls share a room, so one might know if the other had left the bedroom during the night.

Then, over time, you should teach the child how to be a brother or sister, something he may never have had the opportunity to learn. He may also never have learned how to express affection to family members in an appropriate way. He can learn to read to younger ones, for instance, teach them a game they don't know about or a skill they don't have, bake some cookies for them, or comfort them when they feel down. Since acting like a sibling may seem so obvious as to make it difficult for you to break it down into learning tasks, you'll probably come up with many more specific things for him to do if you think for a while about how you and people you know interact with a brother or sister.

Parents are naturally very concerned for the emotional health of a child who has been sexually molested. But often, we believe, they choose methods of treatment that may be of questionable good and could even be harmful. For example, we doubt that anything helpful can come from having a six-year-old sit on a Saturday morning with a group of kids of varied ages who have also experienced sexual trauma and try to relive her experiences by talking them out. Catharsis does not produce a cure, and it could reignite uncontrollable feelings related to the incident, bringing back into the present something better left in the past. Unless that abuse affects her current functioning, it might be best to put off any therapy she may need until she is older.

However, always be willing to talk to her about it if she brings it up. You may want some counseling yourself in handling her concerns and fears when she brings them up. Should she express some fearfulness that stops well short of incapacitating her, you could respond to it by pointing out how different her present circumstances are from those prevailing when she was abused. Say to her, "You were little when it happened. Now you are bigger and stronger. You can run fast now and get away. You can scream louder and fight harder. You have a mommy and daddy to tell now." Contrast her powerlessness then with her increased size and strength as well as the protection and support she gets from your family.

If early abuse left her feeling powerless, what she needs now are activities that empower her. Anything that bolsters her self-confidence, such as sports, would be in order. One interesting idea we've encountered is to give such children self-defense training in the martial arts.

THERAPY—A TOOL YOU MAY NEED

Kids adopted at an older age are considerably more likely to see a therapist at some point in their lives than children who join their adoptive family while infants. We have provided information about such services in the appendix, and we urge you to keep the information handy just in case. If you live near one of the increasing number of family therapy centers in major cities, you might even want to get in touch with them now to find out what kind of services they offer should you ever need them.

If the youngster you adopted as an older child requires therapy—and it's by no means certain that he will—it's not a negative judgment on you. In one family, the mother taught a large class in an inner-city elementary school and had just been promoted to the rank of assistant principal. But that didn't enable her to stop her adopted son from disrupting first his public school class and then his class in the strict parochial school she had sent him to thinking *they* would certainly be able to control him. She was a skilled professional in working with children, but she knew when she needed outside help.

How do you know if your family needs therapy? If your child is destructive or if you're feeling frustrated and you've tried everything after receiving advice from all quarters and nothing has worked, you should consider the therapy option. Complaints from neighbors or the child's school would also point to a serious enough situation to warrant at least a session or two with a therapist.

When therapy becomes necessary, we urge you, particularly if you adopted an older child, to use a family therapist. Too often the adults in their lives have singled out these kids for negative attention. Family therapy takes the burden off the child and spreads it around, making the job of getting better a family project; and it involves the child in a process that emphasizes her place in the family. When choosing the therapist, ask him if he's worked with child-parent problems like yours and how successful he's been—you'll probably get an honest answer.

At the Center for Adoptive Families about 150 families who have adopted older children have been treated over the past five years. The kids' average age at adoptive placement was older than nine years and they were, on average, twelve years old when they came for treatment. They usually had been in the family for two or three years. Many had been misbehaving over a long period of time, and their offenses were often major. For example, they may have been stealing from the neighbors or expelled from school for serious offenses. About 30 percent of the families had already tried other kinds of therapy, and many of these parents were one step away from reversing the adoption. Yet of these 150 families, only one went through with returning their child to foster care. This child had discovered his birth mother, destitute in a run-down neighborhood, and felt it his duty to go back and care for her.

It should offer you some comfort that even under the worst scenario, violent behavior by your adopted child, a brief course of therapy may be enough to restore her conduct to a level that makes her acceptable to her family, her school, and her community. That did not seem evident to Jane Alsop, however, when she brought her nine-year-old daughter, Marian, in for treatment. Marian had pushed another nine-year-old down a flight of stairs at school. Fortunately, the victim was doing much better than Marian's mother, whose nerves were frayed to the point of snapping. She was even having thoughts of returning Marian to foster care, though she loved her daughter very much.

This was a hard nut to crack; mother and daughter were reluctant to talk much. Finally, to break the ice, a music therapist was brought in. She began strumming a guitar, and soon the girl began singing. Marian improvised lyrics that were to the point: "Mommy, when you took me home you were so happy, but I wasn't. You didn't know how sad I felt about leaving the other family. Because you were so happy, I couldn't tell you how much it hurt."

Marian sang out about the pain of separation from her foster family. Instinctively, her mother picked up the theme and sang: "I never knew you felt that way. I'm really sorry.

I should have listened to you then, but I will now." This operatic interchange wasn't the end of the therapy, but it allowed a more typical outpouring of feelings to proceed and in a few sessions it was clear that the crisis would pass.

Quick therapeutic reversals in conduct can also occur in situations that are nowhere near as dangerous, but extremely demoralizing for families who adopted older children. Most parents, like the Crawfords, would feel that way about a fifteen-year-old girl with a long history of bed-wetting. It was bad enough that Connie had that problem when the Crawfords adopted her at age twelve, but since it is not uncommon among children with special needs they felt that they could live with it for a while. But its continuance was beginning to undermine their faith that their daughter would make a successful transition from adolescence to adulthood. It didn't help that Connie was starting to get into fights at school, losing her temper as well as control of her bladder.

Psychiatrists had told Connie's parents that her bed-wetting—sometimes twice a night—was probably the consequence of her having been sexually abused as a young child. That may have been true, but it didn't end the problem. Nor had the drugs prescribed by other doctors. Mrs. Crawford tried the old standby cures for bed-wetting. She saw to it that Connie had nothing to drink for hours before bedtime. And she and her husband woke the girl up just before they went to bed so that she could go to the bathroom at the last possible moment before everyone went to sleep. But they got no results.

Playing up successes often works well under a variety of circumstances. For Connie this meant asking her to think of the nights when she had not wet her bed. There were none. Finally, Connie was asked if she ever lost control of her bladder during the day. "No," she said. "I'm shy about going to the bathroom at school, so I use the bathroom at home in the morning and then I don't go again until late afternoon, when I get home."

This proved to be the opportunity that led to results. Connie needed to extract herself from the debilitating and seemingly endless habit of bed-wetting, and she wouldn't be able to do it without stepping back and focusing on the times when she did have control. She was enlisted in a "scientific study" of other kids who had this problem and told that she could help because of her amazing bladder control during the day. She was asked to keep a record of how she managed to maintain that control. Keeping that record gave her the perspective she needed and helped her to concentrate on her successes. Within two weeks she was having dry nights, and after a few more sessions of talk her control problem—temper as well as bladder—was in the past tense.

By focusing on the times when they are successful, people can learn to recognize their own latent abilities to deal with their problems. You don't always have to bring emotional conflicts and long-buried anxieties into conscious awareness to resolve the problems they're currently causing, you just have to deal with what they are currently doing when the problem is not occurring and have them do more of it.

Ed Peterson also had a problem. For Ed, a teacher, his seeming inability to get through to Mickey, the nine-year-old he and his wife, Margaret, a public administrator, had adopted, was driving him to distraction. True, Mickey loved to ask his adoptive father to cook the dishes the boy liked best. And he also asked Mr. Peterson to join him working on projects. But then Mickey wouldn't eat the food his father so lovingly and laboriously prepared; and as soon as his dad began helping him with a project, Mickey lost interest and simply walked away. Ed Peterson was not just saddened by Mickey's behavior; he had come to think that his son altogether lacked the ability to establish a relationship, that perhaps he was a defective human being.

In therapy it was explained to Mr. Peterson that it was hardly that serious. He just had to realize that it was not realistic to assume that Mickey would start acting the son to his adoptive father without first learning what the role meant. And, being a teacher, Ed Peterson was in a good position to teach his child how to be the son he wanted.

To break his son's cycle of asking-getting-rejecting and to replace it with one of sharing and respect, Mr. Peterson and Mickey were given an assignment. He and his son were to plan a project together two times each week, but it would not be something they would do right away. They were to wait till the next day, after Mickey came home from school, to work on it. Further, they were to spend only half an hour on the project, and it had to be something that produced a product, like a drawing or a kite.

The point was that instead of asking his father for something, Mickey had to negotiate with him and come to joint decisions on the details, thus giving the son a direct interest in the activity. It also taught Mickey delayed gratification, based on having to wait a day and build up his anticipation of the activity. It was important that they make something tangible both to create a ritual of father-son interaction and to produce a permanent physical embodiment of that cooperation. Every time Mickey looked at that kite it would remind him of the pleasurable experience of building it with his dad.

The plan worked. Ed Peterson felt a renewed confidence in his ability to teach his son what the boy needed to know, and Mickey got an inkling of how much satisfaction he could get by working with his father until they had completed what they started. When last heard from, father and son were planning a fishing trip together.

Of course it's not always this easy; but things are rarely as hopeless as they may seem. We are not suggesting that you rush your child into therapy simply because you adopted him at an age beyond infancy. It's appropriate only if specific serious problems arise at school and in the community and threaten your ability to parent him.

CHILDREN WITH DISABILITIES

Some of the most satisfied adoptive parents are those who have adopted a special-needs child identified as having a disability. Some of these parents already have a child with the same condition and therefore know about his or her special needs and may already have altered their house to accommodate them. The most important problems their child has are usually clearly visible and may even have a name—such as Down syndrome. Nobody blames these parents if their child continues to have limitations, and whatever progress the child can make offers immense satisfaction to the parents and reflects well on them.

Disabilities, however, are often present when they're not so obvious or clearly labeled. These may be a little harder to accept and deal with. Children born to mothers who had little or no prenatal care, or who were alcoholics or drug addicts, for instance, are at high risk for intellectual disabilities. Parents who adopt any special-needs child should be aware that school difficulties could result from such conditions. For example, an I.Q. of 75 or less recorded in your child's case record *may* indicate some mental retardation with which hyperactivity is often associated, although it is by no means a sure thing; and the intellectually stimulating environment that you supply in your home could raise his I.Q.

I.Q.s as low as 50, although pointing to the presence of mild retardation, do not mean that your child will not be able to learn; indeed, one label often applied to these kids is *educable*. Children with this level of impairment can usually learn up to about a sixth-grade level. They can develop sufficient social and vocational competence to make their way in the world, although they sometimes need a little help in dealing with stressful or complicated situations.

Children with I.Q.s ranging from 35 to 49 are moderately retarded and considered "trainable," capable of learning up to a second-grade level and holding down a semiskilled job. They are likely to need guidance to deal with social or job-related pressure.

Severely mentally retarded children, with I.Q.s of 20 to 34, may or may not learn to talk and are likely to have problems with motor coordination. At most they will be able to do very simple work, and even that will have to be supervised. Below an I.Q. of 20, a child is profoundly mentally retarded and will always need help in caring for himself, although even some of these kids have the potential for learning some self-care skills.

If you have adopted a child with a physical or intellectual disability—or both, since the two may be present together—the nature and extent of the disability will have a lot to do with the style of parenting you use and the particular strategies you devise to deal with any difficulties that occur. The nearest group of parents of children with similar disabilities would be one place to go for advice and support in dealing with those complications. Major groups include United Cerebral Palsy, 66 East 34th Street, New York, New York 10016, (212) 481-6300; the March of Dimes, 303 S. Broadway, Tarrytown, New York 10605, (914) 428-7100; the Association for the Help of Retarded Children, 200 Park Avenue South, New York, New York 10003, (212) 254-8203; the Juvenile Diabetes Foundation, 432 Park Avenue South, New York, New York 10016, (212) 889-7575; the American Foundation for the Blind, 15 West 16th Street, New York, New York 10011, (212) 620-2000; and the American Society for Deaf Children, 814 Thayer Avenue, Silver Spring, Maryland 20910. In addition, consult your adoptive parents' group or adoption agency–sponsored support group. *Exceptional Parent* is a magazine for parents of children with disabilities that could also be useful. Your agency and the National Resource Center for Special Needs Adoption are good places to go for further resources.

A parent looking for a pediatrician for a disabled adoptee should keep one important point in mind besides the criteria we offered earlier in this book for choosing a doctor. The doctor you select will have to accept the fact that your child will have limitations. That's not as obvious as it may sound. Many doctors have trouble dealing with a child they can't "cure" and always view that child's health in terms of what further steps they might take to improve his functioning—even if it means the child must endure gruelling tests and painful medical procedures. Of course, if something as direct as surgery or a medication would make a difference, it may be appropriate. But for most disabled kids, their condition will probably require management, and little more.

Many parents—adoptive and birth—sometimes forget that a disabled child is, first of all, a child. He is likely to have more in common with other kids than he does differences, especially in the case of a physical disability. Much of what we've discussed so far in this book is still relevant to your child's upbringing. For a mild disability, it may all apply.

Some points that we have made about nondisabled adopted kids relate even more strongly to adoptees with disabilities. You will have to expend a good deal of energy serving as an advocate for your child in the outside world. For example, in her school you'll need to be aggressive to see that she not only gets whatever special attention she needs, but also that she doesn't get too much of it. If she can benefit from being "mainstreamed" and school personnel automatically want to put her in a special class or program, you will have to see to it that your child's best interests are served.

Talk openly with your child about his disability, just as you do about his adoption. Provide him with opportunities—within the family and with other people who have disabilities—to talk about how people react to this way he differs from them. He needs this just as he needs to express any feelings he has about not growing up in the family into which he was born. But as in bringing up the subject of adoption when he hasn't for quite a while, don't dwell on it obsessively.

If you have other children, try to be sensitive to their

feelings about the special attention your disabled adoptee may require. Encourage them to share with you any thoughts or feelings the subject evokes. Your adoptive parents' group may have a program for siblings of disabled adoptees. Some special schools such as the Eagle Hill Schools for disabled kids in Connecticut and on Long Island also have such programs. One teenager, who had always felt embarrassed by her younger, hyperactive, brain-damaged brother, who she thought of as "dumb," came away from one of these programs with a new appreciation of him. "I never realized how much work it is for him to do things," she remarked after the teacher described dramatically how difficult it was for him to do all the little things she took for granted.

Another way you can make your other kids more comfortable with the idea of having a disabled adopted sibling is to involve them in any special care your adoptee needs.

Although you have demonstrated empathy and caring by adopting a child with a disability, you can't possibly know what it actually feels like to grow up disabled in a world where most people don't have an obvious disability—unless, of course, you have one yourself. So like any adopted child who can benefit from knowing an older person who was also adopted and has thus "been through it," your adoptee can gain much from a similar relationship with a disabled grown-up. The parents' support group concerned with your child's disability should be able to help you with this.

Adolescence can be a very rough time for adoptees who also have a disability. They become very sensitive to the way they differ from their peers. Sometimes their friends of earlier years pull away, shutting them out of their crowd. At a time when sexuality takes center stage for all kids, your disabled adoptee may have a particularly hard time of it, since for some strange reason it's a common attitude that disabled people are asexual. You might want to stay especially alert to conflicts your child has over this issue. Should your youngster appear to be having great difficulty with it, a session or two with a sympathetic counselor or therapist could help.

This may not, however, be the appropriate step to take for an intellectually impaired child. This child needs most to be with others like him- or herself in order to have something approaching a rich social life. To fill this need, inquire at the organizations we've listed for referrals to special camps, schools, and after-school programs. If you live in or near Boston you might also want to write to Project Impact, 25 West Street, Boston, Massachusetts 02111, for further information on this subject.

Although there may not be a lot you can do to ameliorate the specific painful occurrences of the teenage years, you can support your child by reminding her that this too shall pass. Point out that it gets easier once she emerges into adulthood—that's the truth!—and that no slight she endures as a teenager reflects on her personality or character. In other words, be her ally.

Finally, much not terribly useful material has been published about the inevitability of low self-esteem among disabled kids, just as similar theories have been formulated about adoptees in general. Your positive attitude about your child will go a long way toward counteracting any negative influences from the outside world. If you convey to her your optimistic feeling about the nature of her possibilities, she'll believe it.

ADOPTING CHILDREN WITH PSYCHOLOGICAL PROBLEMS

We have often pointed out that children who have been removed from their birth families under conditions of abuse or neglect may have also experienced continued abuse and neglect in foster care. These children have been subjected to inordinate stress during their lifetime and have had to develop ways of coping with this stress. It is not possible to predict how severe individual reactions to certain kinds of stress will be. There are just too many factors involved, including the child's inborn temperament, the age of the child when the traumatic experience occurred, the nature of the child's relationships with others at the time, her later experiences, and a range of other issues. It is important to remember, however, that the loss of a parent is an especially severe stressor. In order to survive the kinds of experiences that are usual for foster children, your child has had to develop certain behaviors. It is obvious that a child raised in a loving and secure home, who receives positive attention from family, neighbors, peers, and teachers, will have certain expectations about the world and where she fits in. A child who has been abused, neglected, lived with different families, and moved from school to school will have different expectations for herself and for others.

It is common for children who have experienced disruption of parenting and/or abuse to have developed certain behavior patterns that are labeled *adjustment disorders* by the American Psychiatric Association. These ways of reacting are just that—reactions. They do not say anything intrinsic about the nature of the child. They reflect his or her reactions to experiences. They can therefore sometimes change over time as a result of a changed, new family environment that is supportive and relatively stress free. The range of symptoms associated with adjustment disorders can change when stressors are removed from the child's life, but it will take time. Some of the symptoms your child may express are sadness, tearfulness, nervousness, worry, jitteriness, truancy, vandalism, fighting, poor academic functioning, and social withdrawal.

If the traumas which your child experienced prior to adoption are grave, such as rape, abuse, serious physical injury, especially head injury, and malnutrition, and were caused by others, especially parents, the child may exhibit symptoms of *posttraumatic stress disorder*. The symptoms of this include vivid memories, dreams and nightmares about the event(s), feeling as if the experience is occurring again when something reminds the child of it, less interest in activities which used to be important, feeling detached from other people, limited expressions of feelings, sleep disturbances, guilt, memory impairment, difficulty concentrating, and avoidance of activities related to the experience. In the chronic stage of this disorder, the child may do quite well for a period and then, from time to time, when something triggers the old memories, she may be flooded with feelings and thoughts related to the trauma. Such a disorder generally takes a very long time to heal. It is important to remember that as the child experiences positive interactions in your family, she will grow to feel protected and stronger and therefore less vulnerable to victimization by others. When she reexperiences the traumas, you should gently remind her of just how different things are now. After all, she is bigger, stronger, and smarter. She now has parents who will protect her against others. She will gradually learn, through her experience in your home, that she has parents who do not hurt children in terrible ways. It is difficult to see your child suffer so much, but it is also necessary to remember that through the constant experience of the difference between what her life is like now and what it was during the times of trauma, your daughter (or son) will be able to develop the strength and resources to balance the earlier experiences.

To our way of thinking, it is unlikely that psychotherapy can completely exorcise her early experiences. They are part of her life. Her more dramatic reactions to these memories will fade with time. What psychotherapy can do is reinforce your efforts to show your child just how different things are now and how unlikely it is that she will ever have to suffer in that way again.

Many adopted children are also diagnosed as having an *attention deficit disorder with hyperactivity*. The symptoms of this syndrome include:

- he fails to finish things
- he often doesn't seem to listen

- he is easily distracted
- he has difficulty concentrating on tasks requiring sustained attention
- he acts before thinking
- he has difficulty organizing work
- he needs lots of supervision
- he can't wait his turn
- he runs about excessively
- he has difficulty sitting still
- he always is on the go

We again suggest you view your child's behavior as a reflection of his early experiences. He may have come from a chaotic family, moved from foster home to foster home and from school to school. It will take time for him to learn that he can depend on things to happen because there is consistency in his new family. You can work with him on activities that will symbolically help him to learn to trust in the predictability of certain outcomes. For a while it will be good to have clear rules, times for doing things, and clear consequences, so that he can grow to trust in the predictability of his new home and family.

Separation anxiety disorder includes a group of symptoms that are also quite reflective of the experiences of many former foster children. A child with this diagnosis is afraid of being separated from those to whom she is attached. She worries that harm will befall loved ones or that they may leave and not return. She may worry that they will be lost, kidnapped, killed, or the victim of an accident. She may fear going to school. She may be afraid to go to sleep and have nightmares. She may also suffer from a number of physical symptoms including headaches and stomachaches to avoid leaving home. She may also be sad, have difficulty concentrating, and have temper tantrums. This disorder is not uncommon among all children and usually follows a life stress such as loss of a relative, illness, a school change, or moving to a new neighborhood. For a former foster child, it is fairly common, especially as she grows to love and trust you and then becomes afraid she will lose you. Again, the predictability of her experience in your family and with you will help her give up these symptoms.

Children may come to you with developmental disorders which range from specific delays in reading, writing, arithmetic, language, and articulation to a combination of any of the above. In many cases these delays are reflective of the child's past experiences which have often included chaotic family life and inner-city schools with far too many pupils for him to receive the individual attention he needs. Although it is more likely that your attention, help, and encouragement will have a greater impact on many of these delays if the child is younger than six when he comes to you, even older children have made remarkable gains following adoption. An excellent school with small classes will further reinforce your work with your child. Please remember that school performance depends on your child's motivation and willingness to learn. If her experiences in schools have been unrewarding, it will take a while to help her establish new expectations about school and schoolwork and about her own skill and competence.

QUESTIONS AND ANSWERS

I just found out that my child was sexually abused by an adult in one of the foster homes in which she lived. I'm wondering if I'm up to the task of parenting a child with that history. How can I tell if I can do the job?

We've seen many families in this situation. After the shock of hearing about it wears off, you'll realize that you've been a good parent and there's no reason why you can't handle even this. In fact, that she feels safe confiding in you demonstrates the trust you have built between you and her. You and your husband may want to have some counseling to help you feel more competent to effectively parent her. Remember that most studies that describe the treatment needs of children who have been sexually abused may not be applicable to your child, since she is no longer living in the family in which the abuse took place. The cues that might remind her of the abuse aren't there. It will probably be easier for her to put this experience in the past and get on with her life than it would be for a child who continues to live in the same environment in which the event took place.

□

My nine-year-old is very sweet and has fit into our family remarkably well. However, she often acts quite immaturely and I'm beginning to worry about this. Am I doing anything wrong?

You are not likely to have done anything to cause this behavior. Children who have been moved from family to family in foster care, or have been physically or sexually abused, as many special-needs kids have been, are often delayed in their maturation. They develop strengths where they need them, sometimes making them seem sophisticated in some circumstances and babyish five minutes later. It will probably take time for your daughter's behavior to even out, perhaps even a few years. In the meanwhile, let her behavior at any particular time suggest whether she needs you to take charge and treat her as a dependent little girl or give her the increased opportunities for self-responsibility of a more mature child.

□

I've read about life books, but the agency from which we got our child did not put one together for him and the social worker did not have the time to do the job once our son was placed with us. Is there anything we can do about this now?

You can get information about putting together a life book from the National Adoption Resource Center (address in appendix). They may even be able to recommend a worker who will contract independently with you to develop a life book with your child based on the information you have and his memories.

□

My seven-year-old has started to wet her bed. Do you think she needs a therapist?

We doubt it. It's not uncommon for children her age to respond to major changes in their lives and the anxiety that often accompanies them with bed-wetting. Have your doctor make sure that this problem does not reflect a medical condition. If it doesn't, it will almost certainly go away with time. Reassure your child that you love her. Adoptive parents in similar circumstances have told us that they have been able to get their child to stop bed-wetting by going into the child's room after she falls asleep and telling her that they love her and that she will always be with them. We're not sure why this works—maybe the child partially awakens and hears it—but it does seem to work for some people.

□

It's been more than six months since our child was placed with us and we don't seem to be any closer to getting his adoption finalized. Every week now he asks, "When am I going to be adopted?" Our lawyer says it's because the papers are just "sitting there" at the court, which has a backlog of cases. Is there anything we can do about this?

Perhaps you could call the adoption clerk at the court and try to find out what is holding things up. If you explain how this delay is affecting your family the clerk may be willing to speed things up. If this doesn't work, ask your lawyer if it would be worth trying a different court. In the meanwhile, you might create your own adoption ceremony with your family, or perhaps arrange for an adoption celebration through your church or synagogue.

□

Our child's foster family was distraught at having to give him up. They were sobbing and crying when the time came for him to leave them, and they implored us to keep them in our child's life. Is that really a good idea?

There's nothing wrong with continuing some contact between them and your child as long as the arrangement you devise is in everyone's best interest. First, make sure your child wants to continue the relationship. Talk to the foster parents to see if they fully understand the importance of strengthening the child's new and permanent ties to you and your spouse. If you don't have an extended family nearby, and if you and your foster parents share certain common interests and beliefs, you may grow into a relationship similar to that of an extended family.

□

We were our son's foster parents prior to adopting him. We therefore know his birth mother and she says she wants to remain in at least occasional contact with us and him. Our son seems a little uncomfortable at this prospect. What do you recommend?

There isn't any one correct course of action for such a delicate situation, since the right thing to do would vary with the particular situation such as the circumstances surrounding the child's entry into foster care and the mother's current functioning. We suggest that you consult your agency about this matter. They should be able to direct you to a foster family who could advise you about how they handled such a situation.

□

In the foster homes in which he lived, our child received corporal punishment when he misbehaved. He seems to have gotten used to it. I sometimes have the feeling that when he acts up he is trying to provoke me into hitting him. Sorry to say, he's come close to succeeding a few times. But we just don't treat kids that way in our house. How can I get him to listen to me without using force?

You needn't feel guilty for having felt pushed to the verge of slapping him. But you don't have to give in to the impulse and you probably will be able to substitute a nonphysical correction and punishment system for what he has known in the past. When you're feeling provoked, remind yourself consciously that that's what's happening. Such awareness usually reduces the pressure to act on the provocation. Make it clear that his misconduct will consistently earn for him a different kind of punishment, say confinement to his room for a specific time period. Let him know that this is in place of the way his misconduct was dealt with elsewhere. Tell him that you are confident that he will soon learn the rules of your family and will get used to the ways that you are different from other families.

□

The special-needs child we adopted has been in individual therapy for some time, starting before he was placed with us. Will it damage him to end his treatment?

Ask your child if he wants to continue treatment. If he does and it seems like he's developed a close attachment to the therapist, discuss with the therapist how you can begin to cut back, over a period of time, the frequency of his sessions with the ultimate goal of termination. One way to ease your child out of treatment is for you to start sitting in on some of the sessions if the therapist agrees to this, so that they take on a family orientation. If your child still feels an attachment to the therapist after ending treatment, you might arrange for the two to occasionally get together for a social visit, maybe going for a Coke at McDonald's if the therapist is willing to do this. You will have to pay for the therapist's time, though. This will give your child the experience of having a relationship with an adult he cares for end in a gradual, nontraumatic way.

9 Single Parents

Jennie, a thirty-eight-year-old woman who works in the field of child welfare, has broken off a ten-year relationship with a man. She's dated some, but met nobody in whom she is particularly interested. Increasingly, she realizes, she wants to be a parent. Although her career demands much of her time and energy, she has reached a point where she can afford to hire someone to help with child care. But she's wondering if it's fair to bring a child into a single-parent family.

An increasing number of women and men in this country have decided to (or been forced to) have and raise children without any intention of ever getting married or living with another adult. These "unmarried parents," as the newest euphemism less negatively puts it, constitute a new kind of family. Unfortunately, single parents can often still anticipate prejudice, such as when their child's teacher ascribes their youngster's misbehavior in school to the lack of two parents in the home. Only recently, because of their numbers, and mostly in urban areas, have these parents begun to make a dent in the stigma on such households.

Single adoptive parents, both men and women, are creating one of the newest of these family groups. Adoption agencies started placing children with single parents about fifteen years ago. Most of the placements have been with women. If we still must cope with a stigma on adoptions, an even greater one on older-child adoptions, and a still larger stigma on single-parent adoptions, you can imagine how hard it is for a single male to negotiate this process. Often there is the unspoken suspicion that this adoptive parent is a potential child molester. Men willing to cope with this must be strong and self-confident. Most men who adopt are social workers, teachers, therapists, or former police officers.

Some speculate that most people find single-parent adoptions more acceptable than single women giving birth. In any case, it's still adoption, with all the prejudice that goes with that process. "Why don't you wait for a man and have a real child," single adoptive mothers still occasionally hear. "How will a man accept this child—you may never get married," goes another of these judgments. For much of the public, adopting without a mate may still suggest a doubly "unreal" family: only one parent and no biological connection to the child.

Reliable studies that tell us how successful some female-headed families have been in raising their children have not yet appeared. The inclusion of teenage mothers has skewed available statistics about this group. Many investigators still assume they are dealing with "broken homes" in most single-parent families. Further, any inquiry into the experience of single adoptive parents has to take into account the large number of special-needs kids raised by these mothers and fathers. Many agencies, viewing the one-parent household as the least desirable kind of home for a child, have been willing to give such parents only those children they could not place with more traditional families.

We have a feeling that when studies come out that separate single parents by choice from the single-parent family in general and single-parent adoptions in particular, they will report a success story. The people now undertaking this parenting are better prepared for it. Because they are often doing it by choice, they tend to have a realistic notion of what's involved. They are conscious of their numbers and often help each other out, and they can draw on the experience of numerous others who came before them. These are active mothers and fathers who know that to make it work they have to do a great deal more than their peers in two-parent families.

We wouldn't want to minimize the work involved. Raising an adopted child as a single parent is difficult even without having to contend with prejudice. The lack of another person with whom to share some of the burdens of child-rearing can seem, at times, like one long struggle. To surmount the logistics of getting the child from one place to another, caring for her when she's sick, providing her with companionship and emotional nurturing—all the while trying to lead your own life as an adult and make a living—can be overwhelming at times.

Single-parent adoption also complicates the already difficult job of adoptive parenthood. As an adoptee, your child may require more parental attention from time to time to ensure that some of her unique needs are met. But you will have less time and energy to devote to fulfilling them than would two parents together. You will also lack the perspective couples can give one another simply by having a second adult in the family. For example, has your child brought up the subject of adoption lately? Perhaps, with all of your responsibilities, you've been so busy that you haven't had time to notice the silence. Yet, as with everything else, ultimately it is your job to keep an eye on that aspect of his development. There's no one else around, at least not full-time, to pick it up.

YOUR SUPPORT NETWORK

Whether a single adoptive parent by choice or life circumstances, you will need outside help in raising your child. Some of that assistance can be institutional. Summer camp is one useful resource—an opportunity for both you and your child to have time away from each other. You might explore an organization like Big Brothers or Cub Scouts which could provide a male role model for your young adopted son if you are a single woman. Other service groups like the Girl Scouts might provide a sense of belonging for your daughter. However, as a single parent you have to be alert to complications that might arise from such participation. How will your daughter handle a father-daughter night if you are a single adoptive mother? It might be wise to decide on a strategy for such occasions before they arise. One way to handle this is to have a male friend or relative fill in for your child's father. Fortunately, many schools and groups, particularly in urban areas, are becoming more sensitive to this situation and are making these occasions "parent night" or "family night."

A single adoptive parent must do whatever she can to avoid long periods of isolation from other adults. If it is only her and her adopted child, a single mother can begin to feel imprisoned. Louise Hogan didn't realize the full significance of coping with an adopted baby by herself until the experience was on her and like a flood it almost swept her away.

In order to spend the first few months of parenthood caring for her child, Louise had taken a leave of absence from her company. The corporation she worked for, like a small number (IBM and Johnson & Johnson, to name two), had granted her the adoption equivalent of maternity leave. Her child arrived in the winter. The bitter cold never relented, making it months before she could even take the baby for a stroll in her carriage. To make matters much worse, her baby was colicky. After three weeks of being cooped up in a small apartment with the incessantly crying infant, it didn't look like Louise would make it to spring with her nerves intact. Finally, on a Saturday morning at 8 A.M., near hysteria, she called her only close friend with a desperate plea for respite. She just had to get away from her child for a while. Fortunately for Louise, her friend managed to create some free hours for the besieged mother by organizing an ad hoc "relief team" of sympathetic women.

Another woman we know who had adopted as a single parent told us how she was also caught unprepared, but nevertheless, although shy, was able to marshal her resources to lift herself out of the isolation trap. For Tracy Brodrick, the experience seemed to come upon her suddenly, even though she had been intellectually ready for adoptive parenthood. There she was with a baby, a small house to take care of, and few phone numbers to call when she needed help. She had taken a leave of absence from work for the first few months she had the child, intending to hire a baby-sitter to take over during the daytime when she returned to her job. But as her adoption leave from work drew to a close, she knew she would be coming home at the end of the work day to a second, and probably harder job: parenting her child. Now finally aware of what she was in for, she felt overwhelmed.

"Looking back on what happened then, I guess it was an example of necessity being the mother of invention," Tracy recalls. Instead of letting her circumstances immobilize her, Tracy got organized. She started a play group for mothers and children in the neighborhood, herself creating an institution she needed, since it didn't already exist. She thought up ideas for kids' parties and similar occasions that would bring her into contact with other young mothers, striking up friendships with several of them. By the time her daughter was in her second year, Tracy had organized a bunch of mothers willing to exchange baby-sitting chores on Saturdays, freeing each to squeeze in some recreation, shopping, cleaning, and decompressing from their week's work.

Shortly before her daughter's second birthday, Tracy joined a nearby adoptive parents' group in which a single-parents' branch had recently been formed. Many couples join adoptive parents' groups to hear how others have dealt with adoption-related difficulties; but single parents, we have found, are even more interested in the social interaction the organizations provide. It's the pot-luck suppers, picnics, and museum days that draw single parents toward such groups. With these new friends, single parents have an opportunity to share their child's milestones—the first sip from a cup, for example—that always call for some kind of public notice and celebration.

Support networks are clearly crucial to single parents, adoptive or nonadoptive. So if, like Tracy, you do not have one in place, you might want to pull people into your life to help out. If you are temperamentally shy, try to approach this network-building task as something necessary for your child's welfare. Just as you would do whatever you had to do to protect her health and safety, no matter how uncomfortable the particular task might make you, you must provide for her and yourself in this way, too.

Some single adoptive parents have even joined with others like themselves to institute a new kind of family. Typically, in this new version of the family, a single woman with an adopted child will join forces with another single woman or a single man who has adopted to provide each other with the kind of help and emotional support that married couples might assume will be forthcoming from each other. For single parents with only one child, this arrangement also permits their children to experience some of the benefits of having a sibling. This family system may get together whenever an occasion seems to call for it—on a holiday, for example—or they may meet regularly for joint activities, such as Sunday afternoon in the park.

Relatives might also constitute an important part of your support network. In fact, a supportive family can make an enormous difference in the day-to-day life of a single parent. It's not always easy, though. In a situation which includes death or divorce, you no longer have a mate to act as a buffer between you and your parents. Sometimes, parents go so far as to treat adult children as children once again. If you adopted as a single parent, this new development might aggravate whatever tensions already existed between you and your parents, possibly reducing the amount of useful assistance you can expect or may want from them.

Ordinary parent-adult child interaction can sometimes add a minor annoyance to the experience of the single adoptive parent. For instance, ask yourself, would it upset you if you leave your child with your mother while you attend to other chores and hear from her when you return: "He never cried for me the whole time *I* took care of him"? Many people feel this is worth no more than a benign grin in response. But if it bothers you, you might want to negotiate with your parent. Tell him or her how much you appreciate their help, but make it clear that the remark just happens to rub you a bit the wrong way and would he or she just not say that, for your sake?

JUST THE TWO OF YOU?

Who says growing up with just one parent doesn't have its advantages? For one thing, your child doesn't have to share you with another adult. For another, children with a single parent, especially an only child, have an opportunity to develop their independence at an earlier age.

Melissa, an only child of a single parent, at the age of twelve planned a vacation for herself and her mother, the kind of thing most of us don't do until we're adults. Her mother was just too busy to work out the details, so she told her daughter to go to the travel agent and make the arrangements herself. At first the agent didn't take the girl seriously, but a call to her mother made it clear that Melissa was authorized to deal with him. Melissa even delivered the check—over a thousand dollars—to pay for the tickets and accommodations. Now a successful professional in her thirties, she still fondly remembers the experience and the self-reliance it taught her. And her mother appreciates how Melissa's independence made life easier for her.

On the other hand, children growing up with one parent and no siblings spend much more time in the company of adults than do other kids, which sometimes causes complications. These children grow up faster than do their peers. By the time your child is about ten years old, she may respond to you in conversation almost as an adult would, thus further encouraging you to treat her as if she were older than her years. The result may be confusing to both you and your child.

As your chief confidant, your youngster may feel a loyalty and protectiveness toward you that could cause difficulties. For instance, she might not come to you with her feelings about an adoption-related difficulty such as bad dreams or a remark somebody made to her about her adoption for fear she will be overburdening you.

How much of your personal life and frustrations do you want to share with your child? How much should you? Will you feel "left out" when your child reaches adolescence and becomes more peer centered? Two children can complain to and confide in each other, and neither will feel pressured to be the most important person in your life. Each is freer to act her age. But even if it's just the two of you, you can still create an atmosphere in your home that will take the pressure off you and your child. First, as we have pointed out, go out of your way to bring other people into your life, and get involved with groups that will provide social outlets for your child as well. Second, make sure you and your child create a sufficient degree of silliness in your house. For example, have a pillow fight once in a while; you'll both enjoy it.

Humor can even work as an effective disciplinary tool. One single adoptive mother we saw had a seven-year-old daughter who bit her when angry. The mother had not yet discovered a way to stop this unacceptable behavior, and none of the advice she had received from friends and neighbors worked. She had tried talking to her daughter as well as administering all kinds of conventional punishments. We suggested that she entirely change the framework in which she was interacting with her child. The mother was to buy a Halloween mask and have it ready to put on the next time the child tried to bite her. If that didn't work, she could try banging on a pot with a spoon. The woman, who was very serious by nature, was somewhat taken aback, but agreed to try it.

The mask worked. Her daughter laughed hysterically—so did the mother—the first time she got this treatment. The shock and surprise took the youngster totally out of the mood that had led to the biting. After two or three similar incidents, the child got the message: the Halloween mask was ridiculous, and so was her biting, which she stopped.

If the responsibilities involved in raising an adopted child by yourself sometimes blunt your sense of humor, you can reactivate it by getting some perspective between yourself and your daily cares. In the middle of a day in which most things are going wrong, you have to be able to step back for a moment and look at what's happening without feeling threatened, worried, annoyed, or defensive. In other words, you need to put some emotional distance between yourself and the hardships of single parenthood.

Jogging, shopping, a glass of wine after work, a long-distance call to an old friend can often do the trick. Pamper yourself; you deserve it.

Distance and perspective are not only prerequisites for maintaining a sense of humor, they are also necessary for effective parenting in general. In two-parent families, the complementary personalities of husband and wife can provide built-in alternative ways of seeing and varying approaches to a child's problem behavior. On a bad day, when one parent has had more than enough, he or she can be spelled by the other.

Bringing two viewpoints and styles to parenting also makes it more likely that at least one parent will be a good match for the way a child acts at a specific age. For example, when Scott Roberts was going through his "terrible twos," his mother Janice, a bookish person, couldn't cope. But her husband Dick, who is more active and impulsive, had just the right response to Scott's shenanigans. He took the youngster's behavior in stride, and his son responded positively.

With an adopted child especially, sometimes you need to see things dispassionately in order to stay alert to the extra complications raised by adoption issues. Since you don't have a mate to check your own perceptions of what's going on in your family, we suggest that you try the following technique to give yourself a more objective point of view of how your relationship with your child is working. It's something to use when nothing, from reasoning with your child to punishing him to yelling and screaming, has worked.

Try stepping back from the immediate, from the emotions of the moment that throw everything out of proportion, overwhelm, and immobilize you. The key to creating the distance you need to put things in perspective is cultivating your powers of observation.

There are parents who come to us with seemingly insurmountable problems. They're tried everything reasonable one could think of, and still can't get their child to behave. We ask these parents to visualize themselves wearing a white lab coat and carrying a clipboard. We ask them to think of themselves as scientists, objective observers paying attention to facts and behavior in their families, not to how they feel at the moment.

We emphasize that this exercise is an experiment and it will last for perhaps a week. And we remind parents that these observations are not designed to cause everything to fall neatly and immediately into place. Family interaction will not be changed instantly for the better because of it. We just want them to look, to observe, as a first step toward a solution of the problem.

The idea is to figure out what works and what doesn't work in your relationship with your child. By taking a step back you can sometimes see the difficulty as a sequence of events: how it begins, what you typically do, what she does, and so forth. Then you can systematically alter the one variable you can control completely: how you respond. Eventually, you will find the response that gets the best results.

Social workers, teachers, ministers, doctors, probation workers, psychologists, and others in the helping professions who have become single adoptive parents sometimes fall into the trap of "therapeutic parenting," substituting professional skills for basic parent-child interaction. For example, when a child misbehaves, it might be more appropriate after you and he have talked it out and that hasn't worked just to send him to his room rather than to engage in a marathon conversation about his feelings. Talking it out at this point might do no more than distract from the issues at hand and give you a false sense that you had dealt with a difficulty.

A therapist friend of ours, a single adoptive parent, has a child who has a good cure for therapeutic parenting. This adolescent knows it when she hears it, and immediately responds: "Mommy, *stop* shrinking!"

Still another way of getting a handle on your difficulties with your child is to realize that there are always alternative explanations for why he is behaving in a certain way. For example, it might be tempting to describe as depressed a youngster who has been walking around with his head down, talking little, and staring out the window. But thinking of it as "depression" might suggest doctors and medication and a problem that could quickly get out of hand, demoralizing any parent. Depression usually involves symptoms such as disturbed sleep (too much or insomnia), lack of appetite, agitation, hopelessness, and helplessness. If that does not resemble what your child is experiencing, it might be more reasonable to describe his behavior in less threatening and paralyzing terms. For instance, he might be feeling blue, sad, or overwhelmed, something that the two of you or your child alone might deal with objectively or will run a natural, brief course and then improve.

In fact, adopted children are often confronting issues which sometimes cause them to be quiet, thoughtful, and sad. They need to be allowed to experience and master these feelings themselves. Redefining behavior may help to put things in perspective and get you back on the track of taking control of your life and acting effectively.

A lack of knowledge can also lead a parent to mistakenly interpret her child's behavior in ways that leave the parent feeling helpless. The executive who came to us not long ago with two adopted children who fought constantly "knew" that the incessant conflict resulted from her having adopted them from different birth families. The way she saw it, such adoption-based behavior was obviously out of control. But this mother happened to have been an only child, we pointed out, and didn't have experience with the usual battling of siblings. No longer viewing her children's behavior as pathological, she could ignore it or contend with it, as she chose. And when the children realized that their mother was not reacting to their fighting as she did before, they did less of it.

Don't automatically trust your first reactions to give you an accurate explanation for what you're experiencing or think you're experiencing when encountering a troublesome incident or pattern of behavior. That's particularly true if you think you've spotted pathological conduct. Check in a child-development book to see if you simply have missed a type of behavior found in many kids of your child's age. Ask friends and relatives to take a look and confirm or correct your perceptions. Consult with your child's teachers and guidance counselor. Only if these steps produce no satisfactory solution do you then need to turn to therapy for help.

HALF FULL OR HALF EMPTY?

Single adoptive parents may have more stress than other mothers and fathers resulting from responsibilities in their lives. That's why so many of them have developed the ability to see burdens, pressures, mishaps, and mistakes in the best light possible. For example, change is always stressful, and when that change involves the impending loss of a job, it can be absolutely terrifying. That's especially true for single adoptive parents like Mary Roberts, who did not have a second income in the family to see her and her child through a period of unemployment.

When we met Mary she was stunned by the prospect of being laid off and could hardly think straight. But after several conversations, another picture began to emerge—one of a woman who had been unhappy in her job for years, and who often found that her job frustrations affected the way she interacted with her daughter. We gradually helped Mary to focus less on the coming loss of her job and more on the opportunity that now presented itself: starting a new career. With the assistance of a loan she is now going to school to pursue an occupation that has her very excited: paralegal work.

Cathy Washington is another single adoptive parent we saw who turned something she regarded with dread into an opportunity. Cathy had an all-too-familiar dilemma: she had never told her now adolescent son that she had adopted him. Guilt at never feeling up to the task of telling him the truth, and the thought that he might no longer trust anything she said if she did tell him, was even now keeping her from breaking the news to him. Our task was to help her understand that she would feel enormous relief once she told him. This, indeed, could be seen as an opportunity to recast her relationship with her son based on frankness and honesty.

It wasn't easy, but eventually she decided to take that step. Now she can't believe she didn't do it sooner. Her son's reaction to his mother's revelation was typical of what many adoptees say when confronted with such information: "Big deal, I've known that for years."

It isn't always that easy. Some children do have a negative reaction for a while. For example, it would not be unusual for a child's grades at school to drop for a term or two while he comes to terms with his parent's disclosure. The disruptive effect of this new knowledge, though, can be eased by a mother or father who then works hard to rebuild the child's trust in his parent. In any case, enduring this temporarily difficult time is still preferable to keeping his adoption a secret.

Approaching life in a way that allows one to recognize small successes has allowed many adoptive parents to cope with serious complications more effectively and energetically. Sharon Jones raised an adopted child by herself that way. She adopted an older child who the agency had not been able to place. Although physically disabled, Billy, her adopted son, was so emotionally troubled that he was still capable of wrecking the house when upset. Sometimes, when things got that out of hand, she would even have to call a man in her adoptive parents' group who had volunteered to come over and hold Billy until he could get his feelings under control.

But Sharon could more often than not focus on the little signs of progress and Billy's accomplishments through all the troubles, such as his learning how to read and how to ride a bike. And she knew that it was only because of her caring that Billy was able to spend most of his time outside of institutions.

Sharon succeeded because she had realistic expectations; she knew Billy's limits and looked for small signs of progress. She knew what was possible for her son. By the time he was fifteen, Billy had calmed down enough for her to feel secure in adopting an infant. Besides giving her the satisfaction of raising a child from infancy who had no serious problems, the baby also brought out her older son's sense of responsibility, furthering his progress. Serving as an assistant caretaker, under Sharon's close supervision, did wonders for his self-esteem, enabling Billy to see himself as much more than just a kid with overwhelming problems.

Sharon is an unusual person; few people could or would take on the task of raising a child like Billy. But her approach to life can benefit any parent who has to cope with more than her share of burdens, particularly a single adoptive parent.

WHEN YOU DID NOT CHOOSE SINGLE PARENTHOOD

If you've become a single parent of an adopted child through death or divorce, adoption complications may demand much from you just when enormous stress may drain you of your customary energy and emotional resiliency. If your mate has died, you will need to comfort and reassure your child, while coping with your own feelings of loss. Every child finds this period difficult, but for your youngster this may be especially true. She has already lost one set of parents, and this most recent catastrophe may invoke fears and fantasies of separation.

However, you should realize that all parents have trouble comforting a child under these circumstances. Nor does the ache of such a loss ever absolutely disappear. One important thing you can do to minimize the trauma, though, is to make sure your child feels free to talk about his loss. Some kids think that they don't have the right to grieve as much as their surviving parent because they perceive their mother or father as having suffered a greater loss than theirs. Under the age of five or six, your child might even think that he had in some way caused the loss of his parent—perhaps by wishing him or her dead in a moment of anger. Younger children may also be excessively fearful of losing their surviving parent—not entirely irrational, since now they know it can happen. You might want to check *Books to Help Children with Separation and Loss* by Joanne Bernstein (R.R. Bowker) in the library for summaries of books for youngsters three to sixteen with a special category devoted to death of a parent.

It's hard to protect children from the tension in a marriage that is failing. Kids are very good at picking up the strains in a relationship, and the weakened marital bond is likely to make them feel anxious. But adoptive parents who finally realize that they do not wish to continue in their marriage need not feel guilty about the temporary disruption and emotional upheaval their children have already experienced. It will pass and their children will regain their equilibrium. Besides, once parents have decided to separate, they can make it a point to cooperate in anything involving their youngsters—no matter how much they disagree about everything else—thus minimizing the strain on their children.

Adoptive parents who divorce should do their utmost to separate with a minimum of strife. If possible, before you separate, try to plan how you and your spouse will handle matters concerning your children. Create a structure in which hostility related to other issues does not spill over into the area of child care. For example, you could agree in advance that when you speak on the phone about the children, that is the *only* legitimate subject of discussion. No matter what your feelings about each other may be, you should stay in contact, if only so your child can't play one of you off against the other. If you're having trouble with any of this, a counselor might be able to help. Remember that the first year following separation is usually the most difficult and things will get progressively easier as time progresses.

Cooperating with your former spouse in anything involving child rearing is crucial, though perhaps difficult, in minimizing the emotional toll the parting takes on your child. Still assimilating the information you have given him about his adoption, your child now has to come to terms with yet another missing parent. He will need to talk about this new state of affairs. How he discusses it and how you should respond will depend on his age and emotional development when you and your spouse parted.

Discuss your divorce with your child as you would his adoption, sympathizing with his sadness and giving him only as much information and explanation as he can absorb. Like adoption, it's a subject that you and he will be coming back to for more clarification as time goes by. Make it clear that he has done nothing to bring about the separation. Whenever he brings up the topic, be honest with him. Avoid giving him the impression that there's even the slightest chance you and your former spouse will reconcile, unless you have reason to think it will happen. Tell your child that both of his parents still love him, but that he will not be living with mommy and daddy together anymore because they just have too many differences. Don't withhold information he obviously wants, since that would compound the effect of his lack of knowledge about his birth, creating still less clarity and more secrets in his life.

You might want to point out other kids he knows, adopted or not, whose parents have divorced. Remind him that they were able to adapt to their new situation and that they are still loved by each parent. Reading together Jill Krementz's book *How It Feels When Parents Divorce* (Knopf) might be helpful. During the separation process, you can go far toward calming his fears by telling him how you and your spouse have arranged for him to see each of you, where he will live and when, where his toys will be, and which school he will attend.

Besides competently raising your child, you have an additional task as a single adoptive parent: leading your life as an adult—in whatever time you can grab from your daily responsibilities. But that, too, will affect your child. Perhaps you will once again become romantically involved with another adult. Your child may also form an emotional attachment to this person. If you are a single woman with an adopted child, this especially presents some potential problems. Your child's birth father is probably a peripheral, hazy figure to her. Other men moving in and out of your (and therefore her) life may cause her to relive fears of abandonment. You may appreciate the possibly temporary nature of these relationships, but she may not be able to absorb and deal with the emotional consequences of still more partings. As she grows older she may assume that men never stay in relationships.

It's not your fault that the facts of your new life could have this effect, but you do have to keep your child's perceptions in mind. While it's understandable that you might want your child to like the current man or woman in your life and that you would find it tempting to integrate that person into your family activities, we feel it's better to avoid it until the relationship has gotten to be both steady and reliable. Unfortunately, that may mean depriving yourself of that person's overnight company.

This is a particularly difficult situation for mothers of adolescent daughters. If she sees you having several relationships, she may ask why it's okay for you and off-limits for her. If she is an only child she may experience a blurring of the lines between herself and you and think herself more sophisticated than she actually is. A professional acquaintance of ours, a single adoptive parent through divorce, recently asked her sixteen-year-old how she would feel if her mother got involved with a man again. The teenager, a girl with a good sense of herself, said that she would probably not be ready for it and hoped it didn't happen until she was away at college.

If you're having any problems with divorce and custodial issues, we suggest that you contact your local branch of N.O.W., the National Organization for Women, or Parents Without Partners, for some practical advice about your particular situation.

Divorced fathers might also want to exercise similar discretion about having their children get to know the new women in their lives. Fathers who do not have custody of their children and see them only on weekends could confine their sleepover dates to weekday nights.

When death or divorce produces a single adoptive

parent, the pressure on the remaining or custodial care-giver to be a superparent can be overwhelming. If that parent is a male, he may suddenly have to learn "mothering" traits his parents never encouraged him to develop. But, male or female, if you have become a single adoptive parent in this way, you may occasionally think that you never would have adopted had you known you would have to do the job alone. Remember that birth parents, too, have such thoughts. There's no law that says you have to make up to your child for the absence of his other adoptive parent. Don't be too hard on yourself, and acknowledge that for at least quite a while it will be complicated for you and your child.

QUESTIONS AND ANSWERS

I'm a single adoptive parent and an attorney with the possibility of becoming a partner in my law firm. I didn't feel guilty when I left my infant in the care of my housekeeper, but now that my child is in his second year I feel like I'm missing some precious time with him when I come home late at night. How can I do justice to both my career and my child?

Instruct your housekeeper to encourage your child to nap early in the evening. Then wake him up at ten so you can spend some time together. Weekends should be split between time spent just enjoying him and time spent just for you with someone to take care of him. When your child gets older, try to coordinate your time off with his school vacations. People on the fast track often have a great deal of energy, so take advantage of this quality.

□

I have a feeling that my four-year-old is in a very unstimulating environment. She spends a lot of time watching soap operas with my housekeeper. What can I do to enrich my child's day?

You could put her in full-day day care or nursery school. Schools of nursing often have student nurses who babysit and enjoy playing with children. Or you could hire a college student to come in for a few hours a week to actively play with your child and to supplement your housekeeper's baby-sitting duties.

□

Since I became a single adoptive parent I rarely go out at night and I hardly get to see my friends anymore. It looks like I'm getting stuck in the isolation you warn about. How can I restore some of my social life without slighting my child's needs?

You do need adult company. It's necessary for your emotional health; if that suffers you'll surely be a less effective parent. Try meeting your friends for weekday lunches or breakfasts. These days, many people do much of their socializing at work. Perhaps you could make an effort to cultivate more friendships where you work. That would make it easier for you to squeeze a social life into your busy day.

□

In the Parents Without Partners group that I joined, I'm the only one whose child does not have a father. At the group's social gatherings, my child is uncomfortable when the other kids talk about their daddies. Is there anything I can do about this?

School-age kids have a need to see themselves as similar to other children. We have a feeling that if you look a little harder into the membership of your group you might turn up either a single adoptive parent or another single parent where there isn't a father around. Perhaps they are members but haven't been to the group's social functions lately. Your single adoptive parents' group is an excellent resource here as well. If there aren't any in your group, at least make sure that you get together with such parents and their kids outside the group so your child does have playmates who also have never known their fathers.

□

I'm a single adoptive parent. I was teasing my nine-year-old son the other day and my mother told me that she thought I was being too sarcastic, possibly hurting his feelings. I like to joke with him; it's an important part of our relationship. Now that I think about it, there are times when I'm not sure if he fully understands my jokes. How can I tell if my humor is going above my child's head?

First, take care that you don't let a little leftover anger from a quarrel slip into your humor. Sarcasm often cloaks such feelings. When you kid around with your child, remember that he's nowhere near as sophisticated as you are. Young children like humor that is broad, obvious, to the point. They also love word-play. This is their level: Why were one, two, three, four, five, and six afraid? Because seven ate nine.

□

I always wanted to have my own child, and it was exciting to find out that I could adopt as a single parent. But I'm a teacher and I have to deal with kids all day. I'm tired when I get home, and I have less patience for "kid stuff" than I would like to have. Is there any way out of this dilemma?

It sounds like you need an hour's break to decompress between the time you finish work and the time you start interacting with your child. Try hiring a baby-sitter for that hour so you can separate your work day from the evening.

□

I'm an adoptive father. I just don't seem to be able to handle work and child-rearing too since my wife died. How can I get some help with this enormous burden?

Single parents' organizations are always especially appreciative of new male members. These groups are good sources of support and advice for people in your position. You might also want to read *Who Will Raise the Children?* by James Levine. It's out of print, but your library may have a copy.

10
The Multiracial Family

When Ken and Sherie Barkley went to the airport to pick up Kim, the Korean baby they had worked so hard to adopt, they made sure that Ken's cousin and his wife, who would be the child's godparents, were right by their side with a video camera. To this day the Barkleys need little encouragement to haul out the two-hour tape and slip it into their VCR for a guest's edification.

Even without the recorded story, they would never forget a detail of that incredible afternoon—their arrival at the airport well before the plane was due, the seemingly interminable wait in the midst of other adoptive parents about to get their babies, and then, as the plane touched down, the woman from the agency commanding them: "Now you stop crying, every one of you, the children will be here in a minute!" And that heart-stopping moment when the door opened and eleven men and women paraded in, single-file, each carrying an infant to new parents and a new life. "Stop crying"? She might as well have ordered Niagara to stop flowing.

Of course, what seemed like a culmination was really a beginning—of a lot of work as well as of pleasure and fulfillment. Raising a child from another culture or race requires adoptive parents to be knowledgeable about and sensitive to the particular issues involved in such adoptions.

Particularly since the civil rights struggles of the 1960s, many Americans have become accustomed to taking pride in their ethnic and racial heritage. At our best we have come to celebrate our differences. But when those differences occur within a family, as they do in many adoptive families where there are children from other races or foreign countries, things get a bit complicated. Although some black and Asian families adopt children of other racial and ethnic backgrounds than their own, much of the transracial adoption that we know about concerns white families adopting children of color from either the U.S. or abroad. A number of interracial couples have adopted interracial children as well.

About 70 percent of the foreign children adopted by U.S. families are non-Caucasian, so there's a good chance that your family is likely to be multiracial if you have adopted at least one child from another country. Even if you don't bother to think of yourselves in that way any longer, others will.

If you have an adopted child of color in your family, whether she was born here or abroad, her road to adulthood will probably have a few more curves in it than the one traveled by other adoptees. Most obviously, she (and you and your other children) will have to deal with prejudice, racial as well as that concerned with adoption. That you can count on.

Prejudice that denigrates her background and geographical separation from her roots will add to your parental tasks. You will have to do what you can to make sure she grows up knowing *who* she is, culturally and racially, as well as confirming her identity as a member of your family.

YOUR MULTIRACIAL FAMILY

Multiracial families have one clear advantage over adoptive families in which parents and kids come from the same general background. In the family of mixed background, there can never be any doubts about whether to tell the child about his adoption. Indeed, the timing of the first discussion is built into the child's development. As soon as he's old enough to notice that he's different from you, or one of his playmates prompts him to notice that difference, you have to talk about it.

But multiracial families have to be prepared to be more than honest with their child; they also have to be ready, as much as possible, to stand in solidarity with him. You will have to be conscious about how society will treat him—and you, since you will encounter some discrimination as a result of being his parent. If you've never experienced discrimination before, this can be especially difficult.

The worst thing you could do in the face of this reality is to deny it, to fall back on platitudes about how we're all the same and therefore think that you have only to treat your nonwhite child as you would a white child and all will be well. Society will not let you do this and your child would suffer as a consequence if you tried. To a great extent, the success of your adoption depends on your absolute willingness to acknowledge the way your family differs from other families and how willing you are to accommodate yourselves to those differences.

A nonwhite child, understandably, will find it hard growing up in an all-white family in an all-white neighborhood going to an all-white school. Before you consider such an adoption you should live in an integrated area and have friends and a lifestyle which includes adults and children from your child's race or culture. Plan to be involved in an adoptive parents' group where your child can associate with other children and adults who look like her. Your adoption agency and adoptive parents' group would be good places to go for suggestions. OURS, 3307 Highway 100 North, Minneapolis, Minnesota 55422, is a good resource for parents of children from foreign countries. If you've adopted an American black child, the North American Council on Adoptable

Children, 1821 University Avenue, Suite S-275, St. Paul, Minnesota 55104, will recommend an adoptive parent group for you. Your local NAACP or Urban League have a number of appropriate activities. You might also want to read black-interest newspapers and magazines to find out about upcoming events that would appeal to your family.

If your family is multiracial, some tensions may arise within your family over the issue of color, and you might have to make an occasional diplomatic intervention. In one multiracial family the nonwhite son, developing a strong pride in his racial heritage, announced that he liked having dark-skinned biological parents because he thought that nonwhite people were better looking than white people. When his white sister objected, their mother tactfully interceded to suggest that her brother was entitled to his opinion and the matter was left at that. In fact, they were also pleased that he had developed a positive sense of himself.

The attitude of strangers will play an important role in your life. As part of a multiracial family, you've lost your anonymity. You'll know that the first time someone comes up to you at the supermarket and says of your child something like, "She's a little tan, isn't she?" Or you may hear what a woman we know heard when shopping with her whole family: "Your kid black? Is that your husband? He's not black." Strangers actually feel free to say things like that!

What's the best reply to such comments? Like responding to boorish remarks about adoption itself, it depends on your mood, temperament, and energy level. Again, humor can help, as long as the comments to which you're responding aren't consciously malicious. When Fred Wilkins brought his adopted black baby to work with him, strapped into the carrier on his back, a fellow worker walked over and asked, "Is that your son?" Fred said "Yes," and looked pleasantly at the other man, who was waiting for the next sentence of explanation that never came. For Fred it was pure pleasure—his sense of humor had an edge to it on this occasion—as the man stood there awkwardly for half a minute at a loss for words and finally turned and walked away.

One young interracial girl we know, adopted by a white family, developed a clever way to answer annoying questions about who was what in her family. If she's walking with her father, she says that her mother is black; when with her mother, she replies that her father is black; and if she's with her grandmother, she says that the other side of the family is black.

As a parent in a multiracial family, you will have to accept that the most innocent of your youngsters' adolescent activities could cause complications in your community. What if, for example, he asks a girl from another race to the senior prom? Should you try to protect him from what might result in a painful experience for him? Your best course of action would probably be no action, unless there were unpleasant consequences. Your child is old enough to make that decision for himself. Back off and let it happen. The possibility of complications in the community is why it is essential that you live in an area that is integrated with people who share your child's racial identity. The experience of being black in this country is largely one of unrelenting racial discrimination. A black youngster cannot grow up with a firm sense of his identity and pride in it without appropriate role models and without acceptance by his peers, an acceptance that is unlikely unless he lives in a neighborhood and attends a school with others of his racial background.

FOREIGN ADOPTIONS

Foreign adoptions began in earnest only in the 1950s with the war orphans from Korea. Children fathered by American soldiers with Korean women had a hard time of it in Korea. Religious groups and public figures such as the

;iter Pearl Buck, who founded Welcome House to bring ar orphans to this country, encouraged Americans to adopt these children. Similar efforts resulted in the adoption of some offspring of GIs and Vietnamese women in the 1960s and 1970s. Today Americans adopt about eight thousand foreign children annually from countries like Korea, El Salvador, the Philippines, India, Sri Lanka, Honduras, Guatemala, Mexico, and Colombia.

If you adopt a foreign child, be alert to any health problems your child might have brought with him that a pediatrician accustomed to treating only U.S.-born children might miss—tuberculosis, parasites, hepatitis, the effects of malnutrition, even leprosy, for example. For an excellent, detailed rundown of everything you should know about this subject, see Lois Melina's *Raising Adopted Children: A Manual for Adoptive Parents* (Harper & Row).

While your doctor will ultimately deal with any medical problems your child may have, ensuring that he grows up with a healthy sense of who he is culturally will be your job. We do not have a long tradition of American parents raising children from other cultures, so it is only in the past twenty years that books and articles on this kind of child rearing have begun to appear in substantial numbers.

Balance is an important factor in providing the right amount of connection between your child and the culture from which he comes. By all means expose him to his heritage even before he's old enough to express his own desires in the matter. Take him to museums which have exhibits on his birth culture, give him children's books that feature the customs of the country from which he came, attend religious services organized by people from the place where he was born or largely attended by them. Then, when he gets older, take your cues from him. Let him decide when enough is enough, but certainly make it possible for him to have friends who share his cultural background in your neighborhood and at his school.

If you push things too far, it will not encourage your son

or daughter to delve further into his or her roots. We have heard many comments from Korean-American adopted kids about being sick of having to go once again to a Korean restaurant instead of McDonald's, which they preferred. "Here go Mommy and Daddy again, being ethnic," is a typical reaction. Still, it's better to overdo it a bit than to not do it at all.

Sometimes parents who have adopted foreign children are so conscientious about maintaining their child's link to the culture she came from that they worry when the youngster seems to be losing touch with it. One mother of a five-year-old Korean child worried that after one year with her adoptive parents the girl had completely lost her ability to speak Korean. But this is common, probably the result of the child not having any opportunity to use her native tongue. She could relearn it in the future, if it became important to her.

Nor should parents worry if a younger child doesn't even realize that there is an important difference between herself and them. For example, a three-year-old may not appreciate that difference. She might need another year or two before she reaches the stage in her development where visible differences take on that much significance for her.

On the other hand, try not to overreact to comments your child makes comparing the way she looks to your appearance. One child we saw told her parents that she wished they were the same color as she was. Initially they were concerned that their child was unhappy in their multiracial family. But when they listened more carefully to what their child was saying, they realized that she was referring to the annoyance of always having to explain that she was adopted. She had no problem with her racial identity; indeed, her comment showed that she had a healthy racial pride. It was an adoption, not a racial complication they were dealing with.

Association with adults who are of his background is important for the child adopted from a foreign country. So make an effort to provide him with opportunities to make such connections. Buddhist temples, Korean churches, benevolent associations, and other cultural and fraternal groups bringing together people from your child's culture are good places for you to ask about activities in which you could meet people from the relevant country.

Prejudice, while perhaps not as large an element to contend with as in the raising of a black child, is always in the background in the lives of these kids. Realistically and painfully, it could begin at home. Did you adopt your child as an infant? Perhaps you didn't think much about what your youngster would look like once he got older. His darker skin tone and deepening ethnic features may really make him look foreign now. Adoptions that don't work are those in which white parents adopted mixed-race children when they really only wanted to adopt white children but couldn't because white children were in short supply. If the only part of your child that you like is the white part, it is unlikely that you will be able to provide a healthy environment for that child to grow in. In a society such as ours, where racism is basic to the experience of people of color, returning to a family in which you are accepted and loved is essential if one is to survive the cruelty of the outside world. Is this possible if a child's parents do not love the most descriptive and visible part of her? It is essential that you work to resolve this issue for your child's mental health and stability through every single method available to you.

None of us is totally without prejudice. If you're raising a child from another culture you have to work diligently to be conscious of any such feelings, especially if you're a white person raising a black child. That doesn't mean you should allow yourself to become paralyzed with guilt if you have a stray thought along these lines. But anything more than that would suggest that you need to work on this immediately, to talk it over with a mate, friend, or therapist.

Sometimes a cultural misunderstanding can get blown up all out of proportion—still another reason you should make a major effort to learn about and understand the customs prevalent in the country from which you got your child. The Albertsons, for example, were in a quandary about what to do about their Korean son, adopted at the age of ten, who insisted on harshly bossing around his younger sister, who was born to the Albertsons after they adopted their son. Understandably, the girl was furious at this practice and relations between the siblings were becoming increasingly strained.

Fortunately, their mother and father had the good sense to ask a Korean adult they knew about what might be causing this clash. He explained that in Korea parents expect the eldest son to act as a parental child, and his siblings to defer to him. The boy is not a true authority figure, so he has to impose his will. Since that would not work in an American family, the parents now knew what they had to do: negotiate with their son to provide him with a role that made both him and his sister comfortable. They pointed out that in their family he didn't have to have the responsibility of parenting his sister. They told him that his sister would respect and look up to her older brother. He could be protective of her, but he also had to respect her rights.

To encounter images that might make her feel uncomfortable about her background, your foreign-born child may not have to do anything more than turn on the television. An eight-year-old from Colombia was watching a program with her adoptive parents when they noticed that she had grown increasingly silent. Finally, obviously holding back tears, she got up, went to her room, and slammed the door shut.

The program they had been watching was a special about the smuggling of cocaine from Latin America into this country. It showed people resembling their daughter being arrested for participating in a drug ring that netted millions of dollars. Later, when she was in a mood to talk, her parents explained to her that only a small percentage of people from her country were involved in the activity. They also pointed out that cocaine was a cash crop in Colombia—that only source of income and survival for many poor people.

Your adoptee could face a difficult time at school, depending on where you live, possibly requiring your intervention. When Harriet Carson's Native American adopted son had to listen to his teacher describe Custer's Last Stand as simply a massacre of American soldiers by "savages," she went to his school and had a long talk with the teacher, citing books—two of which she brought along—that portrayed the incident in a considerably more objective and complex way.

For a child adopted from abroad, searching for a birth parent is problematic at best. Enrique, born in the Philippines, is a teenager who talks of wanting to find his birth mother and speak to her at least once before she dies. He came to this country as an adoptee at the age of three. He knows the general area of the Philippines from which he came, but can't narrow it down any more than that. He does not understand or speak the language spoken there, so he would need an interpreter if he went through with a search.

The chances are slim that he would find what he was looking for, and the search would be much more expensive than that carried out by a native-born adoptee in this country. But nothing is impossible. For example, there's always the chance that somebody in the orphanage that took him in might remember which village he came from.

TRANSRACIAL ADOPTION OF BLACK AMERICAN CHILDREN

Much of what we have said so far about transracial adoption applies to the adoption of all nonwhite children. But the history of oppression and discrimination that black Americans have had to endure requires that white parents adopting a black American child must make sustained efforts to understand what their child may come up against outside the home.

For example, your child will develop a sixth sense about prejudice that you may have to be consciously attentive to in order to pick up. Among things she is likely to notice: disparaging looks from whites when your family walks by, slow and begrudging service from waiters and store clerks, and comments from teachers in which racism lies between the lines. Other people of color may have similar experiences—but these things are likely to happen more often and in a more mean-spirited manner to black Americans.

Black and interracial families adopt at a higher rate than any other groups in our population. These days, all other things being equal, agencies try to place black children with black families. But there are now about thirty-eight thousand black adoptable children—more than minority families can adopt. If they are not to grow up in institutions, many of these children will have to be adopted by white families.

Some people fear that children of one race raised by parents of another race will be psychologically damaged. However, effective parenting of nonwhite kids by white mothers and fathers who realize that they are now a nonwhite family has been shown by several studies to produce psychologically healthy children.

In a study of three hundred Midwestern multiracial families in which white parents had adopted black children, Rita Simon and Howard Alstein reported that the kids, most of them now teenagers or adults already living on their own, felt close ties to their families. Race was often a complication in their upbringing, but usually concerning the outside world, not within their families. Their parents were equally pleased with their experience, and 84 percent of them recommended transracial adoptions.

The children in the study fared as well as other adopted kids. They loved their families, felt loved, and were normal, happy youngsters by any objective measure used by the researchers. They had little problem with racial identification, although the youngsters who appeared white were more likely to identify themselves as white. The parents of these adoptees had raised their children to feel positive and comfortable about themselves.

However, we would not want to underplay the complications involved. Early on your family will have to work out strategies with which you are all comfortable for dealing with prejudice. For instance, even as a young child, as soon as she steps out of the house, your black adoptee could encounter a prejudicial remark from a neighbor's kid. What should you do about this? What if someone pejoratively refers to her as an "oreo"?

We suggest that in such incidents you avoid immediately launching into a lecture to your child about "the way things should be," which many well-meaning people are prone to do. Nor is it a good idea to let your anger eclipse hers. Rather, listen to her and tell her you understand how sad and angry racism makes her feel.

This same low-key approach might also prove useful any time you have to deal directly with possible insensitivity by other kids. For example, Joanne Carter found it helpful one Halloween when she noticed a neighbor's child leaving his house wearing a trick-or-treat costume that included blackface. Not wanting her four-year-old black adopted daughter to have to see her appearance mocked, Joanne took the neighbor's child aside and told him that such a costume would make her feel very sad and would hurt her daughter's feelings. However, she made it clear that she knew that the boy did not mean to do any harm. He took her reaction in the spirit in which she offered it. When he later rang the bell asking for a treat, he was dressed as a goblin.

As he gets older, discrimination directed against your son may take different forms. For example, your child may discover that storekeepers keep a special watch on him when he shops. Some proprietors may refuse to permit a black male to enter their stores, especially at Christmastime. If this happens, he will probably want to talk to you about it. If you want his love and respect, you must be there with empathy and a knowledge of what he faces.

Because of this phenomenon, Mark and Laura Walker put their black adopted son through a regimen whenever he wanted to go downtown to shop for clothes with his white friends. "Do you think you're dressed neatly enough?" his mother would remind him, trying to anticipate the reaction of the storekeepers and department store security people. "Is your hair combed?" she challenged him before he could get out the door. "Aw, Ma, I look just like the other guys!" "No you don't," his mother replied with a trace of a wry grin. He hated the routine; she knew it was unjust and she hated it too. But it was for his own protection, so they went through it.

As with a nonwhite child adopted from a foreign country, your child needs to take pride in her blackness, so you will have to take steps to help her connect with her heritage. Take an interest in black affairs, and discuss them with her when she's old enough to talk about them herself. Also make sure that your youngster has regular contact with children like herself and adult role models of her own race. Make an effort to find black physicians and dentists. If you send your child to camp, be sure it's an integrated one—your black friends and black church groups can probably advise you where to find one.

School could be a series of traps for your child. Overt prejudice aside, you and your youngster may have to contend with the distorted expectations of some teachers and administrators about your child's potential and the significance of any problems he happens to have in his school career. When Nan Miller's black adopted son was a little slow to read, his teacher called in his mother to voice some strong fears about his ability to do the rest of the work coming up in that grade. Nan could hear the unspoken words between the lines: "He is a black child, you know." As a practical strategy, to head off debilitating labels like *slow learner* that the school might be applying to her son before long, Nan took matters into her own hands. She taught her son to read herself. Almost overnight, his teachers' expectations for him shot up.

Even when other students, teachers, and administrators consciously make an effort to be fair to your youngster, they may give her a hard time. For example, if you have the only nonwhite student in town, your child may be made to feel like the school's official person of color. She could be constantly called on to tell what it's like to come from a different racial background and talk about discrimination and tolerance. The office of class president might even be thrust upon her as a matter of course by her well-meaning classmates.

The process of applying for college could turn up some stumbling blocks. Sandy Drummond, a teacher in a large Midwestern city, paid a visit to the guidance counselor at the Quaker school her adopted son attended to see why she had been discouraging the youngster from applying to black colleges. The guidance counselor told her that only one of their students from the previous year had opted for a black school. Then this "professional," naming the student, told Sandy that the girl just dated and partied—implying that this is what black colleges were about.

Private schools and colleges may want your child not so much for her particular talents as for her ability to help them meet quotas. A nonwhite student with middle-class sensibilities may be a hot commodity for them. But will it be an equal bargain? Will they provide her with nonwhite personnel sensitive to her own and other such students' needs? How many members of the faculty are nonwhite? That's something you'll have to investigate carefully if she applies to one of these schools.

QUESTIONS AND ANSWERS

It seems that nobody is talking anymore about white parents adopting black children. I also can find virtually nothing written on the subject. What's going on? I'm beginning to feel as if I don't exist, and our black daughter has also asked about this silence.

What you have noticed is a result of political differences among people who work in this field. Organizations such as the Association of Black Social Workers have taken positions against transracial adoption. Many child-welfare agencies have supported them, although they continue to place black kids in white homes. Despite the large percentage of black families who have adopted, there aren't enough of them to take in all adoptable black children. Tell your child about this; and tell her about the results of the study by Simon and Alstein, discussed in this chapter. Also tell her that you feel that you did the right thing, but that you'll always be willing to discuss the subject with her. Try to reconnect with your old adoptive parents' group to plan a reunion.

□

We don't live in an integrated neighborhood. The other day my neighbor, who has been acting very unfriendly since we adopted our black son, called him a "nigger." What should we do?

Tell your neighbor just how unacceptable you find that kind of language, but don't expect to change the mind of somebody who would talk to a child like that. You can also use this ugly incident as an opportunity to work with your child on ways that he and you can confront the prejudice that your family is likely to encounter. As we have made clear, we believe that it is essential to live in an integrated community so that your youngster has an opportunity to have friends of his background and so there will be adults who are black, as well. It is less likely that your neighbor would have used such language against your child if you lived in a racially mixed neighborhood. A move to a more integrated neighborhood is worth considering, not so much as a response to this one incident, but as a means of providing a more comfortable environment for your whole family. Think of the message you are giving to your child if you choose not to live with people of his racial background.

□

We know that our adopted son's birth father was black and his birth mother was white and Irish-American. Should we be telling our child about his Irish heritage?

Definitely—it's part of who he is. However, the reason you should give greater emphasis to his black heritage is that society will respond to him as a visibly black person and he needs to take particular pride in that identity.

□

We are a white couple who have adopted a black child and we want to move into an integrated neighborhood. What's the best way of finding a house in such an area?

Your local chapter of the Urban League should be able to put you in touch with a black real estate broker who can help you out.

□

I was supposed to meet my son at the toy department of our city's largest department store for a little Christmas shopping. When he was more than half an hour late I went outside the store to look for him and discovered that they did not let black children in unescorted to shop at this time of the year. They claim that black children have a very high theft rate. I was furious at the store's management, but I didn't know what to do about it.

Black people must constantly deal with such slights. We suggest that you talk to a black friend who has a child your son's age to see how he or she would handle this situation. If you don't have black friends, we strongly suggest that you cultivate some. Studies show that black youngsters adopted by whites form the most secure and healthy racial identities when their family's network of friends is integrated.

□

My nine-year-old Korean daughter is an average student but her teacher expects more from her because all of the other Asian-American kids in her class do so well. However, my husband and I are satisfied with our child's progress and we don't want to burden her with unnecessary pressure. What's the best way to handle this?

The best way is the direct way. Tell the teacher that you're pleased with your child's work. As long as she seems to be doing her best you would not want her pushed to achieve levels that might simply be beyond her reach.

□

We have adopted a child who saw horrible events in her native Cambodia, including the murder of her parents. She's wonderful and I'm amazed at how she has progressed at school. But the depth of her tragedy is so obviously with her. I would like to lighten her emotional burden, but I just don't know how. Can you help?

She's not likely to ever completely get over such a trauma. However, because of the nurturing environment you give her she can be a stronger person when something reminds her of those terrible times. As it becomes more a part of her past, it will not have quite as powerful a grip on her as it has now. But, sadly, it will never disappear.

□

My husband has been offered an excellent job in a part of the country where we think our adopted Indian daughter might encounter prejudice. Do you have any suggestions?

NACAC and OURS (see appendix for addresses) can put you in touch with people in that state who can identify the best areas—if they exist—where your family could live.

□

The kids in my Korean son's class have just learned about World War II and they have started to call him a "dirty Jap." What's the best way to put a quick stop to this?

If you child's teacher hasn't picked this up and adjusted her teaching to deal with it, you should speak to her or her superiors about doing it. These kids need not only a lesson about ethnic stereotypes, but also one about differentiating between the various peoples of Asia.

□

We live in a white town. Our dark-skinned Colombian daughter was not asked to her high school prom and she is just devastated. How can we console her?

Tell her you understand how hard it is for her not to be included. Help her to understand how racial prejudice is involved in this issue and that it does not reflect on her personality. If she lived with more people who were similar to her she may not have had this experience. Although it won't make up for it, do something special with her—perhaps a dinner in a nice restaurant—as at least a partial compensation. To minimize the chance of this sort of thing happening as she gets older, start thinking now about helping her to choose a college that has a sizable number of minority students on campus. Many college guidebooks now give for each school the percentage of students who are nonwhite or from foreign countries.

11
Emerging Trends

How much is the family bending under the pressures of the outside world? Where is this venerable institution heading now? *Time* and *Newsweek* seem to ask these questions every few months. Their editors know that we never seem to tire of reading accounts and analyses of the changing relationships between mother, father, and child.

As adoptive parents, you know, perhaps better than your nonadoptive peers, how much the family has borne the weight of change in our society. Originally, you may have adopted because it was the only way you could become parents, giving little thought to the social significance of such a decision. But in doing so society's evolving attitude toward unwed parenthood has become part of your and your child's lives. If you have adopted a special-needs child, you must have been struck by the realities of dealing with one of the possible consequences of poverty—a family's inability to care for their child. Adopting a child who is a member of a racial minority in this country would have brought home to you the meaning of prejudice. And single adoptive parents have pioneered in our shifting notion of what constitutes a family in the first place.

Today, within the community of adoptive parents, there are mothers and fathers who have gone even farther out on the frontiers of expanding family possibilities. Some are creating new family forms and traditions through open adoption. Others are offering a more traditional family setting for children with devastating, even terminal, conditions and diseases. Few would have even considered these children adoptable until very recently. These pioneering adoptive parents have little to guide them; as a result some may need considerable amounts of support. They have succeeded in providing love and nurturance, if only briefly, in a human and personal way, with no expectations.

While our evaluation of these trends and suggestions to participants in them must still be tentative, it's worth noting that there is little happening now in adoption that is entirely new. These trends are variations on and extensions of the kinds of adoptive parenthood we have already discussed—with a few extra complications.

OPEN ADOPTION: A REEMERGING TREND

The couple who had arranged to adopt Patty's baby through a private placement had promised to have their lawyer help the young pregnant woman get counseling before the birth. When Patty came to us, she was near term. During a session, she asked that we meet the people who would bring up her baby. While we had not planned to do this, it seemed to be a reasonable request, and we agreed.

Our conversation with the prospective adoptive mother was particularly poignant. Since she had met the woman whose baby she and her husband would raise, she felt sadness as well as joy at the prospects of becoming a parent. She realized fully that someone was losing something precious in order for her to get a child.

There is much to be said for giving information about birth parents to adoptive parents—or even having the two meet—when a child is placed. Besides providing adoptive parents with important medical information about their child's birth family, and reassuring birth parents that their baby is going to a good home, it may also be more psychologically satisfying for all concerned. The birth parents have a better chance of working through their feelings about having to place their child with other people. The adoptive parents, because they know the identity of the birth mother, will not have to deal with fantasies that someday a stranger will knock on their door demanding the return of her child.

Over the past ten or fifteen years, many professionals in the adoption field have made the point that secrecy is harmful. They urge not a new way of handling adoptions, but rather a return to an old one. Only since 1940 have states kept adoption records closed to protect the privacy of birth parents. Since both birth and adoptive parents have been increasingly urging the opening of these records—not to mention adoptees wishing to search for their birth parents—closed records appears to be an experiment that has not succeeded.

In several ways we appear to be moving away from closed-records adoptions. In most agency adoptions foster parents know about their child's biological family. Evolving state laws regulate private adoptions. This is done to prevent lawyers and others from running a black market in babies. These laws require that babies be placed from birth parents to adoptive parents, with the lawyer serving only to facilitate the process. The adoptive parents receive biographical information from the birth parents, who in turn get to choose who will adopt their baby—sometimes from among several couples. In some private adoptions, birth and adoptive families meet.

One of the oldest adoption agencies in the United States, Spence-Chapin in New York City, has recently begun a program in which birth mothers may choose their baby's adoptive parents. Agencies placing children from foreign countries sometimes stipulate that adoptive parents must agree to continually send photographs and updated information about their child back to their youngster's biological family.

On the broad and developing continuum of open adoption, one of the most open varieties has developed in California. In that state, some birth mothers wanted to remain in contact with the children they surrendered for adoption. Enough adoptive parents seem to have either liked the idea, too, or at least felt they could handle it. Subsequently, they were willing to allow the birth mothers something even more wide-ranging than visitation rights when they negotiated the terms of the adoption. Neither state bureaucracies nor private agencies handed down any of this. It developed to meet a need on the part of the people involved.

When Californians first began working out open adoptions a few years ago, they ran into a few problems. How could an adoptive family guarantee a birth mother access to the child when they could not anticipate what the future would bring? For example, what if they wanted to move out of state? Or how could they justify acknowledgement of the birth mother's interest in staying in touch with the adoptive family in the light of the family's need for privacy? What if the two parties to the agreement later differed on how to interpret their agreement? What if the adoptive family felt that the birth mother was trying to set herself up as a coparent?

Sharon Kaplan often hears these questions. A social worker for almost thirty years, and herself an adoptive parent, she has been at the forefront of the open-adoption movement through the private California adoption services group she founded, Parenting Resources for Growth and Development. Her organization counsels people involved in all types of adoptions, but has gained a reputation for particular expertise in open adoptions. In fact, they have trademarked their term for this process, *Cooperative Adoption,*™ which Sharon Kaplan defines as giving the child access to both families over time. The emphasis, she says, is on cutting children's losses whenever possible and shifting the emphasis from adult needs such as infertility problems to the child's needs and rights.

Kaplan says that those interested in participating in open

adoptions are most likely to succeed if they are trusting by nature, have faith in themselves and a good sense of humor. They should also be self-confident. The ability to negotiate relationships, communicate, and problem-solve are other crucial skills for these parents. These are all teachable.

Adoptees, many feel, gain much from open adoption. Secrecy is difficult for any child to cope with, but especially for an adoptee. Open adoption, by its very nature, banishes the most basic of adoptive family secrets. There are no skeletons in the closet; indeed, there is no closet. These children know who they are and where they came from.

Some speculate that kids raised through this process will have less sense of rejection than do other adopted children. Since they are brought up in this arrangement, it appears to be the most natural thing in the world to them. They might even be less vulnerable to teasing or malicious remarks about their lineage than are other adopted kids. Yes, they have more than one set of parents, but they seem to be comfortable with the notion, which has always been in the open. Besides, given the incidence of divorce in our society, having multiple sets of parents is no longer enough to make them unique.

What kind of relationship develops between the birth mother and the child she places for adoption? While it varies in each case, typically, it seems to resemble one between a child and an aunt or uncle or friend of the family. The adoptee is likely to call his birth mother by her first name and eventually refer to her as "the woman who gave birth to me." There's a good chance that he will not be confused about his relationship to any of the adults on his family tree and will be able to describe each relationship, even when asked to do so at an early age.

The birth mother also seems to gain through open adoption. Some birth fathers also have been more involved in this practice than in traditional adoptions and seem satisfied too. The birth mother often establishes a close relationship with the adoptive parents before she gives birth, which gives her an in-depth look at the people who will raise her child. At the hospital, soon after the baby is born, but not before she has had a chance to spend some time alone with the infant, she gives the child to his new parents in a "handing over" ceremony. This ritual is often recorded on film or videotape. Then, according to observers, for the next few weeks or months, she goes through a grieving process, *not* for the loss of her baby, but for the mothering role she will never have with the child. Counseling, at this point, is very important.

The birth mother stays in touch with the adoptive parents, receiving photographs of her birth child as the youngster grows. She may visit the child regularly, call, or write. The first year and a half or so usually marks the closest period of this relationship. Then, often, the birth mother works through her feelings about her decision and is likely to pull away to some degree from the adoptive family. Now, she is able to proceed with her life, "not feeling like a victim and much more assertive and able to plan her future," as Sharon Kaplan has observed. Four or five years later she may reconnect with the adoptive family, seeing them at holidays or on the child's birthday.

For adoptive parents, open adoption offers the absence of the tension that others sometimes experience when there is a veil of secrecy over the identity of their child's birth parents. There are no worries about what an older child might find if she decided to search for her birth parents. We've even heard stories of adoptive parents who are comfortable with the arrangement and get some unanticipated baby-sitters in the bargain: the birth grandparents.

There are some potential drawbacks to open adoption. For example, parents, birth and adoptive, who have participated in open adoption may experience powerful, turbulent emotions surrounding the issue, feelings that call for some counseling or brief therapy to handle adequately. In one therapy group for birth and adoptive mothers, Mother's Day brought out some of these feelings. Adoptive mothers openly spoke of their jealous feelings toward the birth mothers who were able to give birth to the child; birth mothers also freely admitted their envy of the adoptive mothers who could raise them.

Some professionals in the field suggest that open adoption could interfere with adoptive parents' "claiming" their child as their own. Anyone who enters into an open adoption should be very conscious to avoid the notion that this is some kind of coparenting. One needs to remember always who is the child's legal guardian, who is the only one to make final decisions on how to raise her.

The obligation to uphold the agreement with the birth parent under open adoption is ethical rather than legal, so adoptive parents must carefully consider how far they are willing and able to go to accommodate a birth mother's wishes before agreeing to this arrangement. Of course, you are most likely to stick to an agreement that you take great pains to plan, and living up to such an agreement will ultimately be in the best interests of everyone involved.

LEGAL-RISK ADOPTION

The desire to adopt young children has lately been causing many adoptive parents to take extra risks. For children, placement in a foster home rather than in an institution has traditionally been a tradeoff: never knowing how long it will last, whether this is the final stop or if there will be yet further moves. Now some prospective adoptive parents are choosing to have children placed in their homes before the birth parents have relinquished their parental rights to the child. Agencies placing these kids do so in the belief that the birth parents will eventually surrender these rights or have them taken away by the courts, but it's not a sure thing. These adoptive parents are willing to take the risk that they could lose the child if parental rights are not terminated. Though it's a risky business, many satisfied adoptive parents have adopted in this way and are glad they did.

If you have a child enter your home under these circumstances, you are technically classified as a foster parent. Should you plan to do this, carefully consider whether you can live for perhaps as long as four years with the knowledge that you might have to surrender your child to the birth parent. It does happen, as witnessed by the occasional heart-rending stories on the evening news of preadoptive parents kissing their child goodbye for the last time.

Parents who take this route should look for an agency that seems to have their interests in mind as well as the child's. While the agency will provide an attorney to handle the termination of parental rights, it's a good idea, in addition, to have your own lawyer, to protect your rights to the utmost.

Your lawyer should make sure that the agency makes a diligent effort to provide the birth mother with opportunities to seek rehabilitation and thus become eligible to regain custody of her child. If the agency does not do this, the birth parent might later sue to regain custody on the basis of not having been given a sufficient chance to rehabilitate herself. If you can't afford a lawyer, consult your local Legal Aid Society to see what constitutes a diligent effort. For more information on this subject, inquire at your adoptive parent group or at the Legal Aid Society.

FRAGILE BABIES

Adoptive parents are some of the most highly motivated and dedicated mothers and fathers we have met. Some of them take kids whose birth mother's substance abuse makes their children's prospects for leading a normal life questionable; others adopt and give a loving home to children with terminal illnesses.

In America today, there are an increasing number of

babies who are paying a tragic price for their birth parents' use of crack, speed, angel dust, heroin, and methadone. These children have low birth weights, suffer damage to their central nervous systems, and may not respond well to physical affection. It's often hard to know how to comfort them, which can be confusing and frustrating. Kids afflicted with fetal alcohol syndrome, as a result of their mother's alcohol abuse during pregnancy, are likely to have some serious physical and intellectual disabilities. If you adopt one of these children, you will have to devote much time to her medical care and to intellectually stimulating her. Many hospitals have programs to help you with this task.

You can probably assume that your child has sustained some neurological damage, although he or she might eventually function quite well. The bottom line is that you can't depend on it. However, be cautious about interpreting any studies you see regarding these children. The conclusions of such research generally do not take into account the effects of a warm, nurturing environment on the child's capacities. Such studies are surely needed and will, we hope, eventually be available.

Parents who adopt babies with AIDS or infants who test positive for the AIDS virus may face even more prejudice than they had counted on. Our lack of hard facts about exactly how and under what conditions this disease may be spread has contributed to public fears, and some families have been ostracized. Try to be as honest with yourself as you can be if you are contemplating such an adoption. Can you stand up to the stress to which other people may subject you?

A baby who tests positive for AIDS at birth will not necessarily get the disease. It could be as much as eighteen months before you will know. So adopting such a baby means living with a terrible uncertainty about the infant's prospects. If he does get AIDS, your child will need almost twenty-four-hour attention; he could be killed by common infections that would make other children sick for just a few days, and you will have to stand by while he's subjected to frequent and painful medical tests. And he will die while still very young.

To help you cope with your emotions surrounding death and dying and with the medical procedures necessary for managing the disease, you will probably need counseling. A hospice could be a good source of referrals for this kind of help.

GAY ADOPTIVE PARENTS

Gay men and women have been in the forefront of those offering to adopt children with AIDS, but as far as we can tell society is making it no easier for them to do this than to adopt healthy children. Prejudice against gays is just as pervasive among people empowered to place children for adoption as among the rest of the population. They express fears about the child's sexual development and the possibility that he might be sexually abused by a parent. Studies showing these fears to be unfounded—that gay parents are no more child abusers than are heterosexual mothers and fathers—have done little to change attitudes.

If you are gay and wish to become an adoptive parent, you will have to decide if it's more important to you to make a political statement, doing everything openly, or to take the steps needed to fulfill your practical need to become a parent. Some agencies are less prying than others. To identify them, ask within the gay community. We understand, however, that gay adoptive parents have had the most success going through private adoption. We also hear that they find gay parents' groups and single adoptive parents' groups good sources of support.

QUESTIONS AND ANSWERS

I'm an adoptive mother who knew the birth mother of my child for the last two months of her pregnancy. No matter how much I try not to feel this way, I still think of my baby as belonging to her birth mother, not me. Am I likely ever to feel differently?

The emotional transition from a prospective adoptive parent to the mother of a child takes time. You didn't have the experience of pregnancy and childbirth to help you adjust to the change in your identity. However, we can reassure you that caring for your child over time, while not the same thing as carrying her in your womb, will ultimately serve the same function: establishing close emotional ties between you and your infant.

□

I've heard that some adoptees view themselves as "the chosen baby" and therefore feel compelled to excel. My agency gives birth mothers biographies of prospective parents, from which we were picked by the birth mother of our child. I think I feel something like a "chosen parent," with similar pressure to achieve perfection. Does this make sense to you?

Not only do some adoptees feel this way, first children or grandchildren often feel it too. You may well be experiencing the same phenomenon. Assuming that it hasn't restricted your ability to parent—in which case you might want to discuss it with a family therapist—we would just suggest that you try to remain aware of your feelings. Acknowledging these feelings, perhaps out loud to your spouse or a friend, should keep them from becoming disruptive.

□

Our adopted son is two years old. We have a specific agreement with his birth mother that she can call monthly; but she's been calling more frequently, seemingly whenever she feels like it. We experience this as an invasion of our privacy and we fear it will increasingly get out of hand as time goes on. What should we do?

It's important to remember that you are the legal guardians of your child. If it came down to it, you could unilaterally break off contact with his birth mother, although it's preferable to resolve this problem short of that step. First talk to the birth mother and try to settle what may just be a misunderstanding or differences in your sense of time. If that doesn't work, try having the agency mediate your dispute, or go together for counseling.

□

The birth mother of our child, with whom we have stayed in touch, has gotten pregnant again. We feel that it's important for our child to remain close to his birth sibling, but we're just not ready to adopt again. How does one deal with this?

You shouldn't feel compelled to take yet another of her children. But perhaps you can arrange to establish some kind of ties to the family who does adopt this child, thus keeping your child close to his sibling.

□

We are adopting privately and we've already had some contact with the birth mother. However, we do not want to continue any kind of relationship with her after the child is placed with us. We're a little concerned because she knows what we look like and she will be going to school on a campus near where we live. What should we do if she happens to come across us and wishes to stay in touch?

The encounter you fear is not likely to happen, and there's no point letting the thought of it occurring frighten you. If it ever happens, you'll handle it then. If you find yourself continuing to think about it, remind yourself that you're the legal guardian of your child, with ultimate control over who has access to your youngster.

□

Our six-month-old baby's birth mother was a cocaine addict. We are, indeed, frequently unable to comfort the child. Nevertheless we love him and we want to do absolutely everything we can for him. We've gone from doctor to doctor but none of them has helped much. Is there anything we're overlooking?

We still don't know as much as we need to know about babies with this condition. We suggest that you build a relationship with a major medical center affiliated with a university—travelling to it periodically if it isn't nearby—so that they can track your child's progress. This will enable your child to benefit from the latest research findings and treatments. Current studies of these babies underway now appear to indicate neurological difficulties and perhaps even visual problems requiring sophisticated medical diagnosis.

Epilogue: Therapy

Throughout this book we have periodically dealt with the use of therapy as a resource to help with some of the complications of family life, whether they are directly related to adoption or not. We emphasize that we do not recommend therapy for any adopted child or adoptive parents as a matter of course, only when a situation presents difficulties that need working out. Adoptive families and their children have no inherent pathology that needs to be "cured." On the contrary, we have observed that adoptive parents are among the most involved and motivated parents we've seen. So, as the saying goes, "If it ain't broke, don't fix it."

Should difficulties arise in your family, first try changing the way you've been dealing with whatever is giving you trouble. See what happens when you do something different, and then use what you observe to alter your approach. For example, suppose your child has been cursing and your telling him why you find it offensive hasn't stopped the practice. Instead of appearing shocked, thus letting him get to you, you could try a variety of sanctions. Perhaps writing out the profanity one hundred times will stop him. Or you could fine him, as they do in professional sports for rules infractions—a boy would understand that idea. When you hit upon something that works, try using it for other problematic behavior.

If you can't find something that works, ask friends, relatives, and others close to you and knowledgeable about your family or the difficulty involved for their opinion. The members of adoptive parents' groups are also good sources of experience-based knowledge and counsel when things aren't working the way they should. Ideally, speak to parents with an adopted child temperamentally similar to yours but a few years older. That family may have recently dealt successfully with the very complication that now confronts you. Your child's school guidance counselor is another person to consult if you haven't found a solution yet. And if these steps have not led to a resolution you probably should consider therapy.

As we've pointed out, adoption takes place within a family system. The kind of therapy that makes sense to us in dealing with adoption complications, therefore, is one that acknowledges that adoption affects everyone in the family and problems with any family member affect everyone else in the family to a greater or lesser degree. Systemic, or family, therapy—a usually brief, problem-solving process—recognizes this. Interaction patterns between mothers, fathers, and children can be analyzed and seen as related to the difficulties that arise within the family. Family therapists reject the notion that something inside the adoptee—in his psyche—makes him inherently troubled and therefore the sole proper focus of healing efforts.

The American Association for Marriage and Family Therapists can refer you to a professional in your area who works with this view in mind. The agency from which you adopted your child may also provide some post-adoption services that could include therapy. Group therapy may be helpful for an adolescent, particularly if he or she has little contact with other adoptees.

While we urge you to try to find a practitioner who specializes in treating adoptive families, most family therapists who at least know something about adoption should be able to deal adequately with problems that may arise. If you have any doubts about a therapist's knowledge of and competence to deal with adoption, ask him or her some of these questions: What do you know about adoption? Must adoption result in pathology? What do you think about adoptees and their parents? Do you think adoptive families are the same as other families? Do you think that adoptive families are capable of working out their own solutions to adoption complications? Use what you have read in this book as a guideline to evaluate the answers. If the therapist will not deal with the difficulties until he first analyzes your motives for adopting, or if he thinks that what has happened to your child through the adoption process has caused him irreparable harm, look elsewhere.

For the most part, a therapist should help you to devise your own solutions, not hand down decisions and directions from above. He or she should try to get you to specify what kinds of changes you would like to see in your family, and then help you to work out the small steps you can begin to take to effect those changes. Without specific goals, you can't develop specific solutions. That could leave you feeling helpless, confronting big, seemingly overwhelming problems.

Your therapist should help you to see behavior in your family you've possibly overlooked. As we've noted often, that could involve successes you haven't noticed—accomplishments on which you can build. The more accurate information you can piece together about the way your family works, the more likely you are to make changes for the better. As you create these changes, the therapist should be helping you to see your role in bringing them about. What good is success if you can't take credit for it, empowering you to produce further successes?

Don't be surprised if the heart of your difficulty turns

out to be a parent-child interaction that just happens to take place in an adoptive family, with no further adoption connection. It happens more often than not!

Finally, an occasion may arise in which an adopted child wants or needs individual therapy. Perhaps she just wants to express her feelings about adoption away from the family. Or maybe she has been depressed and needs medication and individual attention. If your special-needs adopted child requires individual treatment, try to delay it until you have established strong ties to her. Rushing a child into individual therapy early in a placement adds an extra adult with whom the child must form a relationship. That could impede the delicate process of building a bond between you and her.

If your child requires or wants therapy, however, there is good news. We have found in our clinical practice that adoptive families are remarkably strong and committed to one another for the most part. We and other researchers have discovered that they respond quickly to treatment, get better faster and stay better when compared to matched samples of other parents and children who seek family therapy.

Resources

ALMA International
Renunion Registry Data Bank
P.O. Box 154
Washington Bridge Station
New York, NY 10033
(212) 581-1568

American Association for Marriage and Family Therapy
1717 K Street N.W.
Suite 407
Washington, D.C. 20006

American Foundation for the Blind
15 West 16th Street
New York, New York 10011
(212) 620-2000

The Association for Children with Learning Disabilities
4156 Library Road
Pittsburgh, Pennsylvania 15234
(412) 881-2253

The Association for the Help of Retarded Children
200 Park Avenue South
New York, New York 10003
(212) 254-8203

Brief Family Therapy Center, Inc.
Adoptive Families Program
6815 W. Capitol Drive
Milwaukee, WI 53216
(414) 464-7775

The Churchill Center
22 East 95th Street
New York, New York 10130
(212) 722-0465

The Foundation for Children with Learning Disabilities

99 Park Avenue
New York, New York 10016
(212) 687-7211

Juvenile Diabetes Foundation
432 Park Avenue South
New York, New York 10016
(212) 889-7575

The March of Dimes
303 S. Broadway
Tarrytown, New York 10591
(914) 428-7100

The Mayo Clinic
200 First Street S.W.
Rochester, Minnesota 55905
(507) 284-2511

National Association for Perinatal Addiction and Research Education
11 East Hubbard Street
Suite 200
Chicago, Illinois 60611
(312) 329-2512

The National Resource Center for Special Needs Adoption
P.O. Box 337
Chelsea, Michigan 48118
(313) 475-8693

North American Council on Adoptable Children, Inc. (NACAC)
1821 University Ave.
Suite S-275
St. Paul, Minnesota 55104
(612) 644-3036

Adoptive Families of America
3307 Highway 100 North
Suite 203
Minneapolis, Minnesota 55422
(612) 535-4829

Project Impact
25 West Street
Boston, Massachusetts 02111
(617) 451-1472

Resources for Children with Special Needs, Inc.
200 Park Avenue South
Suite 816
New York, New York 10003
(212) 677-4650

United Cerebral Palsy
66 East 34th Street
New York, New York 10016
(212) 481-6300

Index

abortion, 150
abused children, 220–226, 230–231, 234, 245–246, 248–249
adolescents, *see* teenagers
adoptees:
 adjustment of, 20, 21
 arrival of, 23–24, 31–33, 34
 birth parents' search for, 185–186
 birth parents sought by, 21, 125, 179–186, 188, 191, 280
 birth siblings of, 177, 184–185, 218–220, 300
 death of adoptive parent and, 264
 discussing adoption with, 16–18, 24–25, 64–68, 75, 186–187, 262–263
 therapy for, 9–10, 20, 231–236, 301–304
 see also multiracial families, adoptive
adoptees, older-child, 10
 adjustment of, 207–213
 arrival celebrations for, 212
 birth siblings of, 217–220
 discipline for, 222–225
 early attachments of, 14–15, 216, 217
 emotional and behavioral problems of, 202–205, 226–231, 241–245, 246
 foster-care experiences of, 192–193, 194, 200, 204, 206, 245
 physical affection and, 209
 school performance of, 213–216
 therapy for, 231–236, 249
 trust of, 204–205, 246
adoptees, of single parents, 250–270
 male role models for, 253
 parental relationships and, 267
adoption:
 of AIDS babies, 207, 297–298
 availability of children for, 193, 281
 of birth siblings, 177
 books for children on, 24, 67, 110, 183
 of children with disabilities, 5, 237–244
 child's life history recorded by, 200–201, 246–247
 finalization of, 207, 247
 of foreign-born children, 6, 8, 271–272, 273, 275, 276–278, 280
 by foster parents, 5, 191, 295, 296
 historical development of, 3–6
 illegitimacy stigma associated with, 7–8, 26
 incidence of, 6–7, 276
 informing schools about, 73–74, 94–95
 legal regulation of, 3–6, 31, 291
 of older children, 191–236
 open, 15, 290–295, 298–300
 of special-needs children, 192–249
 subsidies for, 201
 transracial, 18–21, 27–28, 142, 271–288
adoption day celebrations, 87, 247
adoption registries, state-operated, 181
agencies, adoption, 4–6, 109, 291–292, 296, 302
 postadoption visits by, 50–51
 preadoption involvement of, 198–201, 205–207
AIDS, 22, 28–29, 207, 297–298
alcoholism, 146–147, 157, 297
allowances, 153, 154
attention deficit disorder with hyperactivity, 243

bathroom language, 63
Beavers, W. Robert, 56, 64
bedrooms, furnishing of, 209
bed-wetting, 234–235, 247
birth control, 150, 176
birthdays, 85–87
birth parents, 4, 25, 293–294
 searches for, 21, 125, 179–186, 188, 191, 280
birth siblings, 177, 184–185, 300
 behavioral pattern of, 218–220
black American children, 280–284, 285

bonding, 14–15, 37–41
books:
on adoption, 24, 67, 110, 183, 276
on death and divorce, 264, 266
on sexual maturation, 72, 150
breast-feeding, 35
Brodzinsky, David M., 66

camping trips, 209
Chess, Stella, 41
childproofing, 58–59
child rearing, procedural rules for, 56–58
child-welfare agencies, 4–5
cocaine, newborns and, 77–78
cognitive development, 63, 65–66, 99–101
college, 169–171
community service, 152
criminal behavior, adoption and, 20–21, 26
curfews, 155–156, 165–166
cursing, 301

dating, 176–177, 189
death of parent, 264
depression, 203, 260
development, child, 31, 41–44
sources on, 44, 58, 76, 118
disabilities, adoptees with, 5, 237–241
discipline, 60–62, 82, 89–92, 112–114, 123–124, 166–168, 222–225
for abused children, 221–225, 248–249
humor as tool for, 257–258
divorce, 28, 265–266
drug abuse, 147–148, 190
dyslexia, 101, 102

emotional overprotectiveness, 59

families, adoptive:
child-centeredness of, 58–60
complications vs. problems in, 10–12
counseling for, 9, 231–236, 302–304
different interests in, 115–116
multiracial, 27–28, 271–288
negotiation transitions in, 12
family therapy, 231–236, 301–304
fathers, adoptive, 34–35
single, 251, 267–268, 270

fathers, birth, 25, 103
fetal alcohol syndrome, 297
food, hoarding of, 229–230
foreign children, adoption of, 6, 8, 271–272, 275, 276, 280
foster-care, 4, 5–6, 192–193, 194, 200, 204, 206, 245–246, 295
foster-care parents:
adoption by, 5, 191, 295–296
adoptive parents' relationship with, 217–218

gay adoptive parents, 298
grandparents, 22, 45–47, 74–75

heredity, environment and, 14, 27
high school:
alternatives to, 169
dropping out of, 168–169
household responsibilities, 150–152
humor, as discipline tool, 257–258
hyperactivity, 96–97, 203, 243

illegitimacy, stigma of, 7–8, 26
incest, 71, 87
infertility, 7, 15–16, 36, 50, 54, 55, 121
intelligence, 13–14, 27

junior high school, 136–141

Kagan, Jerome, 38
Kaplan, Sharon, 292–293, 294
Kirk, David, 6, 7
Kral, Ron, 16, 20

laws, adoption, 3–6, 31, 291
lawyers, 4, 6, 29, 291, 296
learning disabilities, 101–102, 105–106
behavioral problems and, 96–99, 104–105, 137, 139, 213–216
life books, 200–201, 246–247
lying, 63, 104, 196

medical histories, 23, 37, 52–53, 290
menstruation, 120–122, 125
multiracial families, adoptive, 27–28
cultural misunderstandings in, 278–279

maintaining ethnic and cultural links in, 276–278, 283, 286
organizations for, 273–274, 285
prejudice and, 278, 281, 282–284, 286–287, 288
residences of, 275, 285–286, 287
tensions in, 274

Nelson, Katherine A., 195
nine-to-twelve-year-olds, 107–128
accommodating interests of, 115–116
appropriate humor for, 270
menstruation in, 120–122, 125
ostracism of, 116–118
setting limits for, 112–114, 123–124
sexual maturity of, 120–123, 125
summer camp for, 118–119, 127
testing of limits by, 110–112, 126–127
testing of limits by, 110–112, 126–127
nursery school, 73–74

one-to-six-year-olds, 54–78
child-rearing tips for, 56–58
cognitive development of, 63, 65–66
discipline for, 60–62
explaining adoption to, 64–68, 75
interpreting behavior of, 62–64, 74, 76–77
peer socializing of, 72–74, 75–76
sexuality of, 71–72, 76
sibling relations of, 69–71
open adoption, 15, 290–295, 298–300

parallel play, 72
parental child, 218–220, 279
parents, adoptive:
child's independence and, 130–131
contact between birth mother and, 248, 294–295, 298–300
death of, 264
of disabled children, 239–241
divorce of, 28, 265–266
empty-nest stage and, 161–162
overprotectiveness of, 58–60, 92
preadoption ambivalence of, 15–16, 21–22
realistic expectations of, 261–264
school system and, 137–138, 213–216, 239
search for birth parents and, 125, 179–186, 188, 191, 280
support groups for, 8–10, 238, 252–256, 269, 273
parents, foster-care, *see* foster-care parents
parents, single adoptive, 250–270
discipline by, 257–258
emotional distance and perspective for, 258–260
career of, 268–269
prejudice toward, 250–251
romantic involvements of, 266–267
support networks for, 252–256, 269
parents of older children, adoptive, 198–217
birth parents as viewed by, 220–221
child abuse accusations against, 225–226
expectations of, 203–205
foster families and, 216–217, 248
preadoptive counseling for, 201–202
school personnel and, 213–216
social worker's relationships with, 198–201, 205–207
pediatricians, selection of, 35–37, 52–53, 238–239
peers, acceptance by, 141–143
posttraumatic stress disorder, 203, 242–243
prenatal substance abuse, 22–23, 77–78, 296–298, 300–301
private agency adoptions, 4, 6, 28, 291, 298
puberty, 134–136

racial discrimination, 278, 281, 282–284, 286–287, 288
rebellion, 167–168, 188–189
relatives, as support network, 255–256
resource list, 305–306
restaurants, 212
retardation, 237–238

schools, 19, 73–74, 92–95, 136–141, 155, 169
  adoptive parents' contact with, 137–138, 213–216, 239
  behavioral problems in, 96–99, 104–105, 137, 139, 213–216
  learning disabilities and, 101–102
  racial prejudice in, 283–284, 287
self-esteem, adoptee's, 158
separation anxiety disorder, 244–245
sexual behavior, 71–72, 76, 87, 148–150, 172–176
  effect of adoption on, 172–173
sexually abused children, 220, 225–226, 230–231, 234, 245–246
shyness, 43, 158
siblings, 16, 69–70, 71, 87, 114–115, 136, 152, 177, 184–185, 218–220, 240, 300
six-to-nine-year-olds, 79–106
  adoption fears and fantasies of, 80–85
  birthdays of, 85–87
  birth mother of, 80, 81–82, 102–103
  birth parents idealized by, 82–83, 103–104
  cognitive styles of, 99–101
  discipline and limits for, 89–92
  learning disabilities of, 101–102, 105–106
  lying of, 104
  physical affection of, 88–89
  school adjustment of, 92–94
  school behavior of, 96–99, 104–105
  sexual curiosity of, 87
special-needs adoptions, 192–249
  children available for, 193
  of children with disabilities, 5, 237–241
  of older children, 191–236
  organizations for, 200
stealing, 111, 227–229
strangers, insensitive behavior of, 49–50, 51–52, 274–275
summer camp, 118–119, 127, 252–253
support groups, 8–10, 273
  for parents of children with disabilities, 238
  for single parents, 252–256, 269
teenagers, late teens, 159–191
  alternative programs for, 169, 170
  birth parents sought by, 179–185, 188
  caring for younger siblings by, 171–172, 186, 263
  college issues for, 169–171
  conflict resolution techniques with, 164–166
  dating by, 176–177, 189
  departure from family by, 177–178, 187–188
  discipline for, 166–168
  identity issues of, 162–164
  openness about adoption of, 177, 189–190
  rebellion of, 167–168, 188–189
  revealing adoption to, 186–187, 262–263
  sexual behavior of, 172–176
teenagers, with disabilities, 240–241
teenagers, young, 129–158
  accommodations for friends of, 143–144
  adjustment to junior high school of, 136–141, 155
  communicating with, 146
  delegating responsibilities to, 150–152
  drug and alcohol abuse by, 146–148
  emotional behavior of, 131–133
  jobs for, 154
  monetary responsibilities of, 153–154
  negotiating with, 156
  peer acceptance and, 141–143
  puberty and, 134–136
  recognizing behavioral problems in, 133
  respecting privacy of, 144–145
  school performance of, 139–141
  sexual behavior of, 148–150
temperament, 13–14, 40–41, 76
temper tantrums, 60, 74
therapeutic parenting, 260–261
therapy, 9–10, 20, 231–236, 249, 301–304
Thomas, Alexander, 41
transracial adoptions, 18–21, 27–28, 142, 271–288

war orphans, adoption of, 275–276

Celeste Ascending

A NOVEL

Kaylie Jones

HarperCollins*Publishers*

OTHER BOOKS BY KAYLIE JONES

As Soon As It Rains

Quite the Other Way

A Soldier's Daughter Never Cries

HarperCollins books may be purchased for educational, business, or sales promotional use. For information please write: Special Markets Department, HarperCollins Publishers Inc., 10 East 53rd Street, New York, NY 10022.

FIRST EDITION

Designed by Nancy Field

Printed on acid-free paper.

Library of Congress Cataloging-in-Publication Data
Jones, Kaylie, 1960–
Celeste ascending : a novel / Kaylie Jones. — 1st ed.
p. cm.
ISBN 0-06-019325-5
I. Title
PS3560.O497C45 2000
813'.54—dc21 99-35290

00 01 02 03 04 ❖/RRD 10 9 8 7 6 5 4 3 2 1

TO KEVIN

All roads led to you

Acknowledgments

I wish to thank Trena Keating, my editor, for her keen and rich observations; my dear friend Shaye Areheart for her fine critical eye; Peter Matthiessen for his kindness and guidance; James Ivory, Ruth Prawer Jhabvala, and Ismail Merchant for their inspiration; David Weild IV for explaining mergers and acquisitions; and Kevin Heisler, whose faith never wavered.

Also Cecile and Buddy Bazelon, Carolyn Blakemore, Gabrielle Danchick, Henry Flesh, Joy Harris, Nan Horowitz, Beth Jones, Gloria Jones, Ellie Weiler Krach, Tim McLoughlin, Kimberly Miller, Haig Nalbantian, Dayle Patrick, Lucy Rosenthal, Ina Shoenberg, Kate Sotiridy, Liz Szabla, Janine Veto, Kathleen Warnock, and Renette Zimmerly for their readership and kind encouragement.

The generous support of the Virginia Center for the Creative Arts, where I spent two extraordinary summers working on the novel.

And my student at MS 54, Derby Clarke, for permitting me, on page 134, to print his poem.

Before Nathan, there had never been this overwhelming feeling of wanting someone so much. Only one other time in my life had I felt so completely alive—the trip my mother and I took around Italy. Both were colored by a certain recklessness. We seemed to be attempting to stop time; but what we feared from the future, I had no idea.

—CELESTE M.

One

I HAD A FRIEND in high school named Sally Newlyn who explained what had gone wrong with God's plan for the world. During one of her schizophrenic episodes, she told me that God had given mankind a finite number of souls. He set them free in the sky where they orbited silently until they were needed for the newly conceived. He intended for the souls to be reincarnated so that humanity would grow more generous and wise with each generation. But God had underestimated man's propensity to go forth and multiply, and so, on our planet today, millions of bodies were roaming the earth searching in vain for a soul.

We were sitting cross-legged in an abandoned shed we'd discovered in the woods, passing back and forth a thermos of rum and Coke. I listened to her with rapt attention, because she often spoke important truths when she stopped taking her medication. Sally's eyes were on fire, and I reached out and felt her pale forehead, but it was cool to the touch.

"That's what's wrong with me, Celeste," she said close to my ear in her small, urgent voice as tears fell from her eyes. "I didn't get a soul."

"Oh, Sally," I said, pulling her into my arms and holding her tightly, as if that could keep her demons away.

* * *

WHEN I WAS a sophomore in college, she killed herself.

I learned of Sally's suicide on a December morning when an old friend called me on the hall phone in the dormitory. Afterwards, I sat alone for a long time in the communal kitchen, listening to the midweek silence. I tried to get on with the day but I couldn't move. I remembered what Sally had told me several years before about God's plan, and I could not shake the thought from my mind.

I began to look into people's faces, searching their eyes for a glimmer of their souls. It became a compulsion; I pictured the inside of their heads as a room—something like the set in Beckett's *Endgame*—with no doors, only two windows looking out onto the world. If I could furnish the room, or at least see the view from the windows, a little corner of their soul was revealed.

I remembered Sally's eyes, and in them I could still see a warm and sunny greenhouse crowded with rare and rich-smelling plants, fragile and in constant need of care. But as she grew ill, the light in her eyes slowly dimmed, and in the greenhouse of my memory the plants shriveled up and died.

I lost my mother when I was ten, and although I remembered her well, I could not recall the event with any certainty. Trying to spare me pain, my father had filled my child's mind with reassuring stories that tenaciously lodged themselves in my imagination, leaving little room for the truth. In my mother's eyes I imagined an exotic French boudoir, with a mauve chaise longue, silk tapestries of naked demoiselles covering the windows, risqué lingerie peeking out from a closet, old clothbound books strewn everywhere, and in a corner, a bar for the many guests she might have had in real life, but never did.

* * *

At twenty-eight, I found myself in a small, dark apartment in New York City, quite alone. Having lost almost every person who had ever meant anything to me, I confronted my own soul-room for the first time. In mirrors, my blank eyes stared back at me. The walls and floor were bare. The windows looked out onto a dirty airshaft, a brick wall.

And then I met Alex, at a Fourth of July party on a chartered yacht, the way people meet in movies.

During the past six months, I had managed to get to my teaching job at Columbia University; to the public school in Harlem where I taught creative writing to eighth graders; and to the Korean deli: familiar places and preplanned destinations.

When summer finally came and I was relieved of my teaching obligations, I locked myself in my apartment, and began putting together my first collection of short stories.

Sometimes, in the evening, I went down the hall to visit my neighbor

Lucia. She was in the throes of a love affair with a rock and roll roadie called Soarin' Sammy. Lucia had met him on the set of one of her music videos.

They had never been outside of her apartment together. It had been going on—off and on, but mostly on—for over three years. I always knew when he was visiting because she would stop answering her phone, and the music would start pounding so that her door would hum with the vibration.

For long stretches there would be no mention of him, then she would begin to expect him again. "Soarin' Sammy should be coming by," she'd say in her heavy voice.

That summer we holed up, waiting for a storm to pass, like two commuters who'd forgotten their umbrellas. We watched old movies on her VCR and drank wine or brandy into the late hours. Around the corner there was a bar I liked, a small, dark place. Sitting in there one night, after we'd both had a number of cognacs, she made me promise I'd accompany her to this upcoming Fourth of July party. The Slimbrand company had rented a private yacht that sailed around lower Manhattan. Lucia, who had produced several commercials for them, had received a gilded invitation in the mail. It was a black tie affair. Last year, she told me, there had been music and film stars, a Top Forty band, and rivers of champagne.

I promised, and forgot about it. But on July third, she called to remind me. I told her I had other plans.

"Yeah, like what," she said. "Like lying around reading Emily Dickinson poems?" She sighed heavily into the phone.

"I like Emily Dickinson," I said.

There was a long pause. Then she said in her lumbering voice, without anger, a mere statement of fact, "Maybe you should go see a shrink, Celeste."

I would never consider it; in my family, we were stubborn and resilient and took our "hard knocks" in silence, with fortitude.

So I put on my best summer dress, low-cut, drop-waisted, emerald-green silk, which I had bought for a cousin's wedding, my high-heeled Evan Picone pumps, which I saved for special occasions, and my mother's long strand of pearls that blushed pink in the light. I braced myself with several shots of frozen Stoli and waited for Lucia to ring the bell. She arrived promptly; dark and sensual with her large mouth painted crimson, she wore a black Spandex dress that accentuated her full breasts and wide hips, fishnet stockings, and big, shiny black pumps like Minnie Mouse wears.

As we boarded the yacht, I wanted to spin around and run back across the walkway. The upper deck was all windows and resembled an aviary crowded with rare birds. The yacht cast off; Lucia and I headed for the bar. On the way, she ran into her Slimbrand executive in black tie and I found a waiter with a full tray of glistening champagne glasses. The band started to play Motown hits. Unable to hear a thing Lucia and the executive were saying to each other, I went outdoors. Manhattan's lighted windows formed a glorious halo in the indigo sky. A tall, wide-shouldered man appeared beside me, elbows leaning comfortably on the railing. His dark blond hair was brushed back from his broad forehead. Little glasses glinted on the bridge of his nose, and below that was a substantial, firm mouth and square jaw. In his pin-striped suit, he seemed poised, content with who he was in the world.

"It's spectacular, isn't it?" he said. I looked over my shoulder to see whom he was addressing, and realized it was me.

"It's overwhelming," I said. "I've never seen it from this perspective before."

"I was born and raised in Manhattan," he said, "and I still think it has the best skyline in the world."

"Better than Singapore?" I said. "I've never been there, but it looks pretty impressive on the Discovery Channel."

"Better than Singapore. I go there quite often on business. I'm Alex Laughton."

He extended his hand and smiled. He had a firm grip and his eyes were steady. Alex's teeth were perfect, not one of them out of line, and very white.

Inside, the band was playing "Respect."

I didn't meet men like him. In fact, I hadn't met any men in a long time. I used to go out on surrogate dates with my best friend Branko, who had been as familiar and dependable as Christmas.

"I'm Celeste Miller," I told him, shaking his hand. I brought my champagne glass to my lips, but it was empty.

A waiter passed by carrying a tray of bubbling flutes, and Alex briskly exchanged my empty glass for two fresh ones. A little nervous, I began to babble. I told him I didn't often go to such parties. He asked me what I did.

"I teach English lit and creative writing at Columbia. I got my Ph.D. there a couple of years ago. Now I'm an adjunct professor. Once a week, I go up to Harlem and teach kids creative writing in a public school. But really I'm a writer."

"What do you write?" His glasses picked up the city lights and glinted as he gazed at me.

Lucia came by, apologized for abandoning me, and explained that the Slimbrand fellow wouldn't stop talking. He was considering her for another job.

"Can you believe this line?" She merrily quoted in a high-pitched singsong, "'Plastic, it's fantastic!'

"They're competing with Playtex," she explained. "Plastic applicators."

"That slogan is obnoxious," Alex said.

He introduced himself to her. Lucia looked him up and down, and finding me in good company, she went back to discuss more business with the Slimbrand fellow.

I asked him what he did for a living.

"Investment banking. I'm a managing director in the M&A group at Griffin Silverstein."

"MNA?"

"Mergers and acquisitions," he said vaguely. Not that a more detailed explanation would have helped clarify this. He might as well have said the Enema Group. There was an uncomfortable silence. Then he said, "My mother is a doctor with Feed the Children. She works primarily in Central Africa. Her job is a little like yours, I guess."

"Just like it," I said with an ironic laugh. "You Wall Street guys think it's a real jungle up in Harlem."

He looked down, blushing, and shook his head. He murmured, "Good one, Alex, you moron."

"I'm sorry," I said quickly. "It's just that I've never had any problems up there at all."

After a pause, Alex asked again, "So, what do you write?"

"Short stories. I've published several stories in magazines. Literary magazines." I felt uncomfortable saying all this, as if it weren't enough, as if I were apologizing.

"I don't know anybody who writes fiction. You must be really good to teach at Columbia."

I didn't tell him that writing well was not a prerequisite for teaching at Columbia, that the university treated adjuncts like slave labor, and we were still grateful to the administration for the job. I liked that he was impressed.

Alex told me he was an only child, that since he and his mother were often traveling, their paths rarely crossed these days. She'd been married and divorced twice. When she was home she descended on the nation's capital like a plague, he said, shouting about the awful living conditions of America's underprivileged masses. Alex admired her. He said he admired women who were ambitious and independent—although politically he and his mother were in different camps.

"I haven't voted since Carter," I said. This fact really seemed to worry him.

"It's our right, our democratic right," he said, looking intently into my eyes. "It's what makes this country great."

"Where's your father now?" I asked, changing the subject.

"He's in Jersey. But he may as well be in Alaska. I've been on my own a long time," he said serenely.

"So have I."

The yacht circled the Statue of Liberty, gleaming like an emerald tower in the sleek black water. Fireworks tumbled from the sky as though angels were emptying their treasure chests, and in the distance, Manhattan twinkled like the palaces in the fairy-tale books my mother used to read to me at night.

I gasped as just above our heads a firework exploded and then whistled dangerously as it careened toward the river. Alex pressed me to his wide chest. He smelled of one of those manly leather-and-spice colognes. I felt small against him. "I saw you as soon as you came in," he said close to my ear. "I thought you were European, French or something."

"I'm half-French," I said, surprised.

A waiter passed close by and Alex grabbed two more champagne flutes. We toasted Independence Day, I held my glass tight in my hand, and with my head all in a whirl, tears threatening to rise, I buried my face in his hard pectoral muscles and breathed deeply.

"I'm sorry. My best friend Branko . . ." my voice trailed off, the right words out of reach. Alex stroked my hair and held me as the city lights flashed by. I felt safe there, as I had when my mother and I rode the Ferris wheel, pressed against each other, screaming out at the night.

The waiter came by and my hand shot out for another glass of champagne.

We must have talked and talked, but what we said escapes me, lost in a swirl of champagne. It seemed no time had passed at all and then the yacht docked and guests began to stumble off. Alex led me through the crowd, across the walkway to the glistening black pavement. Lucia was standing there, looking at us with amusement.

Alex hurried us away from the dock. He said it would be impossible to find a cab there. Indeed, the guests were rushing into the street with their arms up. I wondered if he would ask me to have a drink; go back to his place. I would not refuse. He walked us uptown a few blocks, then stepped out into the empty street and whistled loudly. As if on command, a taxi came careening around the corner and screeched to a halt before us. Alex held the door for Lucia, then me. I hesitated, not knowing what to do or say to him. I was certain I'd never see him again.

"Would you give me your number?" he asked tentatively.

"Got a pen?"

"I have a photographic memory for numbers," he said with a confident smile. I told him my number. He stooped and kissed me with open lips, not at all inhibited by Lucia's watchful gaze. A passionate kiss that lasted many seconds. He stepped away.

"Watch your dress." He shut the door and pressed his hand to the glass for a moment. I watched him through the rear window as he receded, then disappeared into the darkness.

Lucia was telling me that I was silly to have been so scared to go. I was thinking that I would surely never hear from him again.

* * *

THE NEXT MORNING a dozen red roses arrived with a note that said only, "From Alex Laughton."

He must have looked up my last name and initial in the phone book, and searched for the number that matched the one I'd given him. With a last name as common as Miller, this was no small feat in New York City.

I went back to sleep for three hours, unplugging the phone as I always did. When I awakened there were three hang-ups on the answering machine.

"I guess I should tell you I've been married before," Alex said the following evening, a Wednesday, at dinner. He had chosen a California grill on the Upper East Side. The space was enormous and brightly lit by track lighting. I strained to hear him over the din of cutlery and echoing voices.

"Any children?" I asked; the obvious question. He shook his head. I was relieved and hoped my face didn't betray me.

It had taken me a long time to get ready. Alex had no idea how many times I'd called Lucia long-distance. She was away on a job. She'd grown irritated and told me to pull myself together. I missed my old roommate Candace sorely. In the old days, Candace would have picked a dress for me. She might even have come along on the date if I couldn't face it alone. In the stark bedroom Candace and I had once shared, I glanced quickly at myself in the mirror, half expecting her to appear behind me and rearrange my hair. "Where the hell are you?" I muttered. A draft from the air-conditioning passed over me like a flutter of wings, and I began to shiver.

I had asked Alex to come pick me up. I had been afraid to go into the restaurant alone, but I would never have told him this. I realized that he had no idea what he was getting himself into. He thought we were two normal people sharing a nice dinner. I reached for my vodka gibson; the delicate faceted stem of the glass reflected the light like a diamond as I twirled it. The liquor crackled nicely against the back of my throat, warming my chest and stomach. I wanted to down the whole thing, but nursed it instead. Who knew how much Alex drank, or if he'd even order a second cocktail, or wine, or would he drink plain water? It would be impossible for me to sit through dinner on plain water. I decided to order wine by the glass.

He was telling me that his wife had been a part-time model who was trying to finish law school at Fordham. Her name was Mimi.

"What happened?" I asked.

"I don't know. Didn't work out." Since then, he'd been what he called a serial monogamist.

"Better that than a serial polygamist, I guess." A laugh escaped from me. He seemed disconcerted. I composed myself.

"I want to settle down," he said, dead serious. "I want children."

I glanced uneasily at my reflection in the floor-to-ceiling window. I looked poised and sensible, perhaps even beautiful to him, in my pale green cotton sweater and long skirt. A tall, dark-haired woman ambled by behind me in the smoky glass of the window. She wore a skintight, sleeveless emerald green dress. Her arms and legs were thin and taut, and she wore emerald earrings and a matching choker. She was probably a model. I had always wanted to be taller, and bone-thin, straight-haired; in fact, all the things I was not. I turned back to Alex, and felt myself disappear under his gaze.

I took a last sip of my martini and speared the pearl onion, popping it into my mouth. I wanted another drink. Alex had finished his rum and tonic. He called the waiter over and ordered a bottle of California Chardonnay. Thank God. My relief was so extreme that for a moment I couldn't remember what we'd been talking about.

The topaz-colored wine arrived. The waiter poured. I reached for my glass, but the gesture seemed greedy, so I set it back down without taking a sip.

I blurted out, my mouth dry, that I had only been in love once, and that the feeling had lasted for years and years, and that with this fellow, I'd lost a piece of myself that I'd never been able to recover.

"What was his name?" Alex asked, the tips of his ears reddening.

What a lot of heavy baggage I had. I didn't know if I had the energy or the enthusiasm to go through it all again. I didn't want to talk about it, and shook my head.

"I'm going to take care of you," he said. He reached across the table and took my hand. He invited me to have dinner at his apartment on Saturday night. He said he would call me when he was ready to leave work.

"You work on Saturdays?" I asked.

"Well, not always," he said.

* * *

I WAITED BY THE PHONE until he called at nine P.M. He said his secretary had ordered dinner for us and it would be waiting with the doorman when we got there. I imagined that I would be spending the night.

His Upper East Side penthouse apartment was on the thirty-eighth floor and had a large, gleaming white kitchen with an open counter on one side that faced a dining/living room area so long and wide you could have put a bowling alley in there. The tall windows faced southwest, offering a magnificent view of the Manhattan skyline and Central Park. A wide balcony ran the entire length of the apartment. Alex opened a sliding glass door and stepped out. I couldn't, it was too high up for me and I had a terrible fear of heights. I stayed inside and walked around inspecting his things. There were a few large art books on the Chinese coffee table, and a picture book on the history of tennis, but no others.

He had installed track lighting on the ceiling, which carefully highlighted the Oriental rugs over the mossy green carpeting, the Chinese tapestries and scrolls on the walls, the dark cherrywood furniture embossed with gold bamboo leaves and charging dragons. The large, plush couches were a darker, mossier green than the carpeting.

"Nice stuff," I called out to him, thinking that he must have had a designer help him.

"I got most of it in Hong Kong," he said. When I didn't join him outside, he came back in and shut the door. "But it's real, old colonial stuff from the mainland."

A sleek black cabinet ran the length of the far living room wall and in it stood a shiny black TV, VCR, tape deck, compact disk player, an electric guitar and huge amplifier, and all the accompanying paraphernalia. The remote controls were lined up like little coffins on top of the TV. At my place, I had a small black and white with no cable and not even a single coffin.

"You play the electric guitar?" I asked, surprised.

"Not so much anymore," he said.

His secretary, Lorraine, had ordered a crabmeat salad with all kinds of vegetables and greens. Unsure of whether he had wine in the house, or if his secretary would have the good sense to order a couple of bottles, I had brought an expensive white Bordeaux from my grandmother's vineyard. Americans usually dismissed white Bordeaux, but my grandmother had long ago taught me that this was one of the finest wines of France. I was hoping Alex would ask me about my choice, but he just poured liberally, never glancing at the label.

In his hand-carved four-poster king-sized bed, in the dark, my lips reached hungrily for his wide mouth. A rapacious mouth, a predator's mouth. His body was strong and smooth, and he was graceful and sure of himself. An athlete. In fact, I'd learned tonight that he'd been a tennis champion at Yale and at Choate, and a soccer standout before that, in junior prep school.

He liked to kiss, to lick, to suck as much as I did. We were very good together. Excellent, in fact. All-conference, at least. He didn't talk or make a sound. Not a sound. I liked to make a lot of noise, especially in an apartment as big and safe as his, with walls so thick there were no noticeable neighbors in any direction. Several hours passed, and still not a word, not a sound from him, only a hissing exhale of breath, a shudder of his wide back.

* * *

The next Saturday, we had brunch and then walked down Columbus Avenue. I stopped in front of an Italian shoe store to admire the summer pumps.

"You'd look hot in those red ones," Alex said in a murmur that sent a shiver from my throat to my crotch.

"I've never worn red shoes," I said.

He took me by the arm. "Why don't you try them on?"

"I can't afford them, Alex!"

In the store I noticed that women looked at him. He sat back comfortably in an armchair and asked me to walk back and forth in front of him in the red shoes.

"I have nothing to wear with these, Alex!" I protested.

He took a platinum Visa card out of his wallet. "We'll get you something to wear with them."

"God, you landed yourself a jewel," the salesgirl murmured, looking up with big eyes from her crouched position as she slipped the shoes from my feet.

Two

For my birthday, he took Friday and Monday off and we flew to Bermuda for a long weekend. Alex had not taken a single sick day or vacation day in two years and had recently been ordered to take some of the time that was due him.

In our spacious room at the White Bone Beach Hotel, we were greeted by the big red blinking message button on the telephone.

"Shit," Alex said, dropped his sports coat on the bed, and punched in his work number.

"Yes, George," Alex said. "The letter went out to the board of directors, what, on Wednesday? What's the stock trading at today? Still twenty, and we offered to purchase at twenty-five . . . "

I went to the window and opened it. A few hundred feet straight down was a large terrace and a bean-shaped electric blue pool; a few hundred feet farther down some steep stone steps lay the aquamarine ocean and bone-white beach. The sun was hot despite the wind and there were still umbrellas and beach chairs and people swimming in the churning surf. A thatch-roofed bar catered to the guests who were tanning themselves on the chaise longues.

Alex said, "Put a call in to company counsel, ask if they received our letter. Ask if there's a response."

I waited for a while, but Alex had kicked off his loafers and stretched out on the bed. He did not appear to be getting off the phone anytime soon. I opened my bag, took out a bathing suit and the second volume of Marcel Proust's *A la recherche du temps perdu*—nice light beach reading, I now thought. I'd secretly hoped to impress Alex not just with my intellectual acumen but also with my linguistic talents. I changed right there, hoping to distract him. He barely glanced my way.

"You tell them that we're prepared to put out a press release. That we'll contest it in the press. We'll take out a fucking ad in the *Wall Street Journal* and force the issue! We'll squeeze their balls!"

When I was done changing, my wrap snug over my hips and the suntan lotion and other necessities in my new beach bag, I waved to him to indicate that I was leaving. He held up an index finger. Was he indicating that I should wait? I waited.

"Well, you call them, George, and find out what they have to say. I'll wait right here. You call me back and we'll figure it out from there. What else?"

Fifteen minutes later he was still on the phone, so I walked out, shutting the door a little harder than necessary.

* * *

There was a very nice waiter on the beach who wore a blue sports coat over a white shirt and bow tie, white and blue striped Bermuda shorts, and knee-high black socks and dress shoes. He looked like he'd walked out of his house that morning and forgotten to put on his pants. Every time he appeared with his tray and a fresh piña colada for me, I felt like laughing. After a little while I didn't feel angry at all.

The sun was low in the sky by the time Alex showed up wearing long black swim trunks. He had a few inches of fat around the waist, but he was a splendid sight. Still lightly tanned from summer, with large biceps and chest muscles, a tight, round ass and muscular legs, he turned women's heads on the beach. When he sat down at the edge of my chaise longue, I slipped my hand up one of the swim trunks' legs. He grabbed my hand and threw it aside.

"Don't do that, people can see."

"Are you going to apologize to me for ruining this whole day or what?"

"How many of those have you had?" he nodded toward the empty glass.

"Just two."

Ha! Proust lay unopened at my side. Many years of practice had taught me to avoid slurring and to control my muscles so that most people would never even know.

"Good book?"

"Great book!" I said with conviction. When my friend the waiter came back, Alex ordered two piña coladas.

"So did George work out whatever it was he needed to work out?"

Alex shifted around. "Not really. They can't do anything without me, I swear." After a pause he said, "I'm going to play some golf tomorrow. I wanted to go scuba diving but they say it's all fished out around here."

"Whatever," I said gloomily. "I'll just hang here with our nice waiter who forgot to put his pants on this morning."

Alex didn't laugh. Our piña coladas arrived.

"What's the matter, Alex?"

"Nothing," he said. "I'm just not used to being on vacation, that's all."

We drank the piña coladas and then two more.

Later, when we dressed for dinner, I realized why Alex hadn't laughed. He had Bermuda shorts as well, and looked, as the waiter had, as if he'd forgotten to put on his pants.

"Where did you get those?" I said, trying to hold back a giggle.

"Last time I was here," he said, annoyed. He had a habit of stamping his feet and sliding them back slightly, like a bull about to charge.

"And when was that?"

He hesitated. "My honeymoon."

"Well, goddamnit, Alex, couldn't we have gone someplace else?"

"It wasn't the same hotel," he said, straightening his collar. "And stop using that language, Celeste."

"Oh, excuse me. You can swear all you want on the phone with George but I can't use the word *goddamnit* in my own hotel room?"

"That's different," Alex said, "that's work."

It was the beginning of a long night.

After dinner, he gave me a little black box and inside was a pair of ruby studs.

"Wow, they're beautiful. What good taste you have, Alex!"

"I sent Lorraine to Tiffany's during her lunch hour. She loves doing that kind of stuff."

It occurred to me that his secretary had probably been the one who looked up my phone number in the phone book in order to find my address and send me a dozen long-stem roses. Somehow none of this sat well with me but I thought it prudent to keep my mouth shut. Instead I had another after-dinner drink.

Many hours later, we found ourselves in the outdoor disco, set up under a long thatched roof on the beach. A glittering disco ball hung from the center roof beam and showered the empty dance floor with little circles of light. It must have been two or three in the morning; we were the last customers, and the blond Australian bartender, who was also drunk, was telling us Sheila jokes. The music suddenly died, and the lights were turned up, so that in their glare the cigarette-strewn dance floor and bar area, the overflowing ashtrays and empty glasses and sticky spills were a dismal sight. Alex fled, pulling me behind him along the path and up the steep, narrow steps to the terrace and the now dark, bean-shaped pool.

"Oh, Alex, let's go skinny-dipping! There's no one here."

Alex looked around. "No," he said.

"What a square," I said, and jerked free. I dove into the deep end in my black evening dress, sandals and all. The world seemed so quiet and peaceful down there that I considered staying. I wondered if Alex would jump in to save me. When my lungs began to ache for air, panic forced me to push for the surface. I grabbed the edge of the pool and looked around, gasping for breath. Alex had gone.

I have a hazy recollection of standing under a tepid shower with my arms pressed up against the tiles to steady myself, and Alex appearing behind me, naked and hard. He lifted me up and turned me around, thrust himself into me as my back and head slammed into the tiles. Next we were on the floor, wet, then I'm pressed, facedown, over the edge of the bed with him standing behind me.

The next morning I was so sore I felt like I'd been in a rodeo.

"I think we have a fascinating method of communicating," I said to him as I inspected my swollen face in the mirror. He lay prostrate on the bed with a pillow over his head.

* * *

A FEW WEEKS LATER, in the beginning of November, we were watching a late-night movie, *A Kiss Before Dying,* in bed; Robert Wagner was about to push his pregnant girlfriend off the roof of the municipal building.

Alex said, "Isn't it incredible? She has absolutely no idea who she's in love with!"

"I know!" I said. Naked, we'd pulled a sheet up from the floor and twined it around ourselves. His whole apartment smelled of him, of that leather-and-spice cologne. Pillows, sheets, towels, and now, even I.

Chinese take-out containers stood on a tray on the bedside table, and our clothes were strewn everywhere. Alex had just gotten home from work, and I'd come over straight from the bar where Lucia and I had been sitting for several hours.

"How come you never talk or make any sounds when you're fucking?"

"Don't say *fucking*. It bothers me."

"All right," I said, "screwing, then. How come you never make any sounds or talk when we're screwing?"

He was mad now, his face became flushed and a frown crossed his brow. I punched him in the arm, "Come on, lighten up!" Perhaps Lucia and I had had too many cognacs. I was pushing my luck.

"It started at Choate, I guess," he said, and shifted his weight around uncomfortably. "You learn to be quiet."

I laughed, thinking of young Alex Laughton inchoate at Choate. "So you were doing those naughty homosexual things then—"

"Listen, Celeste, I don't like it when you talk like that."

"I'm sorry."

Alex said suddenly, "Why don't you move in? Then you'd be here when I got home. You wouldn't have to travel across town late at night."

I swallowed, and caught my breath. "So soon?"

"Why not? My place is so much nicer," he said simply. Alex wouldn't stay at my apartment. It was cramped and too "bohemian."

"I can make this apartment perfect for you," he said. "And why pay two rents? I'll get someone to build you bookshelves for all your hundreds of books, wall to wall. With an alcove in the middle for your desk. We'll turn the guest room into a really nice library/study. Your cinderblock-and-boards shelves are college stuff, Celeste."

I was mad now. So what if I couldn't afford custom-made shelves? I was doing what I wanted with my life.

"This is a little fast for me, Alex. I can't do things this fast."

A formal shroud of politeness fell over his eyes. He moved away and kept a foot of space between us for the rest of the film. I became frightened.

"I just need a little more time."

As the film credits began to roll, I said, "Maybe I'd better go home."

"If you like," he said in an indifferent voice that I didn't recognize.

I took my time getting my jacket, to give him an opportunity to stop me, to put his arms around me, but he did not.

Even in my own apartment I still smelled of him. That cologne had rubbed off on my hand towels in the bathroom, on my own pillowcases.

I couldn't stand it and ran down the hall and knocked on Lucia's door. She was in her nightgown. The light at her back illuminated the cotton fabric, exposing the dark forms of her wide thighs and large, round breasts.

"Hey," she said in a gloomy voice, "what's up?"

"Let's go have another drink," I said.

"All right; let me get dressed."

Sitting at the bar in the spot we had vacated only a few hours before, I felt much better. I warmed a Martell brandy, twirling the snifter around in my palm, and watched the light glowing amber inside the glass. I took a sip, felt the familiar splash-and-burn make its way from my throat to my esophagus, hit my stomach, and then a feeling of grace wafted over me. *Fuck him,* I thought. *I don't belong there anyway.*

"Let's stay until the place closes!" I said to Lucia.

"What's the matter, Celeste?" she asked. "What the hell happened?"

"Nothing. I'm sick of him," I said. "He's such a tight-ass."

"Yeah, well, Soarin' Sammy he's not," she said, dead earnest.

* * *

Between midnight, when I left Alex's, and ten-thirty A.M., when I came to, there were ten hang-ups on my answering machine. At eleven, Alex finally left a message. I lay in bed and listened as he talked to the machine. An image pierced through the pain and fog: I was dancing to the jukebox, crotch to crotch with a gorgeous Puerto Rican bodybuilder, the lights spinning round and round. Having run his hands up under my shirt, he was just about to unsnap my bra when Lucia grabbed my arm and dragged me away.

I swiftly turned my back on the thought and pulled the pillow over my head.

"Celeste?" Alex's voice rang through. "Call me as soon as you can, okay? . . . Listen . . . I love you, Celeste. I hope you know that. Don't forget, we have that fund-raiser tonight. They're honoring the CEO of Chemical Bank."

My brain was pounding on the walls of my head, trying to get out.

By four o'clock I was able to construct a coherent thought and this was it: this was no way to behave at my age. I called him back.

Ten minutes later, the phone rang again and I didn't pick it up. "Hallo, this is Esteban, we met last night," said a deep, gravelly voice.

My heart started to pound in my throat. How had he gotten my number? Had I given it to him?

I erased the message as soon as he hung up.

* * *

For the occasion, Alex had bought me a tight-fitting black velvet dress with a low-cut tulip-shaped neckline, a matching velvet evening bag and pumps. I wore my mother's pink-hued pearls and antique pearl earrings. We sat at a round table with eight other couples I had never met but whom Alex knew through his business dealings.

I kept my mouth shut and smiled till my ears ached, feeling sure that this way no one would identify me as the impostor I was. The waiters were fortunately quite liberal with the wine.

The man to my left wanted to know how Alex and I had met. I told the romantic story of the Fourth of July cruise. He nodded approvingly. His wife leaned across him and told me conspiratorially that Alex was one of the most "eligible bachelors" in New York City. That she and her husband had been trying to fix him up for years, to calm him down. Her husband nodded. "He works seven days a week," he said with a rueful smile, "sixty, eighty hours, no problem. Married guys with kids, like me, we hate him."

After the steak au poivre, during the champagne and profiteroles, we were shown a video on the life and achievements of Mr. John Fairfax Jr., CEO of Chemical Bank. He was big on giving to museums, and had donated many millions to the Metropolitan Museum of Art.

"The Metropolitan Museum!" I grumbled in Alex's ear. "Jesus Christ, I can think of a few places that could really *use* that money. Like the program I work for in Harlem, The Writer's Way, they could sure use it! Or how about just setting up a fund to send some of those kids to college? Jesus, Alex, the Metropolitan Museum!"

"Shhh," Alex hissed. His glasses twinkled in the candlelight. I couldn't see his eyes. "Museums need money, too."

"Keep the poor in the ghettos, right?"

"Stop it, Celeste. Don't get mad at me, I give tons of money to Feed the Children every year." His jaw was tensing. I could see he was getting angry. "You sound like a socialist."

"I am a socialist!" I said with conviction. I had never given politics much thought, but at the moment, I felt very much like a socialist. The couple I had been talking to looked down, embarrassed. Alex began to laugh, a low, rumbling chuckle I found very appealing. He squeezed my knee under the table and I let out a little cry that made the other couples turn in our direction.

I began to stay at Alex's in the mornings, reading for my classes, trying to get used to the place. There was a closet in the living room, right next to the garbage chute, and every bag that dropped down sounded like a body falling through the floor above.

One night, after I'd awakened in a sweat over a bad dream, I sat in the dark living room and counted the blinking red lights to calm myself: the microwave, VCR, the cable box, the little round lights of the electric mixer mounted on the kitchen wall, the rectangular light on the answering machine, and the digital clock on the coffeemaker. I opened the fridge. A bottle of Moët champagne, a bottle of Evian, and some ancient barbecued chicken wings in a plastic delivery container. It was as if no one lived here.

I came upon the remnants of his former wife, Mimi, in remote corners of the apartment. There were lipstick cases and a little makeup mirror with a flowery pattern on the back in a drawer of an antique vanity that had belonged to Alex's grandmother. I found an eye-pencil sharpener and some perfume samplers—Poison, appropriately—in the back of the medicine cabinet.

Once, while Alex was at work, my shoulder knocked a large, rectangular plastic picture frame off the bathroom wall. The frame fell apart, and a small stack of photos slid out from behind the one of Alex and his mother playing tennis at some club. They were naked photos of Mimi. In one she posed arched and growling, leonine, her blond hair teased out and the eyeliner black and curving to points at the corners of her light blue eyes. Her skin was pale and her body reedlike, her breasts just the right size, a handful. How could Alex have been in love with someone as different from me as this? And why had he saved the pictures?

* * *

NOT LONG AFTER THAT, we went to a dance club on a Saturday night with a friend of Alex's from his college tennis team. The fellow was still in awe of Alex ten years later, sidling up to him like some kind of large dog. He had some Ecstasy and offered Alex and me each a hit. I waited to see what Alex would do. He swallowed the white pill dry, without giving it a thought. Mine went down easily with a shot of tequila.

Alex danced beautifully, lithe and graceful and perfectly in rhythm. He barely moved, but his movements were rolling, coordinated. Even on the dance floor people cleared the way for him.

When we got home I was so high I couldn't sleep after we'd made love twice so I put on the Discovery Channel and watched a show on sperm whales. I felt that the world was a grand and wonderful place.

I said, "All right, Alex, I'll move in. But would it be all right if I put some real food in the fridge?"

"You know I work late almost every night," he said evenly. "And sometimes things come up. Like my boss wants me to take someone out to play golf or to dinner . . . "

"If I cook my boeuf Maringo you'd goddamn well better be home for it, or else!" I said, and laughed. He didn't laugh, so I punched him in the arm.

"I'm serious, Celeste."

"Alex, lighten up, will you? Why the fuck did you ask me to move in if you didn't really want me to?"

"Don't swear like that, it bothers me. I do want you to move in. I just want you to know how things are."

"I know how things are, goddamnit."

"God, you're so crude sometimes," he said.

"Crude?" I cried. "Crude? Well, screw you, Alex. I just told you I'd move in. Isn't that what you want? Make up your fucking mind!" I grabbed my clothes from the floor and dressed to go.

His doorman smirked at me as I marched unsteadily out of the lobby and into the street. A taxi blared its horn.

* * *

Alex usually called every hour, and if the answering machine picked up, he hung up. But this day, there were no calls from him at all. I raised the receiver once to make sure the phone was working. By nightfall, my anxiety had risen to a crescendo and I was pacing the floor.

Someone knocked; I thought it was Lucia and opened the door. It was Ethel, the deaf old lady who lived next door.

On the day seven years earlier that Candace and I had moved in,

Ethel opened her door, peeked out, and said, "I'm dying of cancer so I can't help you." Candace and I stood there, loaded down with boxes, and just stared at the shriveled old woman. Candace's face got blotchy, which always happened when she was trying to control her emotions. "Oh, I'm sorry—excuse me, please," Candace said, and rushed into our apartment with me on her heels.

As soon as the door was closed, she covered her mouth and held her nose to stifle her nervous giggles and slid down the wall to the floor. "What an awful thing to say—I don't mean to laugh, but really."

Now Ethel's clawlike hand gripped the door frame as her knobby foot slipped across the threshold. The scent of stale vodka and cockroach spray clung to her. She glared at me, her face scrunched up in a wince of outrage.

"It's so bad today, Celine," she said, her voice warbling. "My son hasn't called me in three weeks."

Her trouble was always cataclysmic, and never her fault. Often she had the DT's. "There's a crater in my ceiling and water's leaking all over the floor! Rats are crawling down! They let you live like niggers in this building!"

Once she called the firemen in the middle of the night and in their zeal they tore her door off its hinges. Occasionally she ran out of vodka, which was the issue this afternoon.

"Celine," she said, "they disconnected my phone again. I'm entertaining tonight. Call the liquor store for me, will you? Order me a pint of vodka. Smirnoff's. That kind."

As I was making the call to the liquor store, I considered ordering a new bottle of Stoli for me and Lucia, but then I remembered with a shudder the smell of vodka on Ethel's breath, and didn't.

The young German couple upstairs began to fight.

I looked around my crowded living room, at the fold-out futon couch, the dust balls in the corners, the dingy windows, my unpaid bills. No messages blinked on my answering machine, because lately I had neglected friends and family. Against the far wall stood my cinderblock-and-boards bookshelves, so crowded with books that I'd started piles on the floor. I'd kept every book I'd ever read, although a few were missing that people had borrowed and never returned. Long ago when I had thought about the future, I'd dreamed of myself as successful, and married, and safe. Looking at my reflection now in the cheap mirror that hung on the door, I wondered what on earth had happened. Where had the time gone?

Alex had promised to build me wall-to-wall shelves for my books.

Lucia will be home soon, I said to myself. *Don't panic.*

The room grew dark, the radiator hissed and thumped. There was a grille on the fire escape window, and the light across the street projected diamond shapes onto the floor. Ethel was watching *Live at Five,* and the overenthusiastic voices of news anchors seeped through the wall. I remembered that I still had a bottle of Stoli in the freezer. I went into the kitchen and poured a shot into a thin glass and took a long, icy, syrupy sip.

Better.

What now? I thought.

When I was completing my Ph.D. in Comparative Lit at Columbia, I found temp work as a word processor at various law firms at night. My father, an attorney, once said, chuckling at the irony of it all, "You tried to get as far away from lawyers as you could and here you are, working as a lawyer's secretary."

I gazed at him calmly while my heart pumped blood behind my eyes.

"Gee, sometimes you look so much like your mother, you scare me," he said, turning his eyes away guiltily. "You know I'll pay for law school, Celeste. Anytime, anyplace." He said the last magnanimously, and for a moment my system seemed to completely shut down with the realization that I truly did not like this man whose genes I shared. Then he shook his head, as if the whole thing were simply beyond his control. Rage burned in my esophagus like hot soup swallowed too fast.

Thank God *for the money your mother left you,* I told myself again as the old, unnameable fear tightened its grip. She had made me the sole beneficiary of a large life insurance policy that had been supporting me for over a decade, but the money was running out.

You can always sell her emerald ring, I told myself. *You can always sell her pearls.*

But then what? In less than a year, I would turn thirty.

For many years, I had taught at Columbia while compiling my notes for my dissertation on the works of two concentration camp survivors—Primo Levi, who refused to perish at Auschwitz, and Varlam Shalamov, who survived Stalin's Siberian Kolyma camps. I had often considered quitting, getting a full-time job, but Levi and Shalamov kept me from doing so. If two such great writers had managed to survive the worst conditions the world had to offer, their souls intact—*and write such beauty*—who was I to quit? I was nothing but a spoiled, rich girl; I'd never had to fight for anything in my life. What right did I have to quit?

They had described brutality and death, but also the random gifts of life—a scruffy shrub laden with wrinkled, frozen berries that Varlam collected with trembling fingers in a wasteland of snow; a pipe leaking droplets of clean water that Primo discovered when everywhere around him people were dying of thirst. Sometimes the gifts came from the reckless acts of generosity of other inmates, gestures that cost them their lives. In such a wasteland, on some days the tiniest flicker of human dignity had kept them alive, and they had, for me, best depicted the darkness when describing the flickers of light.

I had started many letters in my rudimentary Italian to Primo Levi, but they seemed trite and unconvincing and I never mailed one off. I could not write to Varlam Shalamov because he would never receive my letters. He was imprisoned in a Moscow insane asylum, until his death in 1982. Five years later, in April, Levi died.

The television news had been making me cringe for years: ghetto babies burned to death in firetrap buildings; children raped by their own fathers, burned by their mothers' cigarettes. When Levi died, I stopped watching the news and began to look for a volunteer position teaching in the public schools. For eight months I fought the New York City school system's bureaucracy, and then an opportunity to teach in Harlem just fell into my lap. I had been there for three semesters now, and I was prouder of this than I was of anything else I'd ever done. But today, none of it, not even the kids with their wide-open faces and fresh and gorgeous poetry, could bring me peace, because fear once again had its clawed hands around my throat.

I thought of Alex's warm, bright, sunny apartment, where nothing ever leaked and the floors were straight. He lived in a world where wastelands did not exist, where pain and fear were just obstacles to overcome, like correcting nearsightedness with a handsome pair of glasses.

His life would surely go on without me, barely disrupted; the city was filled with women who would gladly take my place. Rage and jealousy churned in my stomach, my mouth was dry, my knees numb.

It was dark, and Lucia still wasn't home.

I remembered what Lucia had said last winter when in a particularly blue mood. "Oh my God, I'm thirty-three already. I've been living in this dump for ten years! I don't want to be here at forty, fighting with that drunken lout of a super over the fucking heat!"

I went back to the kitchen and poured myself another stout shot. The hours passed. At ten o'clock, I heard the news come on at Ethel's. I could no longer face the black hours before daylight. No amount of Stoli would calm my fears. With a shaking hand, I reached for the phone.

"Hello?" Alex said, and I heard an edge of anxiety in the one word, and I knew everything was going to be all right. I felt drugged, overcome by relief. Suddenly there was no fear, no black hole, and I could no longer remember what had caused me to argue with him the night before. I saw nothing ahead but easy sailing and blue skies.

* * *

I MET ALEX'S MOTHER, Aurelia, on New Year's Eve. She was in town for a few days. We went to a party at the Fifth Avenue apartment of their rich cousin by marriage who had recently sold his business magazine to a midtown conglomerate for an inconceivable sum. His wife had decorated the vast living room with an array of oeuvres by famous artists—Magritte, Calder, Duchamp. Behind the paintings the walls were deep red. The robust couches and armchairs were upholstered in a lush green and red floral pattern. Long, dark green velvet drapes, embossed with gold fleurs-de-lys, hung in folds beside large windows that revealed a beautiful view of the Met and the park beyond. There wasn't a single book in the entire apartment, but there was a surfeit of Dom Perignon champagne. Aurelia and I stood by one of the windows discussing the view while I tried to keep my balance in my high heels by surreptitiously holding on to the thick drapes. Aurelia wore a green and blue sequined jacket over a black turtleneck and slim black slacks. The track lighting ricocheted off the sequins and made little blue and green spots of light dance on her face and neck.

Suddenly she said, "Alex is crazy about you. He's been so lonely. He doesn't socialize much with his schedule. I guess you could say he's a workaholic, like his mother." She smiled. "Be prepared, he's going to surprise you."

Just then Alex emerged from the crowd and strode toward us with a determined expression on his face. He took me by the arm and pulled me toward the window, behind the curtains. He'd timed his arrival so that there were less than three minutes left to the countdown. He kissed me hard as he slid his hand into his jacket pocket and produced a little velvet box. The box remained in my hand, a corner digging into my palm as he held me tightly. When he released me, I opened it and found a large round diamond solitaire, which threw off sparks of color against the black velvet background. *Oh, to have such things,* my mind whispered.

"Marry me," Alex said in a murmur close to my ear. "I've been looking for you for a long time."

"Did your secretary pick this out as well?" I asked him, smiling to show I was kidding. I couldn't resist.

"Actually, she came with me. Just say yes, Celeste," Alex said.

"How old is this Lorraine anyway?"

"She's a grandmother," Alex said, finally cracking a smile.

I could feel his mother's presence behind the curtain; she seemed to be holding her breath.

"Yes," I said, completely overwhelmed. My mind was saying, *Why me? Why me?* As the crowd began to shout the countdown, he kissed me again, not waiting for midnight. We emerged from behind the curtain engaged. Alex was beaming.

"He wanted to surprise you but I told him not to put you on the spot," Aurelia said with a bright smile. Her dark blue eyes were unfathomable.

* * *

In early February, a few days after the announcement of our engagement appeared in the *Times,* the phone rang at eight-fifteen in the morning. Alex had left for work hours earlier. I was sound asleep.

"This is Mimi. Who's this?" she said.

Later, after hanging up, I came up with cutting responses like, "This is Alex. I forgot to tell you, I had a sex change." But at the time, I was so taken aback I simply said, "Celeste."

"Oh. Well . . ." She proceeded to tell me in a high-pitched breathless voice that she wanted to come by and fetch her Christmas tree lights.

"Isn't Christmas over already?" I asked, befuddled.

"Well, honey, they're for a party. But see, I can't come up to the apartment because I have an order of protection against Alex."

An order of protection? What the hell was she talking about?

I mumbled that I'd leave the lights with the concierge in the lobby.

I put her Christmas lights into a plastic bag along with every little feminine by-product I'd found in the apartment since I'd moved in two months earlier.

Once I'd regained my composure, I called Alex at work.

"Alex, what's this shit about an order of protection against you?"

"It really bothers me when you swear, Celeste, you know that."

"Just tell me what the fuck is going on, Alex."

He sighed deeply. "It's nothing. It was nothing. When we were breaking up I got kind of pissed off at her and punched a hole in the wall. Nothing, really. She overreacted."

"All right," I said, unconvinced. "But you could've told me. I didn't need to hear it from her."

"She's high-strung," Alex said, as if that explained everything.

Three

The second week of April was so warm, it broke records. Mostly I stayed in the cool, quiet apartment, watching the world steaming away outside the thick, soundproof windows. Across the avenue, in the canyon between two tall buildings, there was a little public park with benches where business people came to eat their lunches in their shirtsleeves. I wondered what they all did for a living and if they were happy.

* * *

On Friday night, Alex and I drove his shiny black, tank-like BMW to my father and Anna's house in southern Connecticut. It was a grown-up's car, and sitting back against the soft, chestnut-colored leather seats, I felt like a little girl. I can't say that I didn't appreciate how impressed Anna looked standing at the front door, waving to us as we drove up in a sputter of gravel.

Anna was thrilled by my "catch." She had always been certain that I couldn't take care of myself. She'd been calling for days now, insisting that it was time to have my wedding dress fitted, even though the wedding wasn't for another two and a half months. Anna seemed to think that if the invitations were mailed, and the dress bought, and the wine ordered, the chances that the event would take place were greatly improved.

Their large shingled house stood on a hill overlooking Long Island Sound. We had cocktails and a late snack on the wide porch, facing the luminous water. The lights of Long Island's north shore blinked across the Sound. A nice breeze had stirred itself up after the sultry day, and everyone was cool and relaxed.

"I swear, I've never seen an April like this, have you, dear?" Anna asked my father. He seemed to ponder the question as if it were of the utmost importance to give her a precise and definite answer. Such was his habit in all conversations, one I assumed he'd picked up from being a corporate lawyer for over thirty years. Finally he shook his head and asserted that he had not.

"I wonder what this presages for early July?" Anna asked worriedly. She was already imagining rain on my wedding day. The ceremony was to take place in the garden, then we would all gather at the yacht club for the reception.

* * *

Saturday morning, Anna drove me to her seamstress's shop. The dress was an antique eggshell-colored lace gown that clung to my body over a silk slip. Anna had spotted it in a local antiques boutique, and called me immediately. Alex was not thrilled with the idea of an antique, but Anna had been right about the dress. She had insisted that I leave it in Connecticut so that the minor alterations could be done there, figuring that I probably would not have taken care of it in New York until the last minute, if at all.

Anna stood behind me and watched in the mirror as the seamstress stuck pins here and there. Perched on the little stool in front of my reflection, I watched the lovely bride in the large mirror. She seemed perfectly poised and sensible, and I felt I was watching a film of someone else's life. Inside, a strange, hot sensation of embarrassment assailed me.

"Your mother's pearls will look divine with the dress," Anna said. "And what you need to do now, dear, is take a little piece of fabric to one of those shoe stores that specializes in dyeing satin pumps, and you'll be all set. Now, what about a veil?"

"I don't want a veil," I said.

"But you must have a veil!" Anna cried. She had embraced the wedding plans with a passion she had previously shown only for birth control, the pro-choice movement, and golf. She had no children of her own.

"You *are* stubborn!" Anna laughed, crossing her arms and throwing her head back. "When you were, oh, ten, I believe, I took you to Central Park, to the carousel. You got on and I waited for you at the gate. I waited and waited. You wouldn't come off! Do you remember? How you screamed and yelled when I made you leave. I could never get you to listen to me, even back then. All right, you don't want a veil, so you won't have a veil. How about a little tiara of flowers?"

I looked at Anna in the mirror, puzzled. I had no memory of a day at the carousel with her. I remembered vaguely my mother's presence and the carousel, but not Anna. For some reason, this sent a chill through me.

"I never went to the carousel with you," I said in a formal voice that came from the pretty, poised bride in the mirror and did not sound familiar. Anna frowned in midsmile.

"What are you talking about, Celeste? Of course we did."

* * *

I AWAKENED with a start the next morning, in the bedroom that I had slept in for half my life, to the squawking seagulls and the clatter of lawn mowers. Still thinking about the carousel in Central Park, I could not remember the day Anna was talking about. I recalled many other days from that time, but there was a certain haziness to the images.

Who had I been, then? What had been my hopes and fears?

The shelves and walls of my old bedroom offered no clue, for I had come home after my sophomore year of college, and in a moment of resolve, emptied my shelves and closets of all my old belongings. Once and for all I wanted to bury the childish and needy Celeste whom I had never liked much. I unceremoniously packed everything into boxes and shoved them in a dark corner of the attic. Now, as I tried to form a picture of myself as a ten- or twelve-year-old girl, I could not remember the books I had read, the toys I had played with, or the clothes I had worn.

Alex turned over and reached out for me as he opened his eyes. I kissed his shoulder, sat up, threw off the sheet, and got out of bed.

"Where are you going?" Alex asked, sitting up and running a hand through his lovely dark blond hair.

"Up to the attic," I said.

"What for?" he asked sleepily.

"I don't know. I'm not sure. I'll be back in a little while."

The air in the attic was close and still. The early sun shone through the windows in slanting beams that seemed opaque and tangible. Specks of dust danced in the light. The boxes were not hard to find. They were exactly where I had left them ten years before.

I opened the first one and came upon my large, clothbound fairy-tale picture books: the Brothers Grimm, Hans Christian Andersen, Mother Goose. Beneath them were *Les fables de la Fontaine*, and every single French-language version of *Tintin* and *Asterix le Gaulois*, special-ordered by my French mother who had feared that I would grow up "too American"; and below them, my *Bobbsey Twins* and *Nancy Drew* mysteries. I could not remember the plot of a single *Nancy Drew,* only vague images of haunted houses. In the next box were my bears and dolls. They seemed sad, all jammed together and suffocating in the dark. I took them out and made a halfhearted attempt to smooth their fur, hair, and clothes.

In the next box I found my posters: characters from *The Lord of the Rings*; a barefooted Cat Stevens; a miniskirted Carly Simon, and a frizzy-haired Carole King. Folded neatly were my hip-hugger bell-bottom jeans, tie-dyed T-shirts, and Indian beads. I held up the old khaki army satchel I'd used as a book bag, embroidered with butterflies, flowers, and a huge peace sign. At the bottom of the box I found my senior prom dress, a pale blue gown of tulle, wrapped in plastic, along with the corsage of white roses and baby's breath, given to me by my date, Sebastian MacKenna. Beside the dress was a large jewelry box my mother had given me that played a little tune when you opened it while a tiny ballerina twirled around in front of a mirror. The little lock had long ago lost its key. I lifted the lid, but the ballerina wouldn't twirl anymore. The box was filled with Sebastian's letters in their envelopes, held together with a ribbon. Underneath, I found letters from his brother, Nathan.

"You've been up here for ages." I looked up to find Alex standing in a beam of light. I closed the box quietly, putting it aside.

"Hi," I said, and smiled. "I'm sorry, I just started thinking about all this stuff up here. I haven't looked at it in years."

"Getting married makes people nostalgic," he said. Alex crouched down beside me and put a hand on my shoulder. He gazed at the tie-dyed T-shirts strewn by my crossed legs. "Oh God, remember those clothes?" He laughed. "My mother wanted me to have Beatle boots, you know. But I wanted penny loafers, so I could look like my dad. Square at twelve."

His eyes landed on the box filled with picture books. "You should keep these," he said, serious. "One day you could read them to our children and say, 'These were my books once.'"

Children! What a thought. I smiled, nodding foolishly.

Alex reached his hand into the box, and like a cardsharp, drew out a volume that had not been there a moment before: the 1977 *Sand-*

piper, my high school yearbook. How could I have overlooked it? I wrenched the solid navy-blue clothbound book from his hands.

"Oh, come on, let me see your picture!" Alex said, reaching for it. I gripped the book to my chest and sighed as he tried to pry it from my hands. As we struggled over the volume, a cardboard picture frame with a gold lining slipped out. In the cloud of dust our fuss had raised, I watched Alex lean over and pick it up, and unfold the prom photo of Sally Newlyn and Sebastian MacKenna and me.

Sebastian stands in the middle, looking businesslike and in control of matters in a gray fedora and gray suit. On his right arm is Sally, her skin milky white against the crimson velvet of her long dress that fits her perfectly. It was her mother's prom dress, kept in storage for over twenty years. Above her ear, pinned to a barrette, the corsage of red roses Sebastian gave her pokes out. Fine, straight black hair falls to her shoulders. Her oval face, sporting tiny dark freckles at the nose and cheeks, is wide open, her smile immense, verging on an explosion of hysterical laughter. I am on Sebastian's other arm, smiling coyly for the camera in my pale blue dress, overwhelming in its puffs and folds, my white roses pinned above my breast. My Farrah Fawcett hairdo looks like a palm tree, with dark blond fronds falling in layers around my face.

"The three of you went together?" Alex asked.

"Yes. Sally was in the hospital up until a week before the prom. By then everyone was paired up already." Images of that evening came flooding back, the crowded dance floor, the bottle of vodka in Sally's handbag, the lights twirling around us as we danced, the three of us together, except for the slow songs, when Sally and I would take turns with Sebastian. Quickly, I added, "We had the best time. Until the football players pulled the urinals off the wall of the men's room and we all got thrown out of the country club."

"Who's the mortician?" Alex asked with a smile.

"Sebastian MacKenna. Last I heard he was a Navy pilot. He joined up after college. His dad worked for Exxon. His family moved away. They moved a lot."

We sat in silence as the dust settled around us. A frightful pang of anxiety gripped my heart. The yearbook lay in my lap. I opened it to the first page.

SALLY NEWLYN, JUNE 1977, was written there in bold letters.

"This isn't yours," Alex said thoughtfully, pointing to the inscription.

"It must be," I said, but then realized with a shudder that Sebastian and I had bought one yearbook for the two of us, as an act of faith and eternal devotion. After graduation, he had kept it. It was inconceivable to me that I had packed up Sally's by mistake.

* * *

When I had come home for Christmas my freshman year, Mrs. Newlyn called to inform me that her daughter was back in the hospital. Sally had to be put in a straitjacket because she was tearing out her hair, punching the walls, screaming that she had left her yearbook at my house and absolutely had to get it back. Her doctor was adamant that Mrs. Newlyn try to find it.

Mrs. Newlyn said that she'd turned her house upside down, and asked me to look for it at mine. There was a certain iciness in her tone that had been there since Sally's first bout with mental illness. I felt that Mrs. Newlyn somehow blamed me, or at the very least wished that I had been the one afflicted, instead of her own, very good little girl. I had searched everywhere for the yearbook, but never found it.

* * *

"This just can't be," I said to Alex, my voice rising insistently. "It wasn't here. I know it."

He looked at me strangely and said, "You probably just packed it without seeing it, what's the big deal?"

"No!" I said. I sat there, stunned, while Alex took the book from me and silently began to flip through the pages. He came across a large photo of Sebastian, tall and tow-blond, in his baseball uniform, poised at the plate with the bat over his shoulder. Across his slightly bent legs in the white uniform, he had written in his left-hander's tilting script: "Dear Sally—I know this year has been hard for you, but don't forget we love you 4-ever."

All the inscriptions were similar: "Dear Sally, you're the nicest, sweetest person I know, and I know everything will be great in your life from now on." "Dear Sally, remember when you ran the mile in 5:12? You were the greatest." Further on, there was a page-sized picture of our local beach, gray in the winter light, with the Sound almost black beyond it. High above, seagulls hovered, white V's in the dark sky. The yearbook staff had printed a poem I had written earlier that year for the *Sandpiper Press* on the photo. It was about a girl walking alone on a winter beach, looking out at the stormy ocean and trying to picture it on a summer day.

"This is a nice poem," Alex said.

Below it I'd written: "My dearest friend—I know that everything is going to turn out the way you want it to, so don't worry. I'll always be there for you. Remember, 'Winter, spring, summer or fall/all you got to do is call/and I'll be there/yes I will/you got a friend.' —Carole King." It seemed so silly now, attributing the verses to Carole King, as if anybody on the planet wouldn't know, or would accuse me of plagiarism.

Alex turned the pages back to the senior portraits. He was looking through the N's. There was a blank, pale square where Sally's picture should have been. She'd penciled in a self-portrait, with her hair sticking straight out around her head, and her eyes huge, bulging and crossed, and a zero with a bar through it at the center of her forehead. She used to sign her notes and letters with this symbol. I had found this wise and deep on her part. Below the blank frame, the caption read: "Sally Newlyn, Best Girl Athlete, Everyone's Friend. Unavailable for photograph."

"She wasn't there when they took the pictures," I said to Alex. "Something was wrong with her brain chemically. She was in and out of the hospital for most of the second half of our senior year."

"You mean she was crazy?"

I looked at him, his handsome face, so clear in its understanding of things, as though he'd rolled over all of life's sticks and stones like a mountain stream. Our upbringing had not been that dissimilar—he had a stepmother, I had a stepmother. We had never wanted for anything in the material sense. At seventeen, we each were given a car, all that. But he'd never *lost* anyone, and that, I thought, made a big difference in how we perceived the world.

I thought about his question for a moment. Doctors had attached names to Sally's illness, and the names changed, along with her medication. "An imbalance," they said at first, and put her on lithium. When that didn't work, they called it "clinical depression" and put her on some mood elevator. Finally, when nothing seemed to help, they said she was "schizophrenic," and put her on new drugs that made her lethargic and fat. We did not live in a community that liked to delve into disaster. She was ill—this was an accepted fact, but her parents, our teachers, and our friends behaved as if she had a rare but curable infection. We were all afraid of the word *crazy*.

It was, I remembered with a shudder, what my father used to shout at my mother in fits of rage: *You goddamn crazy bitch! You're crazy, Nathalie, you know that?*

Calling somebody crazy was like calling them junkie, faggot, or whore.

"I guess she was crazy," I said, feeling guilty, for I remembered that in the midst of her bouts with despair and madness, she'd said the most brilliant, intuitive, unexpected things. She'd predicted my future with an accuracy that now seemed staggering.

"What happened to her?" Alex asked.

I'd never spoken to him of Sally, or of that period in my life. As I thought about what to say to him, all sorts of images came rushing back, and crowded out my breath.

"She killed herself," I said, attempting to sound neutral. "She jumped off an overpass in New Haven and landed on the highway."

"Jesus, what a horrible thing to do," he said.

"No." I felt I had to defend her. "She did what she felt she had to do. I think it took a lot of guts."

"I know those overpasses," he said. "Jesus."

I'd never belonged to any church. I'd never been baptized. But after I heard about Sally I went to the Catholic church in town and lit candles for her, praying on my knees to God, "Please, if You exist, please let her into heaven." It seemed such an outrage, such a terrible injustice, that she should have to suffer in purgatory for eternity after having suffered so much in life.

"I don't know. Maybe she wasn't planning it," I said. "Maybe she was just out walking over a bridge, and then . . . I don't know."

"No one just goes out for a walk on an overpass," he said quietly.

"What does *that* mean, Alex?" I said in a menacing tone I knew scared him. He looked at me as if he thought I was about to throw one of my "fits." Whenever I felt tears threatening, I would run and lock myself in the bathroom until it passed. He'd sit on the couch and read a newspaper and act as if it never happened. I couldn't stand to have him see me like that. I wanted to change. I wanted, in fact, to become more like him—calm, rational, objective. He'd never seen me cry.

"I'm really sorry," he said. His eyes were dark and luminous and I thought that perhaps he understood, perhaps great pain had not escaped him entirely. We sat in silence a long time.

* * *

For the rest of the day, images of Sally, of my mother, of Sebastian and his brother Nathan, came to me unexpectedly, like impromptu visits from old friends you really don't want to see and so you hide, pretend that you're not home. But they kept returning, especially that night back in our apartment, as I lay in bed waiting for sleep. Not another word on the subject was uttered, yet Alex and I had made love almost violently, throwing sheets and blankets to the floor. Now he was sleeping soundly beside me. After a while I got up quietly and went to the kitchen, remembering that there was half a bottle of white wine in the door of the fridge. I poured myself a glassful, then took the glass to a chair by a living room window and sat in the darkness, trying to make peace with those I thought I'd left behind a long time ago.

Four

My French mother's railing against America had started off as a joke between us, "to break the silence," she said, of our large house. By the time I was eight, an edge of anger and frustration had infiltrated her lightheartedness; and my father, who worked long hours in the city, who was silent and distracted when he was home, moved farther and farther away from us. One day he took a studio apartment in New York and started coming home only on weekends. Then, he'd lock himself up in his study and appear only at meals, safe and formal affairs in which Mathilde, the French cook, would serve us from fancy trays and my mother would never yell because she thought it not *comme il faut* to involve the servants in family disputes.

* * *

I was ten at the time; my brother Jack, thirteen. He was not interested in us, and didn't come home except to change and sleep. My mother had lost control of him, given up hope. She talked incessantly of taking me away to Europe and leaving my brother and father behind.

"What is this sports, sports all the time?" she'd say in her heavy French accent. "They watch the football like it is the great truth of life. I tell you, that is the only way men can talk to one another in this country. They watch the football, sitting in a row so they don't have to look in each other's eyes, and they say 'Ah, nice pass,' and slap each other on the back.

"Your brother is formed already, just like your father, girls and cars and games, games! I met your father on the ski slope in Grenoble. Ah, I was so young and beautiful then. America was everybody's dream. I was so stupid! And he was so handsome with his white American teeth!

Look how strong are his Wasp genes. Out of two, only you look a little bit like me, not much."

I went back to the kitchen for a second glass of wine. The bottle was nearly empty, so I finished it off. I hid it at the bottom of the trash can under some plastic bags, wondering if Alex would notice. On my way back to the armchair, I caught sight of my reflection in the dark window. In a pale nightgown, hair tousled, carrying the wine glass, I looked so much like my mother that for a moment I stood frozen before this apparition.

I sat down and squeezed my eyes shut, fighting back tears.

* * *

My mother is pacing the kitchen in her stained, pale blue bathrobe with safety pins of all sizes pinned to the lapels. Her hair is a mess of thick curls, the color of a freshly plowed field. Fingers of sunlight reach through the jungle of plants that grow in front of the large window and refract off the ice in her amber drink. I watch her from my tall stool at the butcher block in the middle of the room. Beside me, her ashtray is overflowing.

Her voice whispers to me, "You are not too old yet to have your mind opened up. I tell you something, you don't feel like being an athlete, I tell them to go to hell. I write you an excuse to gym class. This world is too small. Nothing exists for these people outside of these walls!"

I understood even then that my mother was terribly unhappy, that my father did not love her the way she wanted, that she had no friends to speak of in our community. She was unhappy, and no one else seemed to be, or if they were, they didn't advertise it. I began to feel uncomfortable at school around the wholesome, happy kids who fit in so easily and seemed to have no time for doubts. And Sally Newlyn, jockette and running champion, who wore the school colors and went to Halloween parties as the Statue of Liberty, was the child I hated and envied most.

I followed my mother around the house in the afternoons. She padded from room to room, the drink always in her hand, inspecting things, paintings, vases, ashtrays, up close, and then squinting at them from a distance.

"All this—" she'd make a sweeping gesture, a cigarette smoldering between her stained fingers, its ashes falling on the pale carpet. "All this means nothing. Don't forget what I am telling you, Celeste. Ah, let's go back to France. Let's *go*!"

But we never did. She raged mercilessly about her own mother, who sat "like the rock of Gibraltar" in an ancient chateau near Bordeaux. "That old woman will die before she sees me again."

She had incurred the wrath of "the rock" by marrying my father, a "low-class American." It didn't matter to my grandmother that his family had been here since the Revolution; all Americans were by nature low-class. My mother and I had tested the waters with a two-week visit to Bordeaux the previous summer, but it had ended in disaster. For my mother, the thought of going home to *her* mother represented failure, and therefore disgusted her. She had never worked, could not conceive of it, so her talk of moving with me to Italy, to Florence, to Venice, to Rome, was just that.

* * *

Spring. I like the walk home in the rain from the school bus stop, just beyond our gate, the sound of rain pattering on the cool green leaves in the garden. I open the kitchen door. No lights are on in the house. I call out for my mother and hear my small voice echoing through the large rooms. Something has happened. I'm afraid to go upstairs. I walk around switching on all the lamps until the whole ground floor is ablaze with light.

My father came home from New York, unchanged, apparently unmoved, except now he seemed tired. He could not look me in the eyes; I wondered if I brought to mind things he'd rather forget.

"Where is my mommy?" I asked this stranger, glaring up at him.

"Your mommy had a weak heart," he told me. "She had a heart attack. But don't worry, she didn't suffer. She simply went to heaven to visit God."

* * *

There was a funeral, of course. Our neighbors and friends were amazed by our courage, our will as a family to go on. A few days later, in school, I was standing by my locker, laughing coyly at something a cute boy had said, when Sally marched up to me in her perfect pleated skirt (she wore shorts underneath as a precaution against exactly such randy boys) and said to me in a shocked little voice, "You shouldn't laugh like that, what's the matter with you? Your mother's funeral wasn't even a week ago."

"Go to hell," I said to her, and watched her coldly as her face turned purple and she spun on her heels and stormed off in a pout.

My father must have given up his studio, because now he was home every evening. I began to water my mother's jungle of plants, and to watch him in silence.

Incapable of showing us affection, he decided to offer us a sense of organization. He told my brother and me that he expected certain changes. Dinner at seven sharp.

This was the new routine:

"How was your day today, Celeste?" he'd ask at dinner, gazing at the plate our new housekeeper Paloma had set before him. Mathilde had quit, just after my mother died.

He'd had his martini or a scotch on the rocks and there was a bottle of French wine on the table. My mother had collected red wine, and it seemed my father was determined to finish off her vast cellar as soon as possible. We were allowed a few drops in our water. I tried always to get more, mostly because it was not allowed, and because I loved the color and the secret magic of the ruby elixir that made my father feel warm and tender toward the world.

"So, Celeste?"

"I'm fine, Daddy," I'd say. "Everything is fine."

"And what about you, young fellow?" he'd ask Jack.

"Oh, I'm fine, too." And to make our father happy, Jack would add something about football practice, or a new organism he'd inspected under the microscope in science class.

"Well, that's terrific," our father would say, nodding with relief, and he would begin to eat. After a while he'd start to relax, the lines in his face becoming softer, less angry. As if by magic, the vague, cold look would disappear from his eyes. He'd talk about the law firm in words that sounded to me like mathematics, which I had already started to fail.

One by one, my mother's plants shriveled up. Nothing I did seemed to help.

A month passed; I had an accident on my bicycle and broke my leg. One day a tall, thin, blond lady appeared in my bedroom and sat down to read me a Nancy Drew mystery.

"Who are you?"

"I'm Mrs. Smith. But you can call me Anna."

"Do you know anything about plants, Mrs. Smith?"

"Anna. A little, why?" She smiled down at me, her eyes curious and alert.

"All my mother's plants in the kitchen are dying."

"I'll take a look." She patted my cast, stood up, straightened her skirt, and was gone. Moments later she was back, this time with a tall, thin frosted glass that smelled bitter and lemony. "You've been overwatering them," she said. "Now, would you like me to read to you? I certainly hope you and I will become friends."

She read me an entire Nancy Drew mystery. It took all day. Every once in a while she'd cry out gaily, "Break time!" and go downstairs to refill her glass.

* * *

Soon the plants were thriving again. She even replaced the ones that had died. But the kitchen lost its jungle look; now it seemed more like an English garden, with carefully arranged flowering plants, all variations of the same hue.

Within a year my father married her.

Once, my mother had told me when I was having a problem with a particularly bossy math teacher, that it was better to kiss the asses of persons of authority if they had the power to control your life. When Anna moved into our house, I did everything possible to gain her confidence. I grew quickly to depend on her for advice concerning minor, everyday obstacles, like needing new shoes, losing a schoolbook, or needing help with homework. But we never became friends.

Apparently my mother had not given Jack the same advice, and from the moment Anna stepped through the door in her white bridal suit and little hat with a sprig of white flowers, the two were at war.

* * *

I came to think of her as a dainty queen from a fairy-tale book, living behind magical fortress walls. She seemed to peer out at the world through the narrow balistrarias, from where she shot poisoned arrows at her enemies. She believed she had a panoramic view of the world from her castle, and no one could tell her that it wasn't so.

* * *

Jack rushed into the kitchen around supper time like a black tornado, filthy from football, and headed right for the fridge. I was sitting at the butcher block, reading one of my Tintin comic books for the thousandth time. I looked up and watched Jack drink from the milk carton. His fingers left black streaks on the white surface. I gasped, for dirt upset Anna more than anything. But he was taking his time, probably hoping that Anna would walk in and catch him. Since she hadn't come in, he put the empty carton back in the fridge and set about making a sandwich, tearing the plastic wrappers off the cold cuts and leaving them on the counter with the open mayonnaise and mustard jars. Just then Anna pushed through the swinging door, making a swish of wind, a tall glass tinkling in her hand.

"Oooh, macho man! It excites me, *Jacques,* to observe such grace and charm!" she cried.

And Jack, who hated nothing—nothing—more than being called by the French name that adorned his birth certificate, burped, smiled, and walked out carrying his sandwich, leaving dirt and grease stains on the swinging door, and a trail of ham and mustard and mayonnaise on the floor.

I watched her reach into the freezer and take out the gin bottle with a dramatic flourish. She poured a generous shot into her glass. Several ice cubes from the ice cube maker followed with a loud clinking splash.

"God knows I try," she muttered, pushing her hair back with the flat of her trembling hand and taking a large swig of the drink with the other.

A year later, Jack took to drinking from a tequila bottle at the living room bar, his eyes glaring at her. He left empty condom wrappers in the ashtray of the car. Anna complained to my father, but he would just laugh and tell her that boys will be boys. As Jack's rebelliousness grew—he quit the football team, started failing classes—Anna's tone became more and more saccharine, even ebullient. Watching, I wondered if he might consider it a victory if she ever wept or tried to hit him. But she continued to pretend that the war did not exist, all the while firing her sugar-coated arrows at him.

I was quiet, reserved, and had few friends. In school I hung out with the exchange students from France, and the precocious "radicals" who at twelve were singing inflammatory songs about Vietnam. I excelled only in language and literature. When Sally—everyone's little darling—saw me coming down the hall, she made a wide circle to avoid me, and walked by with her nose in the air. Her parents had an American flag on the antenna of their station wagon. I'd heard from other kids that her brother was over in Vietnam, a captain in the Marines. Her family went to the Episcopal church on Sundays. Her mother, a little, dark-haired pixie of a woman, was a member of the DAR, the school board, the PTA, and volunteered in all the charities. Sally was the best girl athlete in the junior high and could outrun almost all the boys.

I hated her, foremost because I wished I could run like that.

In phys ed I had always been a failure. It was not so much that I was physically uncoordinated, but rather that I was terrified of failing, of looking stupid, of being laughed at. We were judged by how we performed, and my distinct lack of practice in the gym was an unfortunate handicap that I couldn't surmount. I was picked last for the teams, while Sally was always a captain, usually of the winning team.

Several years passed in this attitude of general avoidance, until, at the beginning of tenth grade, our class was moved to the new high school, an enormous one-story red-brick edifice that spread out across the town's highest hill. It had been built, at great expense to the taxpayers, in a Romanesque style around courtyards, so that from every class we had a garden view. Sally and I were horrified to find that we'd been placed next to each other in homeroom. For the whole year we would share all our classes, except for the electives.

The first day, I said good morning to her in a cool and formal manner. She responded in kind, and soon we were saying hello to each other in the halls. We were like two species of monkeys glaring at each other through the bars of adjoining cages. Sitting next to her day after day, I realized that she was not a phony. She hated gossip. When other girls talked about a "slut" or a "cock tease," which pretty much covered the range of possibilities, Sally would look away uncomfortably and say, "Oh, gad, hang it up, will ya?"

* * *

One morning in homeroom, she reached over and ran a finger across a butterfly I'd embroidered on my jeans.

"How pretty!" she said. "Did you do that yourself?"

"Yes." And then, for some incomprehensible reason, I added, "I'll do one for you if you like."

"I wish I could wear stuff like that! My mom would have a cow. But thanks anyway."

We gazed at each other and there were smiles on our faces. We no longer feared each other, and in that moment I felt redeemed, as if I had passed across some threshold, into a world of happiness and light.

* * *

Later that day, in phys ed, we lined up in the chill October air for a soccer game. I stood at the perimeter of the group, shivering, with my arms crossed over my chest. Sally, captain as always, didn't appear cold at all in just a T-shirt and shorts. She stacked her team with the best athletes, frightening Amazons with muscular legs and arms—and then, she called out my name.

"What, are you totally nuts?" an ox of a girl cried out.

"Yeah, Sal, what's up?" another teammate said in a deep voice.

I tiptoed over to their side, head hanging guiltily as the jockettes peered at me with scorn.

"Look," Sally whispered to me, "you're probably just scared, see. It's easy! Just kick the heck out of the ball. It's fun! It's no big deal if you miss."

Sally flew through the air, yelling orders and flipping her dark hair away from her eyes. Her legs and feet seemed as coordinated as arms and hands; she could do a jig around the ball and keep it moving, kick it anywhere she wanted, even flick it behind her into the goal. She kept sending the ball in my direction, but I invariably froze.

"Come on, kick! Kick it, Celeste!" she cried.

I attempted one good kick. As my leg flew out, I saw my foot dangling there at the end of it, limp and useless. I sent the ball skidding into the legs of the captain of the opposing team.

"It's all right! At least you kicked it! That was good!" Sally cried.

We did not speak much outside of gym class, but there, she had made me her pet project. For our midterm, we were to perform in one of the four gymnastics disciplines—parallel bars, mat, horse, or balance beam. Sally spent entire gym periods helping me with exercises on the balance beam. She was under the impression that I had good balance.

On the day of the exam, the teacher, a tall black woman with a morose face, stood on the sidelines with her arms crossed while Sally directed my efforts on the beam. I managed a fairly steady pirouette, a few good skips, and a meager, shaky somersault without falling off. I received my first B-plus in gym.

Afterwards, I watched Sally tumble across the mat, performing front and back flips, cartwheels, and splits in every direction. She had brought a little cassette recorder from home, and the song "Tiny Dancer" by Elton John bounded off the gymnasium walls. What she lacked in grace she made up for in the sheer strength of her arms and legs. She could jump higher than anyone, and was not afraid to try a somersault in the air. She landed on both feet with a loud thump and an expression of angry concentration on her face. I stood there watching, dumbfounded by my own admiration.

"Why aren't you taking a shower?" she asked me after class while we were both getting dressed.

"I took one this morning," I responded, feeling shameful.

"God, you really *are* French aren't you?" she said with a strange smile.

"You didn't take one either," I remarked.

"I have my period," she said. With that, she took an extremely large Tampax out of her book bag, slammed her locker shut, and headed for the bathroom. A moment later she came back, pinching her fingers together and sniffing at them, making a disgusted face. "I *hate* that smell," she said. "Deodorant tampons don't make it go away at all. I washed my hands about a million times! Being a girl is so gross."

* * *

"***Voolay . . . Voolay voo*** *oon glassay?* Damn, I'll never get this," Sally muttered. We were in homeroom a few days later, and she was poring over her French textbook, pulling on her hair.

I turned to her. "When's your test?"

"Tomorrow. Damn. I hate this foreign language stuff. My dad might get posted to Paris, can you believe this crap? Now they're making me learn frog-talk!"

"I speak French. I can help you."

"Really? That would be so cool."

She invited me to go home with her after school and stay for dinner.

We ambled along the quiet, winding roads. She told me she wanted to be an Olympic long-distance runner. She was on the cross-country team, she said, running five, sometimes six miles a day after school. She ran barefoot like the American Indians. Today, though, she was taking off so that I could help her with her frog-talk. She told me the coach wouldn't let her run more than five miles a day because her bones were still growing, and he wanted her to be the number one runner for the mile in the spring.

"Have you ever smoked cigarettes?" she asked me.

"Yeah, a couple times, with my brother Jack."

"Gee, is he the *cutest*! . . . I really would like to try smoking," she said, "just once, though. Just to try. They say it gets you high the first time."

She told me that besides her older brother the Marine captain, she had an older sister who was married and had a baby. Once we got to her home, a nice, two-story stone house set back in the woods, she got some milk and cookies from the kitchen and took me up to her bedroom under the roof. She played a Carly Simon tape on her little cassette player and showed me an album full of pictures of her five-month-old niece Suzy, who'd been born three months premature.

Sally gave me a face massage, reading the directions over her shoulder in a book and using a cucumber cream she'd bought at the health food store downtown.

"What about your French test?"

"We'll get to it . . . My mom says all this pressure point stuff is hocus-pocus, but I believe in it."

My first face massage was exhilarating. My family never touched one another. This intimacy, which seemed so natural to Sally, made me long for a sister. I felt quite exposed as I lay on her bed with my eyes shut, while she twisted my face into all kinds of odd expressions.

Then she did my nails with a little kit, buffing and filing each one, clipping off the excess skin around the moons.

"You always want the moons to show," she said.

"Why?"

"Because it's chic. That's what my mom says."

Carly Simon was singing, "We have no secrets/We tell each other most everything/About the lovers in the past/And why they didn't last . . . "

"She's so in love," Sally mused. "I feel like I'm in love, but not with anybody in particular, you know. Just in love. Next week I'm going to get my ears pierced. I've wanted to for years but my mom says it's sleazy if you're too young. You look like a foreigner or something." She gasped, then looked to see if mine were pierced. "I used to hate you, you know," she said, not looking up. Her cheeks were shiny and red, like apples.

"Yes, I know," I said.

"I thought you were a snob. Plus, you didn't act sad when your mom—well, you know. It was like you didn't care what anybody thought. Now I think you're the most interesting person I know. Your clothes are so cool and you walk so straight, like you don't have time for silliness. Boys like that, you know, they like girls who don't pay them any attention.

"I found my mother's diaphragm," she whispered suddenly. "I was looking through her underwear drawer, for fun. Did you ever see a diaphragm? It's as big as a salad dish, I swear! How does she get it in there?" She laughed, embarrassed, her face scrunched up into crinkles. Then she winced. "I don't know, the thought of them doing it kind of makes me feel sick. I *hate* it." She looked at me as if she expected a response.

I tried to imagine my father and Anna "doing it," and the thought was definitely unappetizing. I nodded in agreement.

She told me about her brother the Marine. She said her parents were getting very strange letters from him and were worried. "This is a secret," she warned me, a finger over her lips. I nodded solemnly.

"The troops are starting to pull out, but he's got some big job in Saigon so he has to stay. My dad was in World War II, he landed on Omaha Beach five days after D day. My brother's letters are getting so *weird*! In his last one, he said the war was a *mistake*! Can you imagine? He asked my dad to take the American flag off the antenna of the station wagon!

"What do you think we should do?" she asked me, looking very serious.

"I have no idea."

"I told them to take it off. He could *die* over there. But you know what my mom said? She said, 'Everyone will notice!' It's true, isn't it? Everybody notices *everything* in this town."

I just shrugged my shoulders and flipped over the tape.

Five

THE FIRST DAY of school after the Christmas holidays, there was a new boy in our homeroom. The teacher introduced him as Sebastian MacKenna and said he had just arrived from England. His eyes were velvety-brown, soft-looking, and his hair was a straight and silky blond. He looked a little like Robert Redford in *The Way We Were.* He was on the round side, but this only added to his charm. He was simply adorable.

"Sebastian is a pretty unusual name," Sally said, leaning toward his desk.

"My mother read *Brideshead Revisited* and she fell in love with a character whose name was Sebastian," he explained. He pronounced all his consonants, his vowels were sharp. He seemed self-possessed, well-mannered, and slightly shy.

"What were you doing in England?"

"My dad works for Exxon. We move around. In London, my brother and I went to an all-boys school for three years. This is a big change." He laughed and blushed. "My mom was very happy over there, being that she's an Anglophile from way back."

Sally looked at me, I looked at her. Anglophile, that was a new one on us.

During recess, I saw my brother and another boy sneaking off toward the woods to have a smoke.

"That's my brother, Jack," I told Sebastian, nodding in their direction.

"How funny, he's with my brother."

Sally, Sebastian, and I were still standing around when they came out of the woods a while later.

"Hey, Bass, how's your first day?" his brother said. He was a little taller than Sebastian, dark-haired, with similarly shaped eyes, but his were a strange hazel-green with gold specks, and in them there was something mischievous and sharp, something smoldering. He had a rosy mouth, soft-looking lips, and a nose that was not small but turned up slightly at the end. He was wearing a pair of faded blue jeans with holes at the knees and a bald patch right where the bulge was. I had to force my eyes away.

Looking Sally and me over, he added knowingly, "I see you're already making new friends."

I saw from my brother's eyes that they had smoked more than just cigarettes. A strange, acrid odor, subtle and elusive, rose from them. I was about to go into a pout, because I believed that marijuana led people to more serious drugs, as we'd been informed in health class. My brother noted my sour expression and became more considerate than usual.

"Nathan, this is Celeste and this is Sally."

"Ladies," Nathan said, bowing slightly, but never taking his eyes off us. After a moment, he added, rubbing his hands together briskly, "This is going to be a riot. No fucking rules like in London. No fucking A levels! Clear sailing all the way to graduation!"

* * *

A RUMOR BEGAN drifting around school that Nathan had received a genius score on his IQ test, but we suspected he may have been the source. Nevertheless, his British education had put him so far ahead that, according to Jack, Nathan could outtalk his teachers in every subject.

This was certainly true in Advanced French, the only class he and I shared. He had read every book on the curriculum, and would sit back comfortably at his desk, legs spread wide, tapping a pencil on the desktop, and ask Mlle Spiegel questions in French that she was unable to answer.

Nathan and Sebastian were both left-handed, but Nathan wrote in block capitals, even in French. This annoyed Mlle Spiegel, who said there was a *type* of handwriting specific to France. She had forced the rest of us to learn it. My French handwriting was exactly like my mother's, which frightened and appalled me.

One day she handed Nathan back a paper on Sartre and existentialism with a B-plus scribbled on it in red. She'd taken points off for his handwriting. We heard a loud sound of crumpling paper and turned to look. Nathan had made the paper into a ball between his solid hands. Holding it reverently, he threw it in a graceful arc that landed in the wastepaper basket by Mlle Spiegel's desk. There was no expression at all on his face.

I couldn't imagine doing such a thing—what if he'd missed?

* * *

Sebastian was the kind of boy parents *wanted* you to go out with. Teachers, mothers, traffic cops—everyone seemed to like him. He had a sweet, honest face, calm and focused, that made you want to just turn everything over to him. Sally and I talked him into buying us Eve cigarettes—they seemed so chic with a ring of pale flowers around the filter—and of course the saleslady in the drugstore believed him when he said they were for his mother. The three of us rode our bikes to a field at the end of a dirt path in the woods, and smoked until our heads were spinning and our feet could no longer feel the frozen ground. Then Sally and I took turns kissing him with our mouths open, like in the movies.

I could tell that Sebastian kissed me longer, and that his back and arm muscles relaxed with Sally in a way they didn't with me. But it was easy to pretend that his affection was equally apportioned between us.

Sally and I went over to Sebastian's one afternoon. Mrs. MacKenna made us iced tea and put some Oreos on a plate. She was petite, fine-boned, pretty like a porcelain doll. Her voice was low and steady, her movements precise and refined. Sebastian looked very much like her, he had her coloring and her dark brown eyes. He called her "Mother."

Mr. MacKenna, we'd found out just that day from Sebastian, was still in England, "wrapping up loose ends." When we'd asked him why they'd come ahead, Sebastian said it was because of school.

The pale blue living room was crowded with stiff-backed antique furniture. On the baby grand a few school portraits showed the boys as children, along with one family photograph. I was dying to inspect them, believing that some great secret would be revealed to me. Nathan's and Sebastian's youthful faces smiled at me blankly; there were spaces between their front teeth. The photograph of the four MacKennas was a recent formal portrait, probably taken at the photographer's studio. The three men, the father in the middle, stood stiffly around Mrs. MacKenna sitting in a chair; she was the only one smiling. Mr. MacKenna was suntanned and youthful-looking. Nathan had inherited his mischievous eyes.

Nathan's nose, however, came from his mother. It then occurred to me that Sebastian had his father's nose, a fairly substantial, masculine one that was not remotely delicate.

* * *

SALLY TOOK A QUART of rum from her sister's house one Friday night and we drank it with orange juice, the three of us, in an abandoned shed we'd found in the woods. When it began to pour, Sally stood up, tore off her clothes, and ran out into the teeming rain. Sebastian and I sat there, stunned, as her voice cried out some invented Indian rain chant, which drifted in to us on the wind.

"Oh, come on Bass, let's go!" I said, pulling off my clothes.

"If we get pneumonia, don't blame me," he said, and stood, tugging at a sneaker as he fell backwards into a wall.

I couldn't feel the cold, only the rain splattering against me as the whole world lit up to day in a flash of lightning. There was no fear, no notion of danger. I screamed out Sally's Indian chant and danced in circles, arms spread wide.

"I am here, goddamnit!" Sally yelled up at the lightning sky.

"I am here!" I shouted. The treetops swayed black and phantasmagoric against the flash of light. "I am here!"

Soon afterwards, Sally retreated to the cabin and Sebastian followed. I remained outside in the rain. My blood seemed to pulsate with a feeling of power I had never known.

When I finally went in, they were both dressed, and I quickly grabbed for my discarded clothes. Sally, unsteady on her feet, moaned, "I'll never drink alcohol again."

"God, I will," I cried. "That was great!"

* * *

ONCE, WHEN JACK and Nathan were hanging out in Jack's room, the door was ajar so I stood outside, attempting to eavesdrop.

"Hey, Celeste! Come on in!" Nathan yelled. I could hear my brother grumbling.

I knew it was only a reprieve that would be rescinded at any moment, so I sat primly, quietly, on Jack's desk chair and did not wrinkle my nose at the stink of dirty socks and rancid beer emanating from the piles of clothes on the floor. They were smoking cigarettes and drinking beer. That acrid-sweet smoke filled the air, and I knew they had been smoking pot and that

I'd hear about it from Anna later on. Nathan began waxing philosophical on Olivia of the huge jugs, a senior who wore so much makeup she looked twenty-five. He was saying that she gave excellent head. "It's because she's Catholic." He was lying back on my brother's bed with his hands crossed behind his head. "As long as it's not fucking, it's not a mortal sin. I swear to God, though, Catholic girls, if you can get them to do it, are the best."

"What does that mean, she gives excellent head?" I asked.

Nathan turned to look at me and Jack began to laugh. "It means she gives great blow jobs," Nathan said without blinking.

"You're lying," I said.

"I kid you not. Don't you know that song by Lou Reed? 'But she never lost her head/even when she was giving head/she said, Hey babe, take a walk on the wild side . . .'" Then he said with a sharp laugh, "Celeste, we're destined for each other. Do you know we have the same birthday?"

"You're such a liar."

He sat up and took his passport out of his back pocket. I presumed he carried it for identification, since he didn't have a driver's license yet. It was wrinkled and rounded to the shape of his behind. He reached his arm out to me, and as I took the passport our fingers touched. I felt a stab in the heart, not unlike the electric shock I'd gotten when I stuck a knife in the toaster at the age of five, but this one was pleasant.

I flipped to his picture, attempting to calm my shaking hands. And there on the page, grinning up at me, was a younger Nathan in a funereal black sports jacket and tie. His birth date was October fifteenth. He was exactly two years older than I. Expecting him at any second to ask for the passport back, I flipped through it quickly, attempting to gain some sense, some knowledge of him. There were pages upon pages of colorful visa stamps—Paris, Rome, Istanbul, Marrakech, London . . .

* * *

A NUMBER OF WEEKS LATER, I came across him sitting on a rock in a field behind the school. It had just begun to snow and, with a few minutes to spare between classes, I'd stolen out for a moment to look. Nathan was sitting there alone, in a large black knitted sweater and his old jeans, smoking a cigarette. The white flakes fluttered about and landed on his dark hair and sweater. He seemed preoccupied, maybe even sad. I hadn't seen him like this before.

"Hi, Nathan."

He looked up, smiled faintly. I stood a few paces from his rock, hands clasped before me. It was a cold and windless day and neither of us had our coats. "Is everything all right?" I asked after a while.

"I think my parents are breaking up," he said neutrally. "Sebastian doesn't know. Suspects it, I'm sure." He took a deep drag off his Marlboro and then tamped it out against the rock. Then he took what was left of the cigarette apart and scattered the tobacco at his feet. He took the filter apart, too, and scattered that.

After this meticulous operation, he looked at me quite seriously and said, "They don't really talk to us. I mean, my father's supposed to be coming in a couple of weeks, but this morning my mother made it sound like he wasn't going to stay."

"I won't say anything, I swear." It was hard to breathe. I wanted him to trust me.

"I've been watching you a long time and do you know that you're by far, by quantum leaps, the prettiest girl in any room you're in?" he said matter-of-factly. "It's interesting because I don't think you know. Most girls who are as pretty as you are a real pain in the ass. Boys are terrified of you."

Breathless, I said, "Sebastian isn't scared of me."

Nathan just gazed at me with that serious expression, his lips curving into a smile. His eyes appeared particularly green against the backdrop of white.

With my heart in my throat, I told him something I'd never told anyone: that it didn't really matter to me what I looked like from the outside, because inside I didn't exist. "It's like I can't feel my outline in space!" I said.

"I feel that way most of the time," he said. "Some days I feel like a ghost in my house, like my own family doesn't recognize me."

He stood and stretched his legs. "It's damn cold," he said.

I followed him back toward the school. When we approached one of the countless side doors, he stopped, took my arm, and walked me around the corner of the building. There was a dusting of snow on the pebbles that crunched beneath our feet. He pressed me into a corner where the ground was littered with cigarette butts. His tongue, gentle and forceful at once, explored the inside of my mouth, and it seemed to me that I could feel him all the way down to my feet. After a while he looked at me.

He appeared about to say something, but changed his mind. Shaking his head, he walked away, back into the school, and did not look back.

That particular corner of the school became a magical spot, and even the dirty old cigarette butts took a place in my heart, for they and the falling snow were the only witnesses to my moment of utter bliss.

* * *

A LONG, LONG TIME passed and, although he did look at me with a different sparkle in his eye, he never acknowledged what had happened.

"Want to come over?"

Sebastian and I were standing by the school buses.

"Sally's got track practice."

"I know. Want to come over anyway? No one's home. Nathan's got his Harvard interview."

"Good!" I huffed, as my heart sank.

Walking down the dark, wood-paneled hallway of the MacKennas' house, I paused in front of Nathan's closed door. Sebastian put a tentative hand on my shoulder and spun me around so that my back was pressed up against Nathan's door. Sebastian's tongue found mine, circled, waited for my reaction.

I kissed him for a while. Then I turned my face away and placed my head on his shoulder.

"Can I see Nathan's room?"

He pulled back and gazed at me. "What for?"

"I'm just curious."

Sebastian, resigned, pushed the door open and stood aside like a bored old museum guard. I felt sorry, but not enough to stop.

Nathan's room was oddly spare except for one wall, which was lined with books arranged by author. I had never seen so many books in one room. I went and perused the titles, my eyes landed on the S's—*Last Exit to Brooklyn* by Hubert Selby Jr., Shakespeare's sonnets and plays, *The Gulag Archipelago* by Aleksandr Solzhenitsyn, *The Confessions of Nat Turner* by William Styron, Jonathan Swift's *Gulliver's Travels*. My eyes drifted, landing here and there. I saw *Pale Horse, Pale Rider* by Katherine Anne Porter, Plato's *Republic*, poems by Sylvia Plath. There did not seem to be any logic to his taste. I hadn't read any of these books, except for a few of the Shakespeare plays that had been forced upon me in English class, but I had heard of most of these writers, except for Hubert Selby Jr. and Sylvia Plath. Later, during my college years, I made it a point to read every single one of the authors I remembered from Nathan's shelves.

His single bed was covered by a dark blue blanket and light blue sheets. On his bedside table lay *The Happy Hooker*. I'd heard this title whispered among the older girls in the school's bathrooms.

"Oh my God!" I said, remembering Sebastian. "Doesn't he *care* what your parents think?"

"I guess not," said Sebastian glumly.

I perused Nathan's albums, which took up almost the whole length of one shelf. He had records by Lou Reed, David Bowie, Herbie Hancock, Jefferson Airplane, whose hits I'd heard on the radio, and then he had totally unexpected ones by bands like the Beach Boys, and the Supremes, who at that time were uncool even by my incredibly limited standards.

Nathan seemed more enigmatic than ever.

I wanted desperately to search his dresser, look at his underwear and socks and find a secret diary, but I knew this was not possible, and that Sebastian would be irreparably upset.

"Let's go to your room," I said, feeling restless, dissatisfied.

I let Sebastian touch my breasts. I unbuttoned my blouse and lay back, shutting my eyes. His hands were uncertain, shy. I felt he deserved this gift. I liked him a great deal and had no desire to hurt his feelings. Yet it was Nathan I thought of whenever Sebastian's lips touched mine.

I couldn't wait to get into bed at night so that I could replay the fantasy that I had created for Nathan and me. It was exactly like watching a film: It is a warm day in spring, the clearing where the shed stands is speckled with flowers. I ride up on my bicycle, looking for a quiet place to read. Nathan is walking across the field toward me. He smiles, waves. I drop my bike and go to him. Very much as he had that day outside the school, he takes my arm and leads me toward the shed. Once inside, he presses me into the wall and kisses me hard. He lifts my legs and wraps them around his waist, I can feel his cock getting hard against my crotch; he unbuttons my shirt, kisses my neck with his soft wet mouth, my neck, then my breasts; and since I don't know exactly where to go from here, the picture fades to black.

Wanting more, so much more, I'd start it over again at the beginning, adding dialogue—Nathan tells me he loves me more than anything in the world and will never stop loving me. I tell him I feel the same way. When we get to the sex, my imagination overloads and the picture once again fades.

* * *

LATE IN THE SPRING, Jack drove a carload of us to a neighboring town to watch Sally run the mile in the state championships. Once we were seated, I never took my eyes off of her, as if I could make her win by the sheer force of my will. As the runners prepared at the starting line, Sally's expression was so concentrated that she appeared naked, as if she had shed every ounce of propriety and decorum and couldn't have cared less. Her eyes stared at some point in the distance, while her nose wrinkled and her upper lip twisted into an eight. When the gun went off, she sprang ahead, running with her torso slightly forward, her legs and arms pumping so hard she seemed like a film of herself on fast-forward. She tore away from the other front-runners after the first lap.

People were screaming and jumping up and down on the bleachers as she crossed the finish line. The announcer stated her time—5:12. Sally had broken the high school state record. People were saying that in a few years she'd surely be a candidate for the Olympics. I ran down to the field and hugged her. I kissed her sweat-drenched cheek. Her bright red face showed nothing but surprise and elation. I was so proud of her that I forgot I was envious of her for having such talent and determination.

In July Sally's father learned that he was being transferred to Paris for a year. Sally was told that she had to go, because it was a once-in-a-lifetime opportunity, and her parents couldn't bear for her to pass it up. Although her parents promised to find her a place to train, she was disconsolate.

She burst into my house sobbing like someone had died. Naturally, I turned to stone. I couldn't bear tears or shouting. She threw herself facedown on my bed and I sat with my back against the headboard.

"Fuck Paris. Fuck the 'experience of a lifetime,'" she sobbed.

"I'm sure it'll be great," I said. "Don't cry, Sally, please."

She looked up at me, her face contorted and tearstained.

"You're the best f-friend I ever had." Her head dropped, jerked back in a convulsion of sobs, and I forced myself to pat her shoulder, mumbling inanities.

* * *

With Sally in Paris and our brothers in college, Sebastian and I ended up spending all our time together. One day, in the hall, he put his arm around my shoulders as he was telling me some small secret, and I didn't move away. So he left his arm there, and we began to walk around in this manner. Our new status wasn't news to anyone but us. I often told him I loved him, adding quickly, but not *that* way.

* * *

Around this time, his father moved back from London. I sometimes was invited over for dinner on a weekend. To me, Mr. and Mrs. MacKenna seemed like the happiest, most stable couple in the world, always smiling at each other across the dinner table, and calling each other "dear." Nathan was away at Harvard, and my exchange with him outside the school seemed to have left the realm of reality and become only a fantasy.

* * *

I made Sebastian steal Nathan's copy of *The Happy Hooker*. I had him read parts aloud to me when we were alone. There was a section on Xaviera's favorite masturbation techniques that completely flipped me out.

"It's entirely normal to masturbate," Sebastian said reasonably.

"Do *you* do that? I don't!"

"You should," he said.

When Xaviera described female orgasms, I was certain she was making it up and told Sebastian so. But he said it was true, "Women can have orgasms, too."

"Would you know what to do to make that happen?" I asked.

"Probably. But you should experiment by yourself."

I looked at his kind, smooth face and solid, nice thighs in their pale corduroy Levi's. I liked what I saw and I knew now that I had him all to myself, that I could do anything I wanted, cruel or kind, and he'd take it in silence and never walk away from me.

"Are you in love with me?" I asked Sebastian.

"I've been in love with you since the first time I saw you," he said flatly.

"So let's do it."

He sat there, stunned, thinking, then he said, "All right, but we have to plan. We don't want to do anything foolish. Maybe I should call Nathan and ask him about condoms—of course, I'd never say it was you," he added quickly.

"No, don't do that." His mention of Nathan made the air catch in my throat.

"Well, I'll have to buy them, but I really don't know what kind to get," he said thoughtfully. "It's legal, isn't it, if both partners are underage?"

He pulled a bunch of colorful foil packets out of his down jacket pocket and sat on my bed. The entire house was dark except for the bedside lamp. My father and Anna had gone to Bermuda for a long weekend, leaving their thoroughly dependable and studious teenage daughter alone.

"These are lubricated," he said in the soothing tone of a doctor about to administer an injection, "and these are not."

I was in my best Lanz of Salzburg nightie with yellow daisies and lace at the neck. I felt more like I was about to have surgery than sex, and Sebastian's tone was not helping things.

He slowly removed his clothes as he sat on the edge of my bed with his back to me. "Nathan used to say," he mused, "that one should always take off one's socks."

"Bass—" I said quickly. "I need to tell you something about Nathan—"

He looked at me sideways. "No you don't," he said. "You must think I'm completely blind, or stupid."

A dark room, his dark body so close, his head pressed into the crook of my neck. His smell, sweet like shampoo. The silence is frightening, and there's no sound at all coming from us. His movements are gentle, tender; I feel no pain. I feel no elation, no sadness either. Tomorrow I will remember every detail with utter detachment. I don't bleed, but afterwards, in the bathroom, I notice those other lips have changed shape, are no longer flat and smooth but protrude outward as if to give a subtle kiss.

* * *

Some time in April, I was pushing my bike up the MacKennas' driveway when I saw an unfamiliar, dented Volkswagen

Rabbit parked in front of the garage. The front door was open, a pair of blue jean–clad legs and a behind were sticking out. It was Nathan.

"Hi," I said.

Swiftly, he sat up. "Hey, Celeste. Lost my damn hash pipe. How's life?"

His face was sunburned to a baked-clay color; the area around his eyes formed two white circles where his sunglasses always sat. There were clothes, towels, an empty tequila bottle, and beer cans all over the back seat.

"Just drove up from Fort Lauderdale yesterday," he said.

"How's school?"

"Cool in every department except work. I can't seem to get it together." He looked at me for a long moment with his probing eyes.

"You and Bass are fucking, aren't you?"

I opened my mouth to speak but no words came out.

"Thought so. I can see it in his face. Saw it right away. You probably initiated it. Am I right? You've been reasonably careful, I hope?"

I nodded.

"Good." He went back to looking for his lost pipe. From under the dashboard, he said, "I thought it would be me. I guess I have no right to be jealous."

Incomprehensibly, I began to cry. As if he could feel this happening, he immediately got out of the car and came toward me and my bicycle.

"It—it—doesn't feel like anything," I sputtered. When he was within touching distance, I held up my hand, palm flat to his chest. "Stay away from me." I was blinded by tears, incapacitated. I had never cried in front of another person.

"All right," he said. His face had collapsed, as if he'd dropped a mask he'd been wearing, along with his hash pipe. After a moment, he went back to his car, got in, shut the door, and just sat there. I went up to the window and leaned in.

"You're a bastard, Nathan." I did not wait for his reaction, but turned and rode fast down the driveway.

Six

THE DAY SALLY returned from Paris, she ran six miles barefooted with the cross-country team.

On her first Friday back, the three of us went out in Sebastian's parents' Volvo. We squeezed into the front seat and to celebrate, drank a bottle of gin mixed with Kool-Aid. This was our usual entertainment on a Friday night, the quality and quantity of liquor depending greatly on what we could steal from our parents without getting caught. I did not like gin, but it was the only bottle Sebastian had been able to steal from his mother's bar that particular night.

Sally was telling us about the American ambassador's son, Jeffrey Davis, whom she had met at school in Paris and had dated for the entire school year.

"He had a whole floor to himself that was bigger than our entire apartment! Oh God, I can't believe it—but I've got to tell you guys this!" she said, and burst into a high-pitched giggle.

"Come on, out with it," coaxed Sebastian.

"Well . . . I smoked *pot* with him!!"

"Oh *no*!" we cried in unison, "Sally, you bad girl!"

Bass and I had smoked our first joint together some time ago. It was a rare gem given to him by Nathan—Panama Red with a few drops of hash oil. Sebastian hallucinated, while I merely shrank into a corner of the old shed and wept.

"And I let him feel me up!" Sally said with disgust.

I downed my fourth drink, and suddenly angry for no reason, said, "Well, that's nothing. Bass and I slept together."

Sally stopped laughing, her face freezing in an expression of hilarity, and then collapsing as if she'd been slapped.

"You're kidding me, right?"

We were silent. Sebastian looked away. She opened the passenger door, leaned out, and threw up.

"That's disgusting," she wailed. "Gross me out totally! Well, better you than me, that's all *I* have to say."

Sebastian had many friends on the baseball team who would have been thrilled to take Sally out, but she wasn't interested. She kept up a correspondence with Jeffrey Davis, who was back in Washington. His father the ambassador had been forced to resign due to a scandal involving alcohol, a transatlantic flight, and two TWA flight attendants.

I was sitting on my bed on a school-day afternoon in the late fall, looking through college catalogs and applications, when the door flew open and Sally came in, barefoot in her sweat-drenched gym shorts and T-shirt. Her face was pale and drawn.

"What's the matter?" I asked, worried.

"I don't know. I didn't feel like running today."

She had run about five miles with the team, through a wooded area behind the school, and decided to leave the group and run to my house.

"What's wrong?" I asked. "Are you sick?"

She sat down on the rug and crossed her mud-flecked, muscular legs.

"I'm upset, and it doesn't really make sense."

I was afraid this was going to be about Sebastian and me, and I felt myself shutting down, my mind floating off.

"Remember years ago I told you my niece Suzy was born three months premature? Well, I just found out last night that it's not *true*! Marianne was pregnant when she got married." She stood up and burst into tears, clenching her fists. "Sex is disgusting! Those gross positions! All that huffing and snorting and screaming with some guy's fat ass going up and down on top of you! How could you *do* that?" With that, she began to emit the most terrifying high-pitched wails, and dropped to the rug with all her force. Anna came running up the stairs.

"What's the matter?" Anna said. "What on earth is going on?"

I looked at her and grimaced. Sally's face had contorted and she was frantically rocking back and forth, screaming like a person being tortured.

"My mother just let it slip!" she shouted. *"By accident!"*

I sat frozen on my bed. Anna wrapped her arms around Sally's shoulders and tried to hold her still.

"There, there," Anna crooned.

"*Lies! It's just a bunch of lies!* They lie to you your whole fucking life they tell you to be a good little girl and do what I say and then one day they just let their lies slip like they're nothing, nothing! My sister is disgusting. She's a hypocrite! She's been *fucking* Brad since high school!"

She threw Anna's arms off and rose. "Oh, *fuck* this," she said, and stormed out, slamming the door.

Anna and I looked at each other.

"Do you think I should call Mrs. Newlyn?" Anna finally asked. "I hate to get involved."

"I don't know. What do you think?"

"Have you ever seen her like this before?"

I shook my head.

"I think I'd better call Mrs. Newlyn." Anna plucked at her plaid skirt, tucked a curl behind her ear, squared her shoulders, and headed for the door.

Sally became lethargic, moody, disinterested. But she continued to run.

The next Friday night, she drank twice as much as we did. Once in a while she'd laugh ghoulishly to herself. I realized as I sat next to her in Sebastian's parents' car that she was not thinking about her sister Marianne, but about other things, so disturbing that I could not begin to understand, and did not want to ask.

* * *

The following weekend, she got falling-down drunk on eggnog at an early Christmas party. She dragged Sebastian and me outside to look at the stars.

"I'm going to predict your future," she said in a childish voice. "Bass," she punched him hard in the arm, "you'll grow up to marry a nice Wasp girl and have three, maybe four kids. You'll have a nice job with the government—something very boring but solid. You'll never marry Celeste because Celeste is just beginning her journey. You'd be happy enough with her, she'd be bored to death with you.

"Celeste, you're lucky the first one was Bass and not Nathan. If it'd been Nathan, he'd have dumped you by now and you'd be vicious and pissed off and twisted into ugly knots. Nathan is either going to become famous or kill himself with alcohol or drugs. What you want,

Celeste, is danger. You don't want the truth *now,* but someday you will. Do you know what people say about your mother?"

"Stop! Stop it!" I shouted. For a moment, I couldn't breathe, and I knew that if she'd said one more word I would have jumped on her and stopped her with my hands.

"Okay. Okay," she said. "But I have to tell you this—you're going to get swallowed by a sperm whale, just like Pinnochio."

With that, she fell to her knees and threw up on the frozen grass.

"Good," she said, getting up. "Now that's all out of me." And she walked unsteadily away.

She was admitted to the Clearwater Institute for Mental Health on Christmas Day. Her friends were not allowed to visit.

"She talks about you and Sebastian constantly," Mrs. Newlyn told me cryptically over the phone. I wondered if Sally had told her mother or her doctors that Sebastian and I had sex. After a pause, Mrs. Newlyn went on.

"She's very upset about something but we can't seem to find out what. The doctor thinks she needs time away from her friends and family and daily routine." The coldness in Mrs. Newlyn's voice made a large fish start flopping around in my stomach.

A few weeks later, Mrs. Newlyn called to say that Sally had a salt deficiency in her brain and that soon, with lithium, her condition would be under control. Everyone was acting like she had pneumonia or something.

Sally came back to school in February and quit the track team.

"I never ran for me," she said, shrugging. "I did it for everybody but me."

* * *

Sally had been back a week when she turned to me in the crowded hall, her eyes filled with outrage, and screamed, "I bet you didn't tell Bass how you fucked *Nathan* in the shed, did you? I *saw* you!" She was leaning toward me, her hands in fists, like a furious child.

Faces turned and stared. I was paralyzed, and in that instant I began to calculate—how could she have witnessed my fantasy if she was in Paris? Flushed, I watched Bass's face. Doubt scurried across his eyes; I saw its dark presence and gasped. I felt as guilty as if what she'd said was true.

"That never happened!" I protested. "Sally! Did you forget to take your pills?" She banged her head into her locker and remained there, immobile, for a long time. The school bell rang. Sebastian was still looking at me, but his eyes had cleared now. Sally turned to me, pale again and composed, and said, "We're going to be late for class."

For a few days, I held my breath, praying for her pills to work, for whatever it was to go away and leave her alone.

In English class, in the middle of a discussion on *Robinson Crusoe,* Sally turned to me and screamed, *"You bitch! You stole my fucking money!"*

Miss Wilson and the students turned their eyes to me with questioning expressions, as if maybe for a split second reality were standing on its head and they believed me capable of such a thing.

"You're out of your mind!" I protested, "I don't need your money!"

Miss Wilson came toward us with her paperback of *Robinson Crusoe* pressed protectively to her chest.

"I swear I didn't take her money," I told Miss Wilson.

But Miss Wilson was not concerned with that. "Are you all right, Sally dear? Would you like to go to the infirmary?"

"What do you think I am, crazy or something?" Sally shouted.

After the echo of her voice died, there wasn't a sound in the room.

I realized then that none of us were prepared for this. We didn't understand.

* * *

She returned from Clearwater the second time, in April, and we went to a disco party with Sebastian. Without warning she disappeared and I found her in the ladies' room, leaning close to the mirror, apparently applying lipstick.

"You want to go home, Sally?" I asked, concerned. When she turned around I gasped. She had pierced her bottom lip with a safety pin. Blood trickled from the closed pin, down her chin.

"Celeste! Celeste, I'm so glad to see you." She grabbed me by the shoulders and brought her tearstained face close to mine. "I fucked a guy in the nuthouse. We waited till all the nurses and other nuts were asleep, then we'd sneak into each other's beds. Oink, oink, like little pigs. But not as good—never as good—as with this huge cucumber I stole from the kitchen when I was on serving duty 'cause see, they gave *me* responsibilities, 'cause I was *way* normal compared to the others."

Panic-stricken, I ran out to find Sebastian, who was standing just outside the door.

"Help her, Bass," I said, choking back tears. "She's totally flipped."

He went in. A flock of tittering girls came flapping out.

Minutes later, he emerged, grasping Sally firmly by the arm. She looked reasonably calm now, the grotesque safety pin had been removed. The blood and streaks of mascara had been washed from her face. She held a square of toilet paper to her lip.

"We're going home," he said calmly. "This evening is over."

But of course, nothing was over. There were new diagnoses, new pills, new doctors.

She came back to school again late in the spring. It was a glorious day, the three of us were together again. Sally's new medication made her lethargic and heavy. As we sat on the cafeteria steps, taking in the noonday sun, her face wore a contented, relaxed expression.

"Can you believe," she said evenly, "that I'm adopted?"

She explained in neutral tones that she had been the bastard child of an incestuous affair and that just this morning her mother had put drops of arsenic in her orange juice.

"She's so *stupid* to use arsenic, it smells like almonds. Anybody knows *that*." She turned to Sebastian and me with an exasperated smirk. "You don't believe me," she said, searching my eyes. "I know Bass believes me."

Sebastian looked heartbroken in his silence. He stood and walked to the principal's office to call Mrs. Newlyn.

Sally had stopped taking her pills because they made her feel tired and fat, but Mrs. Newlyn convinced her to start again and she came to school the following week.

"Everything is going to be fine, now," she told us. "It really is. We'll be like we were before."

* * *

Sally had no date for the prom, and we could not let her sit at home, so going as a threesome seemed the only solution. Sebastian invited her formally, in a little card with roses on the front.

Her mother got the crimson dress out of storage. Sally was happier and calmer that night than I'd seen her in a long time. Until the football players got rowdy and pulled the urinals off the wall of the men's room. Uniformed guards rushed into the banquet hall and rounded us up like cattle.

Sally's face twisted into a knot of hopeless rage. She went up to the first football player she could find and slapped him hard across the face.

"How dare you act like this?" she hissed between clenched teeth. "Don't you know you'll have to pay for this in your next life?"

* * *

THE DAY BEFORE I left for my Little Ivy League college in Massachusetts, Sally called and asked me if she could stop by. She had taken a turn for the worse again in July and had spent most of the summer at home with her mother, watching television. Mrs. Newlyn said it had a marvelously calming effect on her.

It was raining that day and water flowed from the eaves in a comforting murmur.

She sat on my bed with her yearbook open on her lap.

"Look at all the nice things people wrote for me," she said.

"I know. Everyone has always loved you."

"I think I'll go to the community college for a year, bring up my grades, see what happens. You'll be nearby. And Bass'll be at Columbia—not too far away. We'll get together and it'll be like old times."

I nodded, looking away.

"I see things nobody else sees," she said.

"Yes," I said, "but don't tell me, Sally. I don't want to know what you see."

"I need to tell you one thing—I used to be in love with Bass. I was so in love with him, I thought I was going to die. But I saw how he kissed you, how he looked at you, and I knew I didn't have a chance. I was so jealous!"

"Don't say things like that now, Sally. What's the point?"

"Do you still love Nathan?" she asked me, searching my eyes.

Abruptly she changed the subject. "My mother is a thwarted woman. She never had a life of her own. This whole town is filled with women like her who are afraid. I used to be afraid but I'm not anymore.

"My mother has hidden talents, she can talk to animals, did you know that?"

My heart sank. "Oh, God, Sally."

"It's the truth. But I'm not going to live my life like she did. I'm going to join the Peace Corps."

"That's great!" I said.

She grabbed my arm and brought her face close to mine. "Don't settle, Celeste. Go get what you want. For me, okay? Don't forget what I told you. You have an *ancient* soul. You have to protect it."

"Okay, Sally."

* * *

During the Christmas holidays Mrs. Newlyn called me to tell me that Sally had returned to Clearwater. Months away from home had freed me, and now I didn't want to return to the nightmarish responsibility of being Sally's best friend.

She told me that Sally was in a state of obsession over her lost yearbook, which she was certain she had left in my room the last time I'd seen her. I was equally certain I'd watched Sally put the book in her knapsack, and told Mrs. Newlyn this. But I promised to search for it, which I did. I never found it.

Mrs. Newlyn never forgave me for not finding it, for not going to Clearwater to visit Sally, for not writing.

* * *

It was Sebastian who called me on my dormitory hall pay phone the following December, in the middle of finals week, and told me that Sally was dead. Her parents did not know what had propelled her suicide.

I hoped that she did not think ill of me before she died.

Sebastian had been a better friend to her than I. He had kept in touch. His voice was slightly distant on the phone. I did not blame him.

After I hung up, the phone rang again, and thinking it was Bass calling back, I picked up.

"Celeste, this is Nathan. I heard about Sally. I just thought I'd call."

It did not even seem strange that he knew my voice immediately.

"How are you?"

"Flunking out of Harvard."

"Why?"

"I don't know, I took some time off to figure it out, but it didn't help. So now we're both sophomores, how's that for fate?"

There was a moment of silence in which I could hear his even breathing, and my mind saw his lips pressed against the phone. I felt that jolt of electricity again as my mouth went dry.

"Nathan, I think I'm flipping out over Sally. I can't *feel* anything."

"I need to see you, Celeste," he said in a quiet voice.

"Why?" I asked, confused.

"Because I've never stopped thinking about you and it's time," he said.

"I'm in the middle of exams," I said desperately, trying to anchor myself.

"Drive up after you finish. Please."

"All right," I said. "Tomorrow."

The next day, a light snow was falling as I drove southeast toward Boston. I felt lighthearted, free, filled with trepidation and desire. I did not feel guilty over Sebastian or Sally; I'd left them behind in my dorm room, the way one would an old moth-eaten coat at the first sign of spring.

Seven

Alex and I were on our way to southern New Jersey to spend the night with Chester and Babs, his father and stepmother, who were throwing us an engagement party. Outside the BMW's tinted windows a desert of factories and empty lots rushed past. It was a beautiful spring day, but you never would've known from the dismal landscape. I was sick with a serious cold. I'd awakened that morning with a scratchy throat and pressure in my sinuses; by noon, the virus had launched an all-out offensive.

I pressed my forehead to the glass. Alex was telling me that he loved me in the beige linen suit he'd bought me for the occasion. I felt as though my head were encased in a jug of tepid water.

The suit was expensive, attractive; something you might see on a Wall Street executive—the skirt just above the knees, the jacket with a cinched waist and padded shoulders. It felt like a disguise, but that was all right by me. Mostly I wore long skirts, loose tops, or drop-waisted dresses.

Alex drummed his fingers on the steering wheel, sighed. His new cellular phone rang. It made a bulge like a small handgun in his jacket pocket.

"What is it, George?"

George talked for a while and then Alex said patiently, "That doesn't change anything. If you want to get the bride to the altar, you have to get her wet first. You can't take her by force. Court her."

What on earth was he talking about? Alex listened for a while and then said, "The controlling party is worried about getting senior management positions for his kids, that's all. You know those Latin types. Big families."

Apparently some huge deal was about to go through in Argentina, and George, whom he'd sent down there, couldn't seem to handle things without calling every thirty minutes. I was becoming annoyed.

"What would happen if you just turned that thing off? Would George have a heart attack or what?"

"This is very serious, Celeste," Alex said, containing a sigh of impatience. "The timing couldn't be worse." To George he said, "Well, carve out something that's going to be attractive to them, goddamnit! You know how to do this, George."

"The timing couldn't be worse for me, either. I'm sick as a dog," I said to the window.

* * *

I THOUGHT THAT perhaps he was nervous about seeing his father's relatives and friends all gathered in one place. This hadn't happened since his father's wedding to Babs some ten years before. Maybe it was easier to plan a huge takeover deal over the phone than to think about his family. I didn't mention my thoughts to him, and put my hand on his thigh instead.

I hadn't seen any of my relatives in years either, but I couldn't have cared less what they thought. The only time they had gathered in one room—the Wasp paternal side and my mother's French clan from Bordeaux and Paris—was at my mother's funeral. My French grandmother had not come. She wrote a tight little note explaining that her husband (her third) was ill with gout and couldn't be left alone, but I was certain it was because she was still angry at my mother over the fight they'd had the previous summer. Nevertheless, whatever my grandmother's reasons, I decided on the day of the funeral, at the age of ten, never to see her again.

Alex maintained that all the divorces and remarriages in his family hadn't affected him in the least.

* * *

CHESTER HAD WORKED in the city for thirty years, for a large commercial bank, but had recently been prodded into early retirement. In the ten months I had been with Alex, I had met his mother twice, "between flights"; but I had met his father and stepmother only once, when they drove into the city the day after Christmas and took us to lunch.

It had been my responsibility to find a suitable restaurant, and I chose a nouvelle cuisine French restaurant that was hip, but not too hip for Chester and Babs, whom Alex had described as "a bit square" and not particularly fond of "foreign foods," especially ones that used garlic.

Unfortunately, on the fateful day, I forgot the restaurant's address.

"I'm so sorry," I said from the back of their Buick. "It's around here somewhere."

Babs's gleeful voice jumped in, "But this is *fine*! We're having a little tour!" She had long dark hair twisted up in a chignon that was held together by large silver combs.

"I remember now," I said. "It's not on Third Avenue, it's on Second."

"It's such a beautiful day," Babs mused. "Must be at least fifty degrees. Whatever happened to white Christmases, I wonder?"

"It's sixty-two," Alex pointed out. "Must be the hole in the ozone."

"Is it really sixty-two?" said Babs. "I could have sworn the radio said low fifties."

"Sixty-two," Alex repeated.

"Well, I'll be. What do *you* think, dear? Does this feel like a sixties kind of day to you?" She turned to Chester and with her long red fingernails flirtatiously tickled the hair at the base of his head, which was shaped exactly like Alex's.

"Yes, love, it does seem that look is back," Chester said. "I see girls everywhere in bell-bottoms."

As we perused our menus, Alex said, "The fish here is good. Not too garlicky."

"What will you have, love?" Chester asked Babs.

"Just a small salad." She smiled wanly at the waiter who stood nearby, and absently rubbed her temples.

"Oh no," said Chester, "a migraine coming on?"

"Just sinuses, I think. I'm fine, really." She winced.

Chester ordered a hamburger; Alex and I, the sole meuniere.

We exchanged presents. Alex gave his father, "from both of us," some kind of state-of-the-art tool, incomprehensible to me, for the carpentry workshop he kept in his basement. Chester had a passion for making Quaker-style furniture in his spare time. Alex handed Babs a gift-wrapped Bloomingdale's box that held an imitation Hermès scarf he had bought from a Senegalese street merchant.

They oohed and ahhed for a moment, then fell silent.

Chester gave Alex a complicated, bright yellow scuba diving watch, and Babs handed me a very large hardcover book wrapped in green paper with a big red bow. It was the latest Danielle Steel novel.

"Thank you so much," I said.

"Alex has told us how much you like to read! I *love* her, don't you?" Babs said with a pleased smile. I smiled back and asked about her sinuses.

Alex told Chester about his latest promotion at the investment firm (he was the youngest managing director in the history of the company) and he asked his father about a Mexican television company called Grupo Telemedia that was attempting to buy L.A. television stations from one of America's oldest and most longstanding companies, Chadwick Broadcasting. They talked about this for a while and I stared at them, dumbfounded. Babs, I noted, was covering her mouth and pressing her fingers up under her nose, attempting to stifle a yawn.

Chester had a benevolent, elastic face that seemed utterly unperturbed.

Babs wrapped an ice cube in her napkin and applied it to her forehead, right between the eyebrows. She shut her eyes tightly and winced again.

After a moment, Alex looked at Babs, then said in a honey-coated voice, "If those headaches are as bad as you say they are, Babs, you really ought to see a doctor."

"I've been to *twenty* doctors if I've been to one, Alex dear," she said, sighing.

Alex frowned, looking extremely concerned. "Well, maybe they just weren't the right *kinds* of doctor, Babs. Maybe it's psychosomatic, did you ever consider that possibility?"

Babs laughed through her nose and said, "Alex, you're so amusing!"

"Hey, Dad," said Alex, "I just read the greatest book. You might like it. By Primo Levi; it's called *Other People's Trades*. Celeste gave it to me—"

"*You* read a real book, Alex? It must have been under duress!" Babs laughed. She turned to me. "When Alex was engaged to Mimi—you know, of course, she was a veritable clothes horse (no, I wanted to say, the only photos I ever saw of her were bare-assed naked)—well, she had him reading *GQ* and shopping at Saks! All those little Italian-cut suits with shoulders out to here! Now it's back to Brooks Brothers, thank God. And *books*! This *is* an improvement!" The smile on her face was so sincere and sweet, you'd have thought she was talking about a brand-new litter of kittens.

Alex was frowning at his stepmother, but Babs pressed on with her earnest smile. I looked to Chester for a clue, but he was also smiling, a big, elastic, happy grin that spanned his entire face.

Now as we sat in the car, Alex's cell phone rang again. The thought of being on display with a cold of this magnitude made me disconsolate. "Just do what you have to do, George," Alex said after a while, and closed the phone, a fat, gray rectangular contraption with a long antenna. He turned to me.

"I wonder if Edgar Marx'll come. He's kind of artistic. He's a big producer. He likes young women, if you know what I mean, so watch out. His wife is an alcoholic."

I took out my Neo-Synephrine and squeezed two large shots into each nostril.

"Celeste, you're only supposed to use that stuff every four hours. That's the third time you've used it and we've only been on the road an hour."

"I can't breathe, Alex," I said, irritated.

I tried to sleep. After a while I attained a pain-filled half slumber; I could still hear the rhythmic ticking of the engine, and my sinuses squeaking and gurgling inside my head as if they had indigestion. Then I slipped into blackness, oblivion. I awakened with a start, with no sense of time having elapsed, not remembering where I was. I looked around quickly. There was Alex, sitting beside me, talking to George in Argentina. Relieved, I closed my eyes again.

We drove up to the three-story white colonial with a manicured lawn on a quiet, winding street. Alex was a guest here as much as I. We were offered our choice of room and he chose the renovated attic, since it was the farthest away from Chester and Babs's bedroom. While Alex went off to the country club to play tennis with his father, I collapsed on the bed and slept fitfully for several hours.

Alex finally shook me from sleep thirty minutes before the guests were to arrive.

"Poor girl," he said. "Maybe a hot shower would help." Not just my head felt ensconced in a jug, my whole body seemed to be moving as if through water. I went to Babs for help. Behind her closed bedroom door I could hear her moving around. I knocked, feeling like an intruder. She was still in her bathrobe.

"Babs, I really feel terrible. I'm sorry, I don't know what to do."

"Oh my dear," she said soothingly. "I know what spring colds can be. Here . . ." She led me into her large, white tiled bathroom that glinted in the light, and opened the medicine cabinet. On the marble vanity table were little glass bottles and vials lined up like an Amazon army conscripted in the war against age.

"Here we are. Liquid Sudafed!" she cried. "A miracle drug." She filled the little plastic cup to the brim with the evil-looking red liquid. "Drink up!"

I tossed it back and it hit bottom like molten lead and then spread warmth and comfort upward toward my chest and extremities.

"In twenty minutes you'll be good as new. Now, you must get dressed, my dear. All these people are dying to meet you! What a pity your father and stepmother couldn't come. We would have loved to have gotten acquainted with Charles and—Anna, isn't it?—before the Big Day."

"They were really touched you invited them," I lied. "It's hard for them to get all the way down here from Connecticut." As I said this, my father's irate voice rang in my head: "Oh God, how're we going to get out of this one?"

Babs gave me the bottle of Sudafed "for later" and I took it upstairs to our attic room. The ache began to disperse, and my nose cleared somewhat. I dressed languidly, had trouble with the small details—my mother's pearls, the diamond earrings Alex had given me, my high-heeled pumps. I went into the bathroom to apply mascara, something I did only on rare occasions. My face looked pale and bloated, oily from sickness.

Alex appeared in the mirror behind me, all ready in his gray pin-striped suit and floral tie.

"The suit looks great! Feeling better?" he asked hopefully.

"Yes, actually." I tried a small smile. We heard the doorbell sound. Cocktail party voices greeted each other on the landing downstairs.

"Uh-oh. You're a real sport," he added solemnly. "I love you. I'll go down." He gave me a hug from behind. "Take your time."

Once he was gone, I filled the little plastic cup and drank another shot of Sudafed. It was only as I descended the stairs that I realized I was already quite tipsy, and the reasonable part of my mind was telling me to cool it, that it was going to be one of those unquenchable thirsts, the ones I had been so conscientiously avoiding lately, which ended up with me waking up the next morning with no idea of where I had been. As the reasonable voice said take it easy, the other, stronger voice laughed derisively, because what I wanted now, more than anything, was a drink.

I floated toward the bar, where Babs was playing bartender.

"Thank you so much for the medicine," I intoned. Babs was quite beautiful, with her tall frame and angular face, her perfect chignon, large onyx and gold earrings, matching necklace, and charcoal gray suit.

"Oh, but you're so very welcome, my dear!" Her voice rang in my ears, as if coming from a great distance, down a long tunnel.

"You're beautiful, Babs," I said.

She gasped, not used to candid talk, I suspected, then laughed gaily, blushing. "Compliments will get you everywhere with me! May I fix you a drink?"

"What goes with Sudafed?"

"Let's see, maybe white wine?"

"Sounds great."

She filled a long-stemmed glass to the rim and handed it to me with a little napkin. The wine sparkled like a jewel as it caught the light. "Now relax, dear Celeste. This is a celebration!"

* * *

My wine was too soon gone. I felt bereft. A tall, gray-haired man in a kelly green sports coat was talking to me about golf. It seemed not enough time had elapsed to go back to Babs for more wine, so I waited patiently for him to ask me if I needed a refill.

"Are you a golfer, young lady? Alex is quite a golfer, I'm told. An all-around athlete. When I was younger I thought golf was for old people," he was saying in an incredibly loud voice, the voice of Wasps at the dinner table that reminded me of my departed paternal grandfather. "Now I'm old and I see all these youngsters out there at the club every day. Why did I wait so long, I ask myself?"

"Precisely," I said, smiling.

"So you *are* a golfer!" he shouted.

"No, but my stepmother plays. She's pretty good, too." This was not a lie, but I would not have been above lying, if it meant pleasing him and getting another drink.

"Say, would you like a refill there?"

Congratulating myself, I handed him my glass.

Only a moment later, it seemed to be empty again. This time I went to the bar myself, only to find Chester had relieved Babs.

"Celeste! This is my dear friend and employer, Mr. Hendrake. Please meet Celeste Miller."

Mr. Hendrake's face looked like an enormous pink nipple, everything puckered and scrunched toward his pursed lips that greedily sucked at his glass. I smiled politely at Mr. Hendrake as a dangerous laugh began to rumble in my chest.

Mr. Hendrake told me about computer software. I listened intently until my glass was empty. Chester was generous with the wine; as soon as he refilled my glass, I excused myself with a big smile, and swiftly floated off.

"Ain't that just too cute," I heard Mr. Hendrake say behind me. "She misses him already."

Time stopped. I found myself speaking to the infamous Edgar Marx, producer of Broadway shows.

"I'm the only Jew here," he was telling me as he looked over the crowded room. He was also tall, with silver hair, in a square-cut sports coat. "But I don't take it personally, ha, ha!" I perceived a wink and continued to smile. His face swam before my eyes. I stood, quiet, demure, smiling, leaning up against the grand piano for support.

"I make more money than all of them put together . . . but, you win some, lose some. Name of the game . . . say, did you see *The Secret Sharer* yet?"

"No, but I love the book." Were there actually words emanating from my mouth? It was hard to tell.

"Never read the book. But it's a hell of a play. I'll send you a pair of tickets next week . . . "

I was grateful to hear him responding; I realized that I had indeed spoken and that I was still in control.

"Say, sweetie, can I refresh your drink?" I felt his hand cupping my hipbone.

"Sure," I said, "why not?"

Shortly he was back.

"Have you ever read John Cheever, Mr. Marx?" I was proud of the effort I was making to speak sanely and crisply. I perceived that he had heard me, for he was nodding.

"Call me Ed, please. In the *New Yorker,* sure."

"Doesn't this party seem Cheeveresque?"

"Hahaha!" He paused and looked at me, then said, "In what way do you mean? Oh, here's my wife, Elizabeth."

She descended like an enormous black bird with a jowly red throat and filled up the entire frame of my vision. Her poor face was ravaged by bloat and wrinkles. It was clear she believed her husband was trying to make me.

"This is Alex's fiancée," he told her quickly, an edge in his voice.

"It's so nice to meet you," I said; my words sounded too slow, too enthusiastic.

"Right," she said. "Marx, get me a drink."

While he was gone she said, "I'm not Jewish, you know."

I smiled, speechless.

"Yes," she continued, "and I've learned the hard way that it's a mistake to crossbreed."

I felt my face turn to stone in some kind of gargoyle smile. And here was Alex, to the rescue, hugging me tightly to his side. It was like leaning up against a refrigerator. I looked up at his beautiful face, his perfect features, his expression always so controlled.

"How are you, Mrs. Marx?"

"No better, no worse than the last time you saw me," she muttered. I wanted to run away from this woman as fast as possible, but I feared that if Alex let go too suddenly, I would totter and fall on the floor.

He turned his attention to me. "Are you feeling better, Celeste?"

"*Much* better!" I cried.

"I'm glad!" He smiled. "You're a real sport. Maybe you should slow down on the wine, Celeste. Better get something to eat. Buffet's ready."

Eating was out of the question. What I wanted was another shot of Sudafed, the miracle drug. The room was now spinning like a carousel, tinkling music, laughter, bright clothes, I felt a dizziness close to vertigo, reminding me of somewhere else, a long time ago . . . I smiled reassuringly at Alex. "I'm off to powder my nose," I said, ever so careful to enunciate, because Alex had seen me like this before, and I turned to climb the stairs. Movements ever so precise. Extremely proud. Handling myself like the real sport Alex said.

Carousel. Carousel. Good or bad? Very important, when dealing with memories, to figure that out. I was feeling a terrible knot of anxiety in my chest. I sat on the edge of the bed and it began to rise and fall like the shiny black stallion with the gold saddle and leather reins.

* * *

It's my tenth birthday, October fifteenth. I am on the carousel in Central Park with my mother, who has been laughing and whooping like a cowboy through the whole ride. She is in a short royal blue dress and matching jacket, and tight black leather boots up to her knees. As our horses begin to slow in their rhythmic rise and fall, the merry, tinny music seems sad, filled with a false lightheartedness.

"No! No! Again!" I am starting to panic, because I know that in a moment it will end and my mommy and I will once again be thrown out into the real world, where she is so desperately unhappy.

As our horses come to a halt, the carousel's guardian, a short, round, elderly man with a beret and a ruddy complexion, is standing below us, on the ground, smiling.

"Vous êtes françaises?" he asks my mother.

"Oui, bien sûr."

"I heard you earlier. From where?"

"De Bordeaux!" she cries. "But we live here now. My husband is an American." I fear she might just start to cry, as she does sometimes for no apparent reason. Her pretty, tight dress is hiked up on her thighs as she straddles her gray horse with a silver harness.

"I'm from Marseilles," the old man says. "I am here for fifteen years but still I miss home."

"Ah, yes. I do know," my mother says, laughing sadly.

"You look like Brigitte Bardot," he tells her. "But you are even more beautiful." We've heard this before, and my mother usually cringes, but she takes it as a compliment and offers him her charming, doleful smile. "My little one doesn't want to get off," she tells him.

"Well then, have another spin on me!" he says, tapping the nose of my mother's horse. "Stay as long as you like."

Much later, for we have been spinning for hours, it seems, he waves us off, standing beneath one of the carousel's high archways. Our heads are giddy, our feet unsteady on the ground.

"Come back soon!" he yells after us. "I'm here every day, for fifteen years!"

"We don't get into the city much," my mother calls over her shoulder.

"Just the same," he says, "come back. I'll remember you."

"God bless you," my mother says, and blows him a kiss.

* * *

Not even a year has passed, it is summer, and Anna, my father's new friend, has taken me to the Central Park Zoo. She has been coming around lately, taking on little chores. Anna is hoping this trip will lift my spirits, but the animals appear so sad in their ugly cement cages that I begin to cry. Desperate, Anna suggests the carousel. I assent, suddenly enthusiastic.

We can hear the tinny music from way down the path. I begin to run, run! as if a minute will make a difference in whether or not I'll find the old French guardian there. All at once, it seems of paramount importance, even though I haven't thought of him since that day.

Anna buys me a ticket and sits on a bench with her feet primly crossed in her sensible shoes and I wait, crazed with worry, for the gate to open. But I see him, standing in a far corner of the grand hall, watching serenely as the horses and carriages spin round and round. The music is the same—gigantic, hopeful, filled with loneliness. The platform stops rotating and the chain is unlatched. I run to him.

"*Monsieur! Monsieur!* Do you remember me?"

He looks down at me for a long moment and then his face breaks into a smile. He asks after my mother, *"Ou est ta belle maman qui resemble à Brigitte Bardot?"*

"Elle est morte, monsieur," I say, and can't look at him. The words are new, never spoken by me before. "She is dead. *Elle avait le coeur faible.*" I translate for him what my father has explained to me. "She had a weak heart."

"Pauvre petite," the man says, placing a hand on my shoulder. He murmurs, "I am certain she is happy in heaven with the good Lord. Let me put you on my best horse. He's the fastest of my black stallions and he'll carry you away!"

He lifts me in his arms and I wrap mine tight around his neck. I am so grateful, I can't even tell him that I don't want to ride, I want to stay with him on the ground, watching the others. I bury my nose in his denim shirt and let out a tiny sob for her, the first. It is also the last for many years.

I'd been weeping with my face in a pillow. Raising my head a few inches, I saw through a blur that the pillow was streaked with mascara. I stumbled into the bathroom and vigorously washed my face. Looking at myself in the mirror, I saw that I was basculating as if on a ship. Clearly there was no hope of reapplying mascara. I congratulated myself on my astuteness, and settled for an eye pencil, some rouge and lipstick. I brushed my hair, my teeth. My eyes were bloodshot, but thank God there was Visine in my *toilette* kit. I considered taking another swig of Sudafed but decided that this might not be wise, and instead planned to have another glass of wine.

Light on my feet, fortified by the release, I descended the stairs. I was reminded for some reason of the costume ball scene in *Rebecca,* when the second Mrs. DeWinter descends the stairs in the absolutely wrong, wrong dress.

Fade to black.

* * *

I WOKE UP PARALYZED, bewildered, and uncertain of where I was. I stretched out my arm and felt along the sheet to see if someone was next to me—thank God, I was alone. Then I remembered that I was engaged. Alex was not there.

What on earth could have happened?

He was standing beside the bed. "How are you feeling, Celeste?"

I detected a note of sarcasm in his voice. "I'm sick."

"You certainly didn't act sick last night," he said. My head began to pound as I attempted to formulate a retort, but he threw himself down next to me and kissed me.

Afraid he might smell my breath, I turned away.

"Everyone *loved* you! I'm so proud of you. What a sport."

I decided that the only thing you needed to succeed with this crowd was the ability to smile and shut up. After a moment, he asked, "What were you and Babs talking about in the kitchen?"

What were Babs and I talking about in the kitchen? Was I in the kitchen? I decided to hedge. "Which time was that?"

"Later, when you were helping her clean up."

I tried very hard to form a picture of the scene. Nothing came to mind.

"Nothing special," I said. "I can't remember, really."

"You two were laughing like hyenas. I guess you'd both had a lot to drink by then," he added.

I realized that Alex felt threatened by this budding friendship, but I couldn't appease his anxiety, as my mind was utterly blank.

"Not me," I said quickly. "It was the Sudafed."

Miraculously, my cold was better, or perhaps my hangover was so bad I could no longer feel the pain of my cold. Alex went to the bathroom and came back with two Advils, a glass of water, and the bottle of Sudafed.

"Get that stuff away from me!" I said. Just the sight of it made me want to vomit.

"It's raining," Alex said. "I thought we could take a drive to the mall. I'll buy you a present for being so charming to the old folks."

"I can't, Alex. I'm really sick. What time is it?"

"Nearly noon."

* * *

I SHOWERED, dressed, and made my way gingerly down to the kitchen. Even my fingertips ached as they touched the banister. I felt seasick, heartsick, and ashamed.

Everything was in order. You'd never have known there had been a party here. Babs was sitting in the breakfast nook in her robe and slippers, reading the *New York Times* Arts and Leisure section. Her long dark hair was down around her pale face. She seemed vulnerable without her chignon, and slightly melancholy. When she looked up at me I saw her bloodshot, swollen eyes and imagined she felt pretty much the way I did.

"Good morning, Celeste, dear—or shall I say good afternoon? How's that cold?" She patted the chair beside her. "Come sit next to me. Would you like some coffee?" Babs's smile was generous and intimate. *Good God,* I thought, *what on earth did we tell each other last night?*

A wave of nausea coursed through me as something came to me in a flash: Babs at the sink, washing glasses, while I sit at the counter nearby, incapable of anything but keeping my head propped up on my hands. "Mimi was so stupid," Babs says, "she didn't know the difference between World War I and World War II! How she managed law school is beyond me." She throws her head back and guffaws, a gold molar glinting in the light. Turning back to her sudsy glasses, she adds, "Alex wasn't 'sophisticated' enough for her, however—she had an affair with an Italian count, and Alex was *very* angry *indeed*."

Jittery-kneed, I took the seat beside her in the breakfast nook. I wanted to ask her about the order of protection. But what if she didn't know about it? What if she was Alex's enemy? She might use it against him in some underhanded way.

Alex was down in the basement with his father; the murmur of their voices and the whizzing of power tools seeped up through the floorboards.

Babs and I sat in silence; she continued to read while I watched the rain dribble down the window pane.

"My dear Celeste," she finally said in a low, quiet voice, "I hope Alex will give you what you need . . . I know I'm much too deep for Chester, but then, when I met him I was forty-five, my husband had just left me for his secretary, and I had four teenage children. Sometimes I want to take Chester by the collar—" She lifted the newspaper and shook it. She stopped, stared at it, then crumpled it and threw it aside. "But then, I suppose, denial can be a blessing. It's so much easier to live that way. It's just that—well—Alex is so violent-tempered. And you are truly a dear, sweet young woman." After a pause she added, "I'm sorry about that Danielle Steel novel. Sometimes I'm such a bitch, I just can't stop myself!"

I smiled weakly with what I hoped was an understanding look. What did she mean by "violent-tempered"? I was afraid to ask.

"I lost my mother too at a very young age," Babs went on. "I'm still avoiding that pain."

I gazed at her, bewildered, as tears rose to my eyes. Had I told her about the carousel? I could not bring myself to ask her about this either, and not remembering seemed a calamity. I swore to myself I would never drink liquor with Sudafed again. I would not drink any alcohol for a month. Say, three weeks. Well, perhaps two. Now, at least, I knew I would never wake up in a stranger's bed. There would always be Alex to lean up against, pillar of stability that he was.

"Oh, God, Babs." I covered my face and breathed to calm the panic and bile that kept rising in waves to my throat. "I don't know what I'm doing."

She took one of my hands and held it in her lap.

I laughed mirthlessly. "I'm a coward," I told her. "I'm afraid of being alone."

"Then that must make me one, too."

We sat in silence for a long while and watched the rain pelt the window as the coffee cups grew cold in our hands.

Eight

A TERRIBLE LETHARGY overcame me after Chester and Babs's party. My cold had set up camp for a long siege inside my head, but I didn't mind. For five days I stayed in bed, relishing the fact that I had an excuse. I read, and watched the Discovery Channel, where I learned about life in far-off places and scientific facts about the behavior of sharks, dinosaurs, ants, crocodiles, wild dogs, and apes. I felt soothed and mentally nourished.

By the following Saturday I was ready for an outing, and Alex suggested we go back to Bloomingdale's to continue our registering extravaganza. Already the gifts had started to arrive. I never opened the boxes, but waited for him to get home from work. It was amusing to watch him rip open the wrappings with a child's voracious enthusiasm. Sometimes I'd tease him, and he'd call me a Trappist monk and grin sheepishly.

For years I'd lived sleeping on a futon and watching a black and white TV. I had lived with just enough money to survive with the basic comforts, and the riches that populated Alex's life were still foreign to me. While his concerns had been to fill his life with such riches, mine had been simply to survive long enough to complete my work, and become a writer.

Yet that Saturday, as we walked slowly through the Bloomingdale's living room and bedroom displays, the back of my throat began to ache with an incomprehensible longing. On a waxed wood dining table spotless crystal glasses and silverware gleamed near deep red plates, spotlighted like jewels from some ancient and revered culture. I felt like an intruder in an opulent world of order and satiety.

I went and sat on the couch and crossed my legs. Alex sat in the armchair beside me. We smiled at each other in silence. I caught a glimpse of us in a large gilded smoky mirror that hung on a nearby wall and for a moment was overwhelmed with happiness for the nice, serene young couple I saw there. I smiled at our reflection; Alex reached for my hand, squeezed it tightly.

As we continued to explore, the Positano display caught my eye and I stopped. We had registered for these dishes. I had liked the simple, childlike, indigo blue fish hand-painted along the borders of the plates and mugs. I picked up one of the large plates and admired it, trying to imagine what I would cook to serve on it.

"I like these, Jane," a young man standing next to me said to his companion.

"They're *Italian,*" Jane responded dismissively. "We're going to *France* on our honeymoon, Howard. Daddy said we could go to *Limoges* and pick out our dishes there."

"Will they be that much cheaper in Limoges, though?"

"Who cares! We'll be able to *say* we got them in *Limoges.*"

I put the dish down and looked at the couple from the corner of my eye. Howard was a dark-haired man in his late twenties, probably a businessman attempting to look relaxed in his weekend Gap bermudas and cotton oxford shirt. Jane was in khakis and a pink Lacoste shirt with the collar turned up, her very blond hair pulled back tightly in a ponytail. She wore a gold Cartier watch, and her diamond solitaire was what Alex would call a skating rink. Like mine, in fact. On most days I looked at it with surprise and awe, as if I still could not believe that it belonged to me. I looked down at my dress, one of my favorites, a faded Putumayo floral print that was five years old, and Portuguese espadrilles whose rope soles had started to unravel.

What the hell am I doing here? I thought, and hurried away.

I found Alex in the cookware section, examining an enormous Le Creuset orange pot that cost $300. "Wouldn't you like to have this? You could make dinner for tons of people. We could have big dinner parties . . ."

We went upstairs to the restaurant for lunch. We stood in line for twenty minutes while the two ladies in front of us discussed how it was nearly impossible to get a good manicure anymore since the Koreans had taken over the nail salons. By the time we sat down, I'd lost my appetite.

Alex paused in midbite of his big chicken salad sandwich on a baguette. "What's the matter?" he said worriedly.

"I—I don't know." My face felt cold, I probably looked pale. "I feel like I don't belong here, Alex."

"You belong wherever you are," he said. "I've worked like a dog to be able to afford whatever I want in life. Just enjoy it, Celeste. Don't think so much."

* * *

ALEX LEFT FOR MEXICO on Monday. He would be gone four days. Restless, I went over to visit my old neighbor Lucia that afternoon and we sat on her couch and smoked a joint. I rarely smoked pot. Soon, troubling thoughts began to invade my mind. *You don't miss him. You should be missing him more.* I remembered too late how the last time I'd smoked pot with Lucia I'd sworn I would never smoke again; and now, here I was, stoned and unable to undo it. I felt like my skin was transparent and she could see everything that was going on inside me. The sharp tang of his cologne suddenly wafted over me. I sniffed at the ends of my hair, my hands. Where was it coming from? Had it permeated my pores? Lucia was staring at me with a concerned look.

"Let's go get some food. I'm freaking out over here," I said.

We went around the corner to the Yellow Rose cafe for an order of deep-fried morels. We sat at the bar. Lucia ordered a frozen margarita. Patrick, our handsome, fortyish bartender-actor friend, waited for my order. Lucia waited too. Everything was happening in slow motion, the pause so pregnant with innuendo it was like a badly directed Pinter play. I was sure they were thinking that everything in my future hinged on my decision of whether or not to have a drink. I had not had one since Chester and Babs's party and it seemed a good idea to continue on this track; yet this endless silence was unbearable and I decided that a margarita would surely help me get unstoned. And there was that leather-and-spice smell again, driving me crazy.

"Lucia, do I smell like him? Like that aftershave or whatever it is he wears?"

She came forward and sniffed me like a big dog. "I can't smell anything," she said. "But then my nose is always stuffed up."

A while later, halfway through the drink, I began a litany of unhappy complaints. I noted foggily that my tolerance to alcohol must definitely be waning. I couldn't believe I was telling Lucia in detail about Alex's ex-wife Mimi and her order of protection.

"I fucking hate that he didn't tell me!" I cried in conclusion.

"I'd be a little more concerned about what he did to her," Lucia intoned.

"He said he didn't do anything to her."

Lucia just stared at me. "Right. One word of advice . . ." She popped another mushroom in her mouth and chewed it with great relish. "Forget it."

"That's two words!"

Patrick, who had been eavesdropping on the twists and turns of our lives for the past several years, came over with two fresh, frozen drinks and set them in front of us on little white napkins.

"Congratulations," he said to me. "These are on the house."

How could I say no? It was unthinkable. So we sat there and discussed marriage in general, and mine in particular, with Patrick, who from time to time would empty the bottom of his margarita blender into our glasses after he'd filled an order, until it occurred to me, sometime after the dinner crowd had dispersed, that I was drunk. Alex would be trying to call from Mexico. How many hours ago had I left home? Perhaps four . . . There would be at least five hang-ups on the answering machine by the time I got home. He would think I was having an affair. I felt guilty for no reason.

I put a quarter in the phone and called his voice mail at work.

"Hi, Alex," I enunciated very clearly. "Listen, I'm with Lucia on the West Side. She is on the verge of a mental collapse—I may end up staying on her couch tonight. Well. Good-night. I love you."

With that, I hung up and breathed a sigh of relief. I went back to the bar and bought a pack of cigarettes from Patrick, who reminded me that I had quit smoking over a year ago. Alex had once said that it was a good thing I didn't smoke because the taste of tobacco in a woman's mouth made him feel sick.

"What the hell," I said. "It's just one night."

"Gimme one," Lucia said, reaching for the pack. "You know what's wrong, Celeste?" she said in her saturnine way. "You're getting cold feet."

On Wednesday a Federal Express package arrived from Lucia—twenty individually gift-wrapped pairs of socks; gold socks, silver socks, neon socks, gym socks, socks with stars and stripes, in fact, every kind of sock imaginable. Her note read: "Celeste, for your cold feet."

I was laughing with a certain amount of uneasiness when the phone rang. It was Alex in Mexico.

"Hey listen, I want you to come meet me down here."

"Down here where?"

"Well, in Mexico. This deal just went through between Grupo Telemedia and Chadwick Broadcasting and these Mexican guys are really happy. They offered me airline tickets and a great place to stay for a week. It's a resort they own somewhere near Matlan. Best diving in the Western Hemisphere. I'll fly to Matlan from Mexico City. Meet you at the airport."

A free trip to Mexico. I'd never traveled on the spur of the moment in my life. "But what about my kids up in Harlem? I have class with them next Tuesday."

"Your *kids*?" he said with a chuckle. "They won't even notice. It's *spring,* the term's almost over. They don't want to be writing poetry in this weather."

It was true that they were getting harder and harder to control and their attention span was shrinking. On days like that they ran my battery down so low, I came home wondering what the good of it was anyway.

"Come on, Celeste, let your hair down," Alex said. "It's beautiful down here."

I decided to call Ellie Horowitz, their teacher, and find out if I could reschedule my class for Thursday or Friday of next week. When that turned out to be fine, I had no more excuses.

* * *

The Aero Zapata plane descended toward Matlan in a torrential thunder and lightning storm. A crack of lightning split open the charcoal-colored sky. It struck the wing, which sizzled white and neon blue in the darkness. I screamed, jumping out of my seat.

I closed my eyes and saw the plane falling, falling, and all the people screaming, bags tumbling down on our heads—and then the crash, the explosion and death. I envisioned my father and Anna hearing the news over the phone, their faces draining of color as they attempted to react without embarrassing themselves. How would Alex respond?

The thought of oblivion did not seem unpleasant or threatening, especially since no one would ever blame me for dying. The plane swooped low and then at the last minute rose again and continued circling and shuddering in the storm. A child in the back began to scream. Across the aisle a woman held a rosary in her hands, her lips moving silently. The pilot tried another pass at landing, but he pulled the plane up once again and circled. It took four attempts before he managed to continue his descent and land. When the plane came to its screeching halt there were loud cheers and clapping.

Alex rushed toward me as I came through the gate. My knees gave way just as his big arms encircled me.

He drove the rented VW Golf on the two-lane road through the steaming, squat jungle toward the ruins of Chichén Itzá. Alex calculated the miles and his speed on his new dive watch, determining exactly how long it would take us to get to the hotel, so that we could see the ruins in the afternoon. On our way to Hol Cha the next day, we would need to leave by dawn to see the ruins of Cobá. Hol Cha, Alex had learned from his Mexican business associates, was one of the last great secret diving meccas on the east coast. The lagoon was so small, it did not even warrant a mention in the guidebook, which excited Alex, because it meant fewer divers to threaten the delicate reefs. Alex told me he had learned to dive on the Great Barrier Reef while on a business trip to Australia.

"Great white sharks live there," I muttered apprehensively.

"Didn't see any," he said with a smile. He told me that now he never missed an occasion to dive. His favorite diving experience so far had been a two-hundred-and-fifty-foot chasm off of Andros Island.

"You get narced out at a hundred and fifty feet," he said excitedly. "It's like being bombed under water."

"You're shitting me, right?" I said.

"I shit you not."

This is an improvement, I thought quickly. *He didn't tell me not to swear.*

We drove on, pursued by thunderstorms that clattered above our heads and then galloped off, leaving behind a dazzling blue sky and thirsty sun. The steaming road and jungle glittered in the haze like a fairyland half-shrouded in clouds. By two o'clock the earth was baked dry and we arrived at Chichén Itzá in a swirl of dust. The world seemed empty of people.

We waited for a long time at the front desk in the quiet, airy hotel for someone to show us to a room. There was no ceiling over much of the courtyard and the hallways were like balconies, open to the sky and jungle and in the distance, the great pyramids. Alex wanted to go to the site immediately, but I thought it was too hot. It would be stupid to get sunstroke on our first day. He agreed.

Our large room had clay-colored walls and a smooth tile floor. I stretched out on the double bed and listened to the hot wind blow through the wooden slats in the shutters. Alex opened his big, manly, leather overnight bag and that leather-and-spice smell, now cool, piquant, wafted out at me. He stretched out alongside me and lightly touched my breasts through my T-shirt. My mouth watered with desire, not just for him, but for all the world's exotic, far-off places, like this one, where I had never been. Alex's soft, wet mouth pressed mine. I pulled the shirt over my head and lay back, a stranger to myself.

We followed the dirt path through a tunnel of squat, thorny jungle trees and stepped out onto a flat, sandy expanse as enormous storm clouds tumbled in overhead. The city of pyramids stood before us, the same purple-gray color as the clouds. A gust of wind blew dust everywhere. I had read that the whole city of Chichén Itzá had been excavated from the jungle by Western archeologists, and reconstructed stone by stone to appear exactly as it had over two thousand years ago. A bolt of lightning cracked the sky, and for a moment I was acutely aware of the millisecond of geological time in which I existed. What had happened to the arrogant, powerful people who had built this place? I thought of home, and wondered if a new culture of indomitable giants would be digging the ruins of our skyscrapers out of the wilderness someday.

No rain fell and the storm moved on. In moments the sky was blue again and the land and the pyramids appeared dust-colored and tranquil.

I gripped the enormous corroded chain that ran up the center of the steep, high steps of Kukulcan, the largest pyramid, and facing forward, I began to climb, following Alex upward. I was out of breath long before I reached the platform at the top, on which stood a little square edifice with arched doorways on two opposing walls, a temple or shrine to the ancient gods. I rose to my full height and, looking down, realized I couldn't see the steps I had just climbed. The platform appeared to be suspended in the sky. I broke into a sweat, convinced that I was going to fall hundreds of feet to the thick jungle canopy below. My knees collapsed and I found myself crawling into the little shrine. The whole pyramid seemed to be rocking madly as if it were trying to shake me off.

I'd had a nightmare like this before, of being at the top of something extremely high that was rocking, and holding on with my fingertips, unable to climb down. I crouched in a corner, my back pressed into the wall, and squeezed my eyes shut.

"Just look at this view, Celeste!" Alex called from outside. I could hear the click of his camera.

"Alex," I said, but my voice was hardly a whisper. "Alex!" I cried hoarsely.

He came in and stood over me. "Montezuma's revenge already?"

"No, it's not that. I—I can't see the steps. I can't move."

"You're acrophobic. You have to reason your way out of this, Celeste. The fear is all in your mind. Tourists have been climbing this thing for years."

"It doesn't matter. I can't."

He sat down beside me and crossed his legs. "This happens to people all the time. They never have it, then one day they do. It's nothing to worry about. But you're going to have to get down off this thing, Celeste. So let's just talk about it for a minute. There's that chain down the middle of the steps, remember the chain?" He was talking to me as if I were five years old. "You can just keep listening to me and go backwards. Back yourself right off this thing."

A memory flashed through my mind. It is summer and I am nine. My mother and I have left my grandmother in Bordeaux and we are in Italy, traveling from city to city, spending her meager savings in fancy hotels and restaurants and clothes shops. In Pisa, we walk around the very top of the Leaning Tower. This is before they put up a railing. My mother leads me by the hand. I feel no fear at all because she won't let me fall.

I started to cry.

"I can't." The terror and the panic were familiar.

"Give me your hand," Alex said gently, calmly. I forced myself to give him my hand.

He guided me backwards and I crawled with eyes closed to the edge of the platform and onto the steps. He placed my hands on the chain and said, "Go." I could hear people's voices, questioning, curious, but nothing mattered at that moment but getting back down to the ground. Slowly, my face to the stone, eyes screwed shut, I crawled downward. As I slowly, cautiously moved backward Alex talked, his calm voice complimenting me on how well I was handling the situation.

When we reached the bottom, it was a good five minutes before I was able to speak.

Alex gazed at me with a mixture of concern and curiosity. This was not the Celeste he knew. This was a surprise to him. I felt vulnerable, and that made me angry.

* * *

I WAS LYING PEACEFULLY on a towel on the hot, white sand reading *Wide Sargasso Sea,* a better choice, certainly, than Proust. Just behind me was our large, whitewashed cabin with a thatched roof, one of maybe ten, but almost all were empty this time of year. Above my head the palms rustled in the breeze, and tiny waves licked at the shore. Suddenly Alex came running down the beach, back from his first excursion to the Hol Cha dive shop, and I could tell by the look of excitement on his face that I wasn't going to like what he had to say.

"For only two hundred and fifty dollars you can pass the PADI certification course in three days," he said, not even slightly out of breath, "and you can be my dive buddy forever!"

My heart started pounding. "Oh, Alex," I said lightly. "I think I'll just sit here on the beach and read."

His face collapsed in disappointment. "Celeste, just try it. Once. For me, please?"

Feeling put-upon and under scrutiny, I consented. After yesterday's fiasco, I didn't want him to think I was a wimp. "Okay, but if I hate it, I'm not going to go through with it."

"Good girl!" he cried. "If you absolutely hate it, you can quit. At least you'll have tried, right?"

"Right."

Dive number one: The dive master, Dave Francisco, was as big as a baby whale, and so serene he reminded me of a Buddhist monk. We were floating in the perfectly clear, calm bay in six feet of water. I wore the cumbersome scuba vest called a "buoyancy compensator," which was pumped full of air. Strapped to it on my back was a heavy air tank. The weight belt, cinched tight around my waist, dug into my sides. He was telling me in a jovial voice that he was from Santa Cruz,

California, and that Hol Cha had the best diving he'd ever seen in his life. For love of diving, he'd given up civilization and now lived in a trailer on the beach with a pet iguana and a parrot for company. He said that he had better conversations with the parrot than with most humans he knew, and that although the parrot's English was still limited, his Spanish was flawless.

I kept nodding, smiling, while telling myself there was nothing to worry about, all was well. I was sweating so heavily that my mask had already fogged up. *I don't want to fail and look like a coward and a fool!* I thought.

Dave gave me the okay sign, which he had just taught me, index finger and thumb in an O; I returned it, and abruptly he let the air out of my vest. I sank to the bottom.

I knew that I was supposed to breathe through the regulator that I held clamped between my teeth for dear life, but I couldn't seem to. My lungs seemed to explode, and wriggling like a dying fish, I paddled frantically for the surface. My dive master pulled me panting and heaving toward the beach. I washed up at Alex's feet. I looked up and saw his crestfallen face.

"Don't worry about it," my dive master said, "this often happens the first time out."

Yes, of course, I thought, *it must happen all the time because what fool would want to do this?*

"You want to take a break?" Dave asked.

I shook my head. I'd rather have drowned than face Alex, so I pushed off and we paddled back out for try number two.

This time it was only a question of pride winning out over sheer terror. I forced myself to breathe through the regulator. The air felt cool and very dry in my mouth and seemed to rush into my lungs and expand there without any effort on my part. A strange sensation, breathing under water. Listening to my lungs working was even stranger. I sat on the bottom and thought, *Okay, so far so good,* and did not see a thing but sand flying around and my dive master's masked face and wavy black beard. He kept giving me the okay sign, so I figured I was doing fine—quite well, in fact, for a person with advanced agoraphobia, nascent acrophobia, and incipient hydrophobia.

Lunchtime. We sat at the al fresco bar under a thatched roof, and Alex was swearing to me that diving was one of the coolest, greatest experiences he'd ever had in his life.

"I want a margarita," I said, turning to the waiter. "Excuse me, sir? Could I have a margarita please?"

"You can't have a drink before your afternoon dive session," Alex said.

"I'm not going back this afternoon, Alex, so you'd better just shut up and leave me alone if you want me to continue doing this."

He sat there sulking as I sipped my drink, feeling like I'd won a small victory, though certainly not the war.

Fortified, with Alex long gone on his excursion, I decided to go back for my second dive. This time, after the drills, which involved taking off the vest under water, taking off the weight belt and putting it back on, and clearing my mask of water, my dive master led me on an underwater tour of the shallow bay. There were some beautiful little fish, indigo blue, gold, silver, rainbow-colored, and several larger yellowtail snappers who were fearless and came right up to my mask and peered at my face. I also saw a flounder and a small stingray that quickly skittered off, leaving a tiny cloud of sand. It was interesting, but a religious awakening it was not.

We returned to the dive shop and there was Alex with the other certified divers, elatedly discussing the five-foot moray eel they had scared out of its hole, that had sliced a bait fish in two with one snap of its jaws.

"How was it, Celeste?" he asked me hopefully.

"It was fine," I mumbled, rinsing out my equipment in the freshwater trough, like my dive master had shown me.

"Give it a chance," Alex said, and squeezed my shoulder.

* * *

With every dive, the underwater drills grew more complicated and depth increased; I had to take the regulator out of my mouth and blow bubbles, inflate my BC through my mouth, share a regulator with my dive master, and ascend slowly. I had to take my mask off completely and put it back on, emptying it of water by blowing air out my nose. All these drills, he told me, were so I would know what to do in case anything ever went wrong.

"Like what?" I asked him.

"Oh," he said in that calm voice, "you know, getting caught on some coral at the bottom, or running out of air, things like that."

"Does it happen often?"

"Nah," he said vaguely.

* * *

THE NEXT DAY, I had my first open water dive. After the compass drills, Dave and I cruised around in about forty-five feet of water. We came upon a sea turtle swimming lazily through the deep blue. We tried to follow, but it moved away too fast.

Back on the motorboat, Dave told me that this species of sea turtle was almost extinct, due mostly to overfishing. There was a rescue operation taking place just down the beach. Experts were gathering the turtle eggs and delivering them to hatcheries, where the baby turtles were kept until they were big enough to fend for themselves in the harsh world.

That afternoon, I passed my openwater test, and afterwards saw the most incredible thing—three four-foot spotted eagle rays swimming together like birds in formation, their black-spotted wings flapping in slow motion, disturbing nothing. They were so unlike anything I'd ever seen, they could have been from another planet, another galaxy entirely.

When we returned to the dive shop, Dave handed me the written exam to take home and told me with a grin that I was on my honor not to cheat. Alex did offer to help me with the math problems involving the dive tables. But that was only after I threw the PADI book against the wall and threatened to tear up the exam.

Later that evening, Dave, Alex, and I celebrated at the outdoor bar.

"Tomorrow you'll be a certified diver, and you'll love it, you'll see," Alex said. He was so proud of me he let me order a fourth margarita.

"Mm-hm," I said.

"You know, you really should try a night dive while you're here," Dave said.

"What a good idea!" Alex said.

"You're nuts," I cried. "I won't dive at night! In the dark!"

* * *

ALEX AWAKENED in a good mood and stated that as recompense for my passing the PADI test, we would drive to Matlan and spend the day exploring.

The main street was lined with tall buildings and the tourist shops carried overpriced Mexican clothes and amulets. We bought presents for our families, earrings for me, and a big white cotton shirt for Alex.

Gazing up at the tall hotels along the beach, I imagined them under water. "How tall is that building, Alex?"

"Oh, about a hundred feet."

Tomorrow I would be diving as deep as that building was tall. My heart began to beat hard, my mouth went dry.

At sunset, we found a crowded bar on the beach that had an uncrowded veranda. Why would they huddle inside, I wondered, when this was so much nicer?

Just as the waitress went off with our order, a loudspeaker announced the beginning of the bathing suit contest. Everyone began to cheer and shout. Annoyed, I looked out at the horizon in the fading light. The water and sky were the same silvery-taupe color, one a shimmering reflection of the other.

About twenty feet in front of us, a lone couple lay stretched out on the beach. The fellow had straight brown hair, the ends sun-bleached to pale gold. He was leaning back on his elbows, his large shoulders hunched. There was something familiar about the folds of skin around his neck and the angular shape of his shoulder blades. He turned his face toward the girl and my breath stopped.

"What's the matter?" Alex asked.

"Nothing. I think maybe I know that guy." I gestured with my chin. "Remember Sebastian from the picture? Well, I think that's his brother. I'm not sure."

I was sure, I just wasn't sure I wanted to talk to him. I hadn't seen Nathan for over seven years.

"Go take a look," Alex suggested.

I got up, slipped off my sandals, and walked on the soft sand that was fine and cool. I skirted the couple but watched them in my peripheral vision, and went down to the water. They were kissing now, and he was not paying attention to me at all. The water was so warm, it was warmer than the air. *Should I go up to him?* I wondered.

The sky glowed a strange greenish hue in the west. To the east, the world was darkening quickly to purple. I waited a moment, and then, resolved, turned and started back. They did not look up from their kiss.

I sat down across from Alex and sipped my margarita. I was strangely out of breath, as if I'd run a long way.

"So is it him?"

"I'm not sure."

"Why not call him, yell, 'Nathan,' and see if he turns around?"

Nathan took a long swig off his beer bottle and put it in the sand, next to several empties that stuck out at strange angles, like old gravestones.

I had once heard that it takes seven years to overcome heartbreak. I supposed that must be right. Seeing Nathan brought to mind again that December day during my sophomore midyear finals, when Sebastian called with the news of Sally's suicide, and how I sat in stunned silence until the phone rang again and it was Nathan, and upon hearing his voice, I decided to visit him up at Harvard.

Nine

After the calls from Sebastian and Nathan, I sat for a long time in the dormitory kitchen. Everyone had gone to the libraries or to exams and I was alone. When I stood up finally, my knees were shaky and my head whirling. I went to my room and gathered up my books, and walked across the frozen green to the Science Library, which stayed open all night. There was no need for me to stay in there all day and then pull an all-nighter, I was prepared for my exams. But I had to keep my mind occupied.

I fell asleep in a leather chair sometime near dawn, and dreamed I was standing at one end of Sally's overpass, behind a tall fence. I couldn't see the road below, but I could hear cars rushing by. Across the way, Sally was walking slowly toward me, down a green sloping lawn. She was wearing shorts and a T-shirt, despite the cold. The noise of cars was deafening. She was taking her time crossing the overpass, looking around as if enjoying the scenery. Then she smiled at me and beckoned for me to join her. Still smiling, she lifted one leg over the railing, then the other, then gripping the rail firmly behind her, took an indecisive step. My fists beat against the fence. She turned her face toward me once more, but it was no longer her face, it was my mother's, and her expression was so desolate, so filled with pain, that I tried to cry out, "No! Wait!" but my voice failed me. Then she let go, and I started screaming. I woke up soaked through with sweat. There was no one around; above the long empty stacks the fluorescent lights droned like beehives.

Shaken, I went home and got into bed. I had the same dream again, but this time Sally was running. She did not stop, or seem to notice me standing on the other end of the bridge. Gripping the overpass railing, she swung both legs over at once, without hesitating. At the last moment she turned her head toward me, and again, it was my mother's face, wearing that look of utter hopelessness and devastation.

* * *

With only two days left before Christmas Eve, I phoned Anna and told her that I had some work to make up at school and I'd arrive home in time for Christmas Eve dinner. I ran back to my dorm after my last exam and packed up my car and drove up to Cambridge.

A wet and heavy snow was falling when I parked at the end of Nathan's street of old brownstones. My stomach was cramping with anticipation. As I locked up it occurred to me that I hadn't thought of Sally all day—only Nathan and what it would be like to be with him.

The door to his apartment was open. I walked in. Nathan sat on a tired old couch in the small living room, framed by his two longhaired roommates. Nathan was taking a hit off a foot-long bong pipe. He looked me over blandly, holding his breath, and exhaled a cloud of smoke that enveloped his head.

"Hey, Celeste," he said, and coughed. He pounded his chest with a fist. "Take off your coat. Have a seat."

I felt ill at ease. The three of them were looking at me in silence. The short walk in the snow had drenched my coat. My boots dripped onto the floor, my hair was plastered to my head in long patches. He introduced me to the two fellows, who shook my hand and left, muttering some excuse.

"Want a hit?" he asked me.

I shook my head. He put the bong away behind the couch. "How about a drink of something? Rum? Vodka?"

"Either."

He got up and went into the kitchen. I heard him opening and closing cabinets, the fridge.

"Nathan, do you think this is a mistake? Because I can leave."

"Absolutely not."

He came out extending a drink to me. It was dark rum and tonic with a wedge of lime floating in it. I took a sip and looked at him.

"What happened to Sally really sucks," he said. "But it wasn't your fault."

I went to the window and looked out at the wet flakes falling heavily against the darkness. Only a few cars were left on the street, there was an end-of-the-semester feeling in the air.

He walked up behind me and began nuzzling the back of my wet head. His arms reached out and held the windowsill on both sides. The old longing came back, hard as a knot, powerful, pulsating in my lower abdomen. *So this is it*, I thought.

He left and returned a moment later with a warm towel, probably left on a radiator. He began to dry my hair with both hands, encircling my head with the towel. He led me back to the couch and we sat down facing each other. He kept rubbing my head until my hair was dry and fluffed out wildly around my head.

"There," he said. He looked at me closely. "When you were fourteen you had a baby face, with little pudgy cheeks."

Abruptly I remembered the discussions he used to have with my brother about girls. "Did you ever screw Olivia?" I asked.

"Who's Olivia?"

"You know, the Catholic one who wore all the makeup and gave blow jobs."

He laughed. "You remember everything! That was just talk. We *heard* she gave blow jobs."

"What about your IQ, was that true?"

"That was true," he said solemnly, as if he were admitting something unpleasant about himself.

"So what was your score?"

"One-eighty." There was a pause. "What's your brother doing these days?"

"Oh, he's going to go to law school in the fall—finally—like my dad always wanted."

"Surprise, surprise," Nathan said. "Sally was sick, Celeste. You couldn't do anything for her."

"I have these dreams—" I started, but couldn't finish. "Oh my God," I put my face down on his lap and was overcome by tears. His hands passed gently through my hair as I cried.

"I've thought about you so much," he said. "Once I even borrowed a friend's car and started down to your school, but I chickened out. I figured, oh shit, I don't know. I figured Bass would never forgive me."

"He will," I said. "He always forgives everybody."

He lifted me easily and carried me into his bedroom. It looked just like his room had at home, with a dark blue spread and bookshelves all along one wall, lined two deep with books. Another wall was covered with photographs: his family standing in front of the Eiffel Tower, in a market in Marrakech, Nathan and Jack and me at one of Sally's running meets. He's shoving an ice-cream cone in my nose, and Jack is laughing. Sebastian must have taken the picture.

Nathan smelled exactly as he had so many years ago—of tobacco, of pot, of some mild soap, of his skin-smell, which was a little like a brand-new clothbound book.

He was tender but not deferential. He lifted my sweater over my head, then unsnapped my bra in one swift click. He lowered it off my shoulders, staring at me without guile. I felt embarrassed and crossed my arms. He moved them away and started licking my nipples slowly, going from one to the other as if they were two different flavors and he couldn't make up his mind.

For me there had been only Sebastian and a boy at school who'd walked me home after we'd both had quite a lot to drink at a party. But there had never been this overwhelming feeling of wanting someone so much. I now felt I understood *Romeo and Juliet* and *Tristan and Isolde*. Their behavior seemed oh so sane. I believed then that there was always a price to pay for great love, that no one ever got anything that extraordinary for free.

I wondered if Nathan felt it too. Or if this was just the way he was with everyone he slept with. I felt crazy jealous, and afraid.

"Nathan, stop—I—"

"Shh," he said. "Don't get up, Celeste."

Off came my jeans and panties in his firm hands. I lay back and watched him as he knelt between my legs.

"Nathan, the door—"

"Oh yes, the door," he said, and got up to close it. In a moment he was back. He pulled me by the hips to the edge of the bed and pushed my knees up to my chest.

"From now on it's just us and whatever happened before doesn't matter," he said, and began to lick me. Soon I was telling him to fuck me, which he did, by pulling me onto his cock as he sat with his legs spread on the floor. It seemed that we shared one mouth, one heart, one sex organ. Like the intersecting circles I used to love to draw with my compass as a child, each overlapping section belonged no more to one than to the other. Our outlines appeared to have merged too and I could no longer tell where I ended and where he began.

* * *

"CELESTE?" Alex asked, reaching for my hand across the table. "Is something wrong?"

All at once, I noticed how dark it had become. The couple had not budged. Nathan placed his large tanned leg over the girl's thighs, and she laughed as he whispered in her ear. Inside the bar the patrons were shouting and jeering at the bathing suit contestants.

"No. I'm sorry. I was just wondering if it's him. I haven't seen him in six or seven years. Anyway, he looks busy right now."

I watched them, feeling aroused but not jealous, just curiously detached.

The winner of the competition was announced. She came outside and stood on the veranda among her admirers. Loud voices congratulated her. I turned to look. She was in a string bikini and had blond hair piled high on her head. She was apparently a bodybuilder. Her muscles looked chiseled and hard.

"God, that guy and his girlfriend look like they're about to do the wild thing right here on the beach," Alex said, laughing.

"Come on, let's get another drink," I said.

"I thought you hated this place."

"It's all right."

The breeze raised the hairs on my arms and I shivered.

* * *

IN MY MIND'S eye I could still see Nathan's college room perfectly.

His bed was a wreck, the blankets and sheets on the floor, and I sat hugging my knees and shivering as he returned carrying drinks and jumped up on the bed. He pulled the sheets and blankets off the floor and arranged them carefully around me and then around himself. We sat there, looking at each other in silence. His hair was hanging down in front of his eyes, making him look youthful and innocent.

"I love you, Celeste."

"Not as much as I love you. And anyway, I've loved you longer."

"Bullshit," he said, and laughed. "What do you want for dinner?"

"Do we have to go out?"

"No, Chinese or pizza delivers."

"Chinese!"

We stayed in bed for two days. At some point the roommates must have come and gathered their things and left for Christmas. I never heard or saw them again and didn't care at all if they heard us. We never left the room except to use the kitchen or the bathroom. On the first morning he ran us a bath with strong-smelling sea-kelp bath salts and he carried me in and deposited me into the old, high tub that had feet. Naked, his penis swinging from side to side, he went out and returned carrying a frosty bottle of Veuve Cliquot and two tall champagne glasses. He'd been working part-time at a liquor store and had hoarded quite a reserve.

He got into the tub, handed me the glasses, and popped the cork on the bottle. The champagne flowed into the bath. He filled our glasses and we drank. Then he put the bottle and the glasses on the floor and began to wash me from head to foot with a soft sea sponge.

As I lay back in the warm, steamy water, he told me that he was thinking about quitting school and traveling. He wanted to go to Central and South America and study those cultures by *being* there, not by reading *One Hundred Years of Solitude* and learning Spanish by parroting a gringo.

"Would you come with me?" he asked.

I just stared at him and smiled, dazed.

"I don't know," I finally said.

The mind, he told me, was a great incomprehensible mystery.

"Magic exists, it's just a manifestation of the side of the mind we don't understand. About a year ago I taught myself to read the Tarot. I've read every fucking book on the Tarot I could find." He lifted my foot and began to scrub the bottom. "The Queen of Swords kept coming up in my spread," he continued. "I kept wondering who the hell she was. This unknown Queen of Swords. What were she and the Death card doing in my spread? And the Eight and Nine and Ten of Swords—nightmares, insomnia, worry kept coming up. Love, the Queen loves the King of Swords, that's me. Well, you're the Queen. That's absolutely sure. Air sign, a worrier, one who has suffered losses and is going to suffer more of them in the future. Definitely you."

"Jesus, you sound like Sally, Nathan. Stop already."

"Do you want me to read your cards for you?"

"No!" I cried, unglued by his description of his cards.

After carrying me back to bed, he stood naked at the stove and made corned beef hash and fried eggs. He brought them in on a tray and we ate in silence. I thought I had never tasted anything so good in my life.

I knew that if an angel offered me a chance to be anyplace in the universe, I would not leave.

* * *

Alex had been talking but I hadn't heard a word he'd said. Just as the waitress brought us another margarita, Nathan and the girl stood and playfully swatted the sand off each other's bodies. They put on T-shirts and began to collect their empty bottles.

"Nathan!" I shouted, without thought. He straightened and made a slow circle, looking around, tottering as if he were standing on a rope bridge. The girl looked right at me; taking his arm, she pointed. Nathan pushed his hair away from his eyes with the back of his hand and squinted. I waved. His face lit up, and he laughed. He came toward us, weaving slightly, and said, "Well, I'll be goddamned."

The girl walked up behind him. Her tousled, sun-bleached blond hair hung in front of her unlined, darkly tanned face. She was young, perhaps twenty, and her skin was smooth and taut.

"Giovanna," he said, "this is—a very old friend of mine."

"Old is how I feel," I said.

Giovanna looked from him to me to Alex with a perplexed but friendly expression. Nathan said to her in Italian, "This woman is the only woman I've ever truly loved." Giovanna smiled understandingly.

"Giovanna's from Milan," he said to us. "I'm helping her with her English and she's helping me with my Italian."

"I see," I said with good humor.

She said, "She's very beautiful," in Italian and laughed. Alex stood up and extended his hand over the veranda's railing.

"I'm Celeste's fiancé, Alex Laughton."

"No way!" said Nathan.

"Way," said Alex.

"Well, congratulations!" Nathan said. He looked Alex over carefully, but then his eyes focused on me with a fierce intensity. "Of all the places in the world to run into you. Come have dinner with us! A little place down the road."

Alex called the waitress over and paid the bill with his American Express platinum card, and I felt ashamed.

"Sounds good to me," Alex said. "But we've got a long drive back to Hol Cha, so we shouldn't stay out too late."

We followed Nathan's Suzuki motorcross bike down a winding dirt road through the canopy of trees. Nathan was flying over bumps and holes, raising dust and zigzagging all over the place.

"He's a wild one, isn't he?" Alex said.

* * *

I WAS NINETEEN when I spent those two days in Cambridge with Nathan, and up until then, there had been only one other time in my life when I'd felt completely happy to be alive—the trip my mother and I took around Italy when I was nine. Both times had been colored by a certain recklessness, by heavy drinking (in Italy, by my mother; in Cambridge, by Nathan and me), and by an intangible sense of impending doom. On both, we seemed to be attempting to stop time; but what we feared from the future, I had no idea.

Late the second night in Nathan's bed, I curled into a ball and hid, wrapped tightly in a cocoon of sheets, frozen, unable to express the pain I was feeling. The next day was Christmas Eve, and I would have to leave him. He stretched out alongside me and held me firmly, not saying a word.

"I'm supposed to fly to Houston tomorrow morning," he finally said. "But if you want, I'll just blow it off. We can stay here. Or I'll come home with you. Is that what you want? I'll do whatever you want."

"And then what?" I asked. "And then school starts again and you'll be gone."

"Time and distance are just concepts," he said. "It's all relative. Nothing on this planet short of death could stop me from being with you."

My heart fluttered with joy at his romantic words, but in my mind, I clearly heard the word, *Bullshit. Bullshit. Bullshit.*

* * *

ANNA DID NOT say much when I called to tell her I was bringing Nathan MacKenna home for Christmas. The news of Sally's death had given me a certain leeway. Driving down I-95 with Nathan, I felt that I'd been given a reprieve from the grayness of reality, and I decided to try not to think about the future for at least a few days.

We stopped in town to buy presents for my family. Snow was falling. The sounds of Salvation Army bells filled the frosty air, which bubbled and popped and tickled the nose like champagne. For once, the couples and children did not make me feel lonely and excluded, for

I too felt loved. Nathan held my hand as we gazed, stupefied, into store windows.

"What do you want for Christmas, Nathan?"

"You. Just you. Every night, all night long. I swear I've never felt this good in my life." He kissed my face, my hands, his warm mouth leaving wet trails on my skin that stung in the frosty air.

Later, we got into my car loaded down with silly gifts for my family, and kissed again, our thick coats keeping a distance between us. Slowly Nathan slipped his hands inside my coat, encircling me tightly. Snow was falling heavily, and I felt like we were kids kissing behind a curtain at a party.

Our lips separated, we breathed in the cold air, looking at each other in silence. On the sidewalk just outside the window, Mr. and Mrs. Newlyn—Sally's parents—materialized out of the snow. They were walking slowly, arm in arm.

"Oh, my God," I whispered.

Nathan looked. They were staring straight before them, as if focusing on some point in the distance. Their faces had aged twenty years since I'd last seen them, the lines hardened into masks of perseverance that revealed their grief and shock. They looked like refugees from a war-torn country. Were they out Christmas shopping? They still had another daughter, and a grandchild. People, I realized, didn't stop living when tragedy struck. It stopped my breath. A gust of wind blew snow against their faces, and Mrs. Newlyn winced and gripped her coat collar shut over her throat. Mr. Newlyn put his arm protectively around her back and guided her slowly past our car windows.

I never saw them again. I wrote them a formal, careful letter on Christmas day, and received in response a printed letter that they had apparently sent out to friends and family, signed by Mrs. Newlyn in her girlish, rounded script.

Later that night, Nathan, my brother Jack, then twenty-two and about to enter law school, and I were watching a late-night rerun of *Star Trek* in the den when the phone rang, and I heard Anna answer it. Shortly she opened the swinging door to the kitchen in her bathrobe and slippers.

"It's for you, Celeste. It's Sebastian calling to wish you a merry Christmas."

Nathan and I looked at each other. My brother grinned evilly.

I went into the kitchen, picked up the receiver, took a deep breath, and said hello.

"How are you doing?" he asked. "I was worried about you after I called you the other day. I called later on, but no one seemed to know where you were."

"Bass, listen. Nathan's here."

"With Jack?" Sebastian asked evenly.

"With me."

"Okay," he said slowly. "Okay. I understand."

"Do you want to talk to him?"

"Does he want to talk to me?"

I didn't know if he did or not. "Yes," I said.

I went out to the den. "Nathan," I said. He got up and followed me into the kitchen, where the receiver lay on the counter. He picked it up.

"Hi, Bass," Nathan said evenly.

I left him alone. I don't know what Nathan and Sebastian said to each other; I never asked. I went back to *Star Trek,* the episode where Captain Kirk has been thrown back in time. He's forced to decide between letting the woman he loves die, thus saving humanity; or saving her, which by some cruel twist of fate would cause the Nazis to win the war, changing the course of history.

Nathan came back looking solemn, his eyes dun-colored and impenetrable. His conversation with his brother did not stop him from sneaking into my room later and pulling the mattress off my bed and laying it on the floor. He pulled me down on top of it and pulled off my nightgown with his smooth, unwavering hands.

* * *

The Mexican restaurant was tiny and had a dirt floor. Christmas lights were strung across the tops of the screen windows. As we entered Alex warned me not to drink the water.

We sat down, Alex and I on one side of the rickety table, Nathan and Giovanna on the other. Alex and Nathan glared at each other calmly, like the two skinny wild dogs at Hol Cha who circled each other tirelessly in their eternal search for food.

Nathan was apparently a regular, and chatted in Spanish with the waitress. He ordered four shots of Quervo Gold. Giovanna smiled all the time and seemed to be listening, although how much she understood is anyone's guess. I decided to pretend I didn't understand Italian in case they said anything that I should know.

The shots arrived. Nathan shook some salt onto the back of his hand

and raised his glass. He licked the salt and said, "To you guys." I licked the salt from my hand and we clinked glasses and drank. Alex dispensed entirely with the salt thing, tipped his glass, and downed the shot without the slightest change of expression. I stuck a wedge of lime in my mouth and sucked on it. The tequila finally hit bottom and exploded, sending a wave of warmth through my legs and chest. Nathan ordered four more, and a round of beers.

"I just read a book," Nathan said, "about the Burgess Shale."

We looked at him in silence.

"This guy who wrote it, I studied with him at Harvard for about twenty minutes. It's the best goddamn book I ever read. Well, one of them."

"I think I read a review of it in the *Times,*" Alex said. "They found some strange fossils there, right?"

"Right. Well, the proposition is as follows: Homo sapiens evolved due to a total accident of fate. This shale is chock-full of previously unrecorded, presently nonexistent phyla. Like twenty-six varieties or something. There are only four phyla in the entire insect kingdom, by the way. Totally weird stuff—so why did all these phyla die off suddenly and this one little wormlike creature evolve into man?"

"But one book doesn't discount hundreds of years of scientific study and almost two thousand years of theology," Alex said. I wanted another shot.

"It sure as shit does," Nathan said. "People didn't listen to Galileo at first, did they?"

"How's Sebastian?" I asked, changing the subject.

Nathan looked away for a moment, his eyes vague. "Paquita! *Quatro mas, por favor!*

"Bass is fine," he said, turning back to me. "Navy's putting him through law school. He married a girl—get this—named Sebastianna. Sebastian and Sebastianna! Isn't that the greatest!" He slapped the table and laughed. Paquita set down four fresh shots, and Nathan slid one toward me and one toward Giovanna.

Alex drank his down and said, "That's it for me. I've got to drive."

"To Sebastian," Nathan said, his eyes misty and unreadable. We salted our hands and tossed back the shots. The warm glow was beginning to darken the corners of my vision, and to my relief, the pounding of my heart was finally subsiding. I wanted him to order more.

"Paquita!" Nathan yelled. *"Tres mas, por favor."*

"Don't overdo it, Celeste," Alex murmured in my ear.

When Paquita put the drinks down, Giovanna reached for hers hungrily and tossed it back without salt. Her enormous hair, sandy-colored and jungle-like, was falling across her eyes now. She looked at Nathan, then at Alex, and licked her lips.

My vision was closing in. The room became hazy and a feeling of goodwill toward all overcame me.

"I just got my scuba certification!" I cried out.

"No way!" Nathan said.

"Oh, yes, way," Alex said.

"You're pulling my chain, Celeste."

I felt Alex's back and arms tense beside me. I shook my head.

Nathan told us that he led dive tours for one of the local shops once in a while, when he needed cash. Mostly he bartended in one of the big hotels. This was not what I'd imagined for his future.

"The tourists are jerks, specially the Japanese," Nathan said. "They step all over the reefs!"

Paquita brought the menus and more shots. I had to close one eye in order to read the print.

"Yes, well, if I had to do it all over again," Nathan said, as if continuing a previous discussion, "I'd be a marine biologist. We're destroying our environment and it's so apparent in the ocean. Global warming is killing off the plankton and pretty soon we're going to be fucked, my friends, *fucked*! When I dive I never touch anything, not even empty shells," Nathan concluded gloomily.

Alex stared at him for a moment and said, "What a bunch of horseshit. I hunt, I fish. I pick up whatever I want when I'm diving."

I felt terribly confused.

"It's a miracle we're not living in a fucking wasteland. If everybody was like you, we would be," Nathan said.

"I'm going to the ladies' room," I said, and pushed my chair back. I found it difficult to walk.

"Don't put any toilet paper in the john!" Nathan yelled after me.

I heard Alex ask Giovanna, speaking very slowly and loudly, "Howa. Longa. You. Beena. Here?"

"Sree," she said. I glanced back. It looked like she was holding up three fingers.

Above the sink was a dirty mirror cracked down the middle. I turned on the faucet. The water was piss warm and smelled like sulfur. I splashed some on my forehead, and looking up, saw two fractured and disconnected sections of my face staring back at me. I couldn't remember what I was doing here. I leaned against the grimy wall to think.

* * *

THAT SPRING semester of my sophomore year, he was at my college more than his own, staying for long weekends that stretched from Thursday to Monday. Lying on my bed, he would read poems by Frederico García Lorca, Octavio Paz, Neruda, and César Vallejo; and sometimes Theodore Roethke, while I studied at the desk.

He'd read a verse or two aloud in a slow, undulating voice. Often it would be Lorca.

Great stars of white frost
come with the fish of darkness
that opens the road of dawn . . .

Although he never wrote his own papers, he thought I took too long to write mine and decided to help me. He asked me what had interested me most in *Anna Karenina,* and I said, "The death of Levin's brother."

"Okay, so we'll do a comparison between the death of Levin's brother and the death of the Master in *Master and Man.* That's short, you can read it in an hour. And we can throw in Ivan Ilych too." He thought for a few minutes, then dictated my opening and closing paragraphs. The paper began something like this: "In Tolstoy, Death comes wearing different masks. At times his face is that of the Grim Reaper; other times, an angel bringing an epiphany of light . . . "

Now it was a simple matter of filling in four pages of illustrative quotes. What before had taken me an entire weekend of working day and night to accomplish now took only an evening.

After reading my paper, my Russian Studies professor suggested that my senior thesis be an exploration of death throughout Tolstoy's fiction.

* * *

SOMETIMES, in the afternoon, we'd lie on my single bed and talk about concentration camps. My obsession with them had started long before my current class in Twentieth Century Europe. As a child I'd often dreamed of dying in a gas chamber.

"In another life, maybe you did," Nathan said.

He brought me books by Hannah Arendt and Primo Levi and told me about the different philosophies on the nature of survival. Nathan believed the writers who said that hope was the prisoner's worst enemy. Seeing a blade of grass on a spring day could kill a person, he told me gravely, whereas oblivion, nothingness, could keep you alive.

"You would have survived," I told him, "I know it."

"Who'd want to?" He shook his head. "I would never have allowed them to separate us. Fuck them, the sick sons of bitches. I would have refused and been beaten to death or shot," he said matter-of-factly.

Ten years had passed since that year, yet there were still certain songs I could not listen to without remembering those late winter days—the taste and smell of Nathan lying beside me, the faded daylight coming in through the blue Indian tapestries we'd tacked up for curtains over the large windows. There was Sting's clear, lamenting voice singing "The Bed's Too Big Without You," which amused us, given the size of the single bed in my dorm room; and the country and western singer Emmylou Harris, Nathan's favorite, singing,

There he goes gone again
same old story's gotta come to an end . . .

I knew that I was buying time. I knew he was flunking out and Harvard would ask him to leave sooner or later. But it was better to forget about such things. I still hoped he would somehow catch up on his courses. Our favorite songs were about heartbreak and being out in the world alone, but for the moment, I was neither, and the songs made me painfully grateful for my own happiness.

And years later, hearing even one bar of these old melodies on the radio, I still rushed to change the station, refusing to remember.

* * *

On a crisp, bright day in April, Nathan stopped by, unlocking the door with the extra key we'd made him. He looked like he'd stopped at a bar downtown after arriving on the Greyhound bus. It was the middle of the afternoon and I was sitting at my desk, reading for the third time Prince Andrew's death in *War and Peace.* Prince Andrew in his final moments dreams that Death is knocking at the door, and he feels he must get up and keep the door from opening, but he can't. When Death arrives, he is liberated from the weight of his earthly existence, and feels sorry for his loved ones who stand around his bed, weeping. He tries to be gentle and communicative with them, but knows he has already left them behind. Tears were streaming from my eyes.

I wiped them away quickly, watching Nathan as he crossed the room and sat heavily on the bed.

"I'm through," he said. "Harvard asked me to leave."

He told me he'd decided to go down to New Orleans for Jazz Fest, and then he was going to travel through Mexico to Central and then South America. Keep on going south till he hit the tip, he said with an uneasy smile. He didn't know when he'd be coming back.

"Come with me," he added after a pause. My pulse quickened.

"Why can't you just pass your fucking classes?" I cried. "You're smarter than everybody else! What the hell's wrong with you?"

"Why does it have to be bad? You can't imagine what a relief this is to me." His tone was calm, his eyes red-rimmed, as if he hadn't slept. His face was set, determined, his eyes inscrutable.

He's leaving me, I thought, panic-stricken. *He says he loves me but he's leaving me. If he loved me he would stay. Therefore he doesn't really love me.* Nothing would allow me to escape the logic of this syllogism and it made me sick to my stomach. My mouth went dry and I clutched the edge of my desk till my knuckles turned white.

"You're just going to leave me, that's it?" I said, my voice shaky.

"I asked you to come with me."

"I can't just walk away from my classes! From my life!"

"Why not?"

"Because this is where I'm *supposed* to be!"

"You want to marry a banker or a lawyer, is that it, Celeste? Because if that's true, it's not me you want."

I'd never thought that far ahead. I'd never really believed that our relationship would be allowed to last. It seemed to me that God was the biggest tyrant of all, lining people up at His giant station, separating wives and husbands, mothers and children, and deciding with the flick of a finger who would live and who would die. I watched Nathan as he sat at the edge of the bed looking at me. *He's weak,* I thought coldly. *He's unreliable.* Yet I was filled with admiration for him. What courage—to walk away from all responsibilities, to shrug off life's burdens, disregarding the consequences!

This is a fork in the road, I thought with awe. My consciousness seemed to lift out of me and float high above the scene. I felt detached, yet I was aware of the enormity of my next words, whatever they might be. Two futures stretched before me and nothing in the distance was clear. I wanted to know the outcome. I weighed the choices coolly. Life on the road with him. I had some money from my mother, much more than he probably had—his parents were paying for Harvard, but they had no intention of subsidizing his peripatetic journeys—I had the semester to finish, classes had already been paid for. But, my God, to be free, with him, unencumbered by responsibility, by the past . . .

"Read my cards," I said abruptly.

"Maybe this isn't a good time." He looked uncertain, boyish, and I didn't recognize him.

"Read them. You believe in them, read them."

Thoughtfully, he reached in his backpack for the leather pouch he kept the cards in and handed them to me.

"Shuffle them," he said, and sat cross-legged on the floor. I sat down across from him and did as he said. "Think about what you want to ask," he said. "Cut the deck in three with your left hand."

I did. He moved so that he was beside me and laid the cards out in a fan, seven across, five down. There was too much to take in. I did not know the cards but I recognized the Death card. I saw another with three swords crossing through a red heart. A charioteer in armor with a crescent moon over his head. An upside-down queen holding a wand. An old king looking into a cup. I saw many, many swords: a knight brandishing a sword, riding a winged horse; a woman sitting up in bed, gripping her hair while swords flew overhead. In the last row was a card of a beautiful woman standing in a vineyard, and all around her hung large clumps of purple grapes. She wore a gauntlet on which a hooded falcon perched.

"What's this one?" I asked, pointing to the card.

"Your benefactress."

My grandmother, I thought. *She lives in a vineyard*. A disconcerting longing for her overcame me.

"Let's start at the beginning," Nathan said, taking a deep breath. "Here's your past—your mother, the Queen of Wands. Fiery, fierce, loyal, beautiful, unreliable. But she's still in your present, still very much on your mind."

"What does that mean, Nathan?"

"I don't know what it means, I'm just telling you what the cards say. You're going to have more sadness. But you're going to survive it and eventually you're going to be happy. You need to look within yourself for the answers to your questions. Who is this older man here? Is there some man in your life I don't know about?" He said this with a slight smile, knowing that we were so obsessed with each other, the thought of someone else never even crossed our minds. "The King of Cups—not your father, surely. The World card just behind him indicates he's come from far away, a foreigner. This is a man with heart and spirituality."

"Maybe Viktor," I said, referring to Viktor Bezsmertno, a Soviet political refugee who was being sponsored by Rudy Brown of the Russian Department. Viktor had survived World War II as a child, only to end up in a Siberian work camp in the early fifties, for writing and publishing harsh facts about life under Stalin. Once, he had escaped and tried to hijack a plane to the West. In all, he'd spent twenty-two years in Siberia and the last four in exile in Gorky, trying to emigrate to the U.S. He was a tall, gap-toothed, gray-bearded man whose eyes were blue and wise.

Rudy Brown had been bringing him to our Second Year Russian class to help us in conversation practice. He was the first Soviet Russian most of us had ever met, and we discovered that he had an affinity for scotch. He hated vodka. A few days after his first visit, my five classmates and I took a bottle of Johnny Walker over to his small, barren apartment. He insisted we stay and drink it with him. The only thing he'd brought from Russia was his dog Bika, a huge sheepdog who wagged her tail hard. Viktor told us, after several big glasses of scotch which he drank warm and straight, that he'd gone to prison so young he'd never had a chance to make love with a woman. Now, he said, it was too late.

"It's never too late!" one of the boys blurted in his rudimentary Russian. We all laughed and Viktor smiled, blushing. The boy was right. There were too many strong-willed divorcées and widows around the college; Viktor's days as a virgin were surely numbered.

He said that while in jail, he'd often considered suicide, but instead he had kept faith that God would reward him, in heaven if not on earth.

"Nu, kto eto, Bog?" But who is God? I asked in my halting Russian.

He looked at me for a long moment. *"Kto eto Bog?"* he said, nodding his head thoughtfully, *"Bog—Bog!"* God is God.

Viktor had survived the unimaginable, and now he was starting life in a new country, in a new language, with absolutely nothing. He poured the last drops of scotch into our glasses and asked us to come back tomorrow. He told us we made him feel useful.

* * *

"Well," Nathan continued, "this Viktor is going to be important to you somehow."

A few months before, Viktor had introduced me to Varlam Shalamov's work. A single mimeographed story from an underground Soviet press. He held the pages and turned them with tenderness and care. When he handed them to me to take home, it was as if he were trusting me with a newborn child. For years I would pursue the elusive Shalamov, until he became one of the subjects of my Ph.D. dissertation.

"This is me, I guess," Nathan continued, tapping a card. "I'm in your obstacle line. The Knight of Swords charging off. But I'm not leaving your life, Celeste, I'm all over your future, too. See, here, I become the King of Swords. And then you've got this benefactress who's going to play a role."

"So?" I said in a controlled, calm voice.

In a tone sapped of all its strength and energy, he said, "I don't see any obvious travel cards in the immediate present, but that doesn't mean anything. We make our own futures, Celeste."

I nodded slowly. I realized then that I had known all along what the cards would say. He came toward me, his face serious and sad. We kissed and stretched out on the rug among the cards. We undressed each other hurriedly. He pulled me astride him and held my hips as I wrapped my arms tightly around his neck and shoulders. He let out a small cry, but I didn't loosen my grasp. I felt like I'd been given my death sentence and I saw no reason to deal with it decorously.

* * *

"**Do you want** me to stay a few more days?" he asked as we lay on my bed at sunrise, each having feigned sleep for most of the night. The syllogism would not leave me in peace—*He says he loves me but he's leaving me. If he loved me he would stay. Therefore he doesn't really love me.*

"What for?" As I heard the coldness and anger in my voice, I couldn't imagine why I'd said that, because I wanted him to stay more than anything else in the world.

"I'll always love you, Celeste," he said in a hushed voice.

"Just go," I told him, rolling against the wall and covering my head. Soon I heard the lock click softly behind him. I lay there for hours, thinking there was still time to change my mind, to catch him. I did not leave my room for the rest of the day and night, even when Candace, who lived two rooms down on my hall, knocked at dinnertime and then later in the evening when she was heading out to the pub. I kept wondering where Nathan was now. Was he packing? On a bus? Was he thinking of me?

When the sun rose the next morning and I was still lying there, staring at the ceiling, I realized I had no choice but to get up. That afternoon I went to a doctor in town who, it was said, was good for a prescription of sleeping pills. He was an elderly man whose hands shook. Broken blood vessels made a landscape of red rivers and tributaries of his nose and cheeks. I told him I needed something to help me sleep. He assured me it was the anxiety and pressure of classes. I told him I didn't care what it was, I couldn't sleep. He reluctantly gave me a prescription for Valium and scribbled down the name of a local psychologist.

I went back to my room. There was most of a bottle of Nathan's rum on a shelf and I drank half of it and felt absolutely nothing. So I took a Valium, and another, then a third, washing the little yellow pills down with the rum.

Someone knocked on my door after eleven and said I had a phone call. I stumbled down the hall and dropped the receiver before getting it somewhere near my ear.

"Celeste? It's Sebastian. My parents just called and told me Nathan left Harvard. Is he with you?" For a second his voice had sounded so much like his brother's that I gasped, and let out a small cry.

"I guess not. Are you all right?" he asked.

"Fuck no," I said, and laughed dryly. "Sally had the right idea, you know." I hung up and made it back to my room without another thought for Sebastian.

He borrowed a car and showed up at my door three hours later. He made coffee as I ranted and raved and threw things around the room.

Sleep finally came, and I dreamed of my mother's cool arms embracing me, of Nathan's long solid body lying in my bed. But even in sleep I knew that they were gone, and a cold, bone-aching wind crept into my dreaming room and I awakened screaming.

Later, when the morning sun broke through the spaces between the curtains, I sat up, startled, and found Bass asleep at my desk. Scanning the room with throbbing eyes, I saw a pair of Nathan's shoes sticking out from under the dresser, old Docksides, the outside heels worn down from the way he walked slightly bowlegged, heel to toe. He'd probably kicked them under there long ago, on his way to the bed. My heart seemed to stop and I gasped at the enormity of my loss.

Sebastian opened his eyes with a start.

"Oh, Bass, I'm so sorry to put you through this."

"Don't say that. You'd do the same for me."

I blinked at him, wondering who he thought I was.

* * *

For years afterwards, I obsessed about the day Nathan left and tried to imagine how life would have turned out if I'd gone with him. The notion of packing up a few things and cleaning out my bank account seemed so romantic. I couldn't figure out why on earth I hadn't gone with him.

His long, arduous, passionate letters began to arrive, filled with our secrets. They gave me hope, and hope brought on despair.

Nathan was standing in the hallway when I stepped out of the little bathroom, my face oily with sweat.

"Are you all right, Celeste?" he asked, studying me closely.

"I'm just fine!" I said too loudly, staring back.

"He's okay. At least he doesn't look like you could fuck him in two," he said matter-of-factly.

"You know what? Go to hell, Nathan." I tried to push past him but he blocked the passage with his arm.

"Are you serious, Celeste? Do you love that man? Are you really going to marry him?"

"Yes," I said, but I turned my face away. He was too close, I could smell him, feel the heat of his skin.

"You could stay here with me," he said evenly.

"Yeah, right. You, me, and Giovanna."

"Giovanna's just here on vacation. We like each other but it's not serious between us, Celeste."

"But Alex and I are serious," I said with a shrill laugh, "we're engaged to be married."

Back at the table, our lobsters had arrived. Alex was trying to explain to Giovanna mergers and acquisitions.

"Cerveza. I buy cerveza," he said, grabbing a bottle of beer and one of hot sauce. "Cerveza, y I buy Tabasco, y I make Cerveza-Tabasco *compania mucho grande. Comprende?*"

"Aha," she said, nodding with a small frown. Abruptly, she grabbed his beer out of his hand, drank a large swig, and licked her lips, smiling.

"Bbrrrr," Alex stuck two fingers above his head like antennae. "Televisiono," he said. "You know Grupo Telemedia? Me," he pointed to his chest, "me make Grupo Telemedia mucho grande."

She smiled nervously. Nathan ordered another round of shots.

As I picked up my glass, Alex swiftly moved it out of my hand and slid it away. I tried to get it back but he took me firmly by the wrist and held me close. He called Paquita over and crisply handed her his Platinum card, which she accepted and brought back a few moments later. Giovanna and Nathan gazed at us with detached curiosity, in silence. While Alex read over the bill I grabbed the shot and downed it. He looked at me for a long moment without saying anything and then turned to Nathan.

"I'm very sorry to break this up, but we've got to get back to Hol Cha," Alex said pleasantly, pulling me out of my seat. Through a blurry, wet haze of lights I saw Nathan and Giovanna stand up.

Outside, the crickets were loud and the night smelled of flowers and the sea.

Nathan came out and stood in front of the screen door. "If you want to write me, Celeste, write in care of the Grand Hotel. Grand Hotel, Matlan, Mexico, okay?"

"'Kay, Nthn."

Alex got into the car and slammed the door. For a moment, I hesitated. I saw myself stepping off of fate's path; all I had to do was walk ten feet. I could say to Alex, *I'm sorry. You are wonderful but I have to stay here now. This is where I belong.* I had lots to say, to Nathan, to Alex, but I found I couldn't at that moment talk at all.

I fumbled for the door handle, tripped and fell, and Nathan came running toward the car. He lifted me to my feet, opened the door, and helped me inside. "Oops, there you go," he said gently.

"Thnmn."

Alex stared straight ahead and I could feel his anger crushing me and squeezing the air out of the car, the way the sea presses in on you as you drop deeper, deeper . . . I leaned up against the door to get away from it.

The drive home was utterly silent, the little car a submarine floating through inky blackness.

"Will you be able to dive tomorrow?" he finally asked in a controlled, even voice, as we drove through the luminous whitewashed gates of Hol Cha.

"'Course!" I said, and slid into blackness, aware only that I wanted to cry.

* * *

I CAME TO OUT of the blackout facedown in the bed. I was crying, sputtering, mumbling, "How could you do this to me? How could you do this to me? Has no time passed at all? Why am I here?" Suddenly someone was on top of me.

"Nathan?" I mumbled. An arm locked hard across my throat. I could barely breathe. I struggled to free myself but the arm squeezed more tightly and I began to gasp for air. He pushed into me, his cock like sandpaper against my dry walls.

I tried to cry out, to tell him to stop, I shook my head to get free of his bulging arm. He grabbed a fistful of my hair and held my head still. I gave up, went limp. Still with one arm around my throat, all of his weight pressing down on me, he let go of my hair and began to slap my ass and thighs, hard. I started to cry. When he was done, he shoved me away, and I slipped right off the bed. He turned his back and went to sleep. I lay curled in a ball on the cool, smooth tiles, unable to move.

The next morning I awakened with the shakes, feeling like I'd taken a hit of speed. My body smelled of something turned, of sweat, sex, booze, and underneath all that, his cologne gone bad. I wanted to throw up. My eyes burned like there was sand in them. There was blood on the sheets. Alex was gone. I looked around the room and was relieved to see that his belongings were still there, my fear of being left alone, penniless, in the jungles of Mexico, greater than the prospect of facing him.

I stumbled into the shower and stood under the hot jet for a long time. Then I slipped on some shorts and a T-shirt and went to find him.

He was in the restaurant, sitting by the open shutters, talking on his cell phone. Outside, palm trees rustled in the blinding sunshine. He acknowledged me by pushing a chair out with his foot. He talked for a minute more, but then he must have seen something disturbing in my face and abruptly said, "I'll call you back," and put the phone away.

"Alex, what the hell was that?" I asked. I was shaking so badly I could hardly lift my glass of orange juice. I put it back down, not wanting it anyway. I felt guilty, and ashamed, as if I'd been punished for doing something terribly wrong.

"What are you talking about?"

"Last night."

"I thought you wanted it," he said simply. He surreptitiously buttered a roll and popped half of it in his mouth.

I put my head between my hands. I felt too sick, too weak, too guilty, to argue with him.

"You were pretty toasted. I guess you're too hungover to dive."

My mother had once told me that one of the ways you can tell if you have a drinking problem is if your drinking starts to impede your daily plans. I was not about to let last night's binge affect today's dive.

I looked up at him, my eyes aching. "I'm not hungover, Alex. I only had three shots."

Alex tossed slices of papaya into his mouth with brusque, staccato gestures. "Four shots," he said matter-of-factly, "and two margaritas before that."

"You're angry because of Nathan, is that it?"

"He was your lover, wasn't he?" There was a cynical bite in his tone, an icy look in his eyes.

"He was my love," I said quietly, and pushed my chair back. I rushed out into the brain-splitting sunlight as tears began cascading from my eyes.

* * *

Sweating, nauseated as I sat on the undulating dive boat with the heavy equipment on my back, I ignored Alex beside me and looked down at the deep blue water. My heart and bowels constricted. I had visions of monsters rising up from the depths and taking away my legs. When the dive master counted three, I held my mask to my face and my regulator tight in my mouth and threw myself backwards off the boat. There was a splash and a moment of deep confusion, then I straightened out and looked around. I let the air out of my BC and sank, watching Alex beside me.

My mind went blank. I became a spaceship swooping down toward an unknown planet, enveloped completely in the silent, deep blue womb of the cosmos. There was no sound except for my lungs breathing and the air bubbles escaping from the regulator.

Just beyond the reef, the bottom dropped away suddenly, straight down for thousands of feet. I floated out above the last coral growths, into the open void. It was like jumping off a cliff and not falling, flying like I did in dreams. Beyond the hundred feet or so of visibility, the blue turned into a dark and threatening void; I swam back to the plateau. At the crest of the drop, schools and large solitary fish passed by, following the current. Hundreds of little neon blue fish rose and fell in cloud formation. Yellowtail snappers came up to my mask by the dozens and looked into my eyes. *Hi there*, I waved to them. In a flash they moved off, a yellow tornado through the blue. A group of barracuda passed by like a moving, glinting silver wall. At the mouth of a cave the dive master left some bait, and a huge green moray eel came out and snapped it up in its sharp-toothed jaws.

Feeling more secure, I swam off by myself to inspect some long neon yellow tubular sponges that were growing perpendicular to the ninety-degree incline. About sixty feet away, slinking toward me through the blue, was a large gray shark. I saw a white patch on the tip of the dorsal fin. I screamed into my regulator but there was no one around to hear. The smaller fish did not seem disturbed, nor did the shark know the terror it caused in me. It passed close, the sleek body pulsing with muscle. *Everything here is as it should be*, I thought, bewildered by its beauty. The shark was simply part of the fine, serene order of this universe; and so was I. I lost all perspective for a moment and felt no fear, no anxiety about the future. Only now—this instant—seemed important.

Alex was not close-by, so I swam after him, and as though in slow motion grabbed his arm and pointed, but by the time he turned and looked, the shark was gone.

I did not become frightened until after I got back on the boat.

"I saw a big shark!" I said to Alex as a chill crept up my spine.

"How big?" he asked, impressed.

"More than six feet." I held a hand high above my head.

"What did it look like?"

"It had a white mark on its dorsal fin."

"A white-tip reef shark," he said with awe. "Did you like the moray eel?" He was smiling proudly, pleased with me. I felt redeemed.

I nodded, smiling foolishly. I sat back and breathed in the warm air. The ocean had washed away the vestiges of the rancid smell. The fierce sun immediately began to dry my diveskin suit. The boat rocked gently beneath me.

Everything is back to normal, my mind whispered to me. *Everything is as it should be. He meant you no harm.*

Ten

We'd been back only a week when the deadly lethargy crept back into my bones. I sat on the M11 bus that runs up Amsterdam Avenue, holding my eighth graders' poems and essays in a folder on my lap, and stared out the window in a daze. I'd had a hard time leaving the warm cocoon of my bed that morning, but forced myself because of the kids. A few months before, I'd gone to a party on a Monday night and called in sick Tuesday. The next week, the kids pouted and were sullen and one girl said, "We thought you quit. We thought you change your mind about us." I never went out on Monday nights again. Last week, they'd been angry at me for going to Mexico and changing our meeting day, and teased me about my tan.

Beyond 125th Street, the sidewalks were strewn with litter and some of the buildings had plywood over the windows. I opened the folder and glanced through the kids' poems from last week, making sure I'd picked out the most interesting ones to read aloud to the class.

I had never, after my first visit to the school, been afraid to go there on the bus. Columbia University stretched to 125th Street, if you counted student and faculty housing, so really I was only going ten blocks beyond what was safe and familiar to me. There was an order to the daily routine that I had become a part of, just in my short walk from the bus stop to the school. People hung out on the graffiti-marred stoops, but most of the time danger was not in the air. Some days, something felt off, I didn't know what, but my senses were so attuned to the movements and faces that even the slightest variation made my ears prick up, and then I walked a little faster. But nothing bad had ever happened to me; no one had said an unfriendly word in my four semesters of teaching. I felt protected, as if by a magic aura.

The teacher I worked with was a woman in her mid-forties named

Ellie Horowitz. I'd met her a year and a half earlier at a pro-choice consciousness-raising seminar that Anna had coerced me into attending, at the house of a fairly well known feminist writer. Anna was not a feminist and did not care about feminist issues, but she was adamantly pro-choice and to my father's great chagrin, she refused to vote Republican because of their stand on abortion. Once, he blocked the door when she was heading out to catch a bus to Washington with the "local dykes," as he so graciously put it; she was wearing a straw hat and white gloves and carrying a Statue of Liberty banner with blue writing that said "Keep your laws off our bodies."

"Anna, if you walk out this door," my father had said, his face wild with rage, "I don't know *what* I'll do."

And she responded, "Well, I know what *I'll* do if you don't get out of my way—I'll divorce you."

Now it was just one of the things they did not talk about.

* * *

The issue under discussion at the seminar was how to educate the young underprivileged women of America so that abortions could be avoided in the first place. The people who spoke didn't seem to have a clue about the inner-city kids they were discussing. I glanced at Anna and made a disgusted face.

Then a woman in her mid-forties, with long, dark, gray-streaked hair, wearing a lower-calf-length flowery skirt and Timberland work boots, got up and said, "My name is Ellie Horowitz and I teach at MS 47 in Harlem, and what you're saying is just lovely and full of good intentions, but let me tell you about these kids. I mean no disrespect, but I know these kids and what you don't understand is the problems they encounter every day. You are talking about educating the young women of America, but who are you really talking about? Dalton girls? The communication gap is cultural, and very deep-rooted. And I don't see you ladies of authority and privilege building a bridge between you and them. I don't see you lecturing up in Harlem." She pushed her hair back indifferently, her olive-toned skin reddening perceptibly under the women's scrutinizing glare. "But that's not even the point. What we need in this country is to reach out to these girls on *their* terms, in *their* territory and *in a language they can understand*. And that is precisely what is not happening."

Pleased, I turned to Anna and smiled while inside I gloated with a little evil self-satisfaction. Anna ignored me and sat with her back straight in her prim suit.

I went up to the woman after the meeting and introduced myself.

"I really liked what you said," I told her as she looked me over with suspicious, cool gray eyes. "And I agree, except for one thing. I've been calling the Board of Education for six months, trying to volunteer in the public schools, and all I've been getting is the runaround. They don't want anyone who isn't certified to teach in the public system. It's like *Catch-22*—you can't teach unless you've taught before, and you can't have taught before if you don't have a certificate," I said, blood rushing to my face as well. "I'm a published writer, and I want to teach children how to write creatively. Why do I need a certificate for that?"

She looked at me as if she could tell everything about me in one long glance. "Have you ever taught before?"

"I've been teaching at Columbia for two years."

Abruptly she pulled a notebook out of a large canvas bag and wrote down her name and phone number. "These kids aren't college students, let me tell you," she said. "But what the hell. Come up to the school next week. This year I've got a disruptive class of eighth graders. They're not Special Ed, you understand. Just difficult. Smart as hell, actually. They just get passed along from grade to grade, nobody gives a shit. It's a sin. So now I've got 'em, and they're not ready for eighth grade. Don't expect too much. We'll give it a shot." She shook my hand, holding it firmly.

* * *

My tryout day came in December, just a few weeks before the Christmas holiday. Feeling like a hypocrite, I took a cab. The driver was an elderly black man whose name, I saw from the registration, was Robert Johnson. When we passed 125th Street, he said, "I don't mean to be curious or nothing, but what are you doing up here?"

I told him I was going to try to teach creative writing to kids in junior high school.

"No kidding. What for?"

"You know, to maybe get them to like writing. Write about things that matter to them," I said. I looked at the back of his bald head, but couldn't tell what he was thinking. I asked him, "How dangerous is it up here?"

"Not too bad," he said evenly. "Come payday, Friday, ain't too good. Crackheads mug people for their paychecks. Otherwise ain't too bad."

When I paid him, he turned to me and said, "God bless you, lady, and have a good day."

I walked into the overheated classroom feeling like I wasn't wearing any clothes. There were five rows of desks, seven deep. A rumble of voices slammed into me. Black, gold, and hazel eyes looked me over with amused curiosity. A Hispanic girl was looking at herself in a pocket mirror, combing her hair and slapping at her neighbor, a large-shouldered black boy with a handsome, devilish face. Ellie Horowitz screamed at the class in a loud, shrill voice like a police siren, and they settled back to watch me in silence.

I took a small papier-mâché container out of my bag, along with *The Paris Review* and two other quarterlies that had published my stories over the past few years. They made a small, neat stack on a corner of the desk.

"This may look like nothing," I told them, "but getting short stories published in these magazines is one of the hardest things in the world for an unknown writer to do." I held up *The Paris Review* and opened it to the second page. "These are the stories I've published. Here's my name, Celeste Miller, in the table of contents."

"How we know that's you?" asked the boy who had been teasing the girl next to him. He smiled. His front teeth were broken and jagged.

"Here, there's a picture of me in this one." I handed him *Glimmer Train* and passed the others around, and they glanced at them without much interest. Only the one with my picture captivated them.

I opened the little papier-mâché box filled with colorful metal Soviet pins that I had bought in Moscow in 1984. Printed on them in Russian were slogans like "GLORY TO THE FATHERLAND OF THE USSR" and "THE WORKS OF MARXISM/LENINISM LIVE ON!" and "GLORY TO THE COMMUNIST PARTY OF THE USSR!"

"I brought these pins back from Russia years ago, to give to people as souvenirs. The Russians were very nice to me," I said. "Families invited me to their homes and fed me, often when they didn't have much food themselves. I've never been this far uptown in my life, but I'd like to come back and teach you creative writing. I'd like each of you to take one of these pins as a gift from me to you for allowing me to visit your classroom today."

"How come you starting at the front of the room?" someone called from the back. "That ain't fair!"

I moved to the back, allowing their hands to reach into the box and pick a pin.

"Miss! Hey miss, what's this one?" a girl asked.

"Call me Celeste," I said. The pin was a red star with a photograph of baby Lenin at the center. "That's Lenin as a baby. He was the founder of Russian communism."

"What this one say?" A girl with mahogany-colored skin held up a representation of the world, a blue sphere, with an atom bomb broken in half.

"It says, 'No to atomic bombs!'"

The girl was looking at me with great wary eyes. "I thought they *wanted* to bomb our ass," she mumbled in a tired voice.

"That's like saying that everyone in America agrees with the president."

"Shee-it," she mumbled, and attached the pin to the lapel of her blue-jean jacket.

Ellie Horowitz had brought her little boom box, as we'd planned, and I put in a cassette of a wistful, romantic piano improvisation by Keith Jarrett.

"Okay, everybody, I just want you to close your eyes and daydream."

They started giggling and looking at me as if I were crazy.

"Man, I'm gonna fall asleep."

"Come on, you do it anyway in class and get yelled at for it. Just close your eyes and breathe easily. Breathe in, one, two, three, four . . ."

The eerie, dreamy music wafted through the room. Many glanced at their neighbors to see if they were being made fun of, but slowly they began to close their eyes.

"If any of you really don't feel like doing this, I invite you to step out into the hall or go to the library," I said equably.

Behind me, Ellie Horowitz yelled, "Yeah, and I invite you to go to Mr. Sender's office!" No one moved.

"In a minute I'm going to play the music again, and I just want you to write down what you were daydreaming about. There's no right or wrong about it. Pretend that your hand is getting an electric signal straight from your brain. I don't care about your spelling or your grammar. I want you to break your sentences up wherever you feel like it. If you don't want me to read yours out loud to the class, then write 'Don't Read' at the top. This is between you and me."

When the music ended, there was utter silence. Quickly, I pressed rewind, knowing I could lose them in the blink of an eye. The music began again, wistful, slow, sad. Quietly, they began to write, bent over their desks, covering their words from their neighbors' glances.

"If you have any questions, just raise your hand and I'll come over to your desk," I said.

Hands went up. I walked among the desks, bumping into book bags and legs. Most wanted to ask me about spelling.

"How you spell *heaven*?"

"Spell it any way you want," I said. "I'm the worst speller in the world, so don't ask me."

Shyly, they began to turn their papers toward me as I went slowly through the rows, looking over their shoulders.

Sofyah, the girl who had taken the peace pin, wrote:

I Had a Dream

I had a dream of peace.
Peace everlasting peace.
In this dream all through
out the land was peace.
No killing no drugs
no guns no war.
Just peace.

"It's beautiful," I told her, and placed my hand on her shoulder for a second. She looked at it, looked at me, and smiled faintly with closed lips. I moved on, filled with joy. The handsome boy in the front who'd been teasing the Latino girl wrote a poem called "Alone." His name was Ramel.

Alone

I dreamed that I was homeless on Christmas day
I was walking through an alley
I was all alone
There was no place to go
I was sad and lonely
I was thinking about that night
and how I would feel after Christmas day.

"Sunset" was by a boy who sat by himself, by a window in the very back:

Sunset

As we head off
into the sunset
Who knows what

Lies out there
as we are
on a journey
to a far away place.

After my first semester, Ellie suggested I apply to The Writer's Way for funding. The grant came through, and I started getting paid to teach my class. But the greatest reward was that, this term, I'd found a writer. He was an eighth grader named Derrence Skinner who couldn't spell and never talked in class. He sat staring at the ceiling with a dreamy expression while mayhem raged around him.

Today, after class, I was taking him to apply for a highly coveted spot in a summer program for gifted children. I had broken my own solemn rule to stay out of their lives, and the prospect of spending a few hours with a fourteen-year-old boy who'd never said more than twenty sentences to me was daunting. I didn't know how to talk to him. He made me feel the way I had when I visited my grandmother in France. I could speak the language, but I was never sure that I wasn't using the wrong idiom and inadvertently insulting someone.

Derrence was quiet, shy, well liked. He wasn't a troublemaker but neither was he a good student. Ellie said his grades were mediocre in all his subjects and next year he was going to one of the biggest, roughest high schools in the city. I showed her his work. She agreed that he had an uncanny ability with words, but she couldn't find a way to reach him. He tested badly and hated reading the assignments. Yet when I first read his work aloud to the class, they clapped and cheered. This eighth grade group thought of itself as unflinchingly cool and had never clapped before.

"Does the writer want to identify him or herself?" I had asked hopefully. At the time, I still didn't know all of their names. A hand in the last row went up slowly. A thin, brown-skinned boy with braces put up his hand, staring down at his desk.

"I swear, Derrence, this poem brings tears to my eyes," I said. The kids laughed and jeered.

"You one crazy woman!" a Latino girl in the front said with a smile.

One day, I wrote just one word on the board in capital letters, INJUSTICE, and put a nostalgic Chopin "Impromptu" on the boom box. This was Derrence's response:

We never ran, we never played,
we never got along.
We never looked, we never watched,
but someone always did.
We always smile, with cigars in our mouths.
We never dream, we never sleep,
we never go in peace.

* * *

THEY LIKED TO tease me about the clothes I wore and the expressions I used, like "fabulous," "excellent," and "wonderful," and how choked up I got when I read them something really good. But I knew that they loved the attention and the compliments I paid them. They often wrote about fear, and drive-by shootings in the streets, and ricocheting bullets that killed passers-by, family members, close friends. Some wrote with devotion about their parents, others about how little their parents understood or knew them.

I began to take a group of five or six kids to the library after class to work on extra projects; students who showed particular talent or just enthusiasm, or ones I thought were most neglected. Everyone wanted to go. I felt sick at heart knowing that I had to concentrate on those who would benefit the most.

The first day, the librarian made them all spit out their wads of gum and warned them that if they didn't behave, she'd throw us all out.

In this much more intimate setting, they began to tell me about their lives. Shatisha, a small, skinny, dark-skinned girl with a tuft of wild and wiry hair, told me that she'd been homeless for two years and was now in foster care. Her stories were always about other homeless people, how she felt sorry for them when she saw them in the street. I asked her if she could write about her own experience. She said no. She said she didn't want her classmates to find out.

Rosalia, an A student with waist-length black hair and almond eyes, told me that she was in love with a boy called Alfredo who was in another eighth grade class. "Oh my God," she looked up at the ceiling and pounded her chest dramatically with her fist.

"Oh boy," I said to her, "I remember that feeling."

This made the table of girls giggle and snort.

"You married, Celeste?"

"No. But I'm getting married in July."

"No shit! Who you marrying? Is he cute?"

"Bring him here for show-and-tell," said another girl.

I started to laugh, picturing Alex standing at the front of the room as I described his accomplishments.

Derrence was off in a corner by himself, writing furiously.

On our way out, the librarian said to me, "I don't know what you're doing but I've never seen them like this before. As far as I'm concerned, you can bring them back anytime."

I walked down the hall surrounded by them, feeling like the Pied Piper, light-headed with happiness.

* * *

For the next month Rosalia wrote sexy, passionate, rhyming love poems to Alfredo, but suddenly her poems became filled with tearful recriminations and jealousy. Rosalia liked me, but she pouted and then ignored me when I spent too much time with Derrence. Two weeks before, she'd asked me why I liked his work better than hers. I told her that her poems were excellent but she didn't push herself, that she'd gotten rhyming down, and now she needed to stop the rhymes and concentrate on herself and not Alfredo. Last week she'd handed me a rhyming love poem about José, her latest love interest.

"What about yourself? What about not rhyming?" I asked her.

"Oh, man, it's too hard what you asking for."

I shrugged and went over to check on Derrence. "Where is your family from?" I asked him.

"Costa Rica," Derrence mumbled in a barely audible baritone as I leaned over his desk.

"Your father too?"

"No." He shook his head. A moment later he murmured that his mother was remarried and that he did not get along with his stepfather. For the first time I realized he had a Hispanic cadence to his speech.

"My mother want to send me to summer school to get me out the house. I hate that summer school, man. So boring. Teach you what you already know!"

Without giving it any thought, I asked, "Do you want me to see about getting you into a special writing program? I think there are places like that. Workshops for young people. Something like that?"

"That be good," he said in a neutral voice. I couldn't tell if he really wanted me to go ahead or if he was just saying yes to be polite.

* * *

I MADE PHONE CALLS to different nonprofit organizations for kids and made arrangements with Derrence's mother and the school to take him for a few hours the coming Tuesday. Freedom to Think, a nonprofit Harlem group run by a man named Winston Jones, had seemed the most promising, although Mr. Jones had said that their funding was limited to children who lived in the neighborhood. Freedom to Think was near the school but Derrence lived in the South Bronx.

I'd nevertheless convinced Mr. Jones to at least talk to Derrence and take a look at his work.

Now I got off the bus and crossed the street toward the school. A clammy suffocating haze hung over the city. Entering the building was like crossing into a strange world of noise in which time and space had completely different values. Time was parsed out in fifty-minute segments, and space was what you took for your own. In the dark blue halls I usually had to duck and weave to avoid crashes; the noise level made thinking impossible.

I had a few minutes until the bell so I walked along the hall looking at the artwork that had recently been taped to the walls. There were perspective drawings of buildings and roads; New York cityscapes; mosaics of faces made of little cut-up pieces of magazine paper; paintings of seas crowded with large, frightening fish. I paused at a drawing of skyscrapers. At the forefront, the sharply angled rooftops loomed gigantic, covered with antennae. Way down below at their skinny base was a slim avenue heading straight toward the top of the page, the horizon. I felt a small presence beside me and turned. A boy of about twelve was looking up at me with serious eyes.

"You like it? It's mine's."

My gaze shifted back to the work. "It's magnificent! You have talent." I turned to him, but he had wandered off.

* * *

FREEDOM TO THINK was only a few blocks from the school. Derrence and I stepped out of the noisy, dark-halled school and into the bright midday sunlight. Derrence must have felt at least as strange and uncomfortable as I did, although his face did not divulge anything at all. I saw that he had dressed up for his interview with Winston Jones. He wore new purple jeans cinched with a belt below his hips, the crotch hanging down at his knees, the legs draping in folds over new high-tops with two enormous straps like aerodynamic wings on the sides, and a purple jean vest that matched the pants. Underneath the vest he wore a yellow and purple striped hooded shirt.

"Listen, Derrence," I said, "I'm just trying to offer you some other possibilities here besides summer school. You don't have to say yes to this."

"I know," he said quickly.

"Mr. Jones, the guy who runs the place, he told me they have a photography and poetry workshop that meets twice a week in the afternoon."

"I like that," Derrence said. His voice was so quiet and low, it was hard to hear.

"Do you read books?" I asked him.

"Nah. I watch TV. But I like true books. I don't like ones that's not true."

"They're all true," I said. "Novels just change things a little."

I only had two sessions left with my students, and I knew I might never see him again after that. There was so much I wanted to tell him.

"You know, Derrence, I think you're *very* talented. I think you're a writer. Do you know that or do you just think I'm crazy?"

He laughed without a sound. "No."

No what? I didn't ask. I didn't push.

"Don't be nervous with Mr. Jones," I said, swallowing hard.

The walls of Winston Jones's office were covered with drawings, poems, and photographs by students. There were also love notes to him. "Winston I LOVE YOU!" "Come home and live with us!" Books and folders were stacked waist high on the floor. Before us stood a tall, square-shouldered black man with shoulder-length, light brown dreadlocks. He wore faded jeans, a blue oxford shirt, and a striped blue and red tie. Derrence seemed to be trying to hide behind me. I wished I could have prepared him better.

"I'm Celeste Miller, Mr. Jones," I said, stepping forward and putting out my hand. "This is Derrence Skinner, the student I told you about."

Mr. Jones had piercing, intelligent eyes that looked hard to fool.

"Hey, man, those are some fly shoes," Mr. Jones said to Derrence, who didn't respond. "Do you like to write?" Derrence gazed lazily upward and around at the pictures on the walls and said, "Kinda."

"I brought you some copies of his poems," I said quickly, reaching into my bag. Mr. Jones took the folder and glanced at the copies I'd made, and said, "Mm-hm. You're a good writer."

Silence from Derrence.

"You interested in photography, Derrence?" Mr. Jones asked.

"Yeah," he said vaguely, looking down at the floor now. I wanted to interrupt, explain that Derrence was shy, but I knew it was best if I sat in the proffered chair and stayed quiet. Every once in a while Mr. Jones appeared to glance in my direction, an inscrutable expression in his eyes.

"Where do you live, Derrence?" he asked.

"Bronx," Derrence said.

"That's out of our usual jurisdiction. We take kids just from around here."

My heart sank. "But he goes to MS 47 just down the street. I've been teaching for a while, Mr. Jones, and I really think Derrence has an unusual talent."

Mr. Jones sat back in his swivel chair and smiled. "This workshop teaches you to take photographs and then develop them. You write poems to go with the pictures you take. At the end we have a little show of everyone's work. What do you think of that?"

"I think it's good. But I don't know about taking pictures. I don't have a camera or nothing."

"We give you the camera. *Lend* you the camera. If you lose it, you're in deep shit." He laughed, and Derrence's face remained impenetrable. Mr. Jones leaned back in his swivel chair, crossed his arms, and chewed on the inside of his cheek for a while.

"Well, we got space for you if you want it," he said finally. "But you got to be responsible about it," he warned. "If I give this space to you, that means some kid in this neighborhood who has a right to be here won't get his spot. You interested?"

"Yeah," Derrence said in his flat voice. "I like to try it."

We stood up after Mr. Jones did.

"Ms. Miller," he said, "you're with The Writer's Way?"

"Yes, but I volunteered for a semester at MS 47 first."

"Give me a call sometime. I'd like to hear about your teaching methods."

"I will. And if it's okay, I'd like to come back to see the exhibition after the workshop."

"Of course," he said. We shook hands.

* * *

Out in the street, the sun beat down fiercely. I asked Derrence if he was thirsty. He said yes as I led him toward a bodega. At the door he stopped for a moment to see if I would open it first. When I did, he stayed back and then followed me in.

We stood in front of the glass refrigerator, staring at the soft drink cans. I could see the reflection of the two Hispanic men behind the counter, gazing at us with curious looks. Me in my little black skirt with white polka dots and cotton blouse, Derrence decked out in his new outfit.

"What do you want? A Pepsi? Something else?"

"Coke be good," he said. I pulled out two cans, a Coke and a Diet Coke, and took them up to the counter. One of the men handed me two straws as Derrence stood back and gazed vaguely at the ceiling.

We left and walked in the direction of Broadway.

"You know, Derrence, it's only like twenty blocks to Columbia University, there's a really good bookstore there. I'd like to get you a couple of books. Do you need to get back to school?"

"Nah. Nothing going on there. My mom she don't get home to after five anyway."

"You get along well with your mom?"

"She's okay. Busy. She always wanting me to go to church with her. I hate that church, man. I hate what they say—you don't believe like us, you don't come here every Sunday, you gonna go to hell. You believe that?" he asked, glancing at me out of the corner of his eye.

My head was pounding from the heat and from the realization that he wanted an answer. I thought of Primo Levi and suddenly wanted to cry.

"No, I don't believe that. I don't think God belongs to any one religion or any one group of people. The Christians say he's one way, the

Arabs say another, then they fight over it. Kill each other. I don't believe anybody has a right to tell anybody else what God is. God belongs to everyone. It's people who say God punishes. People fight over God."

"But like, so you believe in God?"

For me God existed in Primo Levi's writing, in the moments of reprieve he described when one human granted another respect in that godless wasteland of cruelty. The skeletons of buildings stared at Derrence and me with their empty eyes. I had to make a choice to face things and try to help him, or live with my own eyes closed. I felt something lift out of me and float above us, watching us walking down the street.

"Yes, I think there is a God," I said carefully. "I don't know who He is, though. Maybe God is kindness. Treating everybody the way you'd like to be treated. You know what I mean?"

"When I go in the store, they always look at me like I'm stealing something. I never steal nothing!" he said, looking at the ground. "They look at me like I be some garbage or something."

I wanted to tell him he was perfect, beautiful, I wanted to hug him. He would have been horrified.

"That's why you have to read!" I said instead. "You have to educate yourself so that no one can hurt you. I'm not talking about what they teach you in school; I wasn't a good student when I was your age. But if you read, you'll be able to protect yourself because you'll be smarter than the people who would just as soon hurt you as let you be."

"I know that!" he said with a burst of emotion.

Enthusiastic, I went on. "I don't know what it's like to be fourteen and black, but I know what it was like to be fourteen and white and a girl without a mother and to feel totally lost and confused."

He said nothing, walked with his face down, sipping his Coke.

"And being scared and angry doesn't help anything. I'm still so damn angry and scared I never have time to feel good!" I said.

"I know what that is," he said. He nodded solemnly and we walked on.

At the bookstore, I let him wander around. I followed him and pointed out a few writers I thought he might like. James Baldwin's *Go Tell It on the Mountain*. Richard Price's first novel about the South Bronx, *The Wanderers*. There was an anthology of minority poetry; a new novel by a Puerto Rican–American about Spanish Harlem and the crack blight. I pointed out Toni Morrison's early novels, the slimmer ones that would not appear so intimidating to him. He took them all off the shelf one by one and looked at the covers, front and back. He looked up at the poetry section and, piling all the books into the crook of his arm, pulled out a thin pink volume entitled, *Love Poems Throughout the Ages*.

"Rosalia like this one."

"Okay. You can give it to her tomorrow." I took it from him and he went back to his pile and tried to make up his mind.

"Take one from each author," I said, thinking what the hell.

By the time we got to the cash register, Derrence was carrying quite a pile of books. He solemnly placed them on the counter in a neat stack and stood back and gazed around with that blank expression. The clerk ran up the bill. I didn't even glance at the price as I handed him my credit card.

"You don't have to read all these now, but they'll be there for you when you want them." I reached into my bag and pulled out *The Paris Review* with my story in it. "Here, you can have this too. I signed it for you last night. You don't have to read this either. I just wanted you to have it."

I walked him to the subway stop at 116th and Broadway. He had a long ride home. At least it wouldn't be dark for a couple of hours.

"Don't be scared of Freedom to Think," I said quickly. "It'll be a lot of fun, I think. Listen, if you want you can call me and we can talk about it. You want to call me?"

"Yeah." He took out his notebook and a pen and started writing my name out carefully. I gave him the number. I hoped he'd call me, but I didn't think he would.

"Be careful on the way home," I said stupidly, and patted his arm. "You know how to get there from here?"

"Yeah," he laughed, and turned to take the stairs. Halfway down he looked over his shoulder and waved.

"Oh please, God," I mumbled under my breath, "please help this child."

Eleven

THE WEATHER FINALLY broke and the following Saturday afternoon was bright and cool. The ladies kept exclaiming as they arrived, loaded down with gift-wrapped packages in fancy shopping bags, "What a perfect day for a bridal shower!"

The windows of my friend Daphne's duplex were open onto the narrow Greenwich Village street. She had the ground and second floors, and from her living room upstairs we could hear birds and leaves rustling in the trees, and conversations and laughter on the street below.

A few latecomers rushed into the room, and as Daphne said, "Everyone's here, let's get started," I found myself looking toward the door. Someone was still missing, but who? It struck me like a blow to the chest. Candace. My bridal shower should have been her responsibility. Somehow I felt I was betraying her, although I knew this was absurd.

With Candace gone, Daphne had volunteered. Although we didn't see each other much anymore, she was still my second-oldest college friend. Daphne had done everything right: gone to Harvard Law School, become a corporate lawyer, bought a Village apartment that had tripled in value. The only thing she had trouble with, it seemed, was finding a husband. Her mother reminded her of this whenever possible, and Daphne would say, "I don't need a husband, I need a wife."

Daphne seated us in a circle, and I was reminded of games of spin-the-bottle. Since my friend had an obsessive passion for organization, she had planned an "hour shower"; giving each guest a specific hour for which to buy me a gift. It didn't make a difference to the ladies—they bought me pastel-colored slips, teddies, and nighties from Victoria's Secret for the morning and afternoon as well—why not? The most amusing gift was Lucia's.

"For 11 P.M.—" her card read, "Something smooth, black and silky."

In the box, wrapped in pink tissue paper, was a Ray Charles compact disk.

Anna's gift was for midnight, a frilly pink negligee and nightgown from Saks, with a card that said I was free to exchange them if they weren't in my taste. None of this stuff was my taste. I slept in old, extra-large T-shirts with the neckline cut out.

When we were finished, there was subdued conversation and finger sandwiches and more champagne.

I wanted to raise my glass to Candace, but I knew they would stare at me, their soft features darkened momentarily by worry. People didn't want to talk about unpleasant things. I chased away these thoughts with a wide, silly smile that made my face ache. As Alex often told me, I was just blowing storm clouds over a perfectly clear blue sky. I drank another glass of champagne, hoping to dilute my gloom.

* * *

It grew dark around seven-thirty and as though on cue, everyone left except for Lucia and me. Daphne popped the cork on another champagne bottle and they began to talk about hitting a nightclub for old time's sake. The wine had not lifted my spirits; it had given me a headache that sat like a loose pack of marbles in the base of my cranium. Feeling dizzy and confused, I told them I was going to lie down for a little while. I slipped away, down the circular staircase to Daphne's bedroom. I could hear them above me, laughing about the old days when the four of us would go to the Ritz on weeknights and stay out till it closed; the manager was a friend and we drank for free. They never mentioned Candace, but I knew they were probably thinking of her, too.

I stretched out on Daphne's queen-size bed on which large pillows were piled, and closed my eyes. I couldn't stop my mind from dwelling on that other time.

Candace and I had been roommates our freshman year of college, thrown together by an exceptionally wise or foolish computer, because we couldn't have been more different.

I arrived first, alone, driving my secondhand Volkswagen. I had refused my father and Anna's help; my family had never been good at transitions, saying hello, saying good-bye. Propelled by some false sense of humility and a desire to avoid making any kind of self-aggrandizing statement, I'd brought one suitcase that held my four pairs of jeans; my large collection of T-shirts, ones for dressy occasions, hanging around, and sleep; a few cotton turtlenecks; four winter sweaters; and an assortment of unattractive bras and underpants. I also had a box containing all the novels I had read in high school, and a portable electric typewriter that Anna had given me the Christmas before.

Candace and her parents, Jacob and Samantha Black, burst through the door fussing and shouting, with four sweating freshman counselors bearing three enormous trunks. Her parents were tall but stoop-shouldered. Samantha wore a velour fuchsia pants suit and expensive gold jewelry. Jacob looked like an undertaker.

"I'm going to see if the bathroom is clean," Samantha announced, turning on her heel and leaving the room. Jacob tried to tip the freshman counselors, who vigorously shook their heads. "Are you coming, Jacob?" Samantha yelled from down the hall. He followed Samantha out without a word.

"I'm an only child," Candace said apologetically, once we were alone. "They're older. They worry."

I gave her an embarrassed smile. While Candace walked around inspecting the room, I noticed that her right hip was noticeably higher, and protruded more than her left, which gave her walk a slightly off-balance, stomping lilt.

"Not much room," she said, and began to unpack. She had planned for every natural disaster—blizzards, earthquakes, hurricanes. She'd brought all the basic things I hadn't thought of—an electric kettle, instant coffee, creamer, five kinds of herbal tea, extra blankets, medicines, a clothesline, and a little color TV. She had at least thirty color-coordinated outfits and ten pairs of shoes.

"I'm so sorry, I'm sort of pushing into your closet space here," she said from behind the closet door.

"Go right ahead," I said. Looking around, my side of the room suddenly seemed desperately empty.

Samantha and Jacob returned from the bathroom and announced that before every shower Lysol should be sprayed, and flip-flops worn at all times. Samantha proceeded to warn Candace about various illnesses that might afflict her over the course of the semester, advised her to have emergency phone numbers at her fingertips, and warned her to stay away from wild boys who would present themselves as respectable.

Finally Jacob said, "Time to leave the honey bee in peace." They sprayed her with kisses and tears. It all made me uneasy, and I sat at my desk, pretending to read.

"Phew!" Candace said as soon as the door was closed. "So where's the liquor store? Let's buy a big bottle of something and celebrate."

With that first shared magnum of white Folonari wine, I felt a great warmth toward her. I had never met anyone so energetic, so filled with goodwill. In a moment of uncharacteristic abandon, I confessed my distrust of people, especially of groups, and that I had never felt I belonged anywhere.

"But you're so beautiful!" she cried. "Let me handle things and you won't feel that way anymore. Pretty soon everyone will want to belong to *your* group."

I had never thought of myself as beautiful. When I looked into mirrors, I only saw my flaws.

* * *

I REMEMBERED with longing the spring days when Candace and I would buy a magnum of white wine, put it in a wastepaper basket filled with ice, and sit with our books on the hilly campus green from noon until the sun went down.

Candace would read her fat economics textbooks and gossip about school affairs with anyone who happened by, while I tried to concentrate on my Russian language or literature notes, terrified of failing even though I had an A average. By midafternoon, I was too loose to be afraid and I would lie back happily and stare at the sky. But Candace would keep on working and talking.

She was involved in every social affair, from organizing the holiday semiformals to running the student union's dances. She went to every party, terrified of being left out. In our senior year she ran unchallenged for class secretary, which insured that she would remain the recipient of juicy gossip and important social events well into old age. I teased her mercilessly over her compulsion to socialize. I didn't understand until she finally took me home. It was during Thanksgiving break of our senior year.

In her little girl's room, still pink and white, a small white vanity stood in one corner and teddy bears and porcelain dolls smiled down from every shelf. She suddenly said, "I want to show you something," and went digging through cardboard boxes stuffed with old clothes until she found what she was looking for—a barbaric contraption, four long metal rods that formed a jacket with a collar at the top. It looked like a medieval instrument of torture. She was shy about undressing in front of people, but that night, stripping quickly down to her bra, she put it on.

"I keep it to remind myself," she said, and laughed good-naturedly at her reflection in the mirror, while I gaped at her in disbelief. "It's a terrific antidepressant. I needed to catch up! For the whole four years of high school I had to wear this fucking thing and I couldn't wear normal clothes. Granny *shmattes* and maternity dresses, that's all. Forget about dating."

* * *

We decided to live together in New York City after graduation. Candace found our apartment through an ad in the *Village Voice*. I let her take care of everything, installing the phone, calling Con Ed, dealing with the landlord, whom she needled into lowering the rent by a hundred dollars.

Her parents, of course, were horrified by our living conditions. Our one-bedroom railroad flat was just off Amsterdam Avenue in the Eighties. There were drug dealers on the corner. Graffiti marred the dirty, skin-colored bricks of the front stoop leading to the heavily barred front door. The walls all leaned to the right. But we could easily afford the six hundred dollars a month rent. I was starting my Ph.D. program in Comparative Lit at Columbia, and she a training program in one of the big corporate banks. The first thing she did was become friendly with the drug dealers on the corner, figuring it was good form. As we were strolling home from a bar late one night, I heard her say, "Hi there, Ace! How's it going? This is my roommate, Celeste. Celeste, meet Ace."

"Yo, baby," said an enormous black man standing in the shadows. "Need any weed? Whites?"

"Maybe another time," she said gaily, pulling me along.

* * *

Candace could drink all night, change her clothes, and go to work with no sleep at all. I would lie there moaning while she traipsed around the room in matching pink towels, one around her torso, one wrapped turban-style around her head, singing, "Oy, oy, oy, oy, a shikker is a goy, oy oy." The old song had become a joke between us; her parents thought I was the bad influence, because they believed Jews as a rule didn't drink. *They* didn't drink at all. But Candace could drink me and ninety-nine percent of the fellows we knew right under the table.

Spring break of senior year, in a Fort Lauderdale bar, she'd won a beer chugging contest against a football player from the University of Alabama. He was a good loser, though. "What the hell school are y'all from?" he said in a deep, sweet voice as he smiled down at us from his formidable height. He had a little upturned Irish nose, a face boiled pink from the sun, and was as wide as a door.

"A fancy-shmancy Little Ivy League school where they teach you how to drink," Candace responded, holding her trophy aloft, an enormous brandy snifter with a chesty purple mermaid plastered on the glass. She had an absurd tan—brown in front and white on the back, like a piece of toast put on broil by mistake.

He invited her to take a stroll down the beach.

She came back to our bungalow hours later without her trophy. As she undressed, sand spilled from her bra but she didn't seem to notice.

* * *

Candace never doubted that she'd made the right decisions concerning her life, while I was constantly doubting myself. I had no idea what I was doing in New York, pursuing a Ph.D. when I didn't want to be a college professor. I wanted to write. I wrote every day; short stories about loneliness, about my father and Anna, about Nathan MacKenna, who'd chosen to travel through Central America instead of finishing college. His most recent letters were from Chile. What he was doing there, I had no clue. In the back of my mind I was always waiting for him to show up at our door like he always had, in his torn-up jeans, unshaven, with his backpack and nothing else to his name but his passport. I imagined Candace would smile at him and say, "Why, Nathan, how nice to see you," as though he'd been by just a few days ago. She'd fix him something to eat and take his dirty clothes down to the washing machine, while I'd sit quietly, inhaling his presence, anxious to take him to bed.

* * *

Candace was the only person I let read my stories. She was a harsh critic, and would not let up until I got something right, but, when we felt a story was finished, she would mail it out to small presses and quarterlies, writing a brilliant, self-confident letter for me to sign. Rejections were finally followed by an acceptance from *The Paris Review* for my best story, about the first time Nathan left me, in the spring of my sophomore year.

I was thrilled that *The Paris Review* had purchased my story; for at least a week, I believed in myself. I felt I had a future as a writer.

Meanwhile, it was inconceivable to Candace that my future would be anything but brilliant. "Oh, come on Celeste," she'd say, pulling me up from my bed. "Come to this party with me. Flirt with the magazine editors! You've got to go for it, Celeste!"

* * *

THAT FIRST YEAR in New York, when the weather changed, Jacob and Samantha drove a small U-haul down from Boston filled with all of Candace's spring and summer clothes. This operation was necessary because we didn't have enough closet space in our small apartment to accommodate her complete wardrobe. For a whole afternoon Samantha and Candace sorted through her winter things, wrapping suits in plastic to take back to Boston, and making a donation pile for the Salvation Army. Jacob sat in the kitchen reading the paper.

"I'll just leave the sweaters in the street, Mom," Candace said. "The homeless will pick them up in a minute."

"No, no, no. I'll take them back to Boston and give them to the Salvation Army, the proper way," Samantha insisted, as if this were a huge burden but one she wouldn't think of refusing. "You don't wear this lovely shirt anymore? What a pity . . . "

That Samantha knew every shirt and blouse and sweater of Candace's, I found astounding. I was certain that my father and Anna couldn't have described a single article of my clothing if a gun were held to their heads.

That night Jacob and Samantha took us out to dinner and at Candace's suggestion we went to Wolf's Deli, a brightly lit tourist trap on West Fifty-seventh Street where the waiters wore tuxedoes. Once we were seated, her parents sat with stiff backs, glaring suspiciously at the waiter and barking out questions about the food, as if certain that caution was all that lay between themselves and food poisoning. Candace ordered a second glass of wine before the food arrived and I noticed her mother wince. I was dying to order another one too, but didn't. Jacob and Samantha kept kosher, but when they weren't around, Candace ate everything. The past Thanksgiving had been my second with them in Boston, and Candace and I had stayed out very late dancing in a club in Faneuil Hall that Saturday night. Early the next morning we were awakened by Samantha's vigorous vacuuming. We stumbled into the kitchen, where a plate of bagels and a crock of butter sat on the counter. "Eat," Candace said to me as she searched the fridge for the Maxwell House can and some juice.

"Knife?" I said, and she indicated the flatware drawer as she went about making coffee; I reached into the drawer and pulled out a steak knife. By the time she turned around it was too late, the butter was smeared all over the jagged edges of the knife. She gasped. Then giggling, she plucked the knife out of my hand and ran with it to the sink. I started to apologize. "Shh," she said, rinsing quickly. "They'll never know." She said a prayer under her breath and put the knife away just as Samantha came into the kitchen, looking grief-stricken and exhausted with black half-moons under her eyes.

"What time did you get in?" she said, her voice quivering.

"Oh, I don't know, Mom, it wasn't that late."

"I stayed up all night worrying!" she said, then burst into tears. I stood against the cabinets, appalled and guilt-stricken. Candace threw her arms around her mother's shoulders and led her away. They sat head-to-head on the living room couch for a long time, Candace cooing and whispering as Samantha continued to weep.

* * *

Candace was on so many political fund-raising and charity committees that there was always a black tie event on Saturday nights. Sometimes loneliness compelled me to accompany her. Afterwards, we'd end up in some crowded bar. I'd attempt to drag her out of the embrace of a sweet-talking drunk man in a rumpled tux, his clip-on tie askew.

They all said the same thing: "I've fallen in love with you. I've never met anyone I could talk to like this." The looks I threw them were so filled with contempt that Candace would turn to me, a hand on their chest, and laugh and say, "I'm just having fun, Celeste."

Finally, I'd leave her in that dark and deafening maelstrom of spilled booze and cigarette smoke, and go outside to find a pay phone. I'd call my best male friend, Branko, another recent graduate, and if he was not otherwise occupied, I'd go to his place and we'd have a few drinks. He had a massive collection of videos, and we liked to make an all-nighter of it, watching both *Godfather*s or both Terrence Malick movies back-to-back.

At daylight, he'd take me downstairs and put me in a cab. If Branko wasn't home, I'd call Joe Coutinho, a man five years older than I who was a producer at ABC News, whom I'd met at one of our college fund-raising cocktail parties. He wore tweed jackets and khaki pants. He had all kinds of good advice concerning my "postpartum" depression. If he wasn't busy, I'd ask him if I could come spend the night.

I don't know where Candace went with the men she met in bars, but she never brought them to our place and never stayed out all night.

The next evening, Candace and I would stay home, silently regrouping, and I'd cook a French meal for us. She loved when I cooked. About eight P.M. the phone would ring, and Candace would jump to get it. But it wasn't for her; it would often be Joe Coutinho, hoping that I'd decided to give up on Nathan once and for all. I'd put him off with vague, friendly talk. Or it would be Branko, checking up on me, making sure I was all right.

* * *

THAT SAME SPRING, I heard about a yoga guru who could fix crippled backs. People said he was a genius, so I convinced Candace to see him, just because she had nothing to lose. Exercise was not her passion, to say the least. But she finally agreed to go, dragging me along. He assured her that yoga would help and she diligently took classes twice a week. She really liked the people she met there and came home full of new information about New Age books, marriages, movies, divorces, and diets. I wondered when she ever had time to exercise.

The guru warned her that recovery would come slowly, and only after a certain amount of pain—he said she had to work through the pain of her childhood—and Candace told him she'd never felt pain in her life.

After a month, she quit.

"Are you out of your mind?" I shouted when she told me. "Are you quitting without a fight? You'll never be able to carry a child unless you develop the proper muscles in your back!"

"I'm never going to have children anyway," she said, brushing it all off with a shrug. She took a swallow of white wine out of a tall, thick, indigo blue stemmed glass. There was always a magnum of white wine in the refrigerator. She said it helped her sleep.

"What do you mean you're never going to have children?" I cried.

"That's ridiculous." I still believed then that all girls found husbands and had babies. It was just that we weren't in any rush to settle down.

"No it's not," she said simply. "I know. Don't tell me how to live my life, Celeste, Madame Babar, Queen of the Elephants. I don't tell you how to live yours."

"Yes you do!"

"No, I don't. I know you're still waiting for Nathan to come back and that you don't love Joe Coutinho, who is as lovely and successful a man as you'll ever find. But I don't judge you. There's a big difference.

"You're lucky, I guess," she said with a sigh, "to love someone like you love Nathan. I've never loved anyone like that."

"What about Brian?" I said, remembering the two-hundred-and-twenty-pound football player Candace had dated our sophomore year.

"Brian!" she threw her head back and laughed. "Brian raped me," she said.

The silence in the kitchen breathed.

"What?" I whispered.

"I never told anyone. You in particular. I didn't want a fuss." She was quiet for a moment. "It was awful," she said. "He hurt me."

Then she told me the story: a classic date rape case—he walked her home and pushed his way into her room. He knew she was afraid, not only of him but of what people would say if she cried out for help.

I wanted to find Brian, wherever he was, and kill him.

Being on the Student Judiciary Committee herself, she'd seen too many cases of girls taking boys up to the student court on accusations of date rape. No one ever believed the charges and the girls became objects of public derision and contempt. So Candace simply ended her relationship with Brian.

"Maybe I led him on," she concluded, shrugging heavily.

For a moment I was unable to speak. "You should've taken the son of a bitch up on charges!" I yelled, making emphatic waving motions with my arms. I knew I never would have told either, and I felt ashamed. "You should've raked him over the coals!" I pounded the kitchen table.

She laughed mirthlessly.

"That's what I love about you," she said. "You never give a shit what people think. I didn't want anyone to know." She gazed at me sadly.

I told her then, in a determined but gentle voice, that she would find the man who was meant for her someday.

Twelve

The headache that had started upstairs in Daphne's living room as a pack of loose marbles had grown big and taut as a bowling ball. The bed was rocking like a rowboat in a storm. Feeling that I might throw up, I went into the bathroom, closed the door, and ran the tap in the sink till the water was ice-cold. I cupped my palms and splashed my face. I looked at my blurry reflection in the cabinet mirror and saw puffy half circles below my eyes and lines curving downward from the corners of my mouth. Mine was not the happy, expectant face of a bride-to-be.

I switched off the overhead light, put the lid down on the toilet, and sat with my elbows on my knees. The rectangular window cast a blue shadow into the small bathroom.

Suddenly those deeply buried emotions exploded within my rib cage and I started to cry. My lungs strained as they expanded; I doubled over, as if to stave off blows. I knew these were the tears I had never cried for Candace, and I wept for a long time.

I remembered a cold, bright winter day, our second Christmas season in New York. We were walking down Fifth Avenue, bundled up in hats and scarves, window-shopping. Candace loved holidays, Christmas in particular. "So what if I'm Jewish?" she told me. "I love the decorations and the spirit." She liked to buy presents for all her friends.

Trump Tower was under construction, and up high on its scaffolding, five men with wind instruments were setting up to play.

"Oh, goody!" Candace said.

"Silent Night" burst forth like a gift from the angels. Stopping dead in my tracks as though I'd encountered a wall, I began to cry. Candace had never seen me cry before. She called my name softly and hugged me to her chest.

"Celeste. I'm here. You're not alone."

"I miss my mother," I wailed. "I miss the way it used to be when I was little. She loved 'Silent Night.'"

"Your mother is with you," she said. A chestnut vendor was staring at us, his weather-beaten face half-covered by a thick blue scarf. She wiped my face with her gloved hand.

"Chestnuts!" she said. "Let's buy chestnuts like we did last year. You love them." She handed the vendor a few dollars and said, "Give my friend your best chestnuts. She's sad today." He handed her a little brown bag and gave her back her money.

"Merry Christmas," he said.

"And Merry Christmas to you, too," she said.

Remembering, I was startled by even more violent tears. I wrapped my arms around my shins, unable to look up. Candace was the closest friend I'd ever had. Everything that was hers was mine, and mine, hers.

Except Ed.

* * *

CANDACE AND I had been living together in the city for almost three years when she met him through some friends in banking, a brother and sister of Nordic descent named Nils and Birgitt, who were, of course, tall, thin, and blond. They, in turn, had a girlfriend and a boyfriend who were also tall, thin, and blond. Ed was curly-headed and dark, like Candace, but they were both tall and thin, too. When I was with the six of them, I felt like a person standing among trees.

Ed was their one struggling artist friend and they always paid for his dinners and drinks. Candace was enthralled by the idea that he was writing a novel. She began to read his early chapters and give him criticism. He'd been working on the same eighty pages for two years, but Candace believed in him without reserve, the way she did in me.

Ed took to spending nights at our place rather than taking the subway home to Brooklyn. She asked me if I would mind sleeping on the futon in the living room. I told her of course not, and Ed began to sleep in my single bed across from hers. When I'd get up to pee in the middle of the night, I'd hear them talking heatedly in low whispers.

I asked her one day why she preferred sharing the bedroom with him rather than the large futon in the living room.

"Would you sleep in the same bed as Branko?" she said, snorting at the absurdity of this thought.

"Of course not."

"Exactly. Ed and I are *friends,* Celeste."

I eyed Ed with suspicion, because I felt uncomfortable around Candace's banking associates, who were too athletic and enthusiastic and had never read a novel in their lives. I couldn't imagine what Ed saw in them.

By then the late-night bars we frequented had begun to depress me. They were packed with people who yelled over the jukebox at the top of their lungs and spilled drinks. Everyone seemed to want to have sex as fast as possible regardless of whether they were incapacitated by liquor.

* * *

One night, we went around the corner to Simpson's for a hamburger and the place was unusually crowded. Candace grabbed the maitre d' by the arm and said conspiratorially, "Ted! Can you do something for me? I don't want to wait." Smiling brightly, she added, "You know I'm a good customer." I was embarrassed. Ted's expression remained aloof, but he seated us at the next available deuce.

The waiter was harried and mixed up Candace's drink order, bringing her gin instead of vodka.

"What is this shit?" she yelled at him, making a disgusted face. When we got the check, she wouldn't tip him.

"Candace, he's tired." I took several dollars out of my wallet and laid them on the table.

"*I'm* tired!" she cried. "I've been working all day, at a *real* job."

"Jesus, Candace," I muttered, shaking my head.

"I'm paying for my meal!" she said. "I expect service!"

"That could be me, you know," I said icily. She stared at me as if I'd just spoken to her in Arabic.

"*I* could be waiting on you." *No, no, that's not true,* my inner voice said, *because at heart you're not courageous. If you didn't have money, you would've gone to law school, like your father wanted.* A chill skittered up my back. The muscles in my face ached with shame.

* * *

For years, I'd studied Russian and I'd longed to go to Russia to improve my skills, and to learn discreetly about Varlam Shalamov, the elusive concentration camp survivor who had written *The Kolyma Tales* and whom no one seemed to know anything about. I applied for a six-week language program in Moscow and was accepted. Then I became afraid of leaving home. I vacillated. The group was leaving on June sixteenth. Candace encouraged me, knowing that for years I had talked about visiting Russia.

"What do you think," she said, "that I won't be here when you get back?"

Memorial Day weekend was approaching. She asked me to go out to Montauk with her, to stay with Birgitt and Nils. Candace and I had spent every Memorial Day together for the past eight years, and she felt it was "bad luck to break old habits." She promised it would be quiet and relaxing. We'd go to the beach, avoid the touristy bars. I agreed, because I didn't want to stay alone in the city and didn't want to visit my father and Anna in Connecticut.

* * *

On Saturday evening we all went to Gosman's dock at the Montauk port and ate lobsters out on the quiet, moonlit deck. Seagulls squawked at us from above, and swans glided by on the still water.

I seemed to be the only one who did not have a clear vision of the future; Ed, even, had his novel. I was intimidated by their clear-sightedness, their calm, self-confident faces. Ed, who had ended up next to me, asked me if I intended to use my Ph.D. in Comparative Lit to teach. I said I wasn't looking that far ahead—I was still doing research for my dissertation, when Candace said gaily, "Celeste had a short story published in *The Paris Review*!"

"I didn't know you wrote," Ed said.

"Well, it's not what you'd call a profession," I said, laughing nervously. The rest of them were staring at me as if Candace had just said that I dove off cliffs in my spare time.

"I know what you mean!" Ed said, and at once we were coconspirators against the rest of them. He asked me who my favorite writers were. I told him that at the moment I was concentrating on Primo Levi and Varlam Shalamov, the subjects of my dissertation. He'd never read Levi and hadn't heard of Shalamov, but wanted me to tell him more. I got enthusiastic, explaining that Shalamov was fairly unknown, even in his own country. I was going to Moscow for six weeks that summer to try to learn more about him. Ed nodded at me encouragingly and began talking about *The Seagull,* saying it was the best play he'd ever read.

"Hey, miss! Miss!" Candace shouted at the waitress who was passing by in the distance with a large tray of drinks. Candace held up her empty daiquiri glass, making an angry, impatient face. When the waitress returned, Candace said, "Damn, a person could die of thirst waiting for you!" and ordered another round for the table. Furious at Candace, I asked for a shot of tequila. Ed said that sounded great and ordered one as well.

The drinks arrived. Time passed and I became relaxed. Ed, who had changed the subject to Martin Scorsese, had begun to seem very attractive.

Just as we were figuring out the check, he kissed me, a long, sweet probing kiss, right in front of his friends, and it never occurred to me to stop him.

* * *

Candace and I followed the others back to the cottage in our rented car. Her silence made me feel defensive. *I hate your yuppie friends,* I wanted to say, *and sometimes I even hate you, because you're changing. You and I are moving farther and farther apart.* I was getting ready to say this, getting ready to fight.

As I took in a breath, she said matter-of-factly, "I *love* him, Celeste. I've never told him. I've loved him since the beginning, but he only loves me as a friend. He confides in me, depends on me. I'm sorry, I should've told you." She sighed. "They *always* want to be my best friend."

How could I not have seen this? "I'm not interested in him," I said quickly.

She said with uncharacteristic harshness, "Don't give me that shit, Celeste."

That night she and I shared a room with cardboard-thin walls. I lay on my back inches away from her, staring at the moonlit ceiling and listening to everybody's breathing, wondering which exhalation was Ed's, where Ed was in the house, and whether he was thinking of me.

* * *

After that weekend, Ed stopped staying over at our place and began to call me during the day, when Candace was at work.

* * *

Thinking back on Ed, which I often did during my worst sleepless nights, when my life's every mistake and regret crouched in the dark corners of my room, I tried to comprehend why I pursued this dalliance with Ed. I liked to think that I had for a moment believed he might be the one I had been waiting for, the one who would make me forget Nathan. Sometimes I thought that together, Candace and I had been building up momentum, like snowballs rolling downhill that would inevitably hit some jagged rocks. Or was it simply that I'd had too much to drink on the two occasions I met with him? This was the excuse I used to shrug off all my misadventures.

* * *

I met him only once after Montauk, for drinks down in the Village, in a dark bar. Knees touching under the table, we talked in low voices like a stealthy, adulterous couple. We drank vodka martinis, discussed our writing and how hard it was to write in a place like New York. Laughing, we made a ghoulish list of all the writers we could think of who had come to a bad end. The two names Ed came up with were the obvious ones (Hemingway and Fitzgerald). I had wanted more originality from him. After our fourth or fifth drink he invited me up to his friend's loft around the corner, to do some lines of coke. He told me he was watching the guy's cats while he was out of town.

I thought about it for a moment. Who in her right mind would turn down a few lines of coke?

The loft was apparently under construction, tall scaffolds stood against the open brick walls. The long, echoing space smelled of an overflowing litter box. There was a film of white plaster dust over everything. Ed sat on the couch and a puff of dust rose around him. He spread lines on a large mirror that had "Budweiser" written in red across the center of it. It was hard to tell the coke from the plaster dust. He passed me the mirror and a rolled-up dollar bill. I sniffed up the lines and handed the mirror back to him.

His face to the mirror like Narcissus at the pool, Ed told me twice that there had never been anything between him and Candace. As he glanced up, a stealthy, guilty look shadowed his dark eyes. A knot of anger formed in my throat. Didn't he care about her at all? It was becoming increasingly clear that he was not the one. I longed for Nathan again, with a pain that tore at my stomach like hunger, or fear.

We kissed for a while on the dust-covered couch and he got a hand up under my shirt and caressed my breast through my bra. Guilt left an evil aftertaste on my tongue and in the back of my throat. Ed stopped to spread more lines. I got up to leave, looking around for my jacket.

"What's up?" Ed asked, pinching his nose and sniffing.

"I've got to go," I said vaguely.

"Stick around, I've got plenty more of this." He held up the dollar bill.

Luckily I was one of those people who could walk away from coke. I could go home to bed while others gnashed their teeth and begged their dealers over the phone to bring more. I picked up my jacket and slipped it on. I began to slap the dust off my arms.

"Well, I guess I'll see you later," I said.

"Let's get together in a couple of days," he said uncertainly. "Like, Thursday?"

"Sure," I said.

He was sitting there dumbfounded, the bill still in his hand, as I turned toward the door.

* * *

Of course, I told Candace I'd been out with Joe Coutinho, the editor from ABC News.

"Oh," she said sweetly, "I thought you were with Ed."

"No," I said. She looked at me for a long moment, searching my face, and I was forced to turn away.

* * *

I had agreed to meet him again, but when the day came I called and left a message on his machine that I was sick. After that, I stopped picking up the phone and let the answering machine take his calls and erased the messages before Candace got home. I don't know if she still saw him with Nils and Birgitt, but he never again spent the night.

Candace and I didn't discuss Ed or anything else that was troubling us. I saw discomfort and pain when I looked into her eyes; I wonder if she saw the same in mine.

A few days passed with no further calls from Ed; then a final message. It was on the machine when I got home from Columbia.

"We had so much fun the other night," his voice whined lewdly, barely recognizable, "I thought you and I really had something going. You were *hot*." He made it sound as if we'd slept together. Furious, I returned his call with my own message. "Listen, you son of a bitch," I said, "if you call me one more time, I'm going to talk to the cops."

I hoped and prayed that would be the end of it.

* * *

I STARTED HANGING OUT with my classmates in the quiet of the West Sider bar up by Columbia. I would put off coming home until I thought she'd be in bed.

One night I had a bad dream. I was alone in the apartment and all of Candace's things were gone. An icy wind was blowing through the empty rooms. I called out to her as I walked, but I couldn't find her. I awakened on the futon, in a sweat, still drunk from the shots of tequila I'd had at the West Sider, but already shaking and hungover. I stumbled blindly into the narrow hallway that led to the bedroom, and bumped into a muscular, naked stranger. He was only a silhouette, all I could see were the whites of his eyes glinting dangerously.

"Who are you?" I said, trying not to let him know how scared I was. "What are you doing here?"

"I have no fucking idea," he muttered angrily. I pushed past him and into the bathroom, locking the door. I sat on the toilet for a while, trying to decide what to do. When I came out, the light was on in the kitchen and the front door was wide open. The silence breathed and ticked. I closed and locked the door and ran to the bedroom. Candace was on her back, spread-eagle.

"Candace!" I shook her. "Candace! Damn it!"

Finally she stirred and opened one blind eye, like a person emerging from a coma. "Candace! Who was that guy? There was a naked guy in the hallway."

"Wha' guy?" She lifted her head as if it were an impossible weight, and looked around. Her clothes were strewn everywhere, her bra hung over the top of the lampshade as though it had caught there in midflight. "No guy here. You mush be dreaming," she said, and her eyes rolled back in her head.

I brought this up again the next day, but she vehemently insisted that there had been no man.

"You brought a total stranger into our house! He could have

killed you! And me! You had a blackout, Candace." I was furious; I wanted her to admit the truth.

"I've never had a blackout in my life," she said, outraged. "I'm not talking about this anymore."

* * *

I DON'T KNOW how long I stayed doubled over like that, weeping in Daphne's bathroom. Finally, exhausted, I felt a certain calm return.

The tiled room was darker, still tinted that disconcerting blue. The faucet dripped. High-heeled shoes were clicking impatiently down the circular stairs.

Daphne found me sitting on the closed toilet with my head cradled in my arms. She flicked on the light, which buzzed to life over our heads. I looked up at her, wincing.

"You're as white as a sheet," she said. "Are you all right?"

"Did you invite Candace?" I asked. Daphne's hazel eyes went round and stared at me.

"No, of course not," she said quickly, and wrapped her arm around my shoulders. She pulled me up and walked me away from the bathroom, as if it were to blame. "I'm sorry, honey," she said.

"I have a headache," I murmured.

Daphne led me back to the bed and gently helped me stretch out on the soft pillows. "I'll get you some Advil." She rushed off, returning in a moment with a cold compress, a glass of water, and two pills. "Here. Just rest a while," she said softly.

I closed my eyes.

* * *

I MISSED CANDACE terribly while I was in Moscow. Varlam Shalamov proved more elusive than I'd expected. Few people would admit they'd heard of him, even fewer that they'd read his work. Once, at a dissident's house, I was shown a mimeographed copy of one of Shalamov's stories. I had seen one once before, while in college. It had been smuggled to the West by Viktor Bezsmertno, another dissident. "Shalamov came home after more than a quarter century in the Kolyma camps," the dissident in Moscow told me. "He was living here peacefully, writing. Then some fucking American professor smuggled *The Kolyma Tales* out of Russia, translated and published them in the United States. As punishment, the government put Shalamov in a mental institution, the worst one we have, right here in Moscow. He died there, without visitors, without friends. Alone."

How many people would remember him? I wondered with a sinking heart. How many would know that he left the single greatest literary testament to the atrocities of Stalinism? It became even more imperative for me to get home and finish my Ph.D. dissertation.

* * *

From Moscow, I sent Candace the most outrageously Communist postcards I could find. Lenin in red addressing the lumpen proletariat; the Soviet flag with hammer and sickle blowing in the wind; Young Pioneers with red scarves tied about their necks, helping the elderly. I wrote her six postcards in six weeks. They'd started out jocular and grew more and more apologetic, until they became hysterical. Finally I begged her to explain her silence.

She never wrote back. I decided that for once I would confront my problems head-on, face to face, as soon as I got home. I'd tell her the truth about Ed. I'd tell her he wasn't worth the saliva I was using up, explaining to her that nothing had happened and he meant nothing to me. I was certain that she would listen to me. It wasn't too late.

* * *

I held our apartment door open with my shoulder and threw my heavy bags in. An envelope skidded across the kitchen floor. In it were Candace's apartment keys and a note.

Dear Celeste,

You must think I'm a total moron. I heard Ed's messages, including the lewd one that said what a good time he had with you that night. You erased them before I got home but I always called in from work to check messages. Why did you lie to me? I could've handled it if you'd told me the truth. I don't want to stay in New York anymore. This is a sick place. I'm going home to Boston where I belong. I had the PO hold your mail. You can go pick it up. Please don't call my parents looking for me because I don't want to talk to you. Who are you? You are not the person I used to know.

Candace

On the kitchen table were the first two of the six postcards I'd sent her from Moscow. The card she'd given me the night before I left stood on the bookcase in the living room. I picked it up. It was a cartoon of a mouse flying on a goose's back, in the midst of a flock. I opened it. The caption read, "Have A Nice Trip!" Below that was Candace's girlish, large round print. "Stick to your dreams and you will find your way."

* * *

I WROTE HER several letters, sending them to her parents' address. They came back to me unopened. I was afraid to call them. I checked periodically, but Candace still did not have a listed phone number in the Boston area.

When I finally gave up the apartment we'd shared to move in with Alex, I found the card again, covered with dust, between the refrigerator and the wall. Jittery-kneed, I sat down on the bare floor. I'd completely forgotten about that card. How had it ended up behind the fridge?

"Have A Nice Trip!"

* * *

TWICE A YEAR, the alumni magazine arrived with Candace's class notes inside, and every time, my heart constricted in my chest. I could barely stand to open the magazine, but did nevertheless. All class mail was directed to her parents' home. She wrote high-spirited, enthusiastic notes, gossiping about who had gotten married and who'd had a baby. She never failed to mention alumni she had run into in Boston, and that she was not married and didn't have any prospects. She was doing well, working in a commercial bank, living alone in the city, and still "partying hardy with my old college buddies."

The day after my bridal shower, I forced myself to call Samantha and Jacob. Samantha picked up, and a moment later, I heard a second receiver click. "Is that you, Jacob?" she asked. "It's me," he said, and that was all.

I told them I was engaged.

"How lovely," Samantha said coolly. "I'll be sure to tell Candace. Well, good-bye then," she said, and hung up.

I held the receiver with a trembling hand. Finally, when the dial tone beeped busy, I set it down.

I went to the window and looked down at Seventy-ninth Street that seemed so tiny, far below. The long, straight canyon stretched all the way to Fifth Avenue and Central Park. If you could see through the tall green trees of the park, you would find a curving path to the West Side and Amsterdam Avenue and our old apartment—cramped, crooked-floored, but filled with our dreams. Where had they all gone? Was I indeed a person whom Candace no longer knew? Did I deserve the punishment she had meted out?

My forehead pressed against the cool glass, I prayed for the first time in a very long while, for God to let the answers come to me.

Thirteen

After my bridal shower, I started napping too much during the day and having insomnia at night. I worried about everything, especially the kids in Harlem. I had one visit left with them the next week, and after that, I'd never see them again. I didn't know if I'd helped them. I had tried to help them. Also, my short story collection was not progressing. Whenever I sat down to write, I found myself weighing what had happened in Mexico with Alex. No matter how often that inner voice chastised me—*it was your fault, you were drunk and you acted like a jerk*—some other part of me would not let it go. Something terribly wrong had happened.

As I lay in bed at night, the anger I felt made my heart beat too fast. I'd put on the headphones and watch the Discovery Channel to calm my jangled nerves, while Alex slept unperturbed beside me.

* * *

Alex's mother called on Friday afternoon while I was napping. Aurelia was in town for a couple of days and suggested dinner on Sunday evening at Nero's, the restaurant where the rehearsal dinner would take place, to go over details with Alex, the owner, and me.

Later I awakened to Alex's handsome, tired face peering over me. The setting sun cast pink ribbons of light through the blinds, onto the wall across from the bed.

"Hey, lazybones," he said. "I figured I'd surprise you and bring home dinner."

"Your mother called before," I murmured, stretching. "She wants to meet us at Nero's for dinner Sunday night."

"Good," he said.

I got up and perched on the kitchen counter with a glass of white wine while Alex took fresh-grilled tuna steaks and a large assortment of seasonal greens and vegetables out of a white paper bag. He got out a salad bowl and poured in the greens and the container of herb vinaigrette.

"Wow, Alex. This is really nice."

When the salad was ready, he carried our new large wooden bowl to the dining table and set it down. He lit candles in our new candlesticks, set the table with our new silverware, new dishes. The table looked pretty, expectant. We sat and ate in silence for a while.

"Alex, I think maybe I should go talk to somebody."

"What do you mean?"

"You know, talk to a shrink or something. I'm just not feeling well. I can't sleep at night and I can't wake up during the day."

"Maybe you've still got that bug," he said. "Why do you think you need to talk to a shrink?"

I treaded gingerly. "Well, for a while now I've been—I've been haunted by all sorts of thoughts . . . "

"Haunted?" He looked away. He took off his glasses and fogged them with his breath, then wiped them with his napkin. "Celeste, listen. Wait till the wedding's over, then do whatever you want, okay? I just don't think it's a good idea to start digging up stuff now. Not right before the wedding." He put his glasses back on, lowered his eyes to his plate, his flushed ears betraying his discomfort.

After a while he said, "It'll be nice to see my mother, it's been since, what, March? I hope she's put together her guest list like she said she would. She's not really reliable when it comes to this kind of thing."

After I cleared the dishes, he took the wedding file out of his briefcase and spread the papers across the table and looked them over. He had computerized the master list, which held the alphabetized names and addresses of people who had been invited, and he had added a little square in the margin where he could "X" in their RSVPs; there was a "Shower" list with all the gifts listed next to the names of guests; there was a "Wedding Gifts" list, which included date of gift received and a check box for when the thank-you note had been sent; and the "Rehearsal Dinner" list, incomplete because his mother had not supplied him with the names of her guests.

Alex's father would not chip in for the rehearsal dinner, so Alex was splitting the tab with his mother. Aurelia, who was ministering to HIV-positive babies in Zaire, had suggested Nero's because she had gone to college with the owner, Maria Nero, who would surely give Alex an excellent price. Alex was not thrilled that the food was Italian, but he asked around and was told that Nero's was an excellent, well-established restaurant, so we went to dinner there several times to taste different dishes and plan the menu.

Alex was a little concerned about the seating arrangement, as both sides of the family were coming and his parents had divorced when he was a small child. They did not see each other and had nothing in common except for Alex.

"I'm glad she's deigned to visit before my trip to L.A.," he said. "This thing has to be finished before I go."

I had forgotten that he was going away for most of next week. I was ashamed at the relief I felt.

Aurelia arrived thirty minutes late, as was her wont. She marched in, Amazonian in height and assurance. "Hello, hello, sweeties!" she cried.

"Hello, Mother," Alex said. She gave him a hug and then me, pulling away just as I attempted to plant a kiss on her cheek. They didn't kiss in his family either. *That's right,* I thought, *it's the French side who kisses.*

"So tell us about Zaire," Alex said when everyone had finally settled down. He crossed his arms on the table and leaned forward expectantly, smiling with his fine white teeth.

"Zaire was terrific, but Uganda! Oh my Lord. In one village, we attempted to demonstrate the use of condoms by sliding one over a broom handle. On our follow-up visit the next day, they proudly showed us their broomsticks with the condoms we had given them stretched over the handles!"

Alex and she chuckled at the same moment. Sitting between them, I had the odd impression of looking at two representations of the same face—one older and more feminine, but otherwise they were nearly identical. They both had short, thick, dark blond hair and unfathomable, deep-blue eyes. On the few occasions I'd spent with her, I'd listened in bewildered silence while she told of meeting Mobutu ("I called him a big ninny, he loved it"); of almost sitting on a crocodile in the Amazon jungle ("Well, I just thought he was a log, you see"); of flying across America in a hot air balloon with a millionaire she'd been dating ("Hank just loved to show off"). She had seen so much that nothing could get a rise out of her anymore except the sight of starving children and oppressed women. I liked what she did. I even liked her politics. But I didn't like the way I couldn't see behind her eyes.

They each ordered a rum and tonic. I ordered a bottle of Pellegrino water, hoping to make a good impression.

"So why were you late *this* time?" Alex asked, and reached across the table and punched her lightly in the arm.

"It was Frederico, of course. He didn't have his keys so I had to wait—"

Alex interrupted her. "Let's talk about the rehearsal dinner."

After they'd finished their drinks, Maria Nero sent over a bottle of Chianti. Alex rushed to fill our glasses. He was clearly in some kind of excited state.

"This is pretty good wine," said Aurelia. "Maybe we could order this for the rehearsal dinner."

She picked up the bottle and topped off my glass, which I hadn't yet touched. It seemed too much trouble to refuse, to say, *I'm trying to cut back,* so I decided to sip it carefully instead, make it last.

Alex had taken several large gulps and was now topping off his own glass.

Our pasta dishes arrived, and Alex began to ask his mother about her guest list. He was planning the order of the toasts and wanted to know if any of his mother's friends were going to speak.

"Alex, I have no idea!" she cried. "That would take the element of chance totally out of it."

"Exactly," Alex said. "I don't want people going on forever about all the stupid things I did in college."

She chuckled amusedly. "Oh, you mean like when you beat the crap out of that football player for insulting your black friend and had to take a leave of absen—"

I looked at him, my mouth agape.

"Mother, I don't mean that *at all,*" he said between his teeth.

"Well, I haven't made a list yet, Alex. And I think I'll just leave it up to you."

Alex fell silent, brooding.

Another bottle of wine arrived, and later, a bottle of champagne with our dessert, three slices of almond espresso cake, the house specialty.

"Maria is spoiling us tonight!" Aurelia exclaimed.

Alex brusquely filled his champagne flute to the top. Bubbles slipped over the rim and down the stem. He filled his mother's glass, then mine.

"Well," Aurelia said, raising her glass, "I'm glad the whole thing is settled, then. To you, Alex, for doing such a good job. You'll organize this much better than I ever could. I just hope you won't invite too many of your father's stodgy friends."

"Of course not," Alex said, smiling gruesomely. He produced a folded sheet of yellow paper from his shirt pocket and slapped it down on the table; the glasses jumped. "This is the list so far. Now, I want you to sit there for a minute and *think* about who you want to invite to this rehearsal dinner."

Aurelia waved it away. "Oh, I'm sure you can do this without me, Alex."

"Mother," Alex said in a pointed tone, "I want you to have a say in this."

"But I just had my say. I have to go to Mississippi tomorrow, and I'll be gone for a week at least, this is very important to me, Alex, I—"

"And this isn't," he muttered, looking down at the table, a flush spreading over his cheeks. In one swallow he finished off his champagne and refilled his glass.

"All right," Aurelia said with resignation, "Let me see who you've got there. You don't like my friends anyway."

The tips of his ears had turned bright red. Something was beginning to surface from the depths of his calm, still eyes. Watching him, I had a sudden, frightful vision of him overturning the table.

Aurelia glanced at the list and slid it away. "Well, we'll have to ask Frederico, of course," she said vaguely. "And the doctors, let's see—Isabel Green . . . "

He drank his champagne down and stared at his mother with watery eyes.

"Oh, Alex," she sighed . . . "stop being such a tight-ass, will you?"

That was clearly the wrong thing to say. A series of sentences shot out of his mouth like bullets, although he never raised his voice.

"When I was a little kid you left me alone with a moronic maid so you could traipse around the world and take care of other people's kids. It's my fucking *rehearsal dinner* and you couldn't even give me an idea of who you wanted me to invite. You can't ever fucking pretend to care. You're the most selfish, self-involved person I've ever met. How unfortunate for me that you happen to be my mother." Then, quite calmly, he added, "Why am I surprised?" and began to tap at the corner of his dessert plate with his small fork.

Aurelia stared at him, startled, her pink lips slightly parted, exposing her small, even white teeth. "My God, Alex. I did the best I could—I was a single mother."

"You weren't single for thirty seconds. Peter, Hank, John, and now,

I'm sorry, what's his name? Oh yes, *Frederico*. You had time for them. You had time for med school when I was a kid and you certainly had time to graduate at the top of your class."

"I played tennis with you, I paid for your tennis camps. I paid for Choate all by myself, for God's sake!"

Alex didn't say anything, but stared down at the crumbs on his plate and began to smash them with his fork.

"And every vacation we went somewhere where you could practice with the best pros. I did the best I could. I had to live my life, too, after all."

Alex filled his glass again and lifted his flute.

"Alex, put down that champagne glass," I said in a murmur.

His head snapped toward me and he eyed me with icy contempt. "The pot calling the kettle black, don't you think?"

"Not tonight," I said, flushing, glancing quickly from his mother to my half-filled glass.

"Whatever," he said, sighing deeply. "It doesn't matter. I'll take care of it. I've been taking care of myself since I was five years old."

His face looked unfamiliar; he'd become a frightened little boy. In the trembling corners of his mouth I saw glimmers of the grown-up struggling to regain his composure. I was disquieted, and afraid of him, and the floor below me seemed to drop away. I reached for my flute and drank the champagne down in one swallow. With a trembling hand, I lifted the bottle and attempted to nonchalantly pour more into my glass.

"I did the best I could," Aurelia said in a quiet voice, staring at me with a pleading look. "His father wouldn't even give him the money to rent a tux for his senior prom. I had to do everything. I don't understand why . . ." her voice trailed off.

"I'm sure you were a terrific mother," I said. "You did a great job." I put my hand over hers and smiled weakly. Her long, thin fingers felt chilled beneath mine.

"Well, if that's all," Alex said, standing up and squaring his shoulders.

And he left the restaurant very much as his mother had entered it.

"Give me a call tomorrow?" I said to Aurelia, and ran after her son.

I found Alex two blocks up, demolishing a bus-stop shelter. He had lifted a metal trash can and was flinging it repeatedly against the shelter's shatterproof glass wall, which was beginning to crack. Empty paper cups, plastic bottles, cans, and food-stained wrappers flew from the can and skittered about him.

"Alex!" I screamed. "Stop!

People across the street were stopping to watch, while on our side, they hurried past as fast as they could. I came up behind him and tried to hold his arm. He pushed me aside as if I were no heavier than a jacket. I slammed into a parked car, my ribs crashing against the hood.

Frantic, as if possessed, he kicked and punched the thick, crumbling glass out of its casing. The chunks of glass tumbled to the pavement like ice cubes from a huge bag. We heard a cop car siren approaching, and Alex suddenly straightened and gazed around him. He grabbed my arm and dragged me running down a side street toward the next avenue. On the next corner he hailed a cab and shoved me in before getting in himself and slamming the door. His liquor-heavy breath came in gasps. The cab driver's eyes glinted in the rearview mirror like fish passing in a dark tank. I gave him the address.

Alex shouted, "Shit!" then buried his face in his bloodied hands. I couldn't tell if he was sobbing or just breathing heavily. I sat pressed against the door, afraid he might explode again.

"They've never given a shit about me, either one of them. I was a mistake," he said between great heaving sighs. "That fuck my father wouldn't even loan me money for MBA school. I didn't ask him to *give* it to me, for Christ's sake. And that cunt Babs! She fucking hates me!"

I sat frozen, stunned. "It's all right," I reassured him. "It's all right."

But he didn't seem to hear me.

* * *

ALEX LURCHED into the bedroom, dropping his clothes on the floor as he went. He shut the door and the line of light beneath the door went dark.

Later, after two large cognacs, I joined him. As Alex slept soundly beside me, I put on the earphones and watched a show on the birth and death of stars. The narrator said in a deep, measured voice that our own sun would nova in approximately 4.5 billion years. I was struck by an image of the bed being sucked into a tiny black hole and the whole room being pulled in behind it, then the building, the city, the continent, and finally the Earth, until all of it was nothing but a speck of dust floating in space.

* * *

I AWAKENED to the sounds of his packing. He was in a hurry. I sat up in bed and watched him glide quickly about the room, speaking to himself, checking things off a mental list. He was in his blue suit, clean shaven, his fair hair slicked back and his little round glasses glinting brightly.

"Alex, are you all right?"

"Socks . . . gym socks . . . I'm fine," he said, looking toward me with a small frown.

"Alex, you were very upset last night."

He stopped what he was doing and stood immobile for a moment, looking down at me. "I'm sorry, I was a little drunk. My mother just . . . sometimes she makes me angry. It's been a long time since . . . listen, I don't want to discuss this now. I'm fine. I don't even remember what I said." He glanced at his watch. His knuckles were bruised and scabbed. "I'm running late." He opened and closed his hand a few times, looking at it as if he didn't recognize it.

"How are you going to explain that?"

"I never have to explain myself. Besides, it'll scare the shit out of the guy across the table."

He stood in the doorway for a moment, seeming so poised, so strong and in control, so grown-up, I felt as though I had witnessed some kind of rip in time, and this reality had nothing to do with the other, dark reality of last night. My ribs ached where they had smashed into the car hood.

He said, "I'll call you from L.A. Okay?"

"Alex, it's not okay!" I said, suddenly hysterical. "You tore down a fucking bus shelter last night! It's not okay at all!"

"Celeste, you don't need to use that kind of language," he said in a calm, fatherly voice. "I don't have time to discuss this right now."

"You never have time, Alex. You *never* have time!"

"You're overreacting, like you always do. Why don't you *do* something today, instead of just sitting here worrying about nothing? Go to a museum or something."

"Don't you fucking dismiss this, Alex. Don't you dismiss me!" I shouted. "You can't leave with this hanging in the air!"

"Why are you shouting, Celeste? You're way out of control."

I wanted to throw the bedside lamp at him. "*I*'m out of control? *I*'m out of control?"

"I can't talk to you when you're like this," he said. He walked out, letting the front door slam behind him.

Fourteen

I HAD TO KEEP BUSY, not think about Alex, so I spent the morning typing the best of the children's poems and stories and gluing their drawings onto the pages, so that I could take the anthology down to The Writer's Way before lunch so they could make copies. I'd pick them up later in the day and take them up to the children tomorrow. I had the whole week to get this done, but now I was on a mission. To *not* think about Alex.

On my way back I stopped at the mailbox. A letter from my grandmother was among the junk mail and bills and wedding RSVPs. I recognized her thin, vertical script on the thick, eggshell-colored envelope.

For the past nine years, my grandmother had sent me a card on my birthday and at Christmas and Easter, and I'd responded from time to time with a saccharine Hallmark card, bearing only my name. Yet I'd sent her an invitation to the wedding with a little note that read: "I do hope you will come—Celeste." I never expected that she would, and now my heart skipped and jumped. I couldn't wait to get back upstairs and open the envelope. The letter was in French. My grandmother had told me that she could read several of the Romance tongues, but she'd refused categorically to learn to write or speak anything but French, which was, in her opinion, the only perfect language in the world.

Chateau Laroq
Cadaujac
7 June

My very dear Céleste,

Please forgive my delay in responding to your invitation; however, I have been waiting to see how my husband Albert is faring after his most recent cardiac arrest. It appears recovery is slow and therefore I will not be able to attend. This causes me sadness and I do hope you will consider a voyage to France to visit me before I die. Your husband of course is welcome as well. One would not make the same mistake twice! (ha ha, a little joke).

So many issues were left unresolved between your mother and me and also between you and me at the close of your last visit. Could it have been nine years ago already? Please do write to me. You may not believe me but every day I expect a letter from you and am always pained when one never arrives. How is it that I have managed to make such a horrendous mess of things?

Regardless, I do remain your loving and devoted grandmother,

Sophie de Fleurance de Saint-Martin

* * *

I READ IT again upstairs, pacing back and forth in the apartment. I didn't know what to do with myself.

So she isn't coming, I thought, and my skin prickled and itched from the inside as impotent rage tried to surface. With that unwanted emotion came dread, and the thought that warned, *This is all wrong. You don't belong here.*

I had never really expected my grandmother to come, so why was I having this reaction now?

I lifted the venetian blinds on the living room window and pressed my face to the glass. The leaves of the ficus tree tickled my neck and shoulder. I'd brought it in from the hall one day; most of its leaves had fallen off and the earth in the pot was cracked and gray. Some heartless person had just left it there upon moving out. Now it was green and well and grateful.

"What do you want?" I said to it as if it had interrupted me. "You want some water?"

I went and got the plastic water pitcher. As I poured, I looked out at the street, stricken senseless by the sun. Inside, cool air hummed quietly through the vents. Way down below, a taxi suddenly swung around the corner and smashed into a red station wagon that was waiting at the light. Both tiny drivers got out swinging their fists and kicking up their legs. It was like watching a battle scene in a silent film. I began to feel dizzy and moved away from the window.

* * *

This Albert was a new husband I had not met. Her last one, the one who had been suffering from gout at the time of my mother's funeral, had died in 1982. My grandmother had written me a short, crisp note informing me of the death of *le Professeur*. Apparently he had died peacefully in his sleep. I didn't know why she called him *le Professeur,* for he had been a pharmacist whose family had fallen on hard times. I had first met him when I was nine and my mother and I visited for two weeks in the summer of 1969, and I retained a vivid picture of him as an old man who looked like a plucked rooster. He had a few tufts of downy white hair on his head and a beak nose and loose, clammy skin. He walked around grumbling as if the world made a full-time job of affronting his sensibilities. All his fingers were webbed except for the thumbs, a congenital defect that he would be happy to tell you went back seven generations. He had fairly good dexterity, however, and liked to grab hold of me and pinch my cheeks between his webbed fingers and his thumb. I was fascinated and disgusted by his hands and stole glances at them whenever I could. His fingers were clearly formed and pressed together under a thick layer of skin that wrapped around his hand like a bandage.

Every Christmas for as many years as I could remember, my mother had sent him a pair of gloves. She searched for the right pair for days, combing the fancy men's departments with me in tow, finally settling on fabulously expensive lambskin designer gloves. She mailed them off in a chic box with a little exuberant Christmas note, and waited impatiently for his response. Invariably, a note arrived in January, thanking her for her lovely and thoughtful gift, but inquiring as to whether the designer might have available in the same size and of similar quality, a pair of mittens. He never returned the gloves.

* * *

At dinner in my grandmother's large, candlelit, echoing dining room, we sat at the long, dark oak table that had been in the chateau for generations and generations.

"Come here, *mon petit,*" my grandmother said in a tender voice, "I want to show you something interesting."

I jumped down off my *annuaires* and skipped over to her side, fluttering daintily in my brand-new lemon yellow tulle dress that had a lace petticoat, sleeves, and collar, and a large bow in back. It had come in a gift-wrapped box all the way from Bélina, one of the most expensive children's stores in Paris—a present from my grandmother, along with an ancient porcelain doll whose blue eyes closed when you laid her down and who had a brand-new yellow dress as well. My grandmother had told me that the doll had belonged to my mother when she was a girl.

My grandmother took my small hand in her strong plump fingers and placed my fingertips over some dark grooves in the wood of the tabletop at the place to her left where no one sat.

"Do you feel the grooves?" she asked me quietly. "There are four of them, just like fingers. Feel how dainty. They were surely made by the fingertips of a lady. A lady from a long time ago who sat next to her husband at this very table and fretted. What about—we don't know. Imagine how long she must have sat here and worried to make such marks! She was one of your ancestors, perhaps Madeleine de Figeac de Fleurance, who died in 1742—"

"Pff," said my mother, blowing air through her pursed lips. "Don't fill her head with such nonsense, Mother!"

"What?" said my grandmother, as if shocked. "It's the truth! You're the one who is unreliable in this family, Nathalie, not I."

Le Professeur clucked heartily, nodding from his seat at the opposite end of the table. I looked at him and felt my heart turn to ice—a big floating iceberg in a dark, cold sea.

"She doesn't lie!" I cried out. "You're the one who lies!" I pointed at him. He laughed, his whole body racked with mirth.

"You're right to defend your mother," said my grandmother. "That's a good loyal girl. But you mustn't point. I wish my daughter defended *me* that way . . ." Her voice trailed off unhappily. "By the way, Nathalie," my grandmother said to her daughter, smiling at me as she rearranged a curl in my hair, "I compliment you on *Céleste*'s proficiency in our language. With a little work, one wouldn't be able to tell that she is not French."

* * *

Although the Chateau Laroq rouge had been rated among the Crus Exceptionnels in the Graves 1953 and 1959 official classifications, my grandmother complained that the rating should have come much sooner and she believed certain of her best years were superior to Chateau Haut Brion's first growths and that her white was always given short shrift for some incomprehensible reason. She was extremely proud of the fact that Chateau Laroq had stayed in the Fleurance family for over four hundred years, never succumbing to the pressures of foreign multinationals, as so many others had in the Bordeaux region. This was what we discussed as my grandmother took me on long late-afternoon walks "for the constitution," through the rows and rows of ripening grapes. The soil, speckled with gravel stones the size of fists, sloped gently toward the banks of the Garonne. The chateau itself stood in the middle of the vineyard, and tame-looking woods and pine forests stretched far into the distance. There was an enclosed pasture behind the chateau where a few old Thoroughbreds wandered aimlessly through the warm, mild days.

"Your real grandfather de Saint-Martin was poor but exceptionally bright and very handsome. He never did a thing but read and study. He read every single book in the library. He was nice to the children and left me alone, bless him." My grandmother leaned over a clump of little green grapes and inspected them closely through her bifocals, ignoring me completely for a long time. "Good," she said, and moved on. "Let me give you a little advice, *Céleste,*" she now said, taking my hand in her plump, dry one. "Although you may be too young for it—marry a weak man. Have your affairs with strong ones, to be sure. But the smart Fleurance women have always married weak men, which is why we have succeeded in keeping the vineyard.

"You are half-French," my grandmother said sternly, "and you must never forget that this place, this land and our wine, is yours, too. Sometimes I wish that your uncle François was less of a cretin and more of a man. I also wish I'd had more children to carry on the tradition. I fear that François will sell after I die—why not? He's greedy and stupid. Your mother is so much brighter than he. A rebel and a wild one, she is, yes, but so much brighter . . . Wouldn't you like to come back and live in France with your old *Bonne-maman* who adores you?"

"Oh yes!" I said. Obviously, the relationship between my mother and *Bonne-maman* had somewhat improved for her to even suggest such a thing. "But what about *le Professeur*?" I asked with a certain concern.

"Ah, lui!" she said, shrugging. "He means no harm. He's just an old fool."

* * *

My memory is filled with mild, sunny days and the smell of rich wine at every meal, poured in great drops into my water glass; the exquisite lengthy meals that ended with *hachis Parmentier* on Sundays, the cook having ground up all the leftover meats from the whole week, covered them with a layer of milky mashed potatoes, and baked the deep dish in the oven. And there were lavish gifts from my grandmother, the best one an enormous brown bear from Le Nain Bleu in Paris, who arrived in a large cardboard box.

"Stop it, Mother, you're spoiling her," my mother said to my grandmother the day the bear came.

"Pff!" said my grandmother. "It won't hurt her a bit. You've picked up that Calvinist ethic, I see," she added pointedly through pursed lips, which made my mother storm out of the room.

"She's not so bad," I said to my mother gingerly that night as she was tucking me into bed. "Why do you always get mad at her?" I had been wondering why my mother had prepared me to meet a monstrous old witch when my grandmother was really a very appealing, kind and generous lady.

"Pff!" said my mother. "You don't know her. She's trying to buy you, can't you see that? She's very charming when she wants, but what a viper!"

* * *

A FEW DAYS LATER, they had a terrible fight. Doors slammed and voices crashed against the stone walls downstairs, echoing up to me in the warm, still night. My mother burst in like a black tornado and packed me up in a rush. She was flushed and distraught and seemed deflated, as if her clothes were suddenly loose on her frame, as if my grandmother had sucked out all her strength.

"What? What?" I cried, sitting up in the large bed.

"We're leaving, that's what," my mother said.

"Can I take the clothes? Can I take the doll and the bear?" I asked apprehensively.

"Not that damn bear, he's as big as you are."

"I'll carry him, I swear!"

"Oh, all right. But if you ask me to carry him just once I'll throw him out. I will," she warned.

Early the next morning Georges the chauffeur drove us to the Bordeaux train station. We got on a train heading for Italy without saying good-bye to my *Bonne-maman*. The bear, whose name was Monsieur Laroq, took up a whole seat himself.

"Aren't we going to say good-bye and thank you?" I asked my mother, because after all, that was what she'd always told me to do.

"No, we are not going to say good-bye and thank you," she said, imitating my whiny singsong and making a face. I wanted to kick her in the shins and run back to my grandmother's house.

Repenting, the lines in her face softening, she said with a coy smile, "But I tell you what we're going to do, we're going to spend all the money I have in my special bank account and we're going to live like queens! Then and only then we'll go home."

* * *

My sophomore year came to a close in a rush of exams and papers. My grades were unbelievable. I'd gotten four A's and an A plus. Only I knew that I had been concentrating so hard on getting through my classes and homework each day so that I could go out drinking with Candace. As a result I hadn't thought about the summer at all. The prospect of three long hot months waitressing again in Connecticut seemed unbearable. I didn't want to sit there waiting to hear from Nathan, whose most recent impassioned letter had come from Oaxaca, Mexico. A feeling of uneasiness and dread came over me whenever I thought of him. I felt we'd left things completely unresolved, and every time he came to mind I broke into a cold sweat of rage that utterly paralyzed me and made me want to jump out a window. It was easier to deal with the loneliness and the sadness of longing for him than to admit to myself the rage I felt toward him.

I seized upon the idea of writing my grandmother a letter asking if I could come visit over the summer holiday. It seemed the perfect escape, and in my enthusiasm I began to remember fondly the large, cool stone chateau with its high slate roof, the pond with carp, the crickets singing all night, the rich, succulent vineyard, the woods, the Garonne River flowing by in the valley below, and my grandmother's old racehorses that roamed long-legged across the field.

She wrote me back a sprawling, enthusiastic letter and enclosed a check for five thousand francs to purchase my airline ticket. She told me she would combine a visit to Paris with my arrival, so that Georges her chauffeur could drive us back and we could avoid the long and uncomfortable train ride to Bordeaux. To my grandmother, taking a plane from Paris to Bordeaux was a sacrilege. Planes polluted the air and made noise. Trains were the only civilized way to travel across land. I wasn't about to argue with her.

* * *

SHE MET ME at Charles de Gaulle Airport, a space age monster that had not been there when I was nine and that frightened me now as I stepped off the plane, hungover from the drinks I'd had to calm my fear of flying. She was standing in front of everybody at the gate, much shorter than I remembered, solid and round as a boulder in her well-pressed dark blue linen suit.

"Bonjour, Bonne-maman," I said in a shaky voice.

"Mon Dieu," said my grandmother with a gasp. *"Mais tu as vraiment mauvaise mine!"* My God, but you look awful! She reached up and placed her small hand on my cheek. "What's the matter, my darling?" she asked.

"Heartbreak," I said indifferently, with a certain bravado. *"J'ai le coeur brisé."* And I laughed, although tears were threatening. In the touch of her hand, the smell of her wrist, I recognized the essence of my mother and realized with a shudder that my grandmother was much more familiar to me than my father or Anna. She was, I saw now, the last link to my mother, whom I had loved with a fierce and terrible devotion that bordered on obsession because I had always feared, from the youngest age, that I might lose her at any moment.

"Mais si, mais si, everything can be fixed, even *le chagrin d'amour,"* my grandmother said with confidence. "Come along, let's get your bags. You have two whole months to tell me about it."

Le Professeur was waiting in the Citroen, she told me, because he could hardly walk, due to his advanced gout.

* * *

THE CHATEAU LAROQ had not changed from my child's memory. Only, the dramatic circular towers with their round, pointed slate roofs that stood at each corner of the main structure did not seem so tall now. The stone terraces that descended in layers to the vineyard did not seem so vast. The wide marble staircase leading from the center of the front hall to the upstairs bedrooms was no longer the formidable obstacle it had once been.

The second-floor bedrooms sprawled out along a wide corridor that split off in two wings from the main structure. The walls and stairwell of the main hall were decorated with ancient paintings. The furniture was a mixture of different *siècles,* mostly Louis XI and Louis XIII. My grandmother pointed to objects, naming their period, and said that the Fleurances had always liked those two Louis. At the foot of the staircase were two incongruous gigantic *Empire* vases that depicted Napoleonic battles in heroic panoramas. I looked back at them as we climbed the stairs and my grandmother said with a shrug, "Oh, those were there before. That was my great-grandfather Alphonse Fleurance's addition—he loved Napoléon, what can one say?"

She put me in my mother's old bedroom, which had a four-poster bed and a view of the horses in the field and the pine forest beyond.

Before dinner we drank an exquisite *apéritif*—some kind of clear liqueur made from plums. *Le Professeur* shuffled around in silence, grumbling and clucking to himself. He stepped between us, in the middle of a conversation, switched on the TV news and sat down, turning the volume up full blast.

"Let's go out to the sunroom," said my grandmother. "The poor old man is as deaf as a pot." She laughed heartily, and for a moment I almost felt sorry for him.

* * *

A WIND RUSTLED outside the glass walls of the sunroom. The sun was a burning orange ember perfectly outlined above the distant woods. It dropped quickly behind the trees until just a tiny sliver was left, then nothing. Above, the sky displayed a vast spectrum of pinks and reds. We had been traveling all day and I was tired and dazed. In a cage above our heads green finches chirped loudly among the jungle of blooming plants. My heart tightened as I remembered the plants at my mother's kitchen window and how she had loved and tended them. My grandmother cooed to her birds.

"We could have a fancy wine-tasting party, how would you like that?" she asked. "Would that lift your spirits?"

"Whatever you like. I'm so happy to see you again, looking so well."

"Pff," she said, blowing air upwards out of her pursed lips, as my mother used to do. My eyes filled with tears.

"I don't know what's wrong with me!" I cried. "I'm sick!"

"Love can make you as sick as *la grippe,*" she said. "Tell me what happened."

So I told her the whole story, starting with Sally's suicide, as I rocked in an ancient wicker rocking chair and watched the stars making their appearance in the darkening sky. I told her about the dreams I'd had of Sally and how suddenly her face became my mother's. I saw something change at once in my grandmother's face. Her skin turned ashen as her eyes hardened to pebbles, her entire body stiffened and became fortresslike. I quickly changed the subject and told her about Nathan; his passion, his wild streak, his brilliance, his sadness.

"He sounds completely mad," she said, her eyes becoming bright once again. "Like a wild horse. Aren't they sexy when they're like that!" She used the English word "sexy," which made me laugh. She never, for example, said "weekend," an expression that was vastly accepted now in French. She would say *fin-de-semaine*. She could not suffer the bastardization of her beloved language.

"He speaks French perfectly, and also Spanish and some Italian. He went to school in England, you see—"

"Good, good." My grandmother nodded approvingly. "Those English schools teach one manners. Where is he now?" she asked, leaning toward me with curious eyes.

"He's in Oaxaca, Mexico. In some hotel. Can you believe, *Bonne-maman,* he already got himself a job working on the excavation site of some ancient ruins."

"Do you want him very badly?"

I stared at her in silence, exposed by my weakness.

"If you really want him badly, I'll get him for you—no, no, don't look so shocked. I'll send him a round-trip ticket and he can fly back to Central America or South America or wherever he wants to go afterwards. He surely wouldn't turn down a free ticket to France, now, would he? Do you know the name of the hotel? Thank God the telephones in this country have improved in the last ten years. We'll call Mexico and talk to him. Surely Mexican hotels have telephones!"

I must have looked stricken, because she hurried toward me, pulling me to her large breasts, imprisoned in their rock-solid brassiere.

"Now now, don't *worry* so. I'll get him for you, I will." After a moment she added, "I think I know someone in Oaxaca. Someone quite important in the government, I believe . . . Don't worry, *Céleste*."

For a day and a night I didn't sleep as my grandmother made international phone calls and attempted to locate Nathan. Finally the Mexican diplomat brought Nathan by chauffeur to his large estate, and when she finally got Nathan on the phone it was past midnight in Bordeaux.

Her side of their conversation was simple and straightforward. Meanwhile, I stood in a corner of the living room, tearing at a handkerchief and biting my nails.

"Young man," she said to him in French, "I am Sophie de Fleurance de Saint-Martin, the grandmother of *Céleste*. It is imperative that you join her here in France . . . Yes, at Chateau Laroq, but really you don't need to know anything except that I'll have my secretary send you an open-return ticket to Paris. From Paris you'll take the train to Bordeaux . . . It doesn't matter to me what city or country you return to—you can go to Devil's Island for all I care . . . No, she's not well at all and I'm terribly concerned. In this case, young man, money is of no concern."

With her money my grandmother could move mountains, or refuse to, which seemed more often the case when she was dealing with the rest of her family who sniveled, begged, and nipped at her heels.

It was precisely the kind of adventure Nathan would not turn down, and I felt ashamed for bribing him this way. But it didn't matter—to see him! I imagined heroin addiction must be like this. The sweats, the fear, the sickness of the spirit; and then, with one shot, your blood commingling with the liquid drug, you become whole again and life turns sweet and beautiful and pain is just a vague memory, obliterated for the moment.

* * *

We were late in arriving at the Bordeaux train station because *le Professeur* had insisted on driving us and at the last minute he could not locate his keys. As I searched the living room and hall in a panic, I was certain that he had mislaid them on purpose and once again felt that old, bitter, icy hatred for him.

My grandmother and I rushed through the crowded station toward the gate in search of Nathan. There he stood, alone and unperturbed among the shorter heads rushing and bobbing past him, ruddy, suntanned, in jeans and a large blue Mexican shirt, his hair long and wild. I felt my knees collapse just as my grandmother's hand grasped me firmly by the elbow. He came toward us, loping, and took us both in his arms. With my face against his shirt, I could hear my grandmother's muffled, embarrassed laughter.

"But this isn't at all *comme il faut*!" she cried.

For an instant I felt at home, at peace, and so close, so very close, to heaven.

* * *

She gave him a room in a distant wing.

"Do whatever you like, just be discreet," she said to me. "The domestics gossip." That evening she went off to bed early and never asked any questions. When we touched, I knew his smell, his curves, his heartbeat, as if we'd been together the day before. He wanted me to make noise, and tried all his best moves to get me to cry out, but I wouldn't. Not in my grandmother's house.

At breakfast the next morning, she offered Nathan a shot of her one-hundred-year-old cognac from a chateau *"pas trop loin d'içi."* She never offered anyone her special cognac, and I was surprised to see two small tumblers on the tray instead of one. My grandmother poured the cognac, a morning ritual, from a crystal decanter into a small, thin crystal tumbler, which she then twirled around and held up to the light. "*Quelles jambes!* Would you just look at those legs!" she exclaimed as the thick, rich liquor dripped in perfectly even, tiny lines down the inside rim of the glass, burning a deep amber color in the early morning sun.

"I find it adds a little something to the day," she said to Nathan, pouring. "But one is enough!" she warned, holding up her plump index finger. "You need your strength, after all," she tittered. Nathan looked up at her with his mischievous eyes and smiled coyly, his nose in the tumbler. I felt uneasy and turned my bright red face away.

"I'm pleased that you are appreciative of such a fine thing," she said, patting his shoulder. "I never trust a man who doesn't like fine wines and good cognac."

* * *

My grandmother, who was extremely well read, spent hours in her sunroom discussing literature with Nathan. For some reason, she reserved these discussions for him, as if she thought I was incapable of discussing literature with her myself, or perhaps she simply thought it wasn't *comme il faut* for a young woman to show off her intellectual capabilities in this manner. I didn't let this bother me and just sat and listened as they argued heatedly about, for example, translations. Nathan insisted that Aylmer Maude's translations of Tolstoy were definitive. My grandmother countered that his point was moot since Tolstoy couldn't possibly translate well into a language as messy as English. Tolstoy, she insisted, had to be read in French. They argued also about the different movements in poetry. My grandmother didn't like *les espagnols,* which for her encompassed all Spanish-speaking poets, because she found all that magical realism too carefully orchestrated. Nathan said he disagreed categorically with that assessment. She told him with a snort that he was a romantic dreamer; he told her with a mercurial smile that she, too, was a romantic dreamer but unwilling to admit it.

"No, no, my dear young man, I'd *like* to be a romantic dreamer but I simply can't afford *not* to be a pragmatic and narrow-minded old lady."

* * *

We drank large quantities of wine, which we chose ourselves from the ancient, dust-covered *caves* with their rows of bottles that my grandmother said had been the favorites of great leaders and kings. She said she only opened them on special occasions and this visit from her beloved granddaughter classified as just that. Nathan became fascinated with the process of wine making and she took us on a long tour of the *chais,* the sheds where the wine was aged in oak casks.

Once, she even let Nathan read her cards. He told her that she would get married again in the not-too-distant future and that her new husband would be energetic and passionate. She liked this very much and opened a very fine bottle of champagne that she had bartered for a bottle of 1968 Chateau Laroq. As we toasted the wisdom of the cards, again and again, I did not tell her that I couldn't tell the difference between this particular champagne and a good Veuve Cliquot.

* * *

She threw a wine-tasting extravaganza, a seven-course dinner, accompanied by wines from all over France. She invited all the friends and relatives and wine connoisseurs from the neighborhood, explaining to us that this was not a real wine tasting, just a faux one. She introduced me to everyone as her long-lost American granddaughter. They told her that I looked very much like her, which pleased her and made her blush. No one ever mentioned my mother. This was not surprising, as the French never discussed family matters such as health, death, or divorce in public.

* * *

Nathan stayed for three weeks. He planned to return to Oaxaca for a few more months and then travel south to Guatemala.

The night before he left, as we lay curled together in his large bed, he told me that no matter where I was, he would always love me and that he admired me for going my own way.

His face was buried in the pillow when he said carefully, "I hope you've started going out with other people."

I threw the sheets back and began to dress in a blind rage.

"Shh," he said, "you'll wake everybody up. Come back here." He got up and pulled me back onto the bed. I struggled and kicked but he held me down. He began to tickle me, and I to punch him, until we both were laughing.

"Just promise me one thing," he said quietly, caressing my neck. "If you meet someone else, you'll let me know."

It seemed to me at that moment that I might wait for him forever.

"I promise," I said.

The next day he took the train back to Paris.

* * *

I WAS IN a torpor for the first few days. Hoping to distract me, my grandmother suggested a shopping trip to Paris, but I didn't want to leave the grounds of the chateau.

I began to dream of my mother again. One night, I opened my eyes to find her sitting at the foot of the large, canopied bed, smiling at me sadly. She wore a loose white nightgown and her thick hair hung limply around her pale face. Her lips were slightly open, as if she were about to speak to me.

"What? What?" I cried out, startled, blinking into the darkness. The white curtains rustled in the breeze.

* * *

WHILE MY GRANDMOTHER and I were walking through the pine forest one afternoon, she asked if I wouldn't like to stay in France and finish my studies at the Sorbonne. I could have her apartment off Avenue Victor Hugo. I remembered the dream of my mother sitting on the edge of my bed.

"*Bonne-maman,* do you ever dream of my mother?"

"Your mother?" She glanced at me suspiciously and there was a hard edge to her voice. "Why do you ask such a question?"

"Lately I've started dreaming about her again. I feel like she wants to talk, but she never does."

"Pff. You mustn't think about the past, *Céleste*," my grandmother warned, and we walked on.

* * *

A FEW DAYS before I was to leave, she again brought up the subject of my finishing college in Paris. She said she would introduce me to interesting people, and in the spring take me to her private box at Longchamps and Auteuil. Feeling fraudulent and unequipped for such a life, I told her with a certain coolness in my voice that I would have gone with Nathan to Mexico if I hadn't intended to return to my school in the States. She became despondent, sitting for hours in her rocking chair with a shawl draped over her shoulders, sipping a large snifter of brandy.

"You're so much like your mother," she muttered sadly.

"What did you and my mother fight about that night, *Bonne-maman*?" I asked.

She sighed deeply. She seemed to be considering the wisdom of telling me.

"It was about you," she finally said. "Nathalie wanted to come back to France with you. She was afraid your father wouldn't give her any money. I offered to give her all the money in the world if she would come back and live here with me. But she wanted to be in Paris, to put you in the bilingual school there, so you could be with other American children . . ." She paused and rocked, taking a small purse-lipped sip of her cognac. "I said I wouldn't have it. I said you would be sent to board at the French girls' *lycée* where all the Fleurance women went. Your mother wouldn't hear of it. So we fought, and then she took you and left."

I remembered my mother's bright, open face as we sat in an outdoor café in a Florence square. The sun was blinding as it ricocheted off the white paved stones and the fountain's lapping water. She sipped Sambuca and I an extra-sweet cappuccino. She asked me in French if I thought the Italian man at the next table was a baron or a count. I glanced at the handsome, curly-haired man with piercing blue eyes.

"He's a prince!" I said in a whisper.

"Well, then!" she said, and stealthily hiked her skirt up over her delicate knees. She glanced at me out of the corner of her eyes, giggling like a little girl.

"Stop it, *maman*!" I said, turning away in embarrassment.

She was so beautiful, he naturally turned his chair toward us and began a conversation. They talked about the museums.

"Do you know what my daughter said today about the Renaissance paintings of Jesus? She said, 'Why don't they let that poor man down?'"

He paid our bill and asked us to join him for dinner. This happened quite often, and my mother was always graceful and aloof, icy but charming with her bright coy laugh.

Only once did she leave me alone, sneaking out of our hotel room after I was asleep. I awakened to find her gone and ran out into the plush, quiet hallway with my bear in my arms. "*Maman!* Where are you!" I cried. Locked out of the room, I stood in the hallway, weeping and howling in terror and banging on the door. Someone must have called the night clerk, for he came and took me down to the kitchen and sat me and Monsieur Laroq up on a chopping block while the cooks and the waiters, off duty now and getting ready to go home, stayed to play with me and offered an array of desserts from the refrigerator. I ate two *bombas,* vanilla ice cream in a puff pastry with melted chocolate on top, and a slice of mocha cake. One young waiter named Antonio, who had a black mustache, made a rabbit out of a napkin and made it jump around.

The night concierge yelled at my mother when she came in, and threatened to call the police.

"Maybe you are French, madam," he cried, "but here in Italy we don't treat our children like that!"

She was humiliated and ashamed and told him to mind his own affairs as she jerked me away from my new friend Antonio and dragged me upstairs.

"We should've stayed with *Bonne-maman,*" I grumbled. "She never left me alone. If she knew you did, she'd be very angry at you."

My mother looked at me wide-eyed, as if I'd kicked her in the stomach.

At the end of August we ran out of money and went home. Our absence had not caused my father to return all worried and remorseful as she had hoped. In fact, he had taken to staying all week in his studio in the city. She did not cry anymore but paced our big, empty Connecticut house in her pale blue bathrobe, smoking and drinking scotch.

* * *

Remembering all this in a flash, I watched my stiff-backed grandmother rocking, a self-righteous look on her face, and I thought, *My God, she could have helped her, but she didn't!* Our lives could have been completely different. I was overwhelmed by a fury so sharp it pierced my chest and I could barely breathe. Having totally let go of my senses, I stood up and, before running from the room in tears, yelled at my grandmother, "If only you had helped! You killed her! It was your fault she died!"

* * *

I CLOSED the blinds, put the water pitcher back in the kitchen cupboard, and went to my desk. The letter I wrote was in French, and took me a long time to compose.

June 12
New York

Dear Bonne-maman,

The past few months have been very difficult ones for me as I've been forced through circumstance to look at the past. Getting married I suspect makes one review things that one doesn't particularly want to review. I was sorry to get your letter because I was hoping beyond hope that you would be able to make it to my wedding. I have no one but you from my mother's side and I feel the lack of contact with you deeply.

I need very much to apologize to you for what I said that day at the chateau. It has been so many years since her death and yet I can't seem to stop missing her. I also can't seem to remember what exactly happened. I would like to get better, to move beyond the past and live a happy and full life. I miss you terribly and often and if you still want me, I will come visit you. We will be in France in the middle of July for part of our honeymoon.

Please forgive me. Your devoted granddaughter,
Céleste

I licked two twenty-five-cent stamps and put them on the envelope. Abruptly, without considering, I took a wedding invitation from the pile of leftovers and stuck it in an envelope. I wrote Nathan's name, in care of the Grand Hotel, Matlan, Mexico, and put two stamps on the envelope. I ran out into the hall and dropped both letters into the mail chute before I could change my mind.

Fifteen

After I distributed the anthologies I asked the kids to sign my copy.

Dear Celeste please come to my high school next year. From Sir.

Thanks for being here. Love Shatisha.

Peace from Jhamal.

I learned so much thanx, Rosalia PS Thanx for the book of love poems. I read it all the way two times already.

Derrence wrote nothing but signed his poems with a grand, impressive signature. I'd printed four of his poems, one more than any other student.

Ellie Horowitz stood in the front, reading the anthology with great interest. "You kids wrote this?" she shouted. "I don't believe it! *You* kids? Jhamal, *you* wrote this beautiful love poem? Hell, I'd go out on a date with you if you wrote me poems like that."

"You wish," said Jhamal.

"Every word is theirs," I said.

"Do I get to sign your copy, too?" she asked.

"Of course." I handed it to her.

Dear Celeste, she wrote, *This isn't good-bye, I'll see you next fall. You're a pleasure to have around. Best wishes on your wedding day—Ellie Horowitz.*

After every student who wanted to had signed my copy, and I'd signed theirs, I stood at the front of the room trying to think of something to say. I knew that the chances of more than a handful of them making it to college were slim to none.

"You're all wonderful bright kids. You deserve prosperity and happiness. I hope you'll go on to college because you have a right to go. And if any one of you ever needs a letter of recommendation, Mrs. Horowitz will know where to find me."

They gazed at me with their inscrutable eyes.

"Okay, well, good-bye, then," I said.

"Good-bye, Celeste!" they shouted.

"Thanks for teaching us!"

"Yeah, thanks!"

"Have a good life and shit!"

I walked out into the hall, still empty and quiet. My heart felt heavy. I peered through the rectangle of glass in the door and saw Ellie Horowitz's mouth wide open in a shout as she resumed her lesson, pointing to something on the board. The kids were at their desks, talking to each other and half listening, looking bored. It seemed as if I'd never been there at all.

I gazed at the drawings on the blue walls of the hallway, listened to the hum of voices behind the closed door, and sighed. It was time to go.

I walked a few paces and a hand tapped my shoulder. I turned. It was Derrence, his gangly arms fidgeting at his sides.

"I read your story," he said in his absurdly low voice. "I liked it. It was good."

"You liked it, really?" I felt my face break into a smile.

"Yeah. It was easy to read," he said. "Now I'm reading James Baldwin. I like it," he said as if surprised. "It's good. Very interesting. I can understand almost everything." With that, he smiled and his metal braces flashed in the fluorescent light.

"Are you going to go to Freedom to Think?" I asked him.

"Yeah," he said vaguely. "And my mom said thank you for the books."

"Thanks, Derrence." I put out my hand and he shook it limply. Our eyes stayed locked for a long moment as we stood there, not knowing what else to say.

"And my mom says you must be one nice lady."

"You can still call me," I said. "Just to talk. About school or whatever."

He nodded gravely. "Thanks," he said. He stepped back and after a moment, waved.

I watched him until he disappeared into the classroom, then I walked out into the sultry day. The sky had turned the color of bruises. The streets and buildings glowed that strange green hue. Just as I got to the bus shelter, the sky opened up with a crack of lightning and rain began to fall with a loud clatter. I hadn't brought an umbrella. Of course. If Alex had been home, he would have reminded me. He listened to the weather report every morning. As I stood in a corner of the bus shelter looking out at the curtain of rain, I wondered why I couldn't remember to do the simplest things by myself.

The Eighty-sixth Street crosstown bus was crowded with sweaty, wet people in a bad mood. I was squeezed in near the back and watched the street to keep my mind off my discomfort. People were running with newspapers over their heads. Some stood under awnings, gaping at the rain. It was dark as nightfall outside.

At Central Park West, a very tall man stepped onto the bus and stood at the front, amidst the crowd of heads. His curly chestnut-colored hair, the designer sunglasses, his tailored European suit caught my eye and made me blink and stare.

Branko—my heart leapt, though I knew it was impossible.

I tried to get a better look at the figure but the crowd up front was too thick. I could not move forward, the aisle was still packed tight with people. As the bus swung around a double-parked car, the heads at the front all swayed at once in a wave and I caught another glimpse of his face. Although his eyes were hidden behind dark glasses, in that moment I saw his hair, the aquiline nose, his thin-lipped mouth again—and he so resembled Branko that my breath caught in my throat.

I kept my eyes on the spot where he stood to see if he would get off right after the park, but he stayed on. When the bus reached Madison, he was one of a torrent of people who poured out onto the sidewalk. Quickly I pushed my way to the back door.

As I stepped into a cold stream of water in the gutter and was hit in the face by a blast of rain, I questioned my sanity. I stood on the sidewalk, circling, looking for him in every direction. At last, I caught sight of his large frame looming above the others, moving swiftly down the avenue. He had opened an enormous black umbrella that swayed along a full two feet higher than the rest. The rain swept horizontally between the buildings, as if sprites were shaking out invisible sheets.

I picked up my pace, but still he remained half a block ahead of me. I followed him for several blocks, dodging umbrellas and passersby who stared at my rain-drenched clothes and face. He turned into a building on the corner and disappeared.

The building was a brick church whose sooty basement windows opened onto the street. The rain suddenly stopped, and I heard clapping from inside. I looked down into the room through a clean space in one of the windows and saw a crowd of people sitting in rows, facing a small podium. It was a peculiar sight, the dank, hot room completely packed with sweaty faces smiling and laughing as if the heat and rain were no bother to them at all. On a side door hung a sign, a white triangle in a circle on a blue background. There were cheers, followed by more clapping.

A man in his forties with a slender build and salt-and-pepper hair stood outside smoking a cigarette, watching me. He was wearing a T-shirt, jeans, and black lizard cowboy boots.

"What's going on in there?" I asked him, out of breath.

He looked me over with a peculiar smile. "A meeting. AA," he said.

"Why are they clapping?"

"They're celebrating people counting days." His dark eyes took me in. My hair was hanging in a wet clump over my face. I pushed it back and wiped water from my forehead with the back of my hand.

"Counting days?" I asked.

"You know, how many days they've been sober," he said. Smiling as he held up the smoking butt, he added, "My last vice." He chucked it toward the gutter. "Time to go in," he said. "Want to come?"

"No thanks," I said, ill at ease, wondering why he'd felt compelled to ask me in. "Did you see a very tall man in a suit go in about a minute ago?" I asked him.

"No," he said with a twinkle in his eye. "This is an anonymous program, you know what I mean?"

"Thanks," I said, a prickly hot flush rising to the surface of my skin. I abruptly turned east down the street.

* * *

A STARTLINGLY CLEAR image of Branko came to mind as I walked briskly toward home. It was of the first time I saw him, the first week of junior year, in my Advanced French Lit class, a fellow so tall he barely fit into the space between the desk and chair and kept shifting noisily, stretching his long legs and grumbling. The professor stopped speaking and stared with annoyance at this newcomer, who kept readjusting his body behind the tiny desk. His hands were gigantic, the white Bic pen he held looked like a cigarette in his fingers. His hair was curly and chestnut-colored, like my mother's. He had a large square chin, a long, narrow mouth, and a small, straight nose, slightly rounded at the end. His features were so perfect, he looked like Michelangelo's David. And like the David, he was enormous. Much too big for someone my size to date.

"That's not a Parisian accent you have," his deep voice boomed high above me as I was gathering my books to leave.

"Bordeaux," I said. "My grandmother owns a vineyard there."

"Really? How interesting."

He told me he'd lived in Paris, on Avenue Foche, from the age of six to sixteen. He'd gone to the Ecole Bilingue, he said as we walked down the hall together.

"I almost went there," I said, surprising myself. I never offered such information to strangers; I didn't like to talk to people I didn't know, so I rarely met anyone new unless I was with Candace, who did the talking for both of us.

Out on the street, he stood calmly, stretching to get out the cricks, in no hurry to go. "This is a gut for me," he said, patting his flat stomach. "I need to get my grades up. I took a year and a half off. Went to Vail. Taught a little skiing. Hiked in the summer."

"I guess that's why I've never seen you before," I said.

"I saw you, though. I saw you the first day of your freshman year when you were registering. My name's Branko Yeretich. B-R-A-N-K-O. Want to smoke a joint?"

"I don't like pot."

"Well, how about a drink, then?"

It was not like me to follow strangers home, certainly not sober. Except that he did not feel like a stranger to me even then; it seemed as if I'd known him for a very long time but hadn't seen him in a while.

He shared an off-campus house with some upperclassmen, a red house that stood on stilts on a steep hill. A rickety outdoor staircase led up to the first floor from the sharply sloping lawn.

He'd turned the downstairs dining room and living room into his "quarters," as he called them. African masks, Indian statuettes, ancient spears and swords hung on the walls. Above the desk was a series of large black-and-white framed photographs of a swarthy man whose features were much like Branko's. In each picture the man was smoking a nonfilter cigarette, holding it in different ways, as if it were a prop. In some he seemed pensive, in others he wore a cryptic smile.

"Your father?" I asked. Branko nodded without looking up. He was busy rolling himself a joint.

"Where did you get all this stuff?" I asked.

"Oh, traveling," he said lightly. Thoughts of Nathan loomed fresh and sharp in my mind.

"So where's the fancy stereo?" I said, and laughed a little. He lit the joint.

"Haven't had time to buy one yet," he said, holding his breath.

Nathan would like this guy, I thought.

"How about a rum and Coke?" he said.

"Sure."

We sat around for the rest of the afternoon, talking about France, and feeling like strangers in both countries, never quite fitting in either place. Finally he glanced at his watch, rubbed his stomach, and shouted, "Dinnertime!"

We wobbled back down toward the main campus, discussing the college's different eating clubs and cafeterias. I told him I hadn't joined an eating club yet.

"Come have dinner with me at Delta Phi. I wouldn't join a fraternity for all the tea in China—but their food is excellent! Be my guest tonight, then tomorrow you can join if you like. Then we can have dinner together every night!"

* * *

A CRACK OF THUNDER jolted me out of my reverie. I found myself standing in front of a fancy bathing suit shop, staring at the headless white mannequins in bright flowery bikinis, my reflection superimposed over them in the window. The rain fell in huge drops around me, my T-shirt and jumper were completely drenched, my hair hung in my face, dripping. *No wonder that man asked you into the meeting,* I thought.

When I got to our apartment, the air-conditioning sunk right into my bones and I began shivering. I stripped off my clothes and got a towel from the bathroom to dry my face and hair. In the mirror, my stunned reflection stared back at me. I looked at myself closely and could not fill in the space between the person I was looking at and me. It seemed someone else was standing behind me, watching.

I put on a bathrobe and went back to the living room, where I noticed the new crystal decanter from Tiffany standing on the bartop, filled with brandy. I took a step toward it. Out of the corner of my eye I saw the red light on the message machine blinking. I went over and rewound the tape. There were six hang-ups, no messages. Alex.

Then I heard Lucia's lumbering, saturnine voice asking why I hadn't called her in a week.

The last one was from Anna, who said she was in town at her sister Theresa's, and asked me to call her back.

I looked up Theresa's number in my phone book.

"Yello-o-o?" Anna's voice sang out after the first ring, startling me.

"Anna, it's me."

"*Yes,* Celeste! Eighteen days and counting," her voice sang. "How do you feel?"

I didn't know what to say. "Alex is in L.A.," I murmured incongruously.

"Celeste? Is something the matter?"

"Yes, in fact, everything is the matter and I don't know *what* is wrong."

"Pre-wedding jitters?" she said sympathetically. "Want to have dinner with me tonight?"

"Must be the week for family dinners," I said gloomily. "Aurelia was in town."

"And how *is* the prodigal mother? Still taking on the Dark Continent single-handedly?" she asked airily. In the next breath she told me to meet her at her sister's at seven.

I had a couple of hours to kill so I stretched out on the bed, where I tossed and turned and fought to rid my mind of images of Branko.

After a while I gave up and lay there as the storm's darkness filled the room.

* * *

The first weekend of junior year, there was a big dance at one of the fraternities. Branko and I stood together by the keg, getting mildly drunk. A premed junior who had been my TA in Psychology came over and started talking to us. Branko ignored him, his gaze wandering aimlessly as the fellow talked.

After a while, Branko said to me, "I think I'm going to go downtown to He's Not Here. Want to come?"

I looked up at him, puzzled. I was having a good time, enjoying the attention. I shook my head. He leaned down and said in French, "If you stay here you're going to get into trouble."

"*Ça va,*" I told him, smiling vaguely.

So he left and I began to dance with the premed student.

"Parlay voo Fransay? Wee, wee, madame. Vous es trez beautifool," said the premed student in my ear. I laughed. As we danced close I thought of how nice it would be to wake up next to someone again, to be held and rocked to sleep. I wanted to make love again.

But when I awakened in his bed near dawn, sick and disoriented, I felt homesick for Nathan. At first light, I left the premed student's ground-floor apartment through the window. He never stirred.

* * *

Tuesday, after French class, Branko caught me in the hall.

"Want to come over?"

"Why not?" I shrugged, trying to be calm, cool.

"You were bad this weekend," he said with a teasing smile, shaking his index finger at me.

"Yeah, well I don't want to talk about it if you don't mind," I said stiffly.

He had bought an enormous sleek black stereo with speakers that came up to my waist.

"Check it out," he said, and put on a record by The Cars. *"I don't mind you coming here/And wasting all my time."* The walls held as the little glass panes in the French doors rattled.

"Jesus Christ!" I yelled over the bass. "I was only kidding about getting a stereo."

He poured rum and pineapple juice in diamond-cut crystal glasses that reflected a rainbow of light.

After a second drink, he said, "We're alike in some ways. It's funny how we found each other."

"I think it's more like you found me," I answered, still peeved that he had mentioned my weekend indiscretion.

"Whatever. We both have French backgrounds. My father died when I was fifteen. We've both lost a parent." He began to roll a joint.

"How do you know about my mother?" I was getting more defensive by the moment.

"Someone told me," he said.

Who knew about my mother? No one knew except Candace. There were several people at the college from my high school. Maybe it had come from them. It annoyed me that people would label me as someone who'd lost a parent, as if that somehow determined my character.

"My mother died when I was ten," I said coolly. "I don't remember her very well."

"Why do you say that?" he asked without malice, bemused by my statement. "Losing my father was the worst thing that ever happened to me in my life. I try to keep his face fresh in my mind. Sometimes he fades, and it scares the shit out of me. That's why I hung the pictures up."

* * *

In October, the trees on campus turned to burnt sienna. Leaves tumbled and waltzed in the wind across the main green. After French class, Branko said, "I have a surprise for you," and led me outside. Parked at the curb was a silver convertible Porsche.

"It's a '65. What do you think?"

"I don't know anything about cars," I said. "It's cute."

"Cute!" he cried. "Come on." He jumped over the door like I'd seen men do in the movies and opened the passenger side for me. I shut the door, took a few steps back, and took a flying leap in myself. Students were stopping to look. I felt like we were in a James Bond movie, escaping.

He drove up to the apple orchard that stood on a hill just beyond the town. It was still warm enough to keep the top down.

"It's good to get away," he said. "See what's going on in the world. That campus is too fucking small." There was a long silent time as the world blurred and roared. "Do you want to go out with me?"

"No," I said. "I'm in love with someone else. It's been six years."

"Ooh," he said, sucking in air. "That's bad."

"It's just love," I said with a trace of cynicism.

"I really like you," he turned for a moment to look at me. "I feel like I can be honest with you."

"I like you too. Going out would just mess things up."

"See what I mean," he said. "We're too much alike." With that, he drove off the dirt road and into the orchard, slaloming between the trees, in and out, going fast. The engine howled.

I felt free for the first time in months. Laughing, I reached up and tried to pull a gold-red apple off a tree. My effort reminded me of the carousel rides of my childhood, how sometimes you got a wooden stick with which you tried to pull down the golden ring. When you got it, you felt special, as if angels were watching over you. As we swung under the branches an apple tumbled into my lap.

"Where did you get the money to buy the car?" I asked him, biting into the gift apple that was sour and sweet and a little hard.

"I have some money," he said evenly.

He told me that his mother's family from Kentucky was wealthy. "They started in the coal business, but now they own racehorses and real estate." He told me his father had been a Serbian prince whose family was thrown out of Belgrade after Tito seized power. His father had then lived in Paris and New York, attended high society functions, and lived the expatriate royal's life. He met Branko's mother at a society ball. The father had named his son after a great-uncle, an enormous bear of a man who had apparently been involved in the conspiracy to assassinate Archduke Ferdinand.

Branko told me his parents had separated after his father came down with lung cancer. "She killed him," he told me, his voice flat. "My mother broke his heart. He was the best man I've ever known. We were like this," he crossed his long fingers, holding them up for me to see. "I miss him so badly that some days I can barely stand it."

* * *

I MET BRANKO'S mother and older brother Roderic in November, during parents' weekend. I had just waved good-bye to my father and Anna and was walking home across the main campus. Mrs. Yeretich and her two sons were strolling up the cement path. The wind was blowing and leaves twirled frantically around their feet. I turned away, uncomfortable in my knowledge, when he cried out to me in his booming voice.

"Miz Miller!"

I stopped as they came toward me. Mrs. Yeretich was tall and thin, blond, with a pale square face and high cheekbones. She wore a dark mink coat and exquisite two-toned Chanel pumps. Roderic looked like Branko, but shorter and darker; he had a tight, closed-lip smile. I felt sorry for anyone who had to spend his life being compared to Branko.

Roderic took my hand and planted a soundless little kiss on my knuckles. Mrs. Yeretich smiled, a wide, luxurious smile that didn't seem connected with anything that was going on. Branko seemed cranky and out of sorts. In the past I'd only seen him like that when he was hungry. I'd learned to get him to food quickly when his mood changed suddenly that way.

The four of us talked for a few moments about absolutely nothing, Branko edgy and fidgety all the while. Before they left, Roderic handed me an engraved card with his name and phone number on it. He asked me to call him if I was ever in the city. "We'll go out to dinner, go dancing or something." There was a suggestive gleam in his eyes. I stood there, stunned, holding his card.

* * *

Branko had a friend in the Navy who sent him postcards of naked girls from exotic ports of call. An auto mechanic named Henry showed up at Branko's off-campus house now and then, smelling of diesel oil. He had also befriended a call girl he'd met at a party in the city a few years before; occasionally she called him collect in the middle of the night to discuss her love life. But certain people simply didn't interest him.

Candace and I lived in a small two-bedroom apartment that year, in a university-owned high-rise. The first time he came to visit, the three of us sat around the kitchen table drinking beers, when she began to talk in her usual loud, enthusiastic voice about the goings-on around campus. Branko pretended interest, stared off, drummed his fingers on the tabletop, stifled yawns.

When he left, Candace told me she didn't like him. "Who does he think he is, just quitting school and going off *skiing* for a year and a half?" He had broken one of her cardinal rules: you don't drop out of school, no matter what is wrong. "He's a spoiled rich kid with an attitude problem," she said dismissively.

Yet she forgave Nathan the same transgression. But then, Nathan had a deep fondness for Candace and thought she had an excellent sense of humor.

* * *

Branko was fascinated by the waiflike girls with shaved heads or green hair or pierced noses, who seemed on the brink of emotional collapse and wore white lipstick and black nail polish and smoked nonfilter cigarettes. Spotting one of them sitting alone in a dark corner of the pub, Branko would get up, stroll over, and engage her in conversation. Having listened in on too many of these discussions, I knew the topics varied from the girls' devotion to punk rock, their militant feminist ideals, their drug-war stories, their infinite boredom with life, to how their daddies were threatening to cut them off. I found that they were always willing to talk at great length as long as it was about themselves. I told Branko that he was wasting his time.

"I don't know, I think she could use Doctor Branko's hot beef injection," he'd say with a smile.

Mercifully, these relationships never lasted more than a few days.

Sixteen

Branko took me to stay at his mother's Fifth Avenue apartment for a weekend just before the Christmas holidays. The apartment had high, eggshell-colored walls with hand-carved moldings and large windows. The living and dining rooms had been carefully decorated in cream and rose. Delicate egg-shaped objets d'art decorated the dark wood side tables, shelves, and mantelpiece.

She threw a dinner party in Branko's honor. Cocktail hour went on forever. Finally, around ten o'clock, Branko and I were directed to sit together at one end of the long oval dining table opposite his mother and Roderic—the host couples at opposing ends of the table. Branko, whose face was flushed from the drinks he'd had before dinner, proceeded to pour us glass after glass of expensive white wine. By the end of the main course he was mumbling and laughing to himself. Suddenly he tipped his chair onto two legs, raised his arms, snapped his fingers, and began to sing a Serbian folk song in his booming voice. Mrs. Yeretich's guests stopped talking and stared at him for an awkward moment, then went back to their conversations as though nothing were amiss.

Once the guests left, I began to wash dishes, hoping to make up for whatever gaffe I had helped Branko commit. Mrs. Yeretich told me in her pleasant, neutral voice to leave it, the maid would clean in the morning. But I insisted, and accidentally smashed to bits her glass espresso decanter from Italy.

"What a pity," she said in that smooth tone, "it can't be replaced."

Later, Branko tucked me into the guest-room bed, which had a big satin spread that matched the velvet drapes. "Good night, little devil," he said, kissing my forehead. "Don't worry about the espresso pot, she'll get over it."

The next day we went shopping on Fifth Avenue. He bought himself a navy blue cashmere coat at Saks that was as big as a blanket, and he bought me a pair of black leather boots that were so soft they felt like socks. At my insistence, we went to six different stores looking for Mrs. Yeretich's glass espresso pot—but she'd been right, of course; it could only be purchased in Italy.

"Can't fly to Milan this weekend!" Branko said, clapping his hands together and rubbing them briskly.

"Branko, it's not funny," I said in a pinched tone.

* * *

After the Christmas holidays, he decided to have a serious relationship. He said he was lonely, and needed to "ground himself a little."

He found Estelle, a tall, green-eyed freshman. She was considered one of the great beauties of the incoming class. I liked her fine, although it seemed fairly apparent that they had trouble conversing.

About three weeks later he stopped by and sat at my kitchen table, all fidgety and unfocused.

"What's the matter, Branko? You're fidgeting like you're in French class."

"I don't want to go out with Estelle anymore but I don't know how to tell her."

"Just tell her it isn't working out."

"Can't you tell her for me? Make something up. Tell her you and I are in love. Hell, she'd never know the difference."

"Come on, Branko. Do your own dirty work."

Then came Titsia, a Dutch girl with impenetrable blue eyes, a great beauty of the sophomore class. She didn't like it when he stopped in the street to talk to me. At parties, she'd stand a little to the side, scowling, as he engaged Candace and me in conversation.

Branko liked to dance with me because my mother had taught me "le rock," the French jitterbug, Branko's favorite. But after he started dating Titsia he never asked me to dance, and this pissed me off.

One day after French class he told me she was crazy.

"I could've told you that," I said with a snort.

"Bat shit," he said. "Completely. Plus, she's a switch-hitter. I don't like that. Too much competition as it is."

In the spring he had a romance with a senior named Margaret. She was his date to the Delta Phi spring semiformal. They stumbled in, laughing as they held each other up. She wore a strapless dress of green sequins. He left her propped against a column and took me out to the balcony that overlooked a garden. He handed me a white pill.

"What's this?"

"A Quaalude," he mumbled. "Great for sex. Margaret's got a dealer in the city. I just advanced her five hundred dollars to buy a pile as high as Mont Blanc. She's going to sell them here and pay me back, and meanwhile I'll get a supply for free." After a moment, he said, "God, I can't figure her out."

"And that makes her interesting, right?" I made a sour face and swallowed the pill with a swig of gin and tonic.

I woke up the next morning beside one of Branko's housemates, a guy named Ned whose father had recently died in a plane crash. At first I had no idea where I was. Then I saw Ned lying on his belly, his pale, high-waisted behind exposed to the world, one arm thrown over the side of the bed. The last thing I remembered was walking out of the party into the crisp spring night and telling him to read Emily Dickinson's death poems because they would help him deal with his grief.

I stumbled out into the hall in my rumpled evening dress and ran smack into Branko, who apparently was just returning from Margaret's, his bow tie askew and his eyes bloodshot.

"Celeste," he said, shaking his head, a deeply pained expression on his face. "Jesus Christ."

"Branko," I said, my voice trembling, "I'm no slut—I've only slept with five guys my entire life!" I ran for the door and didn't look back.

A month later Margaret came back from a long weekend engaged to her ex-boyfriend, Lance, who'd graduated the previous spring and now lived in San Francisco.

* * *

In April, Nathan showed up at Candace's and my apartment unannounced. He was gaunt and unshaven and his skin ashen.

"My God, where have you been?" I said, my stomach knotting as I stepped away from the door. "You look like shit, Nathan."

"We haven't heard from you in months!" Candace added, wringing her hands.

He sat down at the kitchen table. Candace turned to the stove and put the kettle on for tea. She took some whole wheat bread out of the fridge and stuck the slices in her toaster.

"I was in Nicaragua, hanging in the mountains with some Sandinistas. I got dysentery and for, like, a couple of weeks, I thought I was going to die.

"That's why you haven't heard from me," he explained, looking at me with haunted, exhausted eyes.

Branko showed up with a paper he needed to have typed and I introduced them, feeling jittery and confused.

"Yeretich. Yeretich," said Nathan thoughtfully, emerging momentarily from his daze. "You wouldn't happen to be related to the Yeretich who was involved in the conspiracy to assassinate Archduke Ferdinand?"

"In my arms!" Branko cried, coming forward with his long arms outstretched. Nathan glanced at me with mock concern, an eyebrow raised. "That was Great-great-uncle Branko!" Branko reached into the breast pocket of his rugby shirt, "Look here, I have a joint of gold Colombian . . . "

Nathan smiled. "It's good to be back," he said.

"So, the point here," said Candace thoughtfully, "is that in order to get Prince Branko to part with his pot, one needs to be an expert on World War I?"

Branko laughed, and passed Candace the joint first.

A little while later the four of us drove downtown in the Porsche and sat in He's Not Here and drank pitchers of beer and shots. Branko and Nathan played pinball for shots. Nathan lost, but nothing of consequence seemed to be discussed.

On the way home, Branko said, "Now, this is the kind of guy I see you with."

Nathan squeezed me to his bony chest as I sat between them, straddling the gear shift.

"I want to be the godfather of your firstborn child," Branko said.

"You've got a deal," said Nathan. "You can be our sugar daddy."

"Wait a second!" Candace said from the back. "Celeste said I could be the godmother of her first child. Is that going to work out, Prince Branko, or are we going to fight over the poor kid?"

"No fighting allowed," I said.

At that instant, the future seemed perfectly clear and bright. I saw Branko as an important, famous businessman, a philanthropist who would find revolutionary ways to help the poor and suffering; in ten years Candace would be the highest-ranking female banker in the U.S.; and Nathan and I would be expatriates living in some far-off land, raising brilliant bilingual children, and writing novels read by the entire world.

I felt empowered, unstoppable, courageous.

I thought we would accomplish great things. I never imagined that success would come at the price of facing terrible, difficult choices, and taking responsibility for their results.

Nathan stayed a week and then went on to Houston to visit his parents, whom he hadn't seen in a year.

He called from there to tell me he'd decided to stay. His father had gotten him a low-level job at Exxon, and Nathan had enrolled at the University of Houston for the summer semester, to try to make up some credits. When he called me with the news, his voice was flat and toneless.

* * *

THAT SUMMER Branko took me to Block Island, Martha's Vineyard, and to the Hamptons. One Friday he drove me out to Amagansett to stay with a group of friends who'd rented a house on the beach. We left New York at two in the morning. I was terrified of the crazy way he was driving, but I sat back and watched the road fly past, because I knew I would never get hurt as long as I was with him. When I wasn't with him, bad things happened to me. Branko was my guardian angel, even if he made the two-and-a-half-hour drive to Amagansett in one hour and twenty-five minutes.

I remember the white-hot beach, the wind blowing sand into my eyes, the waves big and threatening, and a blue flag flapping above the lifeguard stand.

"Come into the water, Celeste," Branko urged. I shook my head. "Don't be scared, I won't let you drown. It's really thrilling."

In the water, he held my hand. "Okay, we're going to have to go under this one," he said as an enormous wave rushed toward us, foam curling over its crest. We ducked and the wave crashed over, pulling the sand out from under my feet and knocking me over. Branko never lost his balance and never let go of my hand, and I knew as long as I didn't let go, I'd be safe.

* * *

I ALLOWED NATHAN to string me along for one more year, with his love letters and phone calls, and one visit at Christmas. But just before my graduation, he took off for Nicaragua again and I realized that he was never going to settle down. I couldn't support the rage—the sadness was nothing by comparison—the rage was like lye poured into my mouth, and me fighting to spit it out, to not swallow, as it seeped into my esophagus and stomach.

I began to stick very close to Branko, who always made sure I got home at night. Sometimes I slept on his couch when the trip home seemed too much to handle.

One night he found me in his bathroom after a party, my hands wrapped around the toilet bowl; I was retching. He bent down to wash my forehead with a cold, damp cloth.

"You're going to have to let him go, Celeste," he said gently.

I burst into tears and began howling as I crumpled into a ball. Branko stretched his legs out around me and took me in his arms. For a long time he rocked me without a word. Hours later I awakened curled up in his arms. He was asleep, sitting up with his back against the door.

* * *

THAT SPRING I went to visit Columbia University after I'd been accepted into the graduate program in Comparative Lit. Branko suggested I call his brother Roderic, who was still taking courses there as a Continuing Ed student. I was afraid to go up to 116th Street alone anyway, so I did. He offered to give me a tour of the campus.

He didn't like Columbia—the classes were too large, the administration a bureaucratic bourgeois hellhole, the neighborhood rife with drug addicts and bums. He took me to a health food restaurant overgrown with tropical plants and told me he'd given up meat, alcohol, cigarettes, pills, and marijuana. He was studying yoga intensively and sociology casually.

"Is Branko still in denial about our father?" he asked after we'd been served large tumblers of carrot juice.

"What do you mean?" I regretted immediately that I'd asked that question, because I didn't want to hear what Roderic had to say.

"Our father was a playboy and a drunk. He loved Branko—handsome, athletic like him—but he used to force me to ski even though I hated it and had a bad leg. He called me a coward. My mother would take my side against them, that's why Branko is angry at her."

I sat there, mouth agape. Roderic smiled evenly as if he were enjoying himself, but I could see that he wasn't calm, his blood was pumping furiously through the artery in his neck. There was something alight in his eyes.

"My father completely manipulated Branko." After a while he added in a clipped murmur, "God, you really are pretty but you are clueless, Celeste."

* * *

On the last day of exams week, the final deadline for late paper submissions, Branko walked up to me in the post office.

"Celeste!" he said, rubbing his hands together and cocking his head, "I've been looking for you everywhere. How about typing up a history paper for me? I'll pay you."

"I don't want your money, you jerk. Bring it over right now."

"Problem is, I haven't finished it. It's a ten-er. I have four pages done."

I looked at the clock on the wall. It was eleven in the morning. "That's it, Branko baby, you're going to be here another semester for sure."

"Can you come over? I'll write. You type. You can catch a tan on the lawn."

As he finished each page he would run down the rickety steps of his house and bring it to where I sat on a pillow in the grass with the typewriter in front of me on a crate. I was wearing the bathing suit he'd bought me the summer before in Amagansett.

Branko's last college paper was on the social conditions of the peasantry in the prewar Austro-Hungarian Empire. His thesis was that they were to blame for their lack of education, the landed gentry having offered them every opportunity for advancement. He'd found only a few quotes to substantiate his argument, citations taken out of context and originally used in the textbook to prove the converse.

"Branko, your professor isn't going to like this, I'm afraid."

"What do I give a shit if he likes it? My father told me this and it's the truth."

He cracked open our first beers at three o'clock. An hour later, I wasn't even proofreading for typos. At four-fifty, he grabbed the last sheet from my hand.

"Yes!" he cried. "Adios, college!"

* * *

In New York, he worked for an investment bank for a while before starting his own venture capital company called Baobab, after the tree in his favorite book, *The Little Prince*.

Branko gave seed money to companies who built miracle-seeking medical inventions: a leg and back brace for paraplegics that would make them walk again; a "breakthrough" hearing aid that was implanted in the inner ears of the stone deaf. Nothing came of them, but he kept trying, looking. He joined Greenpeace and the Rainforest Alliance; he funded Save the Whales so that the organization could patrol international waters in search of Japanese whaling vessels.

* * *

One day he met a six-foot red-headed model on the subway. He told me their eyes locked above the heads of the other passengers. She got off at the same stop and handed him her phone number. Her name was Josie.

She had a pale face with a perfect, thin nose and large hazel eyes. She was friendly and open and I liked to look at her. She loved to dance, and at parties she and I rolled back the rugs and contorted ourselves into strange invented dances from mythical countries, holding postures as Branko watched from the sidelines, amused.

I told him I thought she was the one. But he shook his head. He told me she was on the rebound. A few months before they'd met, she'd come home and found her husband shot to death. There was blood everywhere, splattered on the walls and floor. Apparently he'd been shot over drugs. Branko was vague. He told me she woke up screaming every night. She wanted no commitments. After a short while, they parted amicably.

* * *

It was my twenty-second birthday and Candace and I were sitting in the kitchen discussing our plans for the evening when there was a knock on the door. We stared at each other for a long moment; the buzzer in the lobby hadn't sounded. She looked through the peephole and opened the door, sighing heavily. Nathan stood there, wearing a leather jacket and biker boots. He was carrying a large black motorcycle helmet.

"You know, Nathan, this is growing old," Candace said quietly.

Without a word he took three bottles of Veuve Cliquot champagne out of his knapsack and placed them on the kitchen table.

"Happy birthday, Celeste," he said evenly.

"Happy birthday, Nathan," I said.

He told us he'd recently taken a job working as the manager of a liquor store in Cambridge. He hadn't liked Texas or Texans, they were loud and obsessed with the size of things. The job at Exxon hadn't worked out either. He was considering reapplying to Harvard. Candace was right, it was getting old.

Much later, we went to bed on the futon in the living room. I was too drunk to be able to appreciate his hands caressing me. He tried everything, but I only lay there as if I were part of the mattress. I thought that his hold over me might be waning.

In the morning, feeling like an old building with no doors or windows to protect it from the wind, I said, "Nathan, I don't want to see you again."

He nodded slowly, and watched me as he dressed, taking his time as if this were the most normal morning in the world. Finally, he took his helmet, and left without a sound.

I lay there in the gray morning light, feeling an emptiness unlike anything I'd known. It seemed I'd finally reached that place called The Future that I had so often contemplated while in college. But The Future didn't look anything like I'd thought it would. I didn't understand what had gone wrong.

* * *

When I came home from my six-week language program in Russia to an empty apartment, to Candace gone, Branko was the only person I called. Two days passed before I was able to face talking to him.

"Branko, I don't know what to do," I said into the receiver. "Candace left for good."

"It's over a guy, right?"

I didn't say anything.

"Just hang on," he said, "I'll be right over."

He arrived with a frosty bottle of Stolichnaya, a welcome-home present. Sitting in the kitchen that was still filled with Candace's presence, I waited for emotion to overtake me. I waited and waited, just sipping at the shot glass of thick, cold Stoli Branko had placed before me.

"Why?" I finally asked him quite calmly.

"Why what?" He waited for my response. I felt exhausted, drained of strength.

"Why anything, Celeste? Why my father? Why your mother?" After a pause he added, "It was always an imbalanced relationship."

Whatever he meant by that, I didn't want to know.

* * *

We resumed our old habit of having dinner together at least once a week, and going to a party or a film from time to time. Several years passed.

Then one lonely night, much like any other night, I didn't want to go home alone. Something about the darkness, the empty streets, the late hour, terrified me. Branko was matching me shot for shot. If only we could stay in the cozy neighborhood Irish bar, McNamara's or whatever, until the sun came up, but they finally turned the lights on and told us to go home. I told him I was afraid and he came back to my apartment.

We undressed in total silence and darkness and stretched out on the futon, where I'd been sleeping since my return from Moscow. I hoped I was doing the right thing. His body was both too familiar to me and too unknown.

Afterwards he lay on his back in the dark for a few minutes, then said, "I have to go."

"Why?"

"My eyes—my contact lenses are going to dry up and blind me."

"Take them out, you can put them in a glass of water or something."

"No. I gotta go. I'll call you tomorrow."

* * *

He didn't call for three weeks. We hadn't gone that long without speaking since we'd met. Furious, scared, I finally made the first move.

"Branko," I said, "what the hell is wrong with you? We've been friends for years. Why are you treating me like a one-night stand?"

There was a long silence.

"We could've at least discussed it," I continued. "You're avoiding me." He didn't say anything for a while.

"I'm sorry, Celeste. I feel like . . . I feel I've done something very, very wrong."

"We were drunk, what's the problem? All these years I thought you wanted to sleep with me."

"My life's completely out of control, Celeste. Listen, give me some time, all right? I need to think about things."

* * *

He disappeared for two more months.

When he finally called on New Year's Day, he sounded as normal as if we'd spoken only days before. I was angry, but also relieved. We agreed to meet at a Mexican restaurant on Columbus Avenue the following evening.

He ordered immediately, two burritos, a taco, an enchilada, and a chili releno. "And make them really spicy," he told the waitress. The whites of his eyes sparkled like new china and for once, there were no purple circles beneath them.

"Anything to drink?"

"A club soda with a lime for me," Branko said, sitting back.

"A club soda?" I said. "Why go to a Mexican restaurant if you're not going to drink margaritas? Come on, Branko, have a margarita with me."

He shook his head solemnly. "I quit," he said. "Just for today."

"What do you mean, just for today? You drank yesterday but you won't drink today?"

"I mean I'm choosing not to drink today."

"Well, do you mind if *I* have one?" I asked irritably.

"Not at all."

I ordered a margarita and a couple of tacos. But he had taken the fun out of it; we would not be partying tonight.

Sitting back in his chair, he sighed, and said, "That night that we . . . you know . . . I felt so horrible about it. It was a real low for me. I care about you, Celeste. You're my friend. I'm so sorry."

"Listen, we've been friends a long time. We had a lot to drink. It doesn't matter."

"But it *does* matter. It matters."

There was a long silence. The waitress brought our drinks.

"You know what else?" he said, drinking half of his club soda in one gulp. "I feel like I haven't accomplished a goddamn thing in my life."

"You're twenty-nine, Branko, don't panic."

"It's not that. If you died tomorrow, you'd leave something tangible. Your stories. That's important. I haven't done anything."

"You've saved a couple of whales," I said, and laughed. He didn't crack a smile.

"I'm serious, Celeste."

Our dinners arrived, covered with brown sauce. We ate for a while without talking.

"Maybe my biggest accomplishment will be to quit drinking," he said.

"I thought you already quit."

"It's been two months, but every day I say it's just for today." After a moment he added, taking a deep breath, "I'm in so much fucking pain . . ." His voice trailed off. After a while he said, "One day you look around and say, wait a minute, where's my life? But I'll tell you something, compared to most, my bottom was pretty high."

"Your bottom was pretty high? What the hell are you talking about?"

He said calmly, "I didn't end up in the gutter like some people. Some people have to lose everything before they quit. Some people never quit. You hit one bottom and then just go right on through, down to the next one. You lose your job, your family. You might end up in the fucking street, and still not stop. It's a total miracle that I quit when I did. And it was all because of you—because of that night!"

"Jesus Christ, Branko, I didn't think I was that lousy in bed."

He smiled, and I noticed in the pale candlelight that he was blushing. I felt like I was ten years old and this grown-up was trying to explain sex to me for the first time. I had only the vaguest idea of what he was getting at.

"What would it take—what would it take, Celeste, for *you* to quit?"

"You are really bumming me out," I said, and tried to laugh.

"You know, we've had some really good times together. I'm going to Vail tomorrow for a while, that place always has a way of rejuvenating me. Will you do something with me when I get back?"

"Sure, what?"

"I'd like to take you somewhere, a surprise, will you just come?"

"Sure," I said glumly. "If it'll make you happy."

* * *

He walked me a few blocks north.

"When you first quit drinking, they tell you to stay away from people, places, and things that make you want to drink."

"Who's they?"

"Other drunks who stopped drinking. For me, you're one of those people I had to stay away from. That's why I haven't called you."

"Jesus Christ, Branko," I said, my voice knocked out of me. "Fuck you."

At Columbus and Seventy-seventh, he stopped. The wind whipped through the deserted school yard on the corner, sending bits of paper and old cigarette butts scurrying through the fence. He threw his arms around me and squeezed me tightly. With my face pressed up against his chest I felt even more like a child. I looked up at him under the street lamp and smiled weakly.

"I love you, Branko," I said, my eyes filling with tears.

"So. I'll call you in a few weeks, when I get back."

"Definitely," I said.

"I love you, too." He stepped back, looked me over with serious eyes. "Be good, Celeste. Try to take care of yourself." With that, he zipped his down coat to his neck. I stood at the corner, watching him stoop against the icy wind as he walked away. At Seventy-sixth he turned and waved.

A strange and frightening thought passed through my mind in that instant: *You'll never see him again.*

I wanted to shout at him to stop, to turn around, come back with me to my place, or come sit downstairs in the corner bar. But I let him go.

I turned and headed home, feeling the icy wind in my bones.

* * *

A week later, in Vail, Branko was skiing fifty miles an hour down a narrow catwalk in over a foot of powder snow when the tips of his skis sank and stuck, catapulting him out of his bindings and sending him headfirst into a tree. His ski partner found him moments later. On arrival at the hospital, Branko was brain-dead, but his heart went on beating resolutely for three days.

Seventeen

I TURNED and looked at Alex's digital clock on the bedside table. It was a quarter to seven; I would be late meeting Anna. I felt exhausted as I dragged myself off the bed and went to the closet to search for something to wear. I slipped a sleeveless dress over my head and went into the bathroom to quickly wash my face and brush my hair.

* * *

THE DOOR OF Theresa's flat was open so I walked in. Anna was standing by the living room dry bar shaking up a jigger of martinis next to two frozen martini glasses. My taste buds ignited, anticipating the sting of icy gin in a frosty glass. The heat and noise outside had been appalling but the apartment was cool and quiet.

"You look lovely. Lovely!" Anna said, setting the jigger down. When she was ebullient it meant something was worrying her. She was dressed in a light green linen suit with a frilly cotton shirt, and pantyhose. Anna always said it was low-class for a woman of a certain age to go out in public without hose.

"Will you have a martini?" she asked.

Why not? my mind whispered.

"No thanks," I said lightly, and changed the subject. "You're all dressed up."

"I just thought we'd live it up! Sure you don't want one? I have this marvelous frozen glass right here."

What's wrong with you? What are you feeling guilty for?

"Okay," I said.

"Good!"

She started in on my brother Jack immediately and I remained silent. She told me he intended to bring his newest girlfriend to the wedding. She was a lawyer at his corporate law firm, Wolfson-Smith, in Chicago.

Laughing lightly, Anna said, "I can just see her—a tall thin girl in jousting armor. He always picks these types . . ." She pushed a blond curl away from her face as she sipped her drink. She looked at me for a long moment. "Well?" she said.

"Well?" I answered. Suddenly this dinner seemed a terrible idea.

We finished the martinis and walked around the corner to her favorite Japanese restaurant. We removed our shoes and sat on cushions at her usual table. Anna ordered a bottle of chilled sake—very chilled, with cucumber slices in the glasses.

We sat quietly for a few uncomfortable minutes.

"Remember when we came here with your father and Larry Sykes, that client friend of his? You must have been, oh, twelve. Afterwards you said he played footsie with you under the table. Do you remember?"

"Of course I remember. You told me he was just kidding around."

She looked at me with a shocked expression. "I did not! If you recall, we never had him out to the house after that—"

"But you told me he was just kidding around."

She said, "What would one say to a child?"

The sake arrived and this gave her stage business for a few minutes. She poured, stirred, proposed a toast to the future. She finally set her glass down and smiled. "So talk to me, Celeste."

"I got a letter from my grandmother. She's not coming."

"Oh," she said, "that's too bad." I could tell she wasn't sorry.

"Listen, Anna, I think I need help."

"What kind of help?"

"Therapy, I guess."

"Is it the wedding?"

"Maybe. I've been thinking about my mother and about . . . Branko. Today I even thought I saw him on the street!" Hesitating, I added, "I've been drinking too much."

"You know Branko is gone, Celeste," she said pragmatically. And then, "What do you mean, too much?" She refilled her glass. I was uncomfortable with this topic, especially with Anna, who drank more than I.

"And I'm worried about Alex. He's too . . ." My voice trailed off. I wanted to say *violent,* but it sounded horrible in my own ears.

"Too what? You know he adores you."

"I can't stop thinking about my mother!" I blurted.

She swallowed hard. "Your mother? I never knew her, you know. Let's go ahead and order."

"I went to Japan once," she told me, picking up a California roll with her chopsticks.

"Really?" I didn't know this, but it didn't seem odd. I knew nothing about her past, or how she'd met my father, or their courtship. I'd always liked it better that way.

"Yes, I went to Japan with my first husband, Jordan. He was a jazz musician and one summer they played in Japan. It was fun. Altogether life was great fun back then—but he was a junkie. I was so young, I didn't know what was wrong with him for the longest time. Why are you looking at me like that? You think your generation invented drugs?"

Her mood went from ebullient to teary. I laid down my chopsticks and took a long, slow sip of my drink.

"Sometimes I feel I haven't been a good stepmother to you. I just never did enough to make us close."

"You did a fine job, Anna, you really did."

She reached into her little handbag for a tissue and dabbed at her eyes. "You never really liked me. I know you loved me—love me—but we were never friends."

A large dish of sukiyaki arrived and was set at the center of the table. She stirred the vegetables and meat with her chopsticks.

"The best one was Branko," she said without looking up. "I always had a secret crush on him. He was rich, handsome, and nice. I never could figure out why you two didn't—"

My heart was pounding against my rib cage, as if fighting to get out.

"How can you say that, Anna? I don't need this shit," I said in a low, cold voice, and pulled my legs out from under the table. "I'm getting married in less than three weeks. What's the matter with you?"

"Oh my goodness! Don't go! I'm sorry!"

I sat back down, angry.

"I just can't bear to think of you making the same mistakes I made. Do you know why I never had kids? I had an illegal abortion years ago and that damn drunken quack botched up my insides. Jordan couldn't have handled kids, he couldn't handle himself.

"Life is all about settling happily for less than one expected," she went on, looking down. "Your father *thinks* he's content. But now he gets these headaches and can barely move from the pain. He's become an avid bird-watcher, did you know that? He says it helps him relax." She raised her eyes and they seemed hopeful and vulnerable. I felt intolerably sad.

"No, I didn't know that," I said in a quiet voice.

"Oh, yes. He's very serious about it. Has these brand-new binoculars, and keeps a little book. He found a baby bird that had fallen out of a tree. He brought it home and tried to feed it, but it died. He cried like a little boy."

I tried to picture my father crying over the tiny corpse of a bird. It was impossible to imagine. When I'd last been home to try on my wedding dress, we'd come across each other in the kitchen. He was getting ice cubes from the freezer.

"How are you, Celeste?" He looked at me expectantly with eyes the color of old jeans.

Hope rose in me. "Well, actually, I'm having an incredible time teaching in Harlem. You wouldn't believe this boy Derrence, Dad, he's so bright! He's been writing poems about . . . "

Watching him closely, I saw boredom already settling over his eyes like a thick fog. I had always assumed that I bored him, but today, lurking behind the fog I saw discomfort. He felt trapped around me. Did he see my mother when he looked at me? Perhaps I reminded him that he had walked away from her in her illness, and ignored his children.

I kept talking but the enthusiasm had drained from my voice; he wasn't hearing me. My voice trailed off. He smiled, nodded, and walked away, through the swinging door.

* * *

I REALIZED as I listened to Anna that I'd treated her much as he treated me, a difficult thing for me to accept.

I sat there, stunned. "Anna," I said slowly, barely audibly, nausea rising in waves from somewhere down in my legs, "Anna, how did my mother die?"

"How did your mother—" she repeated, looking at me and then glancing away.

"I can't remember what happened. My father told me she had a heart attack, I think, but I have this blank in my memory."

"Oh for God's sake, Celeste, all these years I thought you knew and just didn't want to talk—"

"What?" I put down my chopsticks. One rolled off the table and onto my lap. My throat closed as if a fist were squeezing it shut. I picked up my glass of sake and drank it down. Anna immediately refilled it.

"Celeste," she said in a whisper. "You don't know? Oh for God's sake." She lowered her face into her hands. "I thought you knew. Everyone else knows."

And then I said it as if it made the most perfect sense in the world, as if I'd always known it, and the beast of fear who'd hidden for so long behind every unfamiliar corner had known it too and wanted to shout it in my ear.

"She killed herself," I said numbly.

Anna nodded, without looking up.

"How?" I asked.

"She took all her pills and drank a bottle of booze," Anna said quickly. "Apparently it was a miracle that the maid—what was her name?"

"Mathilde."

"—that Mathilde found her before you did. Your father made me swear never to discuss—"

"I was ten years old!" I cried, squeezing my eyes shut. "Everyone was out, they left me *alone*." I saw myself wandering around downstairs, turning on all the lights, calling out, "*Maman! Maman!*" She always waited anxiously by the kitchen door for me to come home, as if the ride on the school bus were a treacherous journey. She never left the house and I knew something was terribly wrong.

"I *waited* for Mathilde to get home before going upstairs. It wasn't a fucking miracle." I took several deep breaths, gathering my wits. "Why did *he* lie to me?"

"To protect you. To protect your feelings. You were just a child."

"No, it's because my father's a coward," I said.

"Your mother was an alcoholic," Anna said, suddenly defensive.

I shouted back, as if she'd just insulted me, "What about you? You drink more than she did!"

"I don't have a problem with alcohol, and certainly not with pills," she said with authority. "I never even take an aspirin! *You*'ll have to watch it, you know, Celeste. These things are hereditary." With that, she refilled our empty glasses and we both lifted them to our lips.

Where did one draw the line, then? Was it in the way one behaved when intoxicated? Toward the end, only one drink would make my mother wild and blue, and she'd repeat the same thing again and again, as if she'd completely forgotten. Anna, on the other hand, could drink and drink and she only became more ebullient and laughed more loudly. Was that it?

Was that the difference? Branko hadn't lost anything, so why had he decided to stop? Because he had fucked his best friend in a drunken stupor? This seemed patently absurd to me.

"Thank heavens that Alex isn't much of a drinker," she added thoughtfully.

"Oh, he drinks," I said. "He's just a control freak. I'm going to go talk to a shrink," I said with renewed conviction.

"If you must, wait until after the wedding. Now," she said, quite satisfied, "want to go to the Carlyle?"

I didn't want to go home to an empty, dark apartment. Even if it was a beautiful space that reigned high up in the New York sky.

* * *

The bar in the Carlyle was no less dark and more brooding. Anna sent a drink over to the piano player, who looked up and waved toward our table after "My Funny Valentine."

"I used to know him in my other life," Anna whispered to me.

I was on my second brandy when the piano player said, "My old friend Anna Carruthers is here, maybe she'd like to come up and sing a song?" Anna smiled, her blush showing even in the dim candlelight, but she shook her head.

"I'd need several more drinks before I'd be willing to do that," she mumbled, clasping the cameo at her throat as if it were a reminder of who she was today. "Ha, ha, your father would have a heart attack!" She slapped the tabletop with her palm and took a sip of her gin and tonic.

After the set, the piano player came and sat with us. He looked much older up close, with a handsome face ravaged by deep wrinkles. He had a quiet, smooth voice.

"Anna, long time no see."

"Pete."

"How do you do?" he said to me.

"My daughter, Celeste," Anna said. "Pete Brown."

"Passing through?" Pete asked.

"Just passing through," Anna said with a smile.

"Well, good to see you, Anna Carruthers. Come up and sing a song."

"It's Miller now. Anna Miller. Those days are long gone, Pete. I don't even sing in the shower anymore."

He tapped the table, and got up. Moments later, the waitress in a tiny black dress arrived with another round of drinks from Pete.

"My darling Celeste," Anna said in a mumble, close to my ear, "you're going to have to learn to forgive. It's so terribly important as you get older to *forgive*."

"*Forgive!*" I cried. "How about learning how to tell the truth first?"

"I know," she said somberly, "being young is so very hard."

Anna and I were weaving by the time we left the Carlyle. Hooking her arm through mine, she led me toward Fifth Avenue through the stifling night.

In the Hotel Pierre, we walked down a labyrinth of corridors until we finally came upon the bar. There were a few couples sitting in dark corners and one lonely fellow at the bar. The bartender approached and Anna said very succinctly, "A Martell and a gin and tonic, please."

She turned to me, cupped my chin in her hand, and leaned very close. "I'm sorry. I'm so sorry that you've had to go through this now. I had no idea you didn't know. I do love you so." A pearl-sized tear fell from her eye.

"Don't cry, Anna," I said, moved by her emotion. "I love you too. Everything's going to be fine now. We can be friends, we really can."

She pressed her cheek to mine and I felt a tear slide onto my hot, damp skin.

"Ladies," said the bartender, looming above us on the other side of the bartop, "we'll have none of that in here."

"Oh, what are you talking about, silly man!" cried Anna. "This is my daughter." She turned my chin toward him. "Look how beautiful she is."

Anna stood in front of her sister's building and waved as my taxi sped away. The streetlights cast a luminescent glow in the thick haze that hung over the deserted avenue. There was no breeze at all.

The taxi stopped at a red light. I was too dazed to think. Just then I caught sight of a very tall figure through the windshield, his outline fuzzy in the haze. Once again my heart recognized him before my mind did. Branko had been dead over a year, I reminded myself. This time the man was wearing jogging shorts and a torn-up T-shirt. My hand instinctively reached for the door handle. Just then he glanced in my direction. Our eyes locked, and I was unable to breathe. He smiled and ran past the cab, tossing his thick curly hair away from his face.

The light changed and the driver turned a corner and sped off.

* * *

At home, I collapsed onto the couch and stared at the dark TV screen. There were eight hang-ups on the answering machine before Alex left a message asking me to call him at his hotel in L.A. It seemed like he'd been away a year. Reflected in the screen I saw the couch and the coffee table and myself, sitting there demurely, all perfect and in order like a commercial for some household appliance. Except my vision kept going in and out of focus. No way was I calling him now.

I picked up the remote control and with a wavering hand flicked to the Discovery Channel.

A mountain of snow was collapsing on the screen. "Avalanches are common in the Himalayas," said the narrator in a confident voice, "and we were unprepared for the losses we suffered. Two Sherpas in the first avalanche, and Krauss, the Pulitzer Prize–winning German photographer, in the second."

A long, bright, orange and red centipede of Sherpas with heavy square bundles on thin brown legs was weaving up a steep, stony incline. The camera cut to two stills of smiling men whose faces were so wrinkled, it was impossible to determine their age. The Sherpas who had perished in the avalanche.

Next came a wide-angle shot of an enormous expanse of snow. Suddenly the white ground opened up, exposing a bottomless ice pit.

"Even more dangerous are the ice crevasses because you never know where one will surface. We lost our best Sherpa to an ice crevasse. A man who'd been climbing Everest for twenty-five years."

I thought the narrator's voice was much too self-confident for someone who'd witnessed so many deaths. I was seeing double, so I covered one eye with my palm, a late-night driving technique during college. I focused on the screen.

Climbers were camped in small Day-Glo orange tents as a blizzard raged around them. They were smiling, their cracked, sunburned faces aglow with excitement.

"Even though I was the principal financer of this Mount Everest expedition, I was not one of the fortunate ones who made it to the peak. You see, being the richest, or the best climber, or the most physically fit doesn't matter here—it's who is in the best position to make that last major effort on the final day. Evans, who planted our flag, was relatively inexperienced, compared to the rest of us. But he was well rested because he hadn't exerted himself as we had on previous days. I was just too damn exhausted by the time we reached the Hillary Step, the last big obstacle. But in the larger sense, it really doesn't matter who planted the flag. It's the team effort that makes such an expedition worthwhile."

I flicked off the television and sat in the dim light, breathing deeply.

A long time must have passed before I stumbled into the old guest room, now my office, where a carpenter had built me wall-to-wall bookshelves. On the bottom shelf was an old photo album I hadn't looked at in years. I opened it at random and came upon a picture of Branko standing proudly, legs and arms crossed, in front of his Porsche. The pages were yellowed and the plastic protective bindings had come loose. As I fumbled to right the pages, pictures tumbled out all over the floor. I threw the album aside, and bending to retrieve the pictures, stumbled to my knees.

I picked up a photo lying facedown on the rug. It was one of Branko and me at the Delta Kappa Half-Assed Semi-Formal. I am sitting on his lap with my leg extended straight out, wearing a black silk décolleté blouse and silk boxer shorts with black lace stockings and a garter belt. Branko is wearing the top half of one of his European suits, complete with vest and tie and button-down cotton oxford shirt and gold cuff links. He's also in boxer shorts, with cowboy boots and an enormous black cowboy hat he'd bought in Colorado. We'd had a good time dancing that night, until I got alcohol poisoning from drinking Purple Jesus, a grain alcohol punch Branko had warned me to stay away from. In the middle of the party, I stretched out on a couch and closed my eyes. Moments later, Branko tried to wake me but I was out cold. I was barely breathing and he couldn't find my pulse. He slapped me, got me to my feet, and poured black coffee down my throat until I vomited. Afterwards, he walked me around the block for several hours.

I picked up another photo. It was of Branko, Candace, and me in our red graduation robes, the silly square tasseled hats cocked on our heads. A large group of us had been up most of the night, drinking champagne, sniffing cocaine, dancing like escaped lunatics on the campus green. Our three youthful, uncomplicated, sweaty faces smiled moonily at the camera. What did we know?

Anyway, I had never believed myself to be one of the strong or the brave.

Eighteen

AT SEVEN on Friday morning, Alex called me from his office.

"Hi there," he said in a shaky voice. "Where have you been?"

I didn't answer. He went on. "I took the red-eye. I wanted to get back. Want to have lunch with me? We could meet in the park."

I thought for a moment, trying to clear my head. "Okay," I said.

I slept for a few more hours, then drew a bath. I washed my hair, taking my time, luxuriating in the feeling that the storm had finally passed and now I was ready to face the blackouts and frayed power lines. I intended to tell Alex about my conversation with Anna, and to discuss with him the issue of my drinking and of my need to see a shrink.

By the time I entered Central Park at Fifty-ninth Street, my courage had waned. I spotted Alex standing down the path by the pony run. He was observing the little children who sat demurely in the pony cart, knees together and tiny hands clasped in their laps. On his face was an amused smile. It was close to noon and the park was crowded with mothers shouting and chasing children, and homeless people resting on the shady benches that lined the walk. Alex was one of the few men in a suit. I saw the young mothers smile at him approvingly. In a moment he turned his head in my direction. Without thinking, I slipped in behind a tall man walking in front of me.

When I reached Alex, he was facing the pony run again, still smiling at the little kids.

"Hi, Alex," I said. I had been completely alone for more than thirty hours, not speaking to a soul.

He took me into his arms and held me close. "This used to be my favorite place when I was little," he said into my ear. His voice had lost the lacquer of testiness that had bothered me so much before his departure, and his spicy cologne smelled reassuringly familiar.

"Want to go to the zoo?" he asked. "I haven't been here since they've redone it."

Glass had replaced all the bars I remembered from my childhood. We sat down on the shallow steps surrounding the tank of seals and watched their feline faces glide by in slow circles. Their movements were as liquid as the water. I thought of scuba diving again and grew excited.

They coasted past, first in one direction, then the other.

"Wouldn't it be fun to dive with seals?" Alex asked, taking my hand and holding it between his soft, dry palms. "There's a kelp forest in northern California that's teeming with seals."

"I saw it on the Discovery Channel," I said. "Great whites frequent that kelp forest, too."

"You and the Discovery Channel," Alex said, smiling. "I've been trying to call you for two days. I was worried."

"I'm sorry. Look! They're watching us!" The seals had come around again and were turning to look at us as they passed by. With the flick of their tails, they sent a shower of water onto our shoes. Alex took out his white handkerchief, wiped off his black wingtips, and dabbed at my tan slingbacks.

"Celeste, I've been thinking," he said. My heart began to pound again. The sunlight seemed awfully bright and I squinted at him. "Everything is not perfect between us," he said.

"That's for sure," I said.

"I don't remember exactly what happened the other night with my mother, but I'm sorry if I upset you."

I could feel rage simmering below the surface of my skin. I kept my voice calm and smooth. "Alex, you scared the living shit out of me. How am I supposed to live like this? Never knowing when you're going to flip out!"

"You're right," he said, surprising me. "I guess I haven't really dealt with that stuff."

"Why do you push me away, why don't you talk to me about things?"

He watched the seals for a while, thinking. I focused on the curve of his ear and jaw, the way his hair ended in a smooth line at his strong neck. He was beautiful to look at.

"I feel insecure around you," he finally said. "Like that time you were reading Proust. How the hell am I supposed to compete with that?"

"It's not a competition, Alex."

"I think you're smarter than I am. You're an intellectual, a teacher."

"I'm not an intellectual."

A crease forming between his brows. The sun glinted off his glasses. "I wanted everything perfect with the wedding. All I wanted was to take care of you, make your life easy. Make you happy. And I think everything I do is just never enough."

"Maybe you wish I were someone else," I said. "Someone without a history. Listen to me, Alex. I had dinner with Anna on Tuesday and she told me that my mother killed herself."

"Oh, Jesus," he said quickly, and pressed me to his chest. "Jesus, Jesus, what a terrible thing."

"They lied to me, Alex," I said, pulling away from him to look into his face. "I just didn't know; they should have told me. I'm going to see a shrink," I added resolutely. The sunlight was so blinding, I had to shield my eyes with my hand. I swallowed and said, "I think we should go see someone together."

"Okay," he conceded. "I think that's a good idea."

We sat in silence. Finally he said, "But not now. Not till after our honeymoon."

"It seems like maybe not such a good idea to start now, you're right. Since we're getting married in just over a week."

"How could your mother do that to you?" he said quietly. "Kill herself like that and leave you, a little girl? What a selfish thing to do."

I swallowed calmly. "It took courage, I think. *I* couldn't do it. When I was younger and in a lot of pain, I thought about it, believe me. But I never could do it."

I wanted to bring up the other thing, the drinking, but couldn't seem to broach the subject.

"No wonder you're depressed." After a moment he added hopefully, "Maybe you need pills."

His words were reassuring for some reason. Pills might fix me, I thought, put everything back in order. Maybe that was the problem. Maybe I'd inherited my mother's depressive condition. In the quiet buzz of noon, I pressed my face to Alex's chest and heard the steady beating of his heart, the small, excited voices of children surrounding us, and water slapping against glass. The children's voices reminded me of the feeling of loneliness and exclusion that had always haunted me, even while my mother was still alive.

"Alex . . ." I started, without looking at him, knowing that what I was about to say could have disastrous consequences. *Alex,* I was going to say, *Alex, my dearest Alex, I have a drinking problem* . . . But this seemed far too cataclysmic, far too definitive. *Now, now, don't overdo it,* my mind warned. *If you tell him that, you'll never be able to take it back.*

So I asked him in a calm, even tone, "Alex, do you think I drink too much?"

"You drink a lot," he said after a moment of thought. "But you're not—definitely not—an *alcoholic* or anything like that. It's not like you drink every day. You're just a heavy social drinker. And you've been going through a stressful time lately. But look how much you've cut back since we've been together. We're going to keep it that way, right?"

He looked at me very seriously. A huge sigh of relief wanted to escape from my lungs, but I wouldn't let it for fear that he would take notice. *Everything is back to normal. Everything is as it should be.*

I decided, just as a precaution, not to drink until the wedding.

Slowly he kissed my cheeks, my neck, behind my ears, my lips. His mouth tasted cool and sweet, like fresh water after a long ocean swim. I felt desire stirring in me, a tiny flame of hope reigniting.

"I'm going to take the afternoon off," Alex said. "Let's go home and go to bed."

"Let's," I said, breathing against his neck. He took his cell phone out of his breast pocket and called his secretary.

"Lorraine."

Apparently she had something very important to tell him because his whole face went rigid in concentration.

"What the hell is he talking about? We went through this yesterday. He's not to talk to their lawyers. I told him not to! Well, just get him on the phone right now . . . I'll hold."

"George again?" I said, aiming for humor. My lips trembled as I smiled. But he had already forgotten I was there.

I waited a half hour while he talked on the phone, trying to fix whatever had gone wrong. I knew that if he took the afternoon off, he would be anxious and ill-at-ease, resentful of me for taking him away from his work.

I put my hand on his arm. I could feel his hard biceps through his light, summer wool suit. "Alex," I murmured, "it doesn't matter. Go back to work."

He looked relieved. "I'll be there in a minute," he said into his cell phone, and folded it back into his pocket.

* * *

Presiding over our rehearsal dinner in Nero's restaurant, I couldn't take my eyes off the mirror that ran the length of the opposite wall. I looked at us, the bride and groom at the center of a long rectangular table, backs to the fresco of Venice, appearing to be seated in a gondola about to pass under a bridge. Beyond the bridge were gondoliers in striped shirts, floating in their gondolas in a sapphire blue Grand Canal. How happy and beautiful the couple looked, he in a new charcoal gray suit and she in a new shimmering blue dress with tiny white polka dots, her new sapphire earrings flashing prisms of light.

On each table, small white candles burned in crystal sconces, their golden flames reflecting in the wine glasses and sparkling off the ladies' jewelry. Laughter and merry voices echoed through the room.

But Alex's voice in my ear brought me suddenly, with a pang of regret, back into the party.

"Why aren't you drinking the wine, Celeste? I ordered Chateau Laroq just for you."

The ruby wine shimmered in the ballon glass just before me, untouched. I looked at it, thought about it from every angle once again. Even my taste buds were screaming in outrage. My stomach churned, my hands and feet itched. I wanted to drink the Chateau Laroq so badly, I could already feel its tangy, velvety sweetness coating the back of my throat, and the burst of heat in my chest on its way down. I hadn't had a drink since my dinner with Anna eighteen days ago.

If you haven't had a drink in eighteen days then you don't have a problem, my mind told me.

But then I thought of what the man outside the church had said: "They're celebrating people counting days." Every day I'd counted off to myself, and every day I'd felt proud, as if I'd accomplished something. Normal people didn't feel that way if they went a couple of days without a drink. They surely didn't *count*.

As each day had passed without a drink, my anxiety increased, along with the rage and self-disgust, and the fear that accompanied them, that pricked at my skin from the inside.

Alex, for some reason, had seemed deeply threatened by my resolve.

* * *

Last Monday, he called from work at ten P.M. and said he wanted me to meet him at a nightclub his coworkers were taking him to. I told him to go without me. I was already in bed and did not want to get all dressed up and go to a club, where there would be lots and lots of alcohol and I would want to drink.

"What the hell is wrong, Celeste?" he said impatiently.

"Nothing is wrong, I just don't want to go out, that's all," I said. He hung up on me, and came crashing in at four-thirty in the morning like some kind of bulldozer. He crawled into bed and I pretended to be asleep. He grabbed hold of the collar of my nightgown and ripped it right off my back. He held me down with the weight of his body. I struggled to free myself.

"Alex," I hissed, "get the fuck off me."

"Don't you swear at me," he said through clenched teeth. His big hands encircled my throat and began to squeeze. I couldn't breathe, felt my face beginning to explode. I reached over and grabbed the bedside lamp and brought it down on his head. It hardly fazed him, but he was surprised enough to let go of my neck.

I sprang out of bed and ran to the bathroom, and locked myself in. He banged his fists against the door. "Don't make me break this door down!" he shouted.

"Go away!" I shouted back, looking for some kind of weapon in the cabinet under the sink. Not much there besides toilet paper. I picked up the plunger. "Go to sleep, you're drunk!"

"I'm going to wait right here till you come out," he said.

I pulled sheets and towels and blankets out of the closet and laid them out on the floor. "That's okay with me," I said. "I'm going to sleep in here."

As I lay on the bathroom floor with the bath mat and a blanket between me and the tiles, the absurdity of the situation was not lost on me: how many times had I passed out cold on a bathroom floor? And here I was, not a drop of booze in me, sleeping again on a bathroom floor.

At six A.M. he woke me up, knocking politely, and cleared his throat. In his most reassuring and sheepish voice, he said that he needed to get his shaving things. I was so angry, I couldn't speak. We passed each other like strangers getting on and off an elevator, eyes never meeting.

* * *

He came home from work earlier than usual that evening, carrying a small, pale blue Tiffany shopping bag, which he handed to me. Inside was a little blue box with a yellow Post-It attached: "Mr. Laughton: I hope this is what you had in mind! —Lorraine." Apparently he had forgotten to remove the note.

Inside the box was a pair of sapphire earrings in the shape of large tears. "They're beautiful," I said glumly. "Lorraine has good taste."

He shot me an angry glance and chose not to say anything.

Knowing that he would not be happy about it, I told him I'd decided I wanted us to take a week of our honeymoon to go see my grandmother in Bordeaux. "I need my family," I said.

"I thought you hated your grandmother," Alex said as he began to take off his suit.

"Of course I don't hate my grandmother," I said. "In fact, I'd like to see her very much."

"I'd like to stick to our original plan if you don't mind, a week in Venice and a week in Capri," he said evenly. "After all, it is our honeymoon."

I told him I wanted to go to Bordeaux.

"I don't want to go to France and sit there like a jerk while you talk to everybody in French."

"So it's the thing of me knowing something you don't," I said dryly. "Anyway, I speak Italian, too."

"I should never have told you that," he muttered. "Let's go out to dinner, I'm going-stir crazy. How about Le Bistro?"

Le Bistro had *great* martinis. I did not want to be tempted. "I'd rather stay home," I said. "I made a *salade Niçoise*."

He looked at me with an annoyed frown. I'd seen him look at the doormen this way, when he was expecting an important package from the office and it had apparently been misplaced. For a moment, I was crippled with the realization that I had absolutely no idea who this man was, and that last night he had almost strangled me.

And for the first time since my dinner with Anna, I suddenly really wanted a drink. There was a bottle of Stoli in the freezer and it was calling to me. My knuckles turned white as I gripped the couch pillow beneath me in an effort to stay seated.

Enraged and disgusted, I refused to back down. "Alex, I want to go to Bordeaux to see my grandmother."

I realized, of course, the argument had nothing whatsoever to do with Bordeaux.

* * *

ALL DAY Wednesday he called me from work, circling me like a shark, coming in for a nudge, attempting different approaches in the hope that, exhausted, I'd finally give up. I decided that I'd fight him to the end.

He said in a honey-coated voice, as soon as he came in from work, "I had Lorraine call the travel agent; she found out it would cost us nine hundred and eighty-six dollars each to change our tickets to fly to Bordeaux."

"Since when do you care how much things cost?" I said in an equally honey-coated voice.

He said, "What if I plan a vacation for us next Christmas to go just to Bordeaux and stay with her for two whole weeks?"

I knew this was a bribe so I said, "Bordeaux isn't at all beautiful in December." I had no idea if this was true, but it sounded fairly plausible to me. He was silenced for the time being.

* * *

"I'M NOT GOING to Bordeaux," he said to me on Thursday morning. This was the night of his bachelor party. His New York friends had waited until the very end so that Alex's best man, James, could arrive from Oregon.

I tried to envision him sitting with my grandmother in her sunroom and a horrible feeling of embarrassment overcame me. He wouldn't be able to discuss literature with her. He'd proudly tell her about mergers and acquisitions and my grandmother would peer at him with her coldest expression, her inscrutable eyes filled with a contempt that Alex would not even recognize.

I knew he would not back down and that I'd lost the battle.

"Okay, Alex," I said, my voice quivering with rage, "*fuck* Bordeaux! Next fall, I'll go by myself."

"You don't have to swear about it," he said.

* * *

Alex came home early from work to help me greet his best man. James had driven his Nissan Pathfinder all the way from Portland. He was a large fellow with fine hair so pale it seemed white, a small upturned nose, and round cheeks. He wore a lumberjack shirt, jeans, and Timberland boots. When he entered the apartment, Alex stood back and frowned, looking him over.

"Jesus Christ, Jimbo, you're taking this nature stuff way too seriously," he said with a chuckle.

"You're darn tootin', Attila," James said, also laughing. "And it's *Doctor* James to you now."

"A man with a doctorate in environmental science is about as useful as a whore with a Ph.D. in public health. Please tell me you brought a suit."

"Don't know if it still fits," James said. They slapped each other on the back, having a good laugh.

They had a few rum and tonics while I sat on the couch with a Diet Coke. Alex got his second electric guitar out of the storage closet and dusted it off. They plugged both guitars into the huge black amplifier Alex still kept in the living room, although he never played anymore, and they began to twang and rift. The bottle of Stoli in the freezer came to mind.

The walls thumped and thudded as a feedback scream threatened to shatter the glassware. The Stoli began calling to me like a homing beacon. I went to the freezer and opened it. There was my beloved friend, Stolichnaya vodka, a dusting of frost covering the bottle. I saw a pint of Rocky Road ice cream and took that, along with a spoon, into the bedroom and put the headphones on and turned on the TV. I could still hear their guitars and them howling, "You neeeed coolin' baby I'm not foolin' . . . "

I watched a documentary on the mating rituals of birds of paradise, taking slow, deep breaths, and prayed for these bad feelings to go away. *You're just nervous,* I kept telling myself.

Shortly, Alex came in to tell me they were off to the bachelor party. I smiled and waved, not removing the earphones.

* * *

They came in at around two and started with the guitars again. "I'm a cowboy with a six-string on my baaaack!"

Later, when Alex stumbled into the bedroom, I attempted to confront him. Perhaps this was not the best moment, but time was pressing. Tomorrow was our rehearsal dinner; the next day, our wedding.

"Alex, why do you hurt me when you're drunk?"

He stood with an arm against the dresser, tottering slightly as if on board a ship. I thought that maybe he might hurt me again tonight, and that James would have to come in and rescue me, and this might not be a bad thing.

"Hurt you? What the fuck are you talking about?" he said with a rapacious smile, his red eyes ablaze. "You know something? You're a total drag when you don't drink."

With that, he pounced onto the bed, rolled over, and passed out.

* * *

Alex had left by the time I awakened the next morning.

I made coffee for James and waited for him to get up. He finally emerged from the guest room/office, his hair standing on end and his big face bloated and pasty.

"Why do you call him Attila?" I asked lightly, fixing him a cup of coffee. The booze he'd consumed the night before emanated from his pores in a toxic mist.

"Oh, you know. He was pretty wild in prep school and college. He had guts, though." James's eyes lit up at some memory, full of admiration. "Took on half the Yale football team one night. I was there, I saw it. They thought he was nuts, started calling him Attila.

"He's calmed down quite a lot. You're a good influence."

I asked, gambling that James knew about this, too, "He told me about his wife. The order of protection and all that." I let my voice drop conspiratorially.

"Oh yeah, that," he said, looking down and shaking his head. "It was an accident. It's really easy to dislocate a shoulder. He never meant to hurt her." After an uncomfortable silence, he said, "Say, is there a gym in this building?"

* * *

And earlier tonight, at our own rehearsal dinner, we stood together, the beautiful, happy couple, greeting our guests at the door. I had promised myself, as a reward for not drinking for ten whole days, that tonight I would have a cocktail.

Hurry up please, it's time, I heard in my head as Alex and I hugged Aurelia and shook hands with her new boyfriend, Frederico, a thin, stoop-shouldered man with a black mustache who was only a few years older than Alex.

"Champagne, madam?" a waiter asked me, proffering a tray.

Take it! Take the glass! But I knew I was in such a state that if I started now, by the end of the night I would be dancing naked on the table, if not in bed with one of the waiters.

"Could I please have a glass of Pellegrino water?" I asked him sweetly, shocking myself. *What? But you said cocktail time!*

* * *

And now it was dinnertime, and we were having our appetizers, shrimp cocktail, which I hadn't touched, for my mouth was so dry I could barely swallow.

I thought that if I reached out and drank down the glass of Chateau Laroq that Alex had just reminded me he'd ordered as a special surprise, my discomfort, my rage, my fear, would instantly abate.

So what the hell is holding you back?

People, places, and things, Branko had said. Here I was, smack in the middle of the maelstrom. No wonder I wanted a drink.

"Celeste?" Alex said again. "I spent a lot of money on this wine."

"Yes, it must have been difficult for Lorraine to get such a big order on such short notice."

I saw rage in his eyes. If we'd been alone, he might have tried to strangle me again.

"My grandmother would've sent you as many cases as you wanted for free," I said, my voice quiet from the knot in my throat. I turned away, glanced quickly in the mirror across the room and saw there a happy, perfect couple smiling at each other. I felt wrenched in two.

Why can't you believe what you're seeing in the mirror? Why can't you just be happy, accept it? Drink the wine and everything will be all right.

I turned back to Alex. "I don't want any," I whispered, smiling so hard, two points of pressure pulsed dully at the base of my skull.

"What the hell is wrong with you?" he said between his teeth, also smiling, eyes on fire.

"I have a drinking problem, Alex," I said smoothly, in an equable tone.

"I already told you, you don't have a drinking problem, Celeste. Why do you always have to ruin everything?"

My heart raced, my ears rang with a rhythmic pounding. I wanted to lift the glass of Chateau Laroq and dump it on his head. My hand reached out and encircled the glass.

Fuck it. Fuck it all! Drink it!

A zephyr tickled my neck and the tiny hairs there bristled, as I remembered what Branko had said: *Some people have to lose everything before they quit. Some people never quit. You hit one bottom and then just go right on through, down to the next one. What would it take—what would it take, Celeste, for you to quit?*

"God, help me," I whispered.

"What?" said Alex, frowning. Just then someone down the table asked him a question about his latest big merger, and he turned away from me. In the mirror, at this distance, his face appeared aglow with happiness instead of rage.

The wine glass still shimmered before me, full and ruby-colored in the light. At once everything became clear, as if the lights had been turned up full blast in the room. I looked around, blinking as if I were seeing them all for the first time. There was Aurelia, one table away, her eyes opaque with boredom as she listened to Aunt Theresa's husband, the plastic surgeon—Alex had put them next to each other because they were both doctors. Theresa's husband placed his hand over Aurelia's and leaned toward her, practically drooling onto her chest. Two tables away, Theresa watched, ignoring the conversation at her own table, stiff and anemic and malcontent. Catching his wife's eye, the doctor pulled back his hand and reached for his wine glass.

At another table, Anna's pale, oval face was smiling frantically at Chester, Alex's father, whose elastic mouth grinned back, oblivious. Nodding at Chester, she lifted her highball glass to a passing waiter and jiggled the ice in a quick, impatient gesture.

I filled my glass with Pellegrino water and took a sip. It had the nonexistent aftertaste of disappointment. I had to think of something better to drink, but what? I couldn't think of a thing. What had I drunk before? As a child? I'd been drinking alcohol for so long, I couldn't remember.

My brother, Jack, sitting at the end of our table, looked old tonight, his skin flaccid and gray. He was drinking double scotches on the rocks, talking heatedly about corporate law to Lucia, whose stolid face displayed quiet surprise that this man was my brother. In a matter of a few years he'd gone from a longhaired, pot-smoking rebel to an overweight, middle-aged man in a suit.

I looked at my father, tall, stately, expressionless in his own dark suit. He hadn't glanced my way once all night. His face seemed bleached, as though he'd been put through the wash with Clorox. He topped off Babs's glass with Chateau Laroq, then refilled his own. He drank it down. I was reminded of those dinners after my mother's death, when he'd drunk away her wine cellar as fast as he could. Maybe he wanted to get rid of the Chateau Laroq tonight as well, another harbinger of bad memories.

Babs smiled at him encouragingly, as if she had made it her mission to bring him out of his shell, as though his shyness were an adorable character trait rather than some kind of malignant deficiency. In the next moment I hated him so much I wanted to point a gun at his head and shout, "Tell me the truth! What do you feel?" But I knew that even with his life threatened, he'd only stare back, confused, and say, "What on earth do you mean? Are you not well, Celeste? Should I call a doctor?"

Of course I'm not well, you son of a bitch! How could I possibly be well?

What a fucking mess, I thought.

No, it's not a mess at all! If they're all fine, then you're fine too. Why won't you believe it? Drink the wine and forget this nonsense. You deserve it, you haven't had a drink in ten *days.*

Fuck you too, I thought. I'm not drinking the goddamn wine.

You're not going to make it. You can't live without drinking for the rest of your life! You're a loser, anyway. Your mother abandoned you and your father doesn't even like you.

But I remembered something else Branko had said that last night: just for today.

Hear that? I thought. It's just for today. Alex turned to me once again.

"You're having champagne when it's time for the toasts," he said in a whisper, close to my ear. "You're embarrassing me, Celeste."

"Go fuck yourself, Alex," I said, smiling at him from ear to ear. His head snapped back as if I'd slapped him. The muscles in his jaw pulsated. My heart began to pound. I felt afraid of him.

"Just shut the hell up, do you think you could do that?" I said, and pushed the wine glass away toward the middle of the table. "And if you tell me not to swear one more time, I swear to God I'll get up and walk right the fuck out of this restaurant."

Nineteen

"**WELL, THAT WAS** a nice party," Anna said from the passenger seat. In keeping with tradition, I was going home with my father and Anna to Connecticut to spend the night. I wouldn't be seeing Alex till four P.M. tomorrow, when he'd greet me in front of the judge in the rose garden at the end of the garden path. From the backseat I watched my father's broad shoulders, his short, pale, graying hair that didn't touch his white shirt collar, as he stared straight ahead at the road. Every once in a while he patted his forehead with a handkerchief. Anna was in excellent spirits and I wanted desperately to shout at her to shut up.

"That Aurelia is really something!" Anna snorted. "Flirting like that with Theresa's husband!"

"I think it was the other way around," I said from the back in a harsh murmur, dangerously close to losing control.

"Pardon?" said Anna.

"Nothing."

I stared at the back of my father's head and imagined taking an ax to it. The thought was somehow comforting. If I opened my mouth and said anything to him, it would surely be terrible. Unforgivable.

Oh my God, this rage, I thought. How am I going to live with this rage?

I sat glaring out at the highway and the black night, watching the yellow lines slip away under the car as Anna chattered on.

* * *

UPON ENTERING the vestibule, my father dropped the car keys into the silver dish Anna kept there, stretched his back with his arms extended, patted me quickly on the shoulder, and said, "You looked lovely tonight. It was a lovely party. Everything was lovely. Well,

I think I'll pack it in. I have a terrible headache. I want to nip it in the bud, so to speak. Tomorrow's going to be a big day for all of us!" He lifted his hand, backed away rubbing his palms together briskly, and turned to climb the stairs. As I watched his tight, square back recede, I imagined firing on him with an Uzi and watching his body roll down the stairs.

"Yoo-hoo, Celeste!" Anna called from the kitchen. "Come join me for a little drink."

I went in through the swinging door. She was pouring gin from the bottle she kept in the freezer into a short glass.

I sat down at the table and dropped my head into my crossed arms.

"Why, Celeste," she said, "what's the matter? Everything was simply lovely tonight."

"Oh, for God's sake, Anna, open your eyes," I said numbly.

I didn't look up to see her expression. I was thinking hard about tomorrow, about the feelings I'd thought I had, was supposed to have, but simply didn't have, for Alex. How could ten days have changed things so much? Why had this happened? Which was insane, to marry him feeling this way, or to not marry him and have everybody think I was crazy?

I looked up. "Listen, Anna," I said. "I'm having serious doubts about getting married tomorrow."

She stood frozen at the counter, her face muscles quivering. She kicked off her high heels, shuffled toward the table, and collapsed into a chair.

"For God's sake, Celeste," she murmured. "My God. It's almost one A.M. I think you need a little nightcap. How about a brandy?"

"Thanks, but I don't want a drink." I kicked off my heels, too. Suddenly the thought of hot chocolate appealed to me. My mother and Anna used to make me cocoa when I didn't feel well as a little girl.

"I want some cocoa."

"Hot chocolate this time of year?" She got up out of the chair and went to the cabinets to look. "Cocoa," she said, shaking her head.

She poured herself another shot of gin while she placed a cup of milk in the microwave. "You know, Celeste," she said airily, "people often get the jitters the night before their weddings. I, for example, took to my bed and cried for three days before I ran off with Jordan." She took a sip of her drink. "But then, of course," she mused, "we were eloping."

She brought the steaming cup back and placed it before me. I took a little sip. It coated my taste buds, my throat, soothingly burned my heart and stomach. It seemed at that moment the best thing I'd ever tasted in my life.

"I can't stand him," I said flatly, my strength returning. I drank the chocolate fast. "I need some more," I said, holding up the empty cup.

"But—excuse me for saying so—couldn't you have realized this before tonight?"

Could I tell her? I waited for my hot chocolate, my face a stolid mask.

"Listen, Celeste, it's late," she said very logically, composedly as the microwave buzzed. She brought me back the cup. "You've been under a great deal of stress—what we talked about that night at dinner, about your mother—well, you know what I'm referring to . . . Think. There's still time. You may wake up with a whole new attitude."

I decided to tell her the truth.

No! No! Don't!

"Anna, I think I'm an alcoholic."

She stared at me for a split second, then threw her head back and laughed. "That's ridiculous, Celeste, whatever gave you such an absurd idea?" She glanced at me suspiciously. "You haven't been going to those religious meetings, have you?"

You see? She's right. Now, put some brandy in that hot chocolate and we'll just pretend all this never happened.

No, I thought. She's afraid.

Oh, right, everyone in the world is wrong and you're right, as usual. Why not have a drink? After all, why not? Why do you insist on suffering?

I considered this for a while.

A loud whining motorcycle engine roared in the distance. It seemed to be coming up the hill. The noise grew louder, until it was in our driveway, and then right outside the house. A strange lightness filled my head.

The engine growled and sputtered one last time and went quiet. I ran to the window and peered out. In a golden rectangle of light, straddling a large dirt bike, was a man in a black helmet, a dusty bomber jacket, black faded jeans, and biker boots. Walking bowlegged toward the kitchen door, he shook out one leg and then the other. He took off the helmet and shook out thick hair that was damp with sweat. It was Nathan. I knocked on the window, laughing crazily as he looked up and smiled.

Anna was just behind me, looking over my shoulder.

"Well, I'll be damned," she muttered, "here comes the cavalry."

"Hey, Mrs. Miller, what's happening?" he asked with a grin, standing in the doorway holding his helmet.

"Hah! What's happening? What isn't happening? Won't you come in, Nathan? Would you like a drink?"

"Sure. Whatever you're having is fine. As long as it's not tequila."

He looked as if he'd had a few drinks already. Perhaps he'd stopped in a bar in town. He looked me over carefully, taking a step into the room. He seemed to be trying to decide if he'd made the right choice, coming by at one in the morning.

"I got your invitation at the Matlan Grand Hotel. I just figured, hell, why not just ride up? I left the day after I got it. I'd been down there too long, anyway. It was time for a change."

Anna handed him a gin and tonic. He took a sip, shifting his weight from leg to leg.

"Am I interrupting anything? I saw the lights on and figured I'd just see who was around." He took a pack of Marlboros out of his pocket and tamped out a cigarette. He lit it with a Bic lighter, inhaled deeply, and blew a stream of smoke out his nostrils. Anna shooed the smoke away.

My small burst of energy had faded. Depleted, I sat down at the table again. My cup was empty.

"Would you like some more *cocoa,* Celeste?" asked Anna pointedly. I held up the cup.

Nathan sat down across the table from me, looking around for an ashtray. His eyes were impenetrable, his face tranquil, unconcerned. Anna put a large glass ashtray down in front of him.

We were silent. The microwave hummed loudly in the room.

"Celeste has just informed me," said Anna in her ebullient voice, "that she is having doubts about going through with her wedding *mañana.* This wouldn't have anything to do with you, Nathan, now would it, hmm?"

He pushed his chair back and leaned comfortably against it with his legs spread wide. "*I* wouldn't want to marry Alex," Nathan said, looking up at the ceiling.

"That's hardly the issue," Anna said acerbically from the counter. She came back with my cup and sat down between us.

Silence.

"I suppose I should be terribly upset and angry with you," she said to me. "But for some reason I'm not. I can't imagine why. Twenty thousand dollars, your father poured into this wedding. The man is going to shit pears if you back out. Pardon my French."

Nathan laughed.

"It's always about fucking money with him," I said, blood rushing to my face.

"What am I supposed to do? Call people in the morning and tell them not to come?" she asked no one in particular. "I mean, some people are coming all the way from California."

"I'll call people," Nathan offered.

"That would hardly be appropriate," Anna snorted. "Oh, the hell with it. I'm too tired and I've had quite a bit to drink. I think I'll go to bed and—as Scarlett O'Hara so aptly put it—I'll think about it tomorrow." With that, she went back to the fridge and refilled her glass. "Ta-ta!" she said, and disappeared through the swinging door.

* * *

Alone, Nathan and I looked at each other.

"What does Alex say about all this?" he asked finally, tamping out another cigarette and lighting it.

I shook my head. "He doesn't know."

"Hmm," he said. He jiggled the ice cubes in his glass, then he got up and went to the freezer.

"Nathan, do you think you could stop drinking? Like, just stop?"

"Hell no," he said evenly. "The thought alone is terrifying."

"Yeah," I said. "For me, too. If I get through tonight, it'll be eighteen days. I don't think I've gone eighteen days without drinking since I was fifteen."

He came back, sat down. "I know I haven't!" He laughed. He reached across the table and took my limp, cold hand in his.

"I thought you were making a mistake marrying him, you know, when I saw you down in Matlan. I guess I came to see it through. I owe you that much. . . . I'm sorry, Celeste," he said finally.

"For what?" I said flatly, but I knew exactly. I believed our souls had merged once, long ago, and when I'd severed from him, a large chunk had been carved out of me. The gaping hole had never properly healed. But the person here was only vaguely connected to the person he had once been to me.

"You expected too much from me," he said quietly.

"All that doesn't matter now, just help me get through this."

"That guy's not good enough for you. Neither am I."

"Don't make me mad, Nathan. Nathan . . . "

Don't ask him that! The voice in my head cried out.

"Nathan, do you think I'm an alcoholic?"

"Did he call you that?"

I shook my head.

"Well, *I*'m an alcoholic," he said neutrally, without remorse, guilt, or even much interest. I'd never heard anyone use the word so easily.

With that, he went to the freezer, took the gin bottle out, and carried it under his arm through the swinging door into the dark house. I followed him to the empty living room. The moon shone pale and creamy on the beige carpet. He sat in a corner of the long couch and I at the opposite end, stretching my legs out between us. He picked up my bare foot and began to rub it, pressing deeply into the tender arch.

"How's Giovanna?" I asked.

"Giovanna?" He seemed lost for a moment. "Oh, right. She went back to Italy."

He slid toward me, began to rub my shoulders. I relaxed under the pressure of his hands. The smell of gin was strong on his breath, but I was not tempted or repulsed by it.

"You've got a lot more guts than I do to stop like that," he murmured.

"My mother killed herself," I told him.

"Yeah," he said.

"You *know*?"

"Everyone knew. At least, everyone hinted that they knew."

"Why didn't you ever tell me that?"

"Oh yeah, right, just like, in regular conversation. 'So, Celeste, I hear your mother killed herself.'"

"I didn't know," I said, perplexed.

"You didn't want to know."

"So what am I going to do now?" I asked him, bewildered, filled with anxiety at the prospect of tomorrow. He didn't say anything.

"I'm so tired, Nathan."

"Go to sleep. I'm here. Everything's okay."

* * *

THE ROOM WAS still dark, except for the creamy moonlight wafting in through the large French windows. Nathan's back pressed up against me on the couch. We'd slept like this so often, it did not feel uncomfortable or strange. I felt someone nearby, watching. I tried to sit up but was pinned down by Nathan's weight. Lifting my head, I saw a woman sitting at the end of the couch, on the armrest. She was wearing a pale blue bathrobe with safety pins all along the frayed lapels. Her long chestnut hair fell in a mass of curls around her shoulders.

"*Maman?* What are you doing here?" I mumbled.

She smiled, seemed about to speak, and I remembered that in all the dreams I'd had of her, she never spoke to me. I became afraid of sending her away with the wrong words.

"Why do you have all those safety pins on your lapels?" I asked her in French.

"Everything is coming apart," she said in English.

"Why did you tell me a knight in shining armor would come and carry me away? It wasn't true."

"I was afraid you'd never be strong enough to take care of yourself. *I* never was strong enough."

"How could you abandon me like that?"

"Pff! What a waste. There is always another way . . . *Retourne à l'église. Ils te diront quoi faire,*" she said. Then, in English, "Don't be afraid. I will always be with you." She smiled, got up, and walked out soundlessly through the swinging door to the kitchen.

"Wait! Wait!" I cried.

* * *

NATHAN SHOOK ME gently by the shoulder. "Still having those nightmares?" he mumbled, half-asleep.

"It's okay," I said, breathing deeply. "She talked to me."

The next time I opened my eyes, I was facedown, my nose buried in Nathan's armpit. He was out cold, his shoulder, arm, and one leg flung over me. The sun was streaming in through the windows, the air thick and hot in our old, un-air-conditioned house. I pushed his arm away, looked around at the living room, the empty gin bottle on the coffee table, and gasped. But I remembered suddenly, with a feeling of elation, that I hadn't had any booze at all in eighteen full days.

"Celeste, dear!" I heard Anna's high, enthusiastic voice coming from the kitchen. She came wafting through the door in her flowery bathrobe and slippers. She swiftly picked up the empty gin bottle and Nathan's smelly, heaping ashtray. "Yoo-hoo, Celeste! It's ten-thirty, time to wake up!"

I grumbled, tried to pry myself loose from under the weight of Nathan's body.

"It seems to me," Anna said, "that given the circumstances, as a family, we're exhibiting a distinct lack of decorum."

Twenty

I RAN UPSTAIRS to my room and threw off the wrinkled, funky smelling rehearsal dinner dress, replacing it with an old yellow sundress that was in the closet. My wedding gown, wrapped in plastic, hung there expectantly.

I went into the bathroom to wash my face and looked at myself closely in the mirror. *Nothing drastic has happened yet*, my reflection said to me with pleading eyes. *You can still go through with it and have all those things you want so much.*

"What things?" I said aloud.

Safety. Respect. Nice jewelry, good clothes. A big, clean apartment. A place to belong in the world.

The temperature seemed suddenly to rise. Cicadas in the garden below burst into frantic song. I ran the cold water tap and put my head under the stream. A flutter passed over my bare back, like angels' wings.

"Who's there?" I whispered, afraid to look up. I heard nothing but the gentle sound of water running, reminding me of the last time I saw Sally, the day before I left for college. Rain was running off the eaves and it was safe and warm inside my room. She sat on my bed, her yearbook in her lap, and gazed at me with pleading eyes. "Don't settle, Celeste. Go get what you want. For me, okay?"

"Okay," I said aloud. In a corner of the mirror I saw Anna standing in the doorway, still in her robe.

I straightened, watching her in silence as I dried my face. I saw that there was something hopeful in her red-rimmed eyes, as if she were trying to determine if I'd changed my mind. She padded in and perched herself on the rim of the bathtub. She was sweating, a watery film covered her face. Soon, my father would be making Bloody Marys in the kitchen. I knew this as surely as I knew that the sun would set today. Apparently she wasn't finding what she'd hoped for on my face. She shook her head sadly.

"Poor Celeste," she said.

"Why poor Celeste?" I said evenly.

Anna placed her elbows on her knees and her face in her hands. "My God, what am I going to tell your father?"

"I'll tell him. It's my problem anyway, not yours."

"All right," Anna said, getting up with a sigh. "Let's not panic. Let's feed him first, that always has a calming effect."

* * *

The kitchen door was open to catch any hint of a breeze, for the midday sun was beating down fiercely on the house. My father had come down shaved and dressed, in khakis and a crisp white oxford shirt. He was not one to ever step out of his bedroom unprepared to face strangers. Nathan was sitting with him at the kitchen table, still in his dusty black jeans and T-shirt. His beard had grown in, dark and grubby.

Nathan was telling my father about the danger of bandits on the Mexican roads. Anna hovered behind them, pouring coffee.

"A breeze will hopefully kick up off the Sound . . ." Seeing me in the doorway, she fell silent. She returned to the stove, where eggs were frying in bacon grease—my father's favorite. Batter specked with nutmeg for French toast lay in a bowl beside the stove.

My father picked up the folded *Times* at his elbow and opened it in front of his face. Nathan sat impassively, watching a fly crawl across the tabletop.

A yellow taxi pulled up in front of the open door and honked.

"Now, who on earth could this be?" my father grumbled, peering over the edge of his paper.

Anna opened the screen door.

The back door of the taxi flew open and two short, stout legs appeared, struggling to get out. My grandmother emerged, straightening her linen ashes-of-roses suit. Her small, delicate ankles and feet clad in pink pumps did not appear capable of sustaining her substantial weight. On her head was a small white straw hat, cocked to the side so that it almost covered one eye. Attached to the ribbon was a silk bouquet of pink roses the size of a grapefruit.

"I am Sophie de Fleurance de Saint-Martin," she announced.

"Goodness!" exclaimed Anna, running out to help her. Taking hold of an ancient Vuitton overnight case, Anna escorted my grandmother into the kitchen, "We weren't expecting you, Madame—uh—Madame de Fleurance."

"Bonjour," my grandmother said stiffly to no one in particular. "Well, me too, I was not expecting me. And now ze taxi refuse my traveler *cheques*."

I couldn't believe my grandmother was speaking English. A laugh burst from my chest. She looked toward me, smiled, then noticed Nathan sitting at the table, and frowned. She said to him, *"Encore vous?"*

Nathan stood up and went to her with his hand extended. *"Bonjour, madame. Ça fait vraiment plaisir de vous revoir."*

"Pff!" said my grandmother as he kissed her hand. And looking around, she said quickly and softly to Nathan in French, "What are you doing here, young man? This is truly not *comme il faut*!"

The cab honked its horn again.

My father abruptly put his paper down with a loud crackle and glared at my grandmother. A bright flush had spread up his cheeks.

"Well, for Christ sakes," he mumbled, and got out of his chair. On his way out the door, he nodded perfunctorily at my grandmother, who nodded perfunctorily back.

She opened her arms to me. *"Embrasse-moi, mon petit,"* she said loudly. I went and threw my arms around her solid little body. We kissed twice on each cheek.

"Qu'est-ce qu'il fait là, celui-la?" she asked, indicating Nathan with a small nod.

"He came last night. I invited him," I told her in French.

"Hmm," she said.

My father entered, carrying a cumbersome white box with a perfect pink ribbon and bow. His face was now bright red.

"That—that cost over one hundred dollars!" he sputtered. "She came all the way from Kennedy in a cab!"

"I pay you wiz the travel *cheques*," my grandmother said, shrugging indifferently as she slipped off her little white gloves.

"Would you like some coffee, madame?" asked Anna, pulling out a chair. Nathan had remained standing.

"Of course," said my grandmother, sitting down. Nathan pushed her chair in.

"I wasn't going to come," she told me abruptly in French, taking my hand in her small, plump fingers. Her wedding ring, which she wore on her right hand, squeezed her finger like a rubber band. "But then I received your letter and changed my mind at the last moment. I remembered suddenly what your grandfather de Saint-Martin used to say—he was well educated, all he did was read—he used to say, '*Carpe diem*—'"

"'*Carpe diem*,'" Nathan said, "'*quam minimum credula postero*.'"

"Bravo!" cried my grandmother. "That is Horace, of course," she told my father.

My father was once again hiding behind his paper.

"Seize the day, trust little to tomorrow," Nathan said, hunched over and gazing into his cup as if he were reading tea leaves.

My grandmother abruptly gripped the top of my father's paper, pulled it out of his hands, folded it up daintily, and hid it on her lap.

"Brunch is ready!" cried Anna hysterically from the stove, coming forward with the frying pan. "French toast and bacon and eggs!"

"*Mon Dieu*," said my grandmother. "*French* toast! Hahahah!"

"I'd like a Bloody Mary," Anna said. "Charles, why don't you make us up a batch of your famous Bloodys—would you?"

My father swiftly got up and went to the cabinets and fridge, his face muscles frozen in a determined look, as if every ounce of his being were fighting to remain indifferent.

"I like the Bloody Mary," my grandmother said approvingly. In French, she added, "Your accent has become terrible, Celeste. You sound like a Canadian. You must come back to France."

"*Ecoutez-moi, Bonne-maman*—" I coughed, mumbling quickly. "*J'ai décidé que je ne peux pas me marier aujourd'hui. Aidez-moi*—"

She answered in French, "Is it because Nathan the Explorer has once again returned to claim you?" She made her hard, pinched little face.

"Not at all, *Bonne-maman*," I said quickly. I saw that Nathan was following this exchange as if it were a Ping-Pong match, his eyes shifting from me to her. "Please listen to me," I continued, "it has nothing to do with him, I swear it to you. I am totally to blame. I made a terrible mistake. I thought Alex would give my life a certain order. But he is very . . . controlling."

"So he isn't weak?" she asked.

"*No!* Or perhaps he is. I don't know. He's strong in all the wrong ways. But, *Bonne-maman*, that isn't the point. I don't know who he is!"

"I see. But excellent marriages are never based on love." When she saw that I was not to be swayed by this argument, she asked, "So what do you want from me, *mon ange*?"

"Just help me with him." I nodded imperceptibly toward my father.

"With pleasure," she said, squaring her shoulders, her mouth a tight little knot.

I looked toward my father and saw that he was hunched over the Bloody Mary pitcher, pouring in the ingredients with harsh, quick movements. In a moment he would pour himself a drink and go lock himself in his study.

I coughed, cleared my throat. "Since you're all here, there's something I have to tell you—" I began in a steely, calm voice.

Everyone gazed at me with alert expressions, except my father, who was now taking the cap off the Tabasco. Nathan nodded encouragingly.

"I've decided that I can't marry Alex."

My father stopped shaking the Tabasco, his hand freezing in the air. There wasn't a sound in the room. The cicadas' loud chirrup crescendoed outside. I went on, glancing from face to face.

"Right off the bat, if you're looking for reasons, let me assure you immediately that Nathan has nothing to do with this. I've been lying to myself for a long time about Alex. I was scared to end up alone and broke. I was drinking too much and I thought he could keep me under control. I'm truly sorry about the money you spent on the wedding. I don't know if you can get it back or not. You can have the presents back. I don't know anything else to say." I paused, feeling choked up; tears filled my eyes. My grandmother patted my hand. "My life's been a goddamn mess for years. I'm sick of living this way," I said, my voice cracking. "I'm tired of lies. Of running away from things."

I looked right at my father and he looked away, his face in a grimace. Anna stood gripping the back of a chair, her face pale and alert. Nathan was staring into his empty cup, tilting it toward him.

"Don't cry, *mon petit,*" said my grandmother in French. "It's not that serious. You might have married him and awakened feeling like this tomorrow. That happened to me once. And it was too late to do anything, being that I am a good Catholic. Thank God he died not long after!"

My father punched the counter with all his might, sending the Bloody Mary glasses and the celery stalks flying. "I won't have this!" he shouted. "I won't listen to this—this—bullshit in my own house! Twenty thousand dollars, this wedding cost, are you out of your minds? You can't back out at the last minute! I won't allow it! Anna, talk to her, will you?" He turned his back to the room and crossed his arms.

"*Mon Dieu,* Charles!" cried my grandmother. "How you could talk about money at this time? Are you entirely a low-class *petit bourgeois*?

We must talk *raisonablement,* we 'ave avoided this conversation for thirty-three years, but unfortunately the time 'as come."

Nathan stood up. "I think I'll go for a ride into town. Anybody need anything?"

No one spoke or moved. He slipped out, quietly shutting the screen door behind him. A moment later we heard his motorcycle roar to life and fly down the driveway.

"Il faut dire que ce jeune homme est très sensé," my grandmother said to me.

"You stay the hell out of this, Sophie!" my father shouted, spinning around. "This is none of your business. I don't know where you find the gall to barge in here after thirty years and tell me what to do. Where the hell were you when Nathalie needed you?"

My grandmother stood up, fingertips on the table, and stared at him with her coldest, most contemptuous look. "Yes. Yes, Charles, I am guilty and ashamed every day. But let us talk about you for a moment. If you want to start parceling out the blame in front of the child, I will meet your challenge. But I will say some sings I am *certaine* you do not want Céleste to hear," she said evenly. "Now, do we speak reasonably, or do we duel? Because if you want a duel, I am ready for you."

"Oh, no, please, Charles," Anna whispered, her body rigid like a column, "please, do let's speak reasonably."

"I have to go call Alex," I murmured, and rose from my chair.

On my way to the door I could feel all their eyes burning against my back. The door swished shut loudly behind me. There wasn't a sound coming from the kitchen. I climbed the steps two at a time.

"More coffee, anyone?" I heard Anna ask finally, as I reached the landing.

* * *

I WENT INTO their bedroom, which had the only upstairs phone, and shut the door. The bed was unmade, the sheets tangled and thrown back. I hadn't been in this room in a long time. Anna had redecorated after she'd moved in. Now it was pale and modern, black furniture, beige rug, curtains, bedspread. I had never much liked to come in here after my mother was gone. My mother had slept in a wooden four-poster canopy bed with lace curtains and a creamy chenille spread. A bed, in fact, not unlike Alex's.

I hated the fact that their bed was unmade, it was like catching my father and Anna in their underwear. I averted my eyes.

I stood by the bedside table, my back to the bed, and lifted the receiver. I dialed our phone number. I listened, my pulse pounding in my throat, as the phone rang once. Then Alex picked up. I wanted to hang up.

"Hello," said his self-possessed voice. Last night's monster was long gone, and I felt confused again.

"It's me, Alex," I said, swallowing. My mouth was completely dry, my tongue felt thick and useless.

"Well, hello there," he said in his honey-coated voice.

"Alex," I said quickly, "I've been thinking about this all night, and I've come to the realization that I can't marry you."

"I won't discuss this over the telephone," he said immediately, without emotion, as if he'd considered this contingency and had prepared for it. His voice had changed suddenly to his crisp, formal business tone, and I wasn't sure anymore whom I was speaking to. "Don't you do anything until I get there," he added.

"Alex, there's no need—"

"Do you hear me? I'm leaving in ten minutes." With that, he hung up. I tried to call back but the phone kept ringing; apparently he'd turned off the answering machine.

* * *

I COULD HEAR my father shouting in the kitchen from the top of the stairs. I descended slowly and stayed quietly on the other side of the door.

"In all my years!" he shouted. "In all my goddamn years! You're telling me to just chuck this twenty thousand dollars away? Is that what you're telling me?" His voice rose hysterically. "Because if that's what you're telling me, you're out of your fucking minds!"

"Mais c'est pas possible!" cried my grandmother. "Shut yourself up, Charles! I always suspected you were narrow-minded and foolish, but I did not imagine you 'ad such bad taste."

"Oh, for God's sake. If it's about money," said Anna in a cold but controlled voice, "I'll transfer ten thousand from my account to yours, Charles. But I have a strong suspicion that it isn't about the money at all. It's about your neighbors and your business associates and your relatives. You are terrified of what they're going to say. 'Look at that family,' they're going to say, 'they're *still* a mess!' I've had enough of this dissembling, Charles. I've had enough. Now, act like a man, for God's sake, and stand by your child."

"Bravo, madame," said my grandmother quietly.

My father said, "You talk some sense into her, Anna. You're a woman."

"The best thing to do," Anna added evenly, "in my opinion, is to offer everyone a drink here, and then sort of announce—anyway, it's too late to call people now. It's past one o'clock. People are coming from all over the country."

"*I* came from France," my grandmother said.

I opened the door and saw that the three hadn't moved since I'd gone upstairs. My father's face was pale and solemn. He glared at me and then looked away.

"Alex is coming," I said helplessly.

"He's coming?" Anna said, eyes going wide.

"He hung up on me. He said he didn't want to discuss it on the phone."

"So you mean there's still hope?" Anna said, her face lighting up. At once my courage evaporated.

You should have a Bloody Mary, I heard in my head. *It would really help you right now.*

I began shivering, a chill rising from deep within my bones. "I need some hot chocolate," I told Anna.

My grandmother glanced at me with concern.

"Hot chocolate! For God's sake, it's ninety-five degrees outside!" Anna said, turning toward the cabinets.

* * *

I STOOD BY my bedroom window, facing Alex. He had arrived in his best pin-striped suit, the one he'd intended to wear for the wedding. He had on his "power" tie instead of the floral Cardin print he'd planned on. It struck me—and I was horrified—that he still intended to get married today. He stood by the door, hands clasped firmly behind him, shoulders squared, wearing a contemplative and serious expression, as if this were an extremely important business transaction.

This side of Alex had always daunted and intimidated me. We'd been staring at each other for only thirty seconds but it felt like an hour had passed. The heat seemed to be stealing all the air in the room.

"So? Talk to me, Celeste," he said smoothly. "This is about Nathan, isn't it? I saw him downstairs. I'm not *totally* stupid," he added, "even if I am not as well read as you."

I turned my face away and stared into the garden below. Not a leaf stirred. At the round cast-iron table under the pink mimosa tree, my grandmother and Nathan sat, sipping Bloody Marys with tall celery stalks in the glasses. I heard her say to him in French, her voice carrying in the hot air, "Your Bloody Mary is much better than *his*."

"He puts in too much horseradish," Nathan said.

"Exactly!"

"I hope I don't have to go up there and beat Alex up," Nathan said contemplatively.

"He's much bigger and—if you don't mind my saying—in much better shape than you," my grandmother responded.

Anna came out from the kitchen. She'd changed into a short, pale blue dress, something noncommittal. The three began to whisper, and Nathan glanced up once at my window.

"Celeste?" said Alex impatiently.

I turned to him. "I didn't want you to come here, Alex. I won't be talked into changing my mind. This has absolutely nothing to do with Nathan. What I can't understand is why you would want to talk me into marrying you, knowing how I feel."

"How should I know how you feel when by your own admission you have no idea how you feel ninety percent of the time?" he said.

"Well, you're right, I've been feeling very confused. Getting engaged brought up things from the past I'd tried to forget, and remembering, I realized that I'm really not okay."

"You're just terrified of commitment!" he said.

"That too, definitely."

He threw his arms up and took a few steps toward the door, but quickly turned back to me. "My father warned me we were too different. I should've listened to him."

"Why *would* you pick someone like me, Alex? Someone as totally fucked up as I am? I'm an alcoholic—"

"Hah!" he cried. "Now, that's a good one! You'll just try any excuse, won't you, Celeste? Why don't you just admit you're still in love with Nathan?"

You can throw words like that around all you like but that doesn't make them true. No one believes you, especially not me!

I sighed and collapsed into the armchair. "God, Alex, I can't talk to you at all."

"I don't understand," he said. "I work long hours but I always make sure to spend quality time with you. I always take care of all your needs—"

"How could you know what my needs are when *I* don't know what they are?" I cried.

"Well, perhaps that's the point," he said, his voice waning, now soft and lulling. "Maybe I know better than you do what's good for you."

He's right. Absolutely right. You don't have the sense of a billy goat.

I looked out at the garden again. People had begun to arrive. I could hear ice tinkling in glasses, hushed voices conversing. A woman passed by in a bright yellow outfit and a large, pale yellow hat.

Alex began pacing. Sensing that he was making progress with the lulling, gentle tone, he waxed romantic about our early days, the moments of tenderness we'd shared; he talked about our apartment and how beautiful my office was now, and the wedding gifts we'd received and had been using and couldn't return. He paused, waited for my response, which didn't come.

I felt my heart, strength, courage, waning. "Alex, let's not talk anymore. Let's just not talk, okay?"

Abruptly he changed course again and became condescending and fatherly. "You have nowhere to go. You have nothing without me . . . "

In the distance, I spied James walking briskly down the driveway in a suit too tight across the chest, dressed for the wedding. My grandmother's quiet voice carried through the open window.

"I was desperately embarrassed when Nathalie married Charles. I begged her not to do it. *Un Américain, mon Dieu!* I thought I'd raised her better. I took it as a personal affront and cared terribly what everyone thought. I turned my back on my only daughter. I have come to the conclusion, in my old age, that the opinion of others is for the dogs."

My brother approached the table. Nathan stood and they shook hands. Nathan turned to my grandmother, his hand on Jack's shoulder, and said in English, "Madame, this is your grandson, Jack."

"Jacques!" my grandmother cried, jumping up. "My grandson . . ." With that, she burst into tears and collapsed in her chair, covering her face with her hands. Jack seemed at a loss, dismayed, but in a moment he took his clean, crisp white handkerchief from his breast pocket and held it out to her.

"Thank you, Jacques," she said, sniffling. "This is too much in one day for the nerves of *une vieille méchante*."

My eyes filled with tears.

"What the hell is so interesting out there?" Alex asked impatiently. "Here we are, our future hanging in the balance, and you're staring out the window!"

Wiping at my eyes, I said in a faraway voice, "Alex, you almost strangled me the other night. In Hol Cha, you raped me."

"Celeste, I think rape is too strong a word."

"A week ago you tore down a bus shelter and the cops came. You're lucky you didn't get arrested. You broke your ex-wife's arm—"

"She dislocated her shoulder in a scuffle."

"Whatever, that's semantics, Alex. Don't you see that you need help, too? I used to think I deserved to be treated like that. But now I see that I don't. No one does."

He breathed heavily, impatiently, and began to pace the room like a caged beast. I became afraid and wanted to call down to my brother and Nathan to come rescue me.

"Listen, Celeste," he reasoned, getting control of himself, "let's get married today. When we get back from Europe, I'll go talk to somebody. We can even go to a marriage counselor. You have my word I'll go. I'll try it out."

What a good idea! You can give it another try . . .

Perhaps he would. Perhaps he'd even change. I turned back to the window. The lawn was shimmering in the heat like a lake. At the end of the driveway, parked cars undulated in clear, oily waves.

"We'll cut back on our drinking . . ." he said hopefully.

My heart sank. It was so clear to me, in that moment, that he didn't understand. I could never cut back. Just one sip and I'd be right back in the bottom of the pit.

"I'm so sorry. I can't do it, Alex."

He began to pace again. "What am I going to tell the office? And what about the plane tickets? We can't cancel them now."

"We'll figure that out. Get a doctor's note or something."

"What are you going to do?" he continued. "Where are you going to go? You don't even have a real job."

I remembered Branko's words: *Maybe my biggest accomplishment will be to quit drinking.* If I did only that today—not drink—it would already be something. Tomorrow, I would go back to the Madison Avenue church basement and ask them for help.

"I'm going to have to learn how to do things for myself," I said, and smiled weakly.

He seemed to be thinking, then said dryly, "Well, I have to ask you to give me back your engagement ring and credit cards." He held out his hand. Nodding, I went to my bag that was lying on the chair and took out my wallet. I pulled out my Bloomingdale's, Visa, and American Express Gold cards. Alex took them and put them in his wallet. I slid the diamond solitaire off my finger and dropped it into his palm. My hand felt much lighter without it.

Alex's fingers closed over the ring. There was a knock on the door.

"Who is it?" I called.

"Uh, Celeste, can I talk to you guys for a second?" Lucia murmured through the closed door. Alex turned on his heels and briskly opened the door. She wore a tight black lace dress and a little black hat with a sprig of white flowers, and was holding a flute of champagne.

"Anna wants to know what to do," she said, standing in the doorway. "Everyone's arriving, the judge is here. They're all drinking champagne. No one knows anything yet. Anna hasn't even called the yacht club."

Alex sat down heavily on the edge of the bed and covered his face with his hands, his shoulders sagging. I went to him and gingerly put my hand on his shoulder. The sounds of laughter and drinks being stirred echoed through the air.

After a few long moments, Alex stood, back squared, face determined, gazed at Lucia calmly, and then turned to me and said, "Celeste and I have come to a mutual agreement that we're not ready to get married. We still care a lot about each other and plan to remain good friends." He paused, searching my face. I saw a hopeful, conspiratorial look in his eyes and understood. I nodded to him.

"Since all our friends and relatives are coming from everywhere to be here today, we think it would be best to have the party. We can't send them home on an empty stomach. We'll celebrate this decision, and our deep affection for each other and our families. Somehow we'll figure out a way to pay Mr. Miller back."

Lucia stared at him, her crimson lips parted, then turned to me with a startled look. I was relieved. Alex had found a solution that was acceptable to him. In time, he would probably believe it to be the truth. What did it matter? Our sense of what was true and what was important had never coincided. But it was fine, I owed him this much.

"Yes," I said, "Alex and I think it would be best." I watched him. He smiled, the corners of his mouth quivering.

"I'll inform them," Alex said, his face composed, almost relaxed now. He nodded once, and left. Lucia stepped into the room. I stared longingly at her champagne glass; she offered it to me, but I shook my head.

"Do you need a place to stay for a while?" Lucia asked.

"I don't know. Probably." My voice didn't seem to be coming from me.

"You're not alone," she said, placing a hand on my shoulder.

"Thank you," I said.

When Lucia and I entered the lobby of the yacht club, my grandmother, my brother Jack, Nathan, and Anna were waiting for us outside the closed French doors that led into the banquet hall. Nathan had finally shaved and changed. He was wearing a morning coat and a white silk shirt embossed with white palm trees, a black bow tie, and black lizard-skin cowboy boots. They all held champagne flutes and their faces seemed less tense. They smiled at me. My brother, in his dark suit, reached out and hugged me stiffly. I was so taken aback by his gesture that my eyes filled with tears.

"No, no, don't cry," my grandmother said, taking Jack's arm. "Why, this is a celebration! It is a great day for the Fleurances when the grandmother meets her grandson for the first time. It is a familial reunion!"

Jack blushed, breaking into a smile. Strains of soft, cocktail lounge jazz and muted chatter drifted out through the closed doors.

"You all right, Celeste?" Nathan asked. I nodded.

I caught sight of myself in the large, gilded mirror, wearing the green silk dress I'd worn last year on the Fourth of July, when I'd met Alex. It had been packed in my "trousseau" for Europe. "Bookends," Lucia had said as she helped me slide it over my head.

"Jacques," I heard my grandmother say, "you must come see your chateau."

"Absolut-ment," Jack said, and lifted his glass.

* * *

Now I saw Alex through the glass in the French doors, slapping the back of a young man who was laughing, and then moving on with a strained smile to the next group of guests. I admired his valiance.

I looked around the crowded room for my father but he was nowhere to be seen. As if she were reading my mind, Anna coughed into her fist and murmured, "Your father's coming a little later. He has one of his migraines and had to lie down. . . ." her voice trailed off and she attempted a wan smile.

He would come, or he wouldn't; if I waited expectantly for him, I would be setting myself up for more disappointment, as my mother had done long ago, and surely nothing good would come of it. Suddenly I felt sad and alone. Anna had told me that I must learn to forgive; I imagined she was right, but the road to forgiveness would be a long and difficult one.

My grandmother took me by the arm. "All these people are supposed to be your friends. In a moment you will learn who is worth his weight and who is good for the trash bin. *Alors*. Good," she said. *"On y va,"* and flung open the doors with a dramatic push.

I walked right to Alex and hugged him, planting a soundless kiss on his big, smooth chin. As he held me for a moment in his strong arms, his familiar leather-and-spice smell wafted over me and I felt a pang of regret, but evaporated quickly and my heart felt light as air.

* * *

My grandmother and I stepped out of the banquet room onto the deck that overlooked the Sound. The sailboards had been stacked for the night on the small crescent of beach, and beyond them in the shallow blue water, dozens of small sailboats rocked gently in the swells, their halyards chiming. Beyond the deck a long, crooked wharf jutted out into the waves.

Inside, everyone was dancing to a big band swing tune. Alex was jitterbugging with his mother, spinning her in and out of his arms. She laughed delightedly, tottering on her pointed heels. The sun was beginning to sink behind the sloping roof.

"It is very pretty here," my grandmother said in French. "But you know, Celeste, you may come back to Bordeaux with me."

"I have things to do here first. But I will come visit, I promise. Thank you, *Bonne-maman*."

"Do you need money?"

"No. Thank you. You've helped me so much." I still had enough money for a few months. I'd find a second job.

Her eyes searched mine for a moment. "Something good has come of this—something wonderful. We've found each other again."

I squeezed her hand as our eyes filled with tears. I turned to the water.

"I'm going out on the jetty," I said. "Would you like to come?"

"I'd break my leg!" She laughed, and turned to go back inside, taking a handkerchief out of her purse and dabbing the corners of her eyes.

I took off my shoes and walked out to the end of the wharf. Glancing back at the yacht club, I saw that a sliver of sun, bright red now, still remained above the roofline. When I closed my eyes, the sliver shattered in a kaleidoscopic pattern. It remained for a while behind my eyelids. When I opened them, the sky behind the yacht club had burst into a rhapsody of fiery oranges and reds, and amidst the white spots that still danced before me, a dark silhouette approached.

Someone tapped my shoulder and I spun around. It was Nathan.

He leaned his hip against the railing and said, "Want to take a trip with me? See the Southwest? I've never been there."

Go! Run with him! There is nothing for you here!

Oh, shut up, I thought.

I looked at Nathan closely. "I can't leave now. Anyway, if I went with you and you didn't stop drinking, I'd drink for sure."

He thought about this for a while, leaning back on the railing with his pointed boots crossed. A breeze rose over the water; a lock of hair fluttered on Nathan's brow.

Finally, he said, "Drinking has never caused me any problems. The day it does, I guess I'll think about quitting."

I nodded, aware of the futility of arguing. His eyes seemed sad, or perhaps just tired. He turned and walked back toward the beach. My brother was standing on the sand by the stack of windsurf boards, a beer bottle in his hand.

"Want to go windsurfing?" Nathan called to Jack, his voice carrying through the air.

"Sure, why not?" Jack replied.

They took two boards from the pile and attempted to attach sails to them. Laughing, Jack fell backwards on the sand. He took off his shoes and rolled up his suit pants. Nathan steadied himself on Jack's shoulder and tugged at his boots. With their dress pants rolled above their calves, they launched the boards into the surf. There was not much wind, and they fell several times in the shallow water. After a while the wind grew stronger and they managed to pick up speed and sail away from shore. Soon they passed the end of the wharf. Jack's tie whipped his face and Nathan's coattails flapped behind him.

Darkness was spreading over the horizon, a purple stain. In the distance the opalescent water and matte sky had become one. High above, gulls swooped and cried in the expanse of blue. Waves lapped at the pylons and the empty hulls of sailboats. I breathed deeply. The sharp, musty smell of algae and fish filled my nose and throat as I ran my fingertips lightly over the weathered railing, feeling the grooves in the ancient wood. Beneath my feet the planks creaked and moaned with the tide's pull; crabs crawled on the mossy pylons, and schools of silvery minnows rocked undisturbed in the swells.

Soon the sails were two small white fins in the distance, slashing the vast, darkening Sound. The wind had picked up, and the sultry haze was lifting.